Behold!

According to *The New Brown-Driver-Briggs-Gesenius Hebrew and English Lexicon* (1979) using Strong's Concordance word #2009 *hinneh* for "behold" defines the word as a demonstrative participle meant to point out a thing or person. With reference to the past or present, it points generally to some truth either newly asserted, or newly recognized. It can also serve to introduce a solemn or important declaration.

Hineni is related to or a derivation of the Hebrew word *hinneh* which means "Here I am." *Hineni* means ready to be fully available, ready to pay attention, or ready to obey instructions. The word carries with it a sense of one's attitude and full presence to comply.

In essence the word "behold" and the phrase "here I am" are indeed related in Hebrew. "Behold" is a call or command for one's attention to investigate, to perceive, to respond, and "here I am" is the expected response to engage. Each reader will decide if this is their call and their response.

BEHOLD!

The Jesus We
NEVER KNEW

God From the Beginning

―――

ANNA A. GOODMAN
with
JEFFREY GOODMAN, Ph.D.

Behold!
The Jesus We Never Knew: God from the Beginning
Copyright © 2019 by Anna A. Goodman and Jeffrey Goodman, Ph.D.

All rights reserved. No part of this publication may be reproduced, stored in a retrieval system or transmitted, in any form or by any means, electronic, mechanical, photo-coping, recording, or otherwise, without the prior written permission of the publisher. Printed in the United States of America.

First printing November 2019

Cover design by SM Savoy Designs

Print ISBN: 978-0-9844891-6-9
ePUB ISBN: 978-0-9844891-5-2
MOBI ISBN: 978-0-9844891-0-7

"Scripture taken from the NEW AMERICAN STANDARD BIBLE®, Copyright © 1960,1962,1963,1968,1971,1972,1973,1975,1977,1995 by The Lockman Foundation. Used by permission."

THE HOLY BIBLE, NEW INTERNATIONAL VERSION®, NIV® Copyright © 1973, 1978, 1984, 2011 by Biblica, Inc.®
Used by permission. All rights reserved worldwide.

Library of Congress Cataloguing-in-Publication Data

1. Jesus 2. Early Christianity 3. Religion 4. Judaism

Published by
Archeological Research Books, LLC. Tucson, AZ

Dedication

*To my L*ORD*, my Love, my King, & Master - my God*

*We must never be afraid of the truth or where the
truth will lead us, because the truth can only
lead us to God and will set us free.*

Me adapted from Him

*He was in the world, and though the world was made through him,
the world did not recognize him.*

John 1:10 NIV

*"For the earth shall be filled with the knowledge of the
glory of the L*ORD*, as the waters cover the sea."*

Habakkuk 2:14

Table of Contents

Acknowledgments · xi
Introduction · xiii
Chapter 1 – Who is Jesus? The Messiah – The Christ · · · · · · · · · 1
Chapter 2 – Jesus – The Prophet · 31
Chapter 3 – The Son of David and The Son of God · · · · · · · · · 45
Chapter 4 – If you knew · 65
Chapter 5 – The Return to Nazareth · 85
Chapter 6 – Why Return to Nazareth · · · · · · · · · · · · · · · · · · · 93
Chapter 7 – Sin-Atonement, Forgiveness & Redemption · · · · · · · 115
Chapter 8 – The Salvation of Simon Peter · · · · · · · · · · · · · · · · 171
Chapter 9 – Easy to Say, Difficult to Do, Unless ... · · · · · · · · · · 179
Chapter 10 – One Day with Jesus · 189
   Part 1 – Don't you care, Lord? I'm drowning here! · · · · · · · · · · 191
   Part 2 – The Divine Appointment · · · · · · · · · · · · · · · · · · · 197
   Part 3 – Daughter! · 203
   Part 4 – But it's My Child, Jesus! · 211
Chapter 11 – Anointing The Anointed · · · · · · · · · · · · · · · · · · 219
Chapter 12 – The Three Gentiles & What They
               Reveal About Jesus · 225
Chapter 13 – Beelzebub & The Sin Not Forgiven · · · · · · · · · · · · 233
Chapter 14 – Teach Us to Pray · 251
Chapter 15 – My Secret Stream of Life · · · · · · · · · · · · · · · · · · · 263
Chapter 16 – More than Bread – The Feeding of the 5,000 · · · · · 265
Chapter 17 – The Resurrection and The Life · · · · · · · · · · · · · · · 277
Chapter 18 – "My God, Why Have You Forsaken Me?" · · · · · · · · 293

Chapter 19 – Was Jesus Fully Human? 305
Chapter 20 – The Son of Man 327
Chapter 21 – No other Name 345

Note 1 – Sabbath Readings 377
Glossary 383

Acknowledgments

First and foremost, this book would not exist if not for the God of the Bible. My sincerest appreciation to my family – those here and those who have gone before me who walk with our Lord, depositing blessings I've had the privilege to draw upon. To my two sisters Jacquelyne Brady and Avara Gritta and brother, Joseph Griggs whose unwavering and persistent support, love and prayers are invaluable. Many times, my husband, Dr. Jeffrey Goodman said, "No, try again," from which the research yielded nuggets of gold. My daughters Joy Paul, Robin Goodman, a writer and editor who speaks Hebrew and Hannah Goodman, another sounding board, with our nighttime ritual of a Bible verse of the day were each tremendously helpful. Often the nightly divine verses came precisely when I needed support or gave insight to the arguments I struggled with at the time. My dearest friend, Estelle Laquatra, listened tirelessly to my discoveries and transformed before my eyes, never faltered in saying, she didn't get it. Her questions pressed me on to discover more. Lee Pastore and Dr. Brandon Brygider are so appreciated for their editing, excitement and encouragement.

Introduction

"You can't be a Christian! You are a Jew!" the mother of a friend said to my husband upon learning he had come to believe Jesus is the Jewish Messiah.

Historically there have been many Christians who have felt there is a distinct and almost incompatible difference between Judaism and Christianity. The difference being there are Jews who do not believe Jesus is the Messiah, and Christians who differ in their opinions about how relevant the God of the Old Testament and His Laws are to their Christian faith in Jesus and the teachings of the New Testament. However, could the Messiah have been born to any other ethnic group? No, Jesus was born as a Jew, to the Jewish people as promised in the Hebrew Bible (Old Testament) scriptures. It can be startling to many Christians to acknowledge Jesus NEVER celebrated Christmas, and NEVER set foot in a church on Sunday. Rather Jesus kept all the instructions, commands, and percepts of *Torah* – the Law of God. He observed all the Sabbaths, holy days/festivals, attended the synagogue weekly on the Sabbath and at the temple when required. No matter how much Bible studying we do, we cannot grasp the fullness of who Jesus is, nor understand the depth of His statements without studying the Hebrew scriptures (Old Testament), the customs and history of the Jewish people.

I have been exposed to a Jewish viewpoint of the Bible through my husband, who as an archeologist, acquired and studied an extensive library of Biblical related material. I have often heard Christians and pastors comment that the Jews at the time of Jesus' ministry were blind and failed to recognize their own Messiah. This type of broad statement is inaccurate and there are numerous scriptures in the New Testament to show otherwise. While it is true today that many Jews do not recognize Jesus as their promised Messiah, there are many who do. The fact that the Jewish people have had a very long history of persecution in the name of Jesus hasn't helped them be receptive to Him. Strangely enough many people who identify themselves today as Christians are just as blind to understanding much of what Jesus said and did because we have not sought to learn and understand the Hebrew culture of the Old and New Testament time. It is not often that we view the stories, conversations, and teachings within the context that Jesus was talking to a Jewish audience who were familiar with scriptures, traditions, expressions, and idioms of their Hebrew culture. Although some people may think, "You can't be a Christian if you are a Jew," perhaps the more accurate statement is you can't be a complete Christian without knowing the God of Israel, without knowing the reason behind His instructions and without knowing what His holy days tell us about Jesus and God.

As I sat down to write Bible stories about Jesus, I tried to view the events as if I were there at that time. I began to recognize details I had never seen before although I had read these stories dozens of times. I was struck most by the gentleness, compassion, patience and profound love of Jesus. I noticed a pattern of His ministry as He began with a gentle quietness of revealing Himself on an individual basis to prodding the religious leaders to grapple with His identity and authority. Then as the cross loomed, I recognized the increasing clarity in which He spoke, stating clearly before the crowds who He is. It served as a wakeup call to see that many of those who had known Him for years and those who had chosen to serve God in the ministry failed to recognize Him as the Messiah. They refused to believe the testimony of His words and the meaning of the miracles. <u>Then without consulting the scriptures, they chose to believe their personal assessment of what was happening.</u> Before we shake our fingers at the Pharisees, priests and scribes, we should admit that among Christians, pastors, Catholic priests, and theologians, we too have been guilty of this same shortcoming of holding onto our interpretation and loyalty to certain tenets and doctrines without searching the scriptures to be sure of our understanding.

Introduction

There are a lot of scriptures cited in ***Behold! The Jesus We Never Knew: God from the Beginning.*** The Bible says a matter is established by two witnesses (Deuteronomy 19:15, Matthew 18:16 and II Corinthians 13:1). Generally, to make a specific point at least two scriptures are cited as support. When stating my opinion, I have tried to make that clear. While I am not a student of linguistics, Hebrew or Greek, on many words I sought a comprehensive definition from *Strong's Concordance* or/and consulted Jewish sources. In some cases, I took the English translated word at face value. As you will see, I quote from the King James Version (KJV), the New International Version (NIV) and the New American Standard Bible (NASB). Authors are limited by the number of scriptures they can use from translations other than the King James Version without gaining publication rights. This is one of the reasons some passages are from the King James, and the NIV or the NASB were used for easier reading.

Today there are many different English translations of the Bible. Some people prefer one translation over another. However, when trying to be specific about what was said or the meaning of a word, the King James version should be consulted since it is one of the oldest English versions of the Bible (completed in 1611) translated from the Hebrew (Old Testament) and Greek (New Testament).[1] The NIV also translates from Hebrew and Greek, but their translators admit the NIV is not a word for word translation. Rather the NIV attempts to capture the Bible's original meaning in natural everyday English.[2] As my husband frequently says, "Every translation is an interpretation." This means that when a translator chooses a word, it is *their* interpretation of what is being conveyed. Psalms 12:6 NIV says that the word of God is flawless ("pure" in the KJV). Therefore, to find the full meaning of a specific word, the King James should be reviewed, then used to locate the Hebrew and/or Greek related word.

---

1 Most of the Old Testament was written in Hebrew and the New Testament in Greek.
2 According to the International Bible Society.

Some Christians hold the view that the Bible is the inerrant word of God. The very fact that there are many English translations proves this concept cannot be true. Bible scholars, historians and examiners of ancient Biblical manuscripts of the New Testament know this evaluation is inaccurate. Even more disturbing is discovering the different beliefs "Christian" groups of the early church held about Jesus and how their beliefs motivated subtle changes to New Testament scriptures to support their viewpoint.[3] So then how does one determine what is true?

Nearly everyone has an opinion about what they believe regarding spiritual matters. What one believes changes only when they have credible new information, explanations and facts. The basis for what is believed about God should not be based on one's opinion, nor based on what someone else has said. Understanding the God of the Bible must be based on what is in the Bible and be consistent through the Old Testaments, the gospels as well as the epistles. This book presents some different views about who Jesus is and what God requires for relationship. Before these viewpoints are considered incorrect, one should determine if the scriptures cited are incorrectly applied or misinterpreted for the points being made. Use *BibleGateway.com* to do word searches and BlueLetterBible.org for translation analysis and to find related scriptures. Read the verses in the King James Version and other translations. Look at the verses before and after the specific verse, then read the entire chapter (and previous chapters if necessary) to be sure of the context. Five things should be considered for researching a topic from the Bible:

1) Who is the audience and what is the context of the passage/chapter/book.

---

[3] Chapter 6 Theologically Motivated Alterations of the Text from the book Misquoting Jesus: The story behind who changed the Bible and Why, by Bart Ehrman, HarperOne Publisher, November 2005.

2) Ideas or concepts introduced in the epistles of the Bible should originate in the Old Testament and be supported or given insight in the Gospels.[4] Otherwise taking a unique statement and making it a doctrinal point can be questionable.
3) Opinions and assessments of Jewish sages on a topic should be consulted.[5]
4) Evaluate how and when the Christian "church" came to a particular belief. If the doctrinal point or explanation of the nature of Jesus was made a couple hundred years after the resurrection, the doctrine must have *Torah*, Old Testament and gospel scriptural foundation or its validity as truth is questionable.
5) What do you think Jesus' response would be to your assessment on a subject?

As this book presents different information about Jesus, some readers may wonder what I believe. Let me be very clear: I believe the One known to the world as Jesus Christ is my God, my LORD and Savior. While I have known a long time that Jesus was not His name, in this book I use the name Jesus as it is the name most people know Him by. I believe in the one God of the Bible (Deuteronomy 6:4 and Mark 12:29). Although I believe the Bible contains the sacred Word of God, I do not believe all verses, translations and interpretations are perfect in conveying what God said. Based on comparisons of early copies of New Testament books, Biblical scholars, professors and theologians know that many passages of the gospels and epistles have been altered.[6]

---

[4] The Bible's Old Testament consists of the Pentateuch (known as *Torah*), the historical books, sacred writings and the prophets. The New Testament consists of the gospels (Matthew, Mark, Luke and John), the Acts of the apostles, the epistles and the Revelation of our Lord.

[5] There have been many great Jewish theologians with decades of study and examination of the scriptures and historical analysis on the Old Testament. The Old Testament scriptures (the Hebrew Bible) were given to the Jews, kept untampered with by the Jews and is written in their native language.

[6] Misquoting Jesus: The story behind who changed the Bible and Why, by Bart Ehrman, HarperOne Publisher, November 2005.

Yet within the imperfections and changes wrought by men, I believe the complete essence of God's message is retained and untarnished.

When I began this book, it was with the intentions of showing how details in the book of Luke provided more information than the books of Matthew or Mark. However, within the first couple of stories, this book seemed to take on a life of its own. It quickly became a revelation about Jesus, His love for mankind and what He wanted us to know about Him. From the beginning of Jesus' ministry, Jesus was revealing Himself as God to those with Him. He taught lessons that are universal and timeless. The stories show us God cares about our life, our emotional pain, broken bodies and minds. We find that Jesus echoes the central message of the Old Testament telling us our greatest goal is to believe, know, love and trust in Him and our greatest responsibility lies in our fair and compassionate treatment of others. This foundational understanding leads to growing in relationship with and knowledge of God, and will achieve a joy and peace we have never known.

As I approached the end of this book, nearly everything I wrote was new and news to me which resulted in me re-writing the beginning of the book. One question led to another, each answer revealed a far greater truth I had no clue existed. These discoveries revealed there are many things Christians believe about "our faith" that are not in scripture. I found the more I learned, the greater God became and my fears and worries shriveled and shrank as I came to know more of the identity, power and love of God.

This book is not written for the unbeliever. It does not try to convince the reader that Jesus really does exist, or that the stories and Jesus' words are real and accurate. ***Behold! The Jesus We Never Knew: God from the Beginning*** starts with the premise that the events recorded in the four gospels really happened. If someone does not believe the events recorded in the Bible, the Bible itself addresses that issue. God says He will be found when you search for Him with all of your heart (Jeremiah 29:13). So, test Him. Begin the journey with a Bible, a prayer to know the truth, and the Creator of the Universe will reveal Himself, and His love. It is my hope that when asked who do you say Jesus is, we will have the same answer as the disciple Thomas in John 20:28. Thomas called Jesus his Lord and his God.

Jesus' life on the timeline of world history testifies that He is not a myth or fantasy. He really did live, just as King Tut, Julius Caesar before Him, and Henry VIII or President George Washington after Him. As Christians have wondered how the Jewish nation failed to recognize their own Messiah, we should ponder how so many people on this earth now in civilized countries have missed the fact that God came to earth in the form of a man with the most important message in the world for all of humanity. Are we blind too? What is our excuse? It is my hope Christians reading this book, will grab their Bible to see if what is written here is true; then make a habit of incorporating the Bible's instructions and messages in their daily lives. We cannot know the Lord God apart from His Word – the Bible.

Writing this book has transformed my understanding of Jesus like nothing else has in the 25+ years I have been a follower of Jesus and has changed my life. It has changed how I respond to others, and how I regard things happening in the world. It has changed the way I pray, eliminated most of my worrying and fears, transformed my understanding of death for a believer and made my worship and praise of Him far more meaningful. Most of all with each new monumental insight about the vastness of the power of God, His perfection, the love and gentleness of God in His dealings with mankind I have discovered that what I have learned is probably only a drop in the ocean of information about God. Truly because of writing this book, He is the Jesus we never knew – God from the beginning.

CHAPTER 1

Who is Jesus?
The Quest to discover who the Bible reveals Him to be

"...then you will know that I am he ..."
— Jesus in John 8:28 NIV

In 1982 I had an argument with my older sister during a family reunion about whether Jesus was God or *just* the Son of God. Funny how although I had never read one book of the Bible, I felt I could argue on a subject of which I knew virtually nothing. The argument ended abruptly when my favorite aunt, a long practicing Christian said to me gently, "Nesha, Jesus *is* God." I have always remembered her answer. Though she gave no explanation for this statement, I believed her because of the person she was and because I respected her word and knowledge of God. There is an important point here. What is true about God and the Bible cannot be based on one's feelings, intuition, vaguely remembered talking points or scriptures partially recalled. Nor can truth about God be based on the opinion of someone loved and respected. A solid foundation about what is true about God must come from the Bible.

"Who is Jesus?" is not a new question. During His ministry and immediately after His ascension into Heaven, this was the central question. The questions on its heels were: Why did Jesus come and what does His death and resurrection mean to those who have come to believe in Him? These are the questions several of the Apostle Paul's letters or epistles sought to answer. By the end of the first century after Jesus' death and resurrection, Christianity had begun to be recognized as a separate religion from Judaism. After the fourth century, the New Testament canon (the books that comprise the New Testament) began to formalize and were becoming recognized as scripture.[7] Two to three hundred years after the resurrection, the early church was plagued by different views and beliefs about Jesus. During this time, there were specific events that took place to cause separation and rejection of Jews and Judaism from the growing number of Gentile followers of Jesus which eliminated any input and insight from Jewish sages and teachers of *Torah* (the Old Testament). "Church" leaders from whom would come the origins of the Roman Catholic Church began to meet to establish the tenets of belief and church practices for Christianity.

How does one determine the answer to the question – Who is Jesus? What did Jesus say about who He is? When we read the Gospels,[8] did Jesus *say* He was God; did He say He was the Messiah? Called the Son of David, the Son of God, Messiah, the Christ, Jesus referred to Himself dozens of times as the Son of Man. What do these titles mean and what do they reveal about the identity of Jesus? Where do we find the answers to these questions? While the early Church moved away from Judaism and the Old Testament, we must recognize and acknowledge Jesus was born into Judaism, the religion established by God and known in the New Testament as God the Father. No prophecy of the Old Testament nor teaching of Jesus proclaimed that God's relationship with the Jews or instructions (laws) for how His people should live would become obsolete or would need to be replaced. Jesus observed

---

[7] According to Merriam-Webster dictionary, scripture is a body of writings considered sacred or authoritative. In Hebrew from Daniel 10:21 scripture is a written edict of royal enactment or divine authority

[8] The New Testament gospels are Matthew, Mark, Luke and John.

Who is Jesus? The Messiah – The Christ

the scriptures and teachings of the Old Testament and in John 5:39 and 5:46 said Moses wrote of Him and the scriptures testified of Him. Therefore, it is from the Old Testament we will find the answers that reveal not only vital information about who Jesus is but discover why He came. We learn that God provided clues all throughout the Old Testament scriptures like the bread crumbs in the children's story of Hansel and Gretel to help us find our way to Him and to recognize Jesus for whom He truly is.

Known to the world as Jesus Christ and debated about by millions of people for hundreds of years – who is Jesus? What do the titles Christ and Messiah mean? What is the difference?

NOTE: While there are a number of names for God in the Bible, it is very important that the reader to be aware of the main name for God as it appears in the Old Testament of the King James Version of the Bible. (The distinction in this name is not always conveyed in other translations of the Bible). That name is recorded as LORD. The name LORD is very different in its definition from the name – Lord, which means lord or master conveying the idea of rulership or dominion. Lord appears in the Hebrew language as *Adonai*. The names of God are detailed in Chapter 21- *No Other Name* of this book. The main name for God is LORD and appears in the Hebrew as *Yehovah*, or *Jehovah* or the I AM and is recognized among some Bible scholars as YHWH. It is from this name *Yehovah* that Jesus' adapted Hebrew name *Yeshua* is based (meaning *Yehovah* or the LORD saves/delivers/rescues).[9] A simplistic definition of the name LORD is it conveys the Eternal One (the timeless One – past, present and future), the Breath (of Life), His nature to cause, establish, and to abide with (as in the promise to never leave or forsake His followers). The name also identifies Him as the Creator and Source of all things. Therefore, take note of verses that refer to God as LORD. In the gospels of the New Testament take note of Jesus

---

9   Jesus' name is the name of the LORD combined with the word save/salvation.

making "I am" statements. This could be taken as showing Jesus proclaiming His Power and authority as LORD. For example: "I am the Light of the Word," "I am the Good Shepherd," "I am the Resurrection and the Life," etc.

The Messiah/The Christ

*He was in the world, and the world was made by him,
and the world knew him not.*

John 1:10 KJV

Years ago, my husband spoke to an old friend about the changes that had taken place in his life after he became a believer. My husband deliberately withheld the name of Jesus as he spoke because of our friend's ethnic history with so-called Christianity. During the 40-minute conversation, our friend exclaimed again and again, "Jesus!" "Holy smoke," "Oh my God!" and "Christ!" Our friend was intrigued and followed the story intently, until my husband mentioned the source of the change - Jesus. I saw our friend straighten and lean back in the chair as he distanced himself physically from the subject just as he had already distanced himself mentally and emotionally from Jesus.

"Christ!" We have heard it said unconsciously as an exclamation, in jest, surprise, pain, fear, horror, and humor. Few who use the name indiscriminately have thought about what the word "Christ" means or what it means when they said it. It is not Jesus' last name, rather it is a title and a position. Christ and Messiah mean the same thing – anointed, as in ordained or commissioned to do a specific task. *Messiah* is a Greek transliteration (which means to represent or spell in the characters of another alphabet) of the Hebrew word *mashiyach*. In Greek, the word meaning "anointed" is *Christos* and its transliteration in English is *Christ*.

BibleGateway.com shows "Jesus Christ" appears 187 times in the English New Testament (KJV), but only five times in three of the gospels (Matthew, Mark and John). What happened in the first twenty years after the resurrection that caused the writers of the New Testament epistles[10] to frequently refer to Jesus as Jesus Christ? As His disciples shared the teachings of Jesus and His life, they became more aware of how many prophecies from the Hebrew Bible (Old Testament) Jesus had fulfilled in front of them. Now they understood who the wondrous acts and His statements had identified Him to be.

It is easy to assume Jewish people knew very little about the coming Messiah. This is not true. It is safe to say that many of the Jewish people living in Israel at that time had more than a basic understanding of their faith. Each time the Gospels say the people asked if Jesus was the Prophet, or called Him the Son of David, or accused Him of blasphemy (to despise, or speak sacrilegiously of God) indicates they recognized His statements proclaimed Him to be the Promised One to come, or that Jesus had made a direct claim of deity.

The scriptures say the Hebrew people were a nation set apart by God. Yet after years of idol worship, the ten tribes of the Northern kingdom of Israel were taken into captivity by the Assyrian Empire (what is now northern Iraq) in 740 BC. In 597 BC the Southern kingdom of Judah (the tribes of Judah and Benjamin) was carried to Babylon for 70 years. Only a remnant of Jews remained in Judah (aka Judea). Throughout the Bible's history of the Jews, tens of thousands of Jews paid the price of disobedience and idol worship with their lives.

By the time Jesus was born (around 4 BC), many Jews from Babylon and Asia Minor had returned to Israel and Judea. Now they lived under the rule of Rome where they had been oppressed, heavily taxed, and unfairly treated. Within the Jewish population were those who wanted to overthrow Rome's rule in Judea, and a religious segment who benefited from manipulating the political system between the people and

---

10 The New Testament consists of the gospels (Matthew, Mark, Luke and John), the Acts of the apostles, the epistles and the Revelation of our Lord. The epistles are letters of instructions directed to a specific group of people.

the Roman officials. Many of the Jewish people knew of the prophecy that God would send the Messiah to save them. They believed when the Messiah came, He would be like their greatest military hero – King David and they expected the Messiah to save them from oppression by the Romans. They knew the approximate time of the coming of the Messiah because the prophet Daniel had set the timing in Daniel chapter 9, and that time was at hand.

There had been much discussion about the coming Messiah, what the scriptures said about Him, and what He would do. In fact, some of the sages thought there might be two Messiahs. One would be the suffering Messiah – Messiah *ben* Joseph (meaning Messiah *son of* Joseph). The Joseph they referred to was Joseph the favorite son of Jacob. His brothers kidnapped and sold Joseph off to Egypt where he endured slavery and imprisonment for years before becoming one of the most powerful men in Egypt (Genesis 37-47). Joseph later ended up saving his brothers and their families from starvation due to a prolonged regional famine. The sages also suspected a second Messiah would come as Messiah *ben* David; a conquering warrior Messiah who would defeat their oppressors and bring justice for God's people, like King David had done. For those familiar with end time Bible prophecy, it is easy to recognize Jesus' first coming in the mode of Messiah ben Joseph who would provide salvation for His brethren and the prophesied second coming would resemble Messiah ben David as a conquering warrior.

Jesus is known as Jesus Christ and is acknowledged as the Messiah among Christians. Yet few understand what that title means, why it is important and how it relates to Jesus. As previously mentioned, the word *"messiah"* means "anointed," one on whom oil or water has been poured symbolic of being empowered and consecrated to serve God or carry out a specific task. In the Old Testament prophets, priests and kings of Israel were anointed as they took on their new calling or position. A prophet was called to receive and convey a message from God to the people. The role of a priest was to officiate during religious services and to mediate between God and people. In the Old Testament the high priest officiated during Tabernacle[11] (and later temple) ceremonies and anointed rulers, judges, and kings. Initially God called all His people to be a kingdom of priests and a holy nation (Exodus 19:6). The king of Israel was to obey God's instructions, seek and consult God for guidance in ruling over and protecting the people of God as God directed in Deuteronomy 17:14-20. The following scriptures are examples of the anointing of priests and kings of Israel.

Exodus 30:30 KJV[12] "And thou shalt anoint Aaron and his sons, and consecrate them, that they may minister unto me in the priest's office."

Exodus 40:15 And thou shalt anoint them, as thou didst anoint their father, that they may minister unto me in the priest's office: for their anointing shall surely be an everlasting priesthood throughout their generations.

I Samuel 15:1 Samuel also said unto Saul, The LORD sent me to anoint thee to be king over his people, over Israel: now therefore hearken thou unto the voice of the words of the LORD.

I Kings 1:34 And let Zadok the priest and Nathan the prophet anoint him there king over Israel: and blow ye with the trumpet, and say, God save king Solomon.

What do the roles of Prophet, Priest and King have to do with Jesus and where is that in the Old Testament? The word "Christ" does not appear anywhere in the Old Testament King James translation.

---

[11] Three months after leaving Egypt, God gave commandments and detailed instructions about building the Tabernacle which served as both a dwelling place for God and a place for the sacrifices and offerings of the people (Exodus 25-27).

[12] When a verse is cited with no translation designated, the King James version has been used.

Who is Jesus? The Messiah – The Christ

Although the word "Messiah" is in Daniel 9:25-26, the word "anointed" does appear several times in connection to the coming Messiah. It first appears in I Samuel 2:10 when Hannah, mother of the Prophet Samuel, prayed. The Messiah is mentioned in the roles of an exalted Judge and King. Then in that same chapter (I Samuel 2:35) a prophet says the Messiah will be known as both "a faithful priest" and as one who is eternal. Later "anointed" appears in Psalm 2:2 and verse 7 where it identifies the Messiah (anointed) as the Son of God.

I Samuel 2:10 The adversaries of the LORD shall be broken to pieces; out of heaven shall he thunder upon them: the LORD shall judge the ends of the earth; and he shall give strength unto his king, and exalt the horn of his anointed.

I Samuel 2:35 And I will raise me up a faithful priest, that shall do according to that which is in mine heart and in my mind: and I will build him a sure house; and he shall walk before mine anointed forever.

Psalm 2:2 and 7 ² The kings of the earth set themselves, and the rulers take counsel together, against the LORD, and against his anointed, saying… ⁷ I will declare the decree: the LORD hath said unto me, Thou art my Son; this day have I begotten thee.

The anointed positions of King and High Priest were very specific titles and offices in Judaism. Some may wonder how Jesus could be a priest, when all Hebrew priests after the exodus were from the tribe of Levi (Levites) and Jesus was of the tribe of Judah. Shortly after the young nation of Israel left Egypt, God selected Aaron (brother of Moses, also a Levite) and his sons to serve as priests (Exodus 28:1). The tribe of Levi were selected because they did not participate in worshipping the golden calf (Exodus 32:26-28). Later God selected the Levites to serve as the first born for all twelve tribes (Numbers 3:12 and 45).[13] However, the Levites were not the only people to serve as priest for God. Before them was Melchizedek.

Melchizedek is the first priest mentioned in the Bible in Genesis 14. The name Melchizedek means "my king (is) righteous(ness)" or "righteous king." The Bible does not tell of his origins or who he really is. Some theologians and Jewish rabbis have speculated Melchizedek could have been Shem (son of Noah). Some pastors, Christians and Messianic Jews have wondered if he could have been an early appearance of Jesus Himself. Genesis 14:18 says that Melchizedek was *king* and *priest* of God Most High, and Abram (Abraham) recognized Melchizedek's authority as priest and gave him his tithe. It was not uncommon in the surrounding cultures of that time for a leader or patriarch of a large group to be called king and serve as the priest. Melchizedek's role takes on additional meaning as king and priest of Salem when we recognize Salem (coming from the Hebrew word, *Shalom,* means *full, complete* and *peace*) by its current name of Jeru*salem* which could be construed to mean: to direct, show, teach or instruct the way of peace or completeness.

The name Melchizedek appears again in the Bible in Psalms 110 where God has sworn to one who is a priest forever in the order or manner of Melchizedek. It is from this verse that the author of the book of Hebrews (Chapter 7) declares Jesus' right as Priest of Heaven and Priest of Israel. Based on the meaning of Melchizedek's name and the place of his kingdom, the One spoken of in Psalm 110 is better understood as the Priest of Heaven and the King of Righteousness and Peace. Here are the related verses from Genesis 14, Psalm 110 and Hebrews 7:

---

13 Reuben was the firstborn son of Jacob, but the spiritual promise to Abraham (Genesis 12:1-3 and 13:15-16) went to Abraham's second son, Isaac then on to Isaac's second born son, Jacob. Jacob's spiritual blessing on his death bed was given to Jacob's fourth son, Judah. After the first Passover, God said all firstborn males (and animals) of Israel belonged to God; He said they were to be set apart (consecrated) for service to God. In Numbers 3:45 God said He would take the tribe of Levi as the firstborn of Israel for the purpose of serving before God (Numbers 4).

Who is Jesus? The Messiah – The Christ

Genesis 14:18-20 And Melchizedek king of Salem brought forth bread and wine: and he was the priest of the most high God. [19] And he blessed him, and said, Blessed be Abram of the most high God, possessor of heaven and earth: [20] And blessed be the most high God, which hath delivered thine enemies into thy hand. And he gave him tithes of all.

Psalm 110:4 The LORD hath sworn, and will not repent, Thou art a priest for ever after the order of Melchizedek.

Hebrews 7:1-3 For this Melchizedek, king of Salem, priest of the most high God, who met Abraham returning from the slaughter of the kings, and blessed him;

[2] To whom also Abraham gave a tenth part of all; first being by interpretation <u>King of righteousness</u>, and after that also King of Salem, which is, <u>King of peace</u>;

[3] Without father, without mother, without descent, having neither beginning of days, nor end of life; but made like unto the Son of God; abideth a priest continually.

Through the prophet, Jeremiah, God spoke of one to come who would be called "The LORD (Yehovah) our righteousness." Note the connection of the meaning of the onetime king of future Jerusalem – Melchizedek's name, which is "my king (is) righteous(ness)" or "righteous king" to the mention of a descendant (a Branch) of King David, the city of Jerusalem, the Priesthood and the connection to eternal God Himself in this passage from Jeremiah 33:14-18 NASB:

[14] 'Behold, days are coming,' declares the LORD, 'when <u>I will fulfill the good word which I have spoken</u> concerning the house of Israel and the house of Judah. [15] In those days and at that time <u>I will cause a righteous Branch of David</u> to spring forth; and He

shall execute justice and righteousness on the earth. [16] In those days Judah will be saved and Jerusalem will dwell in safety; and this is *the name* by which she will be called: <u>the LORD is our righteousness</u>.' [17] For thus says the LORD, '<u>David shall never lack a man to sit on the throne</u> of the house of Israel; [18] and <u>the Levitical priests shall never lack a man before Me</u> to offer burnt offerings, to burn grain offerings and to prepare sacrifices continually.'"

To give some context of the period of this prophetic message, Jeremiah was the prophet chosen to warn the people of Judah of the coming attack and destruction by Babylon due to their continued idol worship. At this time King David had been dead more than 200 years, Jesus' birth would not occur for another 500 years or so, and with the destruction of the second temple (40 years after Jesus' resurrection), the Levitical priesthood would cease to offer burnt offerings and sacrifices. Yet God spoke of a future time when a descendent of David would be the everlasting King of Israel and Judah and the Priest of Israel whose ministry on behalf of people on earth would never end.

The Old Testament provides another indication that God's priesthood would not be restricted to the tribe of Levi. Predating the selection of Levites as priests and ministers to God is the prophecy Jacob made shortly before his death in Egypt. Jacob's prophecy and blessings to his twelve sons is in Genesis, chapter 49. Jacob was the grandson of Abraham. God had promised that through Abraham (and his descendants) all families of the earth would be blessed (Genesis 12:3). Levi and Judah were two of Jacob's twelve sons who would each represent one of the twelve tribes of Israel. Jesus (and King David) descended from the tribe of Judah. It is from this passage of scripture that Jesus is called the Lion of Judah (paraphrased from Revelation 5:5). Note what else Jacob prophesied for the future of his fourth son's lineage, Judah, whose name means "praise." Genesis 49:8 NASB and then verse 10 say:

[8] "Judah, your brothers shall praise you; Your hand shall be on the neck of your enemies; your father's sons shall bow down to you.

¹⁰ "The scepter shall not depart from Judah, nor the ruler's (Lawgiver- KJV) staff from between his feet, until Shiloh (tranquility or rest) comes, and to him *shall be* the obedience of the peoples.

Jacob prophesied that someone out of the tribe of Judah would be a permanent king (the scepter shall not depart), that He would be praised by the Jews (his brothers) and your father's sons (all who become believers) would bow down to Him. This prophecy says that He would be the Ruler or Lawgiver (KJV) until Shiloh (word #H7886 in *Strong's Concordance* meaning tranquility or rest) comes and the people would give him their obedience. The word for lawgiver in Hebrew is #H2710 *chaqaq* in *Strong's Concordance*. The word conveys the idea of one who governs, and decrees inscribed or engraved laws. This prophecy encompasses the future Messiah as coming from the tribe of Judah as King, priest (lawgiver and one who governs), and God worthy to be praised and worshipped. Like Melchizedek, and the fore mentioned prophecies from Jacob and Jeremiah, the one to come would be both a righteous priest and king. One might ask when did Jesus serve as "priest" during His ministry? The answer is His ministry *was* His service as priest.[14] In Matthew 20:28 NIV and Mark 10:45 Jesus said, "the Son of Man did not come to be served, but to serve, and to give his life as a ransom for many." Recall that part of a priest's role was to intercede between God and the people. Jesus served as Priest when He taught, when He healed the broken people and forgave their sins.

Scripture supports Jesus' role as Priest of Israel, but did Jesus have a right to the title King of Israel as well? When the Hebrew people asked for a king, so they could be like the other nations, God told the prophet and judge Samuel "it is not you they have rejected as King, but me" (I Samuel 8:7). While the people rejected God as their King, their rejection did not mean that God ceased to be King, any more than people denying the existence of God make God cease to exist. God selected

---

14   The book of Hebrews chapter 9 speaks of Jesus' role as High Priest in heaven.

Saul as the first captain (ruler) and king of the people (I Samuel 9:16 NIV).[15] After Saul's disobedience, God rejected him as king (I Samuel 15:26 NIV & KJV). God told the Prophet Samuel to select a king from among Jesse's sons (I Samuel 16:1-13 KJV). As Samuel looked at the physical attributes of Jesse's sons, God said His selection was based on the heart of the person, not their outward appearance. What was the difference between Saul and David? Both would sin, both would break God's commands, however, several times the scriptures show Saul was blinded by his power as king and cared more about the opinions of people than God. On the other hand, David was vexed by his sins against the commandments of God. Rather than turning away, David turned to God in his biggest mistakes. The Psalms show David turned to God when he was afraid, troubled, depressed and to express his love for God.

David was a man after God's own heart (Acts 13:22). Throughout David's life are examples of David's profound love for and trust in the power of the Almighty LORD God and his understanding of God's heart and character. It was to David that the prophecy of a future Son would come who would have the rightful claim to be "King" on earth as well as in heaven. The fulfilment of this prophecy would be directed by God ("I will set up") and this unique Son of David would also be to God a Son. The Messiah would not only be the Son of David, thereby inheriting the right as King of Israel (on Earth), but also as the Son of God, He has an eternal kingdom in Heaven. II Samuel 7:12-14 says:

> II Samuel 7:12-14 And when thy days be fulfilled, and thou shalt sleep with thy fathers, I will set up thy seed after thee, which shall proceed out of thy bowels, and I will establish his kingdom. [13] He shall build an house for my name, and I will stablish the throne

---

15 In the King James this word is "captain," #5057 in *Strong's Concordance* which can mean leader, ruler, captain or prince.

of his kingdom for ever. ¹⁴ I will be his father, and he shall be my son....

Many Jewish people came to understand this prophecy to mean that this future Son of David – the Messiah would have the right to the title King of Israel. When the wise men came to Jerusalem, they asked Herod in Matthew 2:2 – Where is He that is *born King* of the Jews? Hours before the cross, Jesus' role as the King of Israel came up again. In mockery, the Roman soldiers called Him the King of the Jews (Matthew 27:29), the chief priests, teacher and elders questioned "if He be the King of Israel" (Matthew 27:42). As Jesus stood before Pilate on His last night before the cross, He admitted His identity as King when He spoke of His kingdom in John 18:33-36 (below). Pilate later had a sign affixed to the cross that identified Jesus as the King of the Jews (John 19:19-22).

John 18:33-36 NIV ³³ Pilate then went back inside the palace, summoned Jesus and asked him, "Are you the king of the Jews?"

³⁴ "Is that your own idea," Jesus asked, "or did others talk to you about me?"

³⁵ "Am I a Jew?" Pilate replied. "Your own people and chief priests handed you over to me. What is it you have done?"

³⁶ Jesus said, "My kingdom is not of this world. If it were, my servants would fight to prevent my arrest by the Jewish leaders. But now my kingdom is from another place."

³⁷ "You are a king, then!" said Pilate.

Jesus answered, "You say that I am a king. In fact, the reason I was born and came into the world is to testify to the truth. Everyone on the side of truth listens to me."

When Jesus spoke of His kingdom, He said His Kingdom was not of this world; that it is from another place. Jesus as Messiah – the One anointed Priest and King of Israel had nothing to do with being recognized by the people as such at the time of His ministry. Being the Messiah revealed and identified Jesus as God – the Highest Authority for all people - Priest and King of the eternal spiritual realm and Kingdom.

At the time Jesus began His ministry in Israel people knew many things about the coming Messiah from *Torah,* the scared writings and the prophets (what we call the Old Testament). Therefore, this should have caused quite a stir when Jesus began His ministry teaching an understanding of the scriptures in a way they had never experienced. He cast out demons who called Him the "holy one of God," and "the Son of God." He healed the blind, deaf, lame and raised the dead. Several times (Matthew 4:17, 10:7, 12:28, Mark 1:15 and Luke 11:20) Jesus announced that the Kingdom of Heaven (God) was at hand; was here![16] His ministry did cause a stir as hundreds and thousands of people began to follow Him. So why didn't the people recognize Jesus as their Messiah? The correct answer is that thousands actually did.

Today, when we read the New Testament with verses from the Old Testament that reference Jesus' fulfillment of certain prophecies, do we grasp the significance that Jesus was revealing Himself as the Messiah? Do we hear Jesus telling us who He truly is? After the resurrection, writers of the gospels realized these scriptures were fulfilled by Jesus and proved Jesus was the Messiah. From His birth in Bethlehem (Micah 5:2), being called out of Egypt (Hosea 11:1), speaking in parables (Ezekiel 20:49), coming into Jerusalem on a colt (Zechariah 9:9) to the events that involved His death on the cross (Psalm 22) were all written hundreds of years before the birth of Jesus! The essential point

---

16 The Kingdom of Heaven/Kingdom of God mean the same thing. God's Kingdom represents His power, authority to reign and God's presence in His Kingdom. "At hand" means to bring near, to draw or make near, to approach, to be in position.

of these scriptures is they were a description of what the Messiah would be like and do so that people would recognize Him when He appeared.

For many Christians Jesus made no straight forward proclamation that He was the Messiah and He did not say He was God. Yet during His ministry, to many of the Jews of Israel He said it again and again. So why have we missed it? One of the reasons is we generally do not know the Hebrew words and ancient expressions; nor do we recognize the humility in which the Jewish culture spoke. However, when we look at the stories in the gospels with the awareness of what the people knew, and when we understand what His statements meant to them, we see events and hear conversations differently. While there are more, here are just five instances that show Jesus either admitting He is the Messiah, or the people's acknowledged recognition to His claim as Messiah by the things they said, did or tried to do.

The first incident appears early in His ministry in Luke 4 involving Jesus' return to His hometown of Nazareth. At the synagogue He read from Isaiah 61:1 KJV, "The Spirit of the Lord G<small>OD</small> is upon me; because the L<small>ORD</small> hath anointed me ...." Jesus said this scripture was fulfilled that day by Him (see Chapter 5 "The Return to Nazareth"). This was Jesus announcing He was the promised Messiah - the Anointed One. During this encounter, the people became very angry and sought to push Jesus off a cliff. The second instance appears in Jesus' conversation with the Samarian woman at the well in John 4:25-26. "The woman saith unto him, I know that Messiah cometh, which is called Christ: when he is come, he will tell us all things. Jesus saith unto her, I that speak unto thee am He." The third instance occurred after Jesus miraculously fed 5,000+ people one year before the cross. After this miracle, many people thought Jesus might be the Messiah. John 6:15 says, "When Jesus therefore perceived that they would come and take him by force, to make him a king, he departed again into a mountain himself alone." Rome had appointed Herod King, but the Jewish people had not had a Jewish king for several hundred years. This verse in the book of John shows there were people waiting for the Messiah and ready to make Jesus their King.

If the people thought or believed Jesus was the Messiah, they would have acknowledged Him in some way. The fourth incident is in John 11 and 12 and occurs shortly after the resurrection of Lazarus and just days or weeks before the cross. In John 11:48 NASB the chief priests and Pharisees said, "If we let Him *go on* like this, <u>all men will believe in Him</u>...." John 12:19 says, So the Pharisees said to one another, "behold, the world is gone after him [Jesus]." These verses show that the Pharisees and religious leaders were alarmed by the growing number of followers who believed Jesus was the Messiah. Their concern was directly related to their plans to arrest, try, and have Jesus executed. Notice in John 11:50 and 53 the statement made by the High Priest and their resolution to find a way to kill Jesus.

John 11:50 Nor consider that it is expedient for us, that one man should die for the people, and that the whole nation perish not.

John 11:53 Then from that day forth they took counsel together for to put him to death.

The fifth instance where Jews heralded Jesus as the promised Messiah and King occurred when Jesus entered Jerusalem for the last time on what we call Palm Sunday. Generally, we do not grasp the enormity of this event described in all four gospels. With Passover being one week away, there were tens of thousands of Jews who had traveled up to a couple of months from other countries to be in Jerusalem for Passover. *Torah* commands all Jewish males to present themselves before the Lord (Exodus 23:17) for the three main Holy Feasts of which Passover is one of them. Jews who lived in other countries tried to come once per year to at least one of the Feasts. For this Passover, there were potentially a couple hundred thousand people in Jerusalem at that time.[17]

---

17 From the Thematic Concordance to the Works of Josephus on Passover by G. J. Goldberg under "The Numbers that gathered in Jerusalem for Passover (c.65 CE)."

John 12:13 says <u>the large crowd</u> who had come to the feast went out to meet Jesus when they heard He was coming to Jerusalem. Like at the Feast of Tabernacles, they took branches of the palm trees and shouted, "Hosanna: <u>Blessed is the King of Israel</u> that cometh in the name of the Lord."[18] <u>As this particular praise was shouted out, calling Jesus the King of Israel, who brings salvation in the power of God, it is an acknowledgment that God is present.</u> Some Pharisees recognized this and asked Jesus to rebuke His disciples for calling out blasphemy. However, in Luke 19:40 NASB Jesus' response was, "I tell you, if these become silent, the stones will cry out!" Covering the ground with their cloaks and waving palm fronds (II Kings 9:13) was a welcome befitting a King. The shouts of praise to the King of Israel (John 12:13) and to the Son of David (Matthew 21:9) were acknowledgements from the people that Jesus was the Messiah.

You may wonder if so many people believed Him to be their long-awaited Messiah, how did Jesus end up on the cross one week later? Was it not the people from this "Palm Sunday" crowd who yelled, "Crucify him!" that comprised the crowd at the crucifixion? No, the tens of thousands of people were not at the crucifixion. A closer look at the scriptures shows "the crowd" was comprised of the Roman military on duty, those who had plotted to kill Jesus (temple guards, some religious leaders, elders, priests, scribes), some of Jesus' followers, and the people who had seen Him on the way to Golgotha. (See Matthew 27:1, 41, 55, Mark 14:43, 15:1, 16, 31, 40-41, Luke 23:1, 10, 27, 48, and John 18:12, 19:6, 15, 21 and 25.) We may be accustomed to thinking that nearly everyone was jeering and taunting Jesus while He

---

18   This saying is a contraction combining Psalm 118:25 and 26. Hosanna means to "Save now!" It has a sense of urgency with its meaning. When it became combined with "blessed is he who comes in the name of the Lord," it became an urgent cry to God for salvation followed with praise at its immediate arriving answer. "<u>Name</u> of the Lord" means an awareness of the reputation, glory, power, authority and eternal nature of God. In essence, "Hosanna: blessed is he who comes in the name of the Lord" means: "Save us now, Lord! for we are blessed when *You* come in power and authority!"

was on the cross, but Luke 23:27 and 23:48 say a large group of people mourned, wailed and beat their chests at the sight.

While many people call Jesus *Christ*, few are aware the Old Testament calls the Messiah (which means *Christ*) the "most Holy," "the Prince", the Lord's Anointed, and the Son of God.

Daniel 9:24-25 KJV [24] Seventy weeks are determined upon thy people and upon thy holy city, to finish the transgression, and to make an end of sins, and to make reconciliation for iniquity, and to bring in everlasting righteousness, and to seal up the vision and prophecy, and to anoint the <u>most Holy</u>.

[25] Know therefore and understand, that from the going forth of the commandment to restore and to build Jerusalem unto the <u>Messiah the Prince</u> shall be seven weeks, and threescore and two weeks: the street shall be built again, and the wall, even in troublous times.

Psalm 2:2 and verse 7 KJV [2] The kings of the earth set themselves, and the rulers take counsel together, <u>against the Lord, and against his anointed</u>, saying… [7] <u>I will declare the decree: the Lord hath said unto me, Thou art my Son; this day have I begotten thee.</u>

As explained earlier, the title *Messiah* and *Christ* mean the same thing – Anointed. Anointing was the sacred consecration for a Priest or King. From the book of Genesis Jacob prophesied that one would come from the tribe of Judah who would be a permanent King and Priest (lawgiver). In Psalm 110 God spoke of one who is a righteous Priest forever. The week before the cross when Jesus rode into Jerusalem for the last time, the crowds heralded Him as King. Did Jesus think He was the Messiah? In the conversation with the Samarian woman at the well (John 4) He said He is the Messiah.

When and How was Jesus anointed?

The answer of *how* Jesus was anointed appears in all four gospels with the account of the baptism of Jesus. *When* Jesus was anointed comes from recognizing the meaning and historical events of the Holy Days God established. Many think the Christian spiritual act of baptism began in the New Testament with John the Baptist. However, the Judaic practice of ritual cleansing called *mikvah*[19] predates baptism. The consecration of the Hebrew people in Exodus 19:10 before God appeared at Mt. Sinai involved the ritual cleansing or *mikvah*.[20] The appearance of God, the giving of the Ten Commandments and the Covenant between the new nation of Israel and God, is recognized in Judaism as taking place on the first Holy day of *Shavuot*. Occurring seven weeks after Passover, *Shavuot* is also known as the Feast of Weeks and by Christians it is known as the Day of Pentecost.

John the Baptist's ministry was in fulfillment of the prophecy for John's life mission – to bring the people of Israel back to God, to turn the hearts of parents to their children, and to prepare people for the LORD (Luke 1:16-17, Malachi 4: 6, Isaiah 40:3). Matthew 3:11, Mark 1:4, and Luke 3:3 say John's baptism of the people was for repentance and forgiveness of sins. In other words, John was preparing the people, then consecrating (cleansing) them before the appearance of God/Jesus just like the events happened at Mt. Sinai. When Jesus appeared before John, John recognized the Holiness of Jesus (see John 1:29-31). When Jesus came to John to be baptized, John hesitated and tried to deter Jesus saying he needed to be baptized by Jesus. Matthew 3:15 NIV says Jesus responded, "Let it be so now; it is proper for us to do this to fulfill all righteousness." To fulfill what righteousness? Jesus' baptism could

---

19 In Judaism the practice of ritual cleansing is called *mikvah* or *mikva'ot* (plural). *Mikvah* is the full immersion in water to gain ritual purity for one who has converted to Judaism, to cleanse a woman after her menstrual cycle or childbirth, or to enter service in the Temple. Also, a *mikvah* was required to regain purity after certain prohibited behaviors.

20 See Chabad.org on *Mkivah* by Rivkah Slonim

not be for repentance or forgiveness of sins nor was it an example to people who were getting baptized. <u>The washing of Jesus by John, the son of a Levitical priest was to fulfill the requirement for consecrating a priest and King</u>. At age 30 (Luke 3:23) Jesus began His ministry at the same age priests begin their service or ministry to God (Number 4:47). God told Moses to "wash" Aaron and his sons with water to begin their service as priests (Exodus 29:4). John's washing of Jesus was to fulfill the instructions of *Torah* for consecrating and anointing a priest and King.

Immediately after the holy consecration something unique happened – His anointing and identity as the Son of God/Messiah was confirmed from heaven! Luke 3:22 NASB says "a voice came out of heaven, "You are My beloved Son, in You I am well-pleased." John the Baptist in John 1:32 NIV says, "I saw the Spirit come down from heaven as a dove and remain on him." Does this mean that up until this point Jesus did not have the Spirit of God upon and in Him? No, it does not mean that at all. Recall the Angel Gabriel said the conception of Jesus was a result of the Spirit of God and Luke 2:80 says the child grew in the Spirit? While the Spirit of God was a part of Him, the encounter at the Jordan River marked a transitional point. Just as 1,700 years earlier on Mt. Sinai the appearance of the LORD on the Holy Day of *Shavuot* marked a new transitional point with the people of Israel, Jesus' anointing at the Jordan River on *Shavuot* marked a new transition point for the people of the world.

The essential point of this chapter regarding the titles Messiah and Christ is when we say "Jesus Christ," what we are really saying is: "Jesus (Yahweh, the Eternal God who saves), is the Righteous King and Priest of Heaven and Earth." Surely the scriptures say He is the Anointed – the Christ/Messiah!

Important points from Chapter 1 The Messiah/The Christ were:
- The titles Christ and Messiah mean the same thing – anointed. Someone to whom oil (and in some cases water) has been

poured to symbolize the sacred empowerment and consecration of service to God.
- Kings and Priests were anointed for their positions
- Jesus was both King and the Priest in heaven as well as on earth.
- According to scripture, Jesus was anointed by the Spirit of the Lord
- Jesus said He is the Messiah
- There were many Jewish people who believed He was the Messiah

The Holy Days of God and their connection to Messiah

The Hebrew word for "feasts" (moadim) means "appointed times." The seven feasts were instituted by God to be observed and remembered by His people. The first three holy days (Passover, the Feast of Unleavened bread and First fruits) occur within a one-week period and the last three (Rosh Hashanah, Yom Kippur and Sukkot) within a 15-day period. The fourth or middle holy day is Shavuot, which is separated from Passover by seven weeks. The holy days commemorate something important from the past and connect to the Messiah. The first festival of the year is Passover, also known as Pesach.

Passover/Pesach
Three of the seven feasts occur in the week of Passover. Passover (Exodus 12) commemorates God saving the Hebrew people from slavery and death on the night the firstborn males died in Egypt. The death of an unblemished lamb (or goat – Exodus 12:5) secured protection for all first-born Hebrew males whose homes were covered by the sacrificial blood of the lamb on the doorway. Likewise, Jesus' death secured protection from death[21] for all

---

21 When the Bible contrasts death versus life, it is not referring to the death or life of the physical body. It is referring to the permanent spiritual death, versus being spiritually

whose hearts and minds are covered by their belief and trust in the eternal life Jesus gives. Just before the Passover when Jesus was executed, He entered Jerusalem on the same day the Passover lambs arrived; Jesus appeared at the temple and was questioned for the same four days the lambs were held and examined at the temple. It is generally known that the Passover lambs were sacrificed at the same time Jesus, "the Lamb of God," (John 1:29) was dying on the cross.

The day after Passover (Leviticus 23:5-6) – the holy day of **Unleavened Bread** *represents no sin (without leaven). The unleavened bread is wrapped and hidden away; like Jesus' body was wrapped and entombed for three days. Shortly after is the celebration of* **First Fruits** *which celebrates the barley harvest that sustains life. Jesus' resurrection took place on First Fruits and the apostle Paul referred to Jesus as the "first fruits from the dead" in I Corinthians 15:20. The holy day of First Fruits reminds us that when we believe, we like Jesus will also rise from the death of our physical bodies to a renewed spiritual life.*

Traditionally the story of Joseph and his brothers is read at Passover. The story of Joseph is told in Genesis 37-50. It is about Joseph (the great-grandson of Abraham) who was rejected, kidnapped and sold by his brothers, and taken into Egypt as a slave. Meanwhile his brothers led their father, Jacob to believe Joseph had been killed by a wild animal (Genesis 37:31-33). By the divine Hand of God, Joseph became second in command in Egypt years later. Even though the sins of Joseph's brothers against him were great, Joseph loved them. Years later when the brothers arrived in Egypt to purchase grain, they did not recognize their brother Joseph. Refusing to keep their money, Joseph saved the lives of his brothers and their families from a regional famine and forgave their sins against him. (The similarities between Jesus and Joseph reveal a deeper understanding of why Jesus came, what He did and thereby His connection to this holy day. Note

---

and eternally alive. For example, see Genesis 2:17, Deuteronomy 30:15, 19, Proverbs 12:28, Jeremiah 21:8, Ezekiel 18: 32, and John 5:24.

the promise of Deuteronomy 18:15 [the prophet prophecy] and John 1:11, "He came unto his own, and his own received him not.")

Shavuot/The Feast of Weeks/Pentecost

Shavuot and Passover are related and connected. Shavuot always occurs 49 days after Passover and celebrates not only the giving of Torah, but also the wheat harvest. The first Shavuot (Feast of Weeks, aka Pentecost) occurred in the third month after the Hebrew people left Egypt. It commemorates the people's arrival at Mt. Sinai/Mt. Horeb (also known as the Mountain of God) and the giving of the Ten Commandments. Moses instructed the people to sanctify (consecrate, purify) and cleanse themselves in preparation for the appearance of God (Exodus 19:10). (One of the customs for celebrating Shavuot and other holy days is to wash in the mikvah,[22] perhaps in harkening back to the first Shavuot.)

At the time of Jesus, the purpose of John's baptisms was to consecrate and purify the people for repentance and forgiveness of sin for the appearance and beginning of the ministry of the coming Messiah (Matthew 3:3, 5-6, and 11; and Isaiah 40:3, Luke 1:16-17, and Malachi 4:5-6). After the resurrection and ascension of Jesus, 3,000 new Jewish believers were baptized (consecrated/sanctified and purified) on Shavuot. It is easy to see a connection between the three Shavuot. The first Shavuot God revealed to the new nation of Israel Torah (Words of Life that are <u>the source of instructions for right living</u>). When Jesus was anointed by John the Baptist, God revealed to the world <u>the Source of Eternal Life - Jesus</u>. Then after the resurrection of Jesus and His ascension at Shavuot (Pentecost), God revealed <u>the source of power in the lives of believers of Jesus</u> —the Spirit of God in people to live a righteous life and overcome the power of sin.

---

22   The Christian baptism is predated by the Jewish *mikvah*, a ritual cleansing to gain purity for one who has converted to Judaism, to cleanse, or to enter service in the Temple. The ritual cleansing prior to Shavuot is mentioned in an article entitled "Learning on Shavuot Night" by Eli Landes which appears on Chabad.org. https://www.chabad.org/library/article_cdo/aid/2156/jewish/Learning-on-Shavuot-Night-Tikun-Leil-Shavuot.htm

Jesus' ministry began with His anointing and coincided with another type of harvest – the harvest of human souls. How fitting that Jesus' ministry would begin after John the Baptist spoke of the Messiah coming who would gather the wheat. During Passover, only unleavened bread is eaten. In Judaism leaven has always represented sin and Jesus' death at Passover was symbolic of His absence of sin. Yet on Shavuot there are traditionally two long loaves of bread which some have theorized could represent that Jesus' ministry is for the righteous as well as the forgiven sinners.

Traditionally the story of Ruth is read on Shavuot. This story is the account of a Moabite woman (a Gentile) who commits to her widowed Jewish mother-in-law, Naomi promising to make the God of Israel her God. God in Isaiah 42:6 and 49:6 promised to send the Messiah as a light unto the Gentiles. Shavuot then becomes a special time to officially begin His ministry to and for the Jew and the Gentile, for the righteous and the repentant sinners.

Rosh Hashanah

Rosh Hashanah, also known as the Feast of the Trumpet (which is actually the horn of a ram called a shofar) is the first of the fall feasts and begins on the first day of the seventh month of Tishri (which means to begin). Some Jewish people and sages have said God created the universe on Rosh Hashanah. The shofar is blown to announce specific events such as the announcement of a King, on Yom Kippur, or as a battle cry. A heavenly trumpet sounded on Mt. Sinai when God appeared (Exodus 19:16) and Revelation 8 says a trumpet will announce the return of Jesus and the battle of the end times. On Yom Kippur the shofar is blown as a call to repentance. <u>On Rosh Hashanah it is the signal to start anew; it is the opportunity for a new beginning in a relationship with God.</u> Tradition says certain future events are determined on Rosh Hashanah for the next year, so people pray for a year of peace and prosperity. As part of the traditional observance of this holiday, apples are dipped in honey and eaten symbolic of the hope that it be God's Will to <u>renew</u> a good and sweet year.

The story read on Rosh Hashanah is the binding of Isaac where the ram was substituted for Isaac. This incident recorded in Genesis 22 is said to have occurred on Rosh Hashanah.

Yom Kippur

Yom Kippur known as the Day of Atonement occurs on the 10th day of Tishrei in the fall of the year and is the second of three holidays that occur within a three-week period. The ten days that separate Rosh Hashanah and Yom Kippur are known as the **Days of Awe**. *These are days in which one searches their soul, reviews their actions, and makes amends to those they have wronged. Considered the holiest day of the year,* <u>Yom Kippur is a call to begin again with a new slate of forgiveness, a new closeness to God</u>. *It is thought that because all of one's sins have been atoned for and they have been forgiven, it is on this day that like the High Priest, they too can enter into the presence of the LORD.*

A specific order of events took place on this holy day of Yom Kippur (see Leviticus 16). Two goats were selected; one was to be sacrificed for the sin offering (Leviticus 16:9). The second goat, the scapegoat was <u>to make atonement for the Lord</u> *(Leviticus 16:10) was led into the wilderness symbolic of the sins of the people being taken away, never to return. In time, instead of the scapegoat being released, it was led several miles away to cliffs where he was shoved off the cliff. At the onset of this journey a crimson (red) cord was tied to the scapegoat's horns, while part of the cord was retained. At this point the red cord kept turned white when the goat died – symbolic that the animal had atoned for the sins of the people and now their sin like blood was removed leaving them pure like snow (Isaiah 1:18).*[23]

The Year of Jubilee *is not one of the seven annual feasts. Occurring once every fifty years on Yom Kippur with the call of a shofar, the year of Jubilee begins. It is a time of great celebration. Torah commands that all males return to their homeland at the start of a year of Jubilee (Leviticus 25:10 and 13). Land and property sold or traded were returned to the*

---

23 Mishnah, R. Ishmael in Book 3, Tract Yomah, Chapter 6.

original owner. Those who had been held captive were set free. At that time, few people lived to be aware of and experience two cycles of Jubilee in their lifetime.

The Feast of Tabernacles/Sukkot

*Five days after Yom Kippur starts the most joyous holiday - the eight-day festival of the **Feast of Tabernacles/Sukkot** (sometimes referred to as the season of rejoicing). It is one of the three required holidays that all males are to return to the temple. During the days of Sukkot, the people are to live in temporary shelters (sukkahs) and have their meals there. Sukkot is a time to rejoice. It is a holiday that commemorates and celebrates the 40 year period of wandering in the desert before entering the Promised Land when God protected, guided, cared, and provided for their ancestors' needs. (It is the holiday where it is remembered that God was with His people [Immanuel – Isaiah 7:14]). As one can see the stars through the roof of the temporary shelter, the people are to remember they are part of a bigger and greater universe. The special plants associated with Sukkot are symbolic to convey the overall message that each individual is unique and essential to God regardless of how much or little they know of Torah or how much good they have done or failed to do.*

During the time of the second temple, the seven-day festival of Sukkot had such large oil lamps in the court of the temple that they illuminated nearly every courtyard in Jerusalem. It was within this context that Jesus proclaimed to the crowds that He is the Light of the World (John 8:12). Great rejoicing went on for hours each night as the people acknowledged their connection to God is so deep, it is like water— a part of our very being and vitally necessary to sustain life. "In addition, the water-drawing [ceremony] was said to be accompanied by a great awareness of G-dliness, to the degree that… along with water, people would 'draw' prophetic revelation."[24] John 7:37-38 says this was when Jesus announced He is the source of Living Water and if any man thirst to come onto Him.

---

24 From www.chabad.org. on *Sukkot*.

The final day of Sukkot is called Shemini Atzert/Simchat Torah (the joy of the Torah) when the last passage of Deuteronomy and the beginning of Genesis are read symbolizing the completion of the year and the new start of the ongoing cycle of Torah reading. Afterwards there is great rejoicing as the men dance with Torah scrolls.

Since it appears Jesus' ministry began on one of the Holy Days, and He was crucified on one of the Holy Days, is it likely that Jesus was born on one of the Holy Days? And if He was born on one of them, based on its meaning, which one would it have been?

CHAPTER 2

Jesus – The Prophet

¹⁵ "The Lord your God will raise up for you a prophet like me (Moses) from among you, from your countrymen, you shall listen to him. ¹⁶ This is according to all that you asked of the Lord your God in Horeb on the day of the assembly, saying, 'Let me not hear again the voice of the Lord my God, let me not see this great fire anymore, or I will die.'

¹⁷ The Lord said to me, 'They have spoken well. ¹⁸ I will raise up a prophet from among their countrymen like you, and I will put My words in his mouth, and he shall speak to them all that I command him. ¹⁹ It shall come about that whoever will not listen to My words which he shall speak in My name, I Myself will require *it* of him. ²⁰ But the prophet who speaks a word presumptuously in My name which I have not commanded him to speak, or which he speaks in the name of other gods, that prophet shall die.'

²¹ You may say in your heart, 'How will we know the word which the Lord has not spoken?' ²² When a prophet speaks in the name of the Lord, if the thing does not come about or come true, that is the thing which the Lord has not spoken. The prophet has spoken it presumptuously; you shall not be afraid of him.

Deuteronomy 18:15-22 NASB

Jesus, the Prophet? Being a prophet does not sound nearly as important or as impressive as being the Messiah, Priest, King, and Son of God. Christianity generally acknowledges Jesus is the Prophet of Deuteronomy 18:15-22, although there appears to be no obvious scriptures in the Old Testament that shed further light on this prophecy. However, in the gospels it is clear a number of Jewish people were anticipating the appearance of this prophet and wondered if Jesus was Him. Could a Jeremiah or Isaiah have fulfilled this prophecy? No, and there are specific reasons why this prophet could not have been Joshua who succeeded Moses, nor any other prophet from the Old Testament. It is not a matter of saying this prophesy is about Jesus, but being able to show how Jesus embodies the description unlike anyone else since Moses.

According to the Hebrew culture, a prophet is someone God has chosen to receive and impart a message. In the case of most of the prophets in the Bible they appear to have been chosen against their own will and they received the inspired message through a dream or a vision.[25] This is how God said He communicates with a prophet (Numbers 12:6: And he said, "Hear now my words: If there be a prophet among you, I the LORD will make myself known unto him in a vision, and will speak unto him in a dream."). God warned that if the message does not come true or the message encourages belief in another god, then the person is a false prophet and they should be put to death (Deuteronomy 13:5 and 18:22). However, this passage in Deuteronomy 18 spoke of a unique prophet, one God said would be *like* Moses but in whose mouth, would be God's Words *spoken in God's Name*[26] (Deuteronomy 18:19). Interestingly enough, people at the time of Jesus' ministry were anticipating the appearance of this prophet as much as they were anticipating the appearance of the prophet Elijah,

---

25 Encyclopedia Judaica on the word, "prophet," Vol. 13, Keter Publishing House, Jerusalem, Israel.

26 When something is requested or done *in the name* of God, it means it is asked or done in all the power and authority of God. (See Chapter 21 – No other Name)

who would precede the Messiah (Isaiah 40:3, Matthew 3:1-3, Luke 1:16-17, 76-77 and Malachi 4:5-6), and the Messiah himself.

To understand what is so important about the prophet in Deuteronomy 18, it helps to know the context in which the prophecy was given. The first five books of the Bible (*Torah*) are thought to have been written by Moses (as directed and conveyed by God) with Moses' own life story told in the books of Exodus, Leviticus, Numbers and Deuteronomy. Although Moses was born to Hebrew parents, he was adopted as an infant and raised by the Egyptian Pharaoh's daughter. Years later when Moses was about 40 years old, he fled Egypt after killing an Egyptian man who was beating a Hebrew slave. For the next 40 years Moses was a shepherd in Midian. At the burning bush incident on Mt. Horeb described in Exodus 3, God called Moses to return to Egypt to lead the Hebrew people out of bondage and out of Egypt. This meeting began Moses' face to face friendship/relationship with God. Moses thereafter became the shepherd/leader to the new nation of Israel in their journey to the Promised Land and the one chosen by God to convey His instructions, precepts and commands for how God's people are to live.

The promise of the coming prophet was at the end of forty years when the people were once again on the brink of entering the Promised Land. God had already told Moses he would not live to enter the Promised Land. The Book of Deuteronomy is Moses' last speech to the people he was about to leave. He gave them an overview of their history after leaving Egypt. Moses reminded them to obey and follow God with their whole hearts. He warned them of situations that could turn them away from God and what their punishment for disobedience would be. After the topics of forgiveness of debts, responsibility to the poor, consecration of the first born, the importance of impartial judgment, and the coming time when the people of Israel would ask for a king (Deuteronomy 15-18), came this amazing prophecy of a future prophet. God said He would bring forth someone like Moses; one of their brethren who would speak God's words in the Name of God.

What things did Moses and Jesus have in common that other prophets did not? First point: when God said the coming prophet would be "like unto Moses," this indicated the prophet would not be like any other prophet. God had acknowledged He spoke to prophets through dreams and visions, yet God singled out Moses as the only one He spoke to face to face (other than Abraham); one who was faithful in all of God's household; the one who beheld or saw God's form (Exodus 33:11, Numbers 12:6-8 and Deuteronomy 34:10). This was true of Jesus. Look at John 5:37 and 8:38:

> **John 5:37** And the Father himself, which hath sent me, hath borne witness of me. Ye have neither heard his voice at any time, nor seen his shape.

> **John 8:38** I speak that which I have seen with my Father…

Second point – God said He would put His words in this prophet's mouth and the prophet would speak <u>all</u> that God commanded in the LORD's name[27] (Deuteronomy 18:18-19). In John 12:49-50 Jesus said He did not speak of Himself but what the Father commanded.

> **John 12:49-50 KJV** For I have not spoken of myself; but the Father which sent me, he gave me a commandment, what I should say, and what I should speak. ⁵⁰ And I know that his commandment is life everlasting: <u>whatsoever I speak therefore, even as the Father said unto me, so I speak</u>.

Third point – Was Jesus like Moses? Jesus was a Jew like Moses. As an infant, Moses was hidden away to save his life from Pharaoh's soldiers in Egypt. Likewise, Jesus was hidden away as His parents abruptly left

---

27 "In the LORD's name" means in the power, authority and presence of the LORD. Chapter 21 – *No Other Name* shows that where God's name is, God is also.

Bethlehem bound for Egypt to save His life from Herod's soldiers. Both were known as leaders, intercessors, and prophets who conveyed God's message not just to a nation but to the world. Moses was the prophet who received *Torah* (instructions on how people are to live). Jesus said His words *are* Life (John 5:24 and 6:63) and that He is the Source of Eternal Life. Through Moses, God provided manna (the bread from heaven) and water from a rock for several million people and animals. In John 6:35 Jesus said He is the bread from heaven. In John 7:37-38 during the Feast of Tabernacles, before thousands of people at the temple Jesus proclaimed He is the source of "living water" that springs up to eternal life. Moses was a shepherd to the nation of Israel. Jesus said He is *the* Good Shepherd; that He has other sheep thereby proclaiming He is the shepherd to the world (John 10:11 and 16). Moses was the prophet God used for the first Passover. On the night of the death of the firstborn, every household who believed and obeyed God's instructions, was saved from death. But for those who did not believe nor obeyed, the firstborn died that night in Egypt. The next day the new nation of Israel was set free from slavery. Reminiscent of the first Passover, Jesus, the Lamb of God (John 1:29) died on Passover. And according to Jesus' words (John 3:16), everyone who believes in who Jesus is will not perish; they will receive eternal life. As firstborns of redemption and salvation, they walk away from their old lives, freed from the bondage and penalty of sin. In conclusion, it is fair to say Jesus is like Moses in several ways.

Fourth point – What happened at Mt. Horeb? God said the coming of this unique prophet was directly related to what happened on Mt. Horeb forty years earlier (Deuteronomy 18:16), when the LORD had sought an in-person relationship with His people (Exodus 19:3-6). In the third month after leaving Egypt (on the first holy day - *Shavuot*, also known as Pentecost),[28] the people assembled at Mt. Sinai (also known as Mt. Horeb and as the "mountain of God" – Exodus 3:1). Moses

---

28 Exodus 19:1 says it was the third month after leaving Egypt that the people arrived at Mt. Sinai. Shavuot, celebrated 50 days after Passover, is generally acknowledged as the day of the giving of *Torah* on Mt. Sinai.

told the people to consecrate themselves for this special appearance of God. Through great thunder, lightning flashes, the sound of a heavenly trumpet and the mountain smoking, God began to recite His Ten Commandments. Out of great fear, the people asked Moses to speak to them instead of God because they were afraid they would die if they continued to hear the voice of God and experience His presence (Exodus 20). Moses gave the people the rest of the LORD's instructions on how to live and treat one another. The people agreed to uphold God's instructions (Exodus 24:7 NASB). "All that the LORD has spoken we will do, and we will be obedient!" Yet shortly after this declaration of intention, the people sinned by not believing in the unseen God of their forefathers, nor obeying God's instructions about not making or worshiping other gods. They fashioned an idol of a calf out of gold, and claimed this was the god that brought them out of Egypt and worshipped it.

What did God want on Mt. Horeb? What was the goal in sending a prophet like Moses? What was Jesus' mission? The goal from Genesis 1 when mankind was made in the image of God to Revelation 21:3 is for mankind to know, love and desire to have a relationship with God, their Creator. Before the people asked God not to speak to them at Mt. Horeb, God told Moses to convey this message to the people:

> **Exodus 19:3-6...** tell the children of Israel: [4] 'You have seen what I did to the Egyptians, and *how* I bore you on eagles' wings and brought you to Myself. [5] Now therefore, if you will indeed obey My voice and keep My covenant, then you shall be a special treasure to Me above all people; for all the earth *is* Mine. [6] And you shall be to Me a kingdom of priests and a holy nation.' These *are* the words which you shall speak to the children of Israel."

Jesus too sought to draw people to Himself. Matthew 11:28-30 records Jesus' most heartfelt appeal when He says, "Come unto me, all ye that labour and are heavy laden, and I will give you rest. [29] Take my yoke upon you, and learn of me; for I am meek and lowly in heart: and ye shall find rest unto your souls.³⁰ For my yoke is easy, and my burden is light." Then as Passover and the cross drew near, Jesus said in John 12:32, "And I, if I am lifted up from the earth, <u>I will draw all men unto Me</u>."

As Jesus traveled around Israel teaching and healing people, the scriptures show there were people who wondered, speculated and even came to believe that Jesus was the promised Prophet of Deuteronomy 18:15. Note that the last two quotes below occurred after the resurrection and ascension. By that time, the disciples were certain Jesus was the Prophet prophesied to come.

> **John 1:45** Philip findeth Nathanael, and saith unto him, We have found him, of whom Moses in the law, and the prophets, did write, Jesus of Nazareth, the son of Joseph.

> **John 6:14 NASB** Therefore when the people saw the sign which He had performed, they said, "This is truly the <u>Prophet who is to come</u> into the world."

> **John 7:40 NASB** *Some* of the people therefore, when they heard these words, were saying, "<u>This certainly is the Prophet</u>."

> **Acts 3:21-25 NASB** [Peter] whom heaven must receive until *the* period of restoration of all things about which God spoke by the mouth of His holy prophets from ancient time. ²² Moses said, 'THE LORD GOD WILL RAISE UP FOR YOU A PROPHET LIKE ME FROM YOUR BRETHREN; TO HIM YOU SHALL GIVE HEED to everything He says to you.' ²³ And it will be that every soul that does not heed that prophet shall be utterly destroyed from among the people.' ²⁴ And likewise, all the prophets who have spoken, from Samuel and *his* successors onward, also announced these days. ²⁵ It is you who are the sons of the prophets and of the covenant which God made with your fathers, saying to Abraham, 'AND IN YOUR SEED ALL THE FAMILIES OF THE EARTH SHALL BE BLESSED.'

Acts 7:35-37 KJV [Stephen] ³⁵ This Moses whom they refused, saying, Who made thee a ruler and a judge? the same did God send to be a ruler and a deliverer by the hand of the angel which appeared to him in the bush (Exodus 3).

³⁶ He brought them out, after that he had shewed wonders and signs in the land of Egypt, and in the Red sea, and in the wilderness forty years. ³⁷ This is that Moses, which said unto the children of Israel, A prophet shall the Lord your God raise up unto you of your brethren, like unto me; him shall ye hear.

Did Jesus <u>say</u> anything that leads us to believe He is the Prophet, the one whose mouth spoke God's Words? He did. Jesus said on several occasions His words were not His own; that He spoke and did what the Father wanted Him to say and do. Look again at what God said regarding this Prophet, then look at Jesus' statements:

Deuteronomy 18:18 NASB "… I will put My words in his mouth, and he shall speak to them all that I command him."

John 5:19-20 NASB Therefore Jesus answered and was saying to them, "Truly, truly, I say to you, the Son can do nothing of Himself, unless *it is* something He sees the Father doing; for <u>whatever the Father does, these things the Son also does in like manner.</u> ²⁰ For the Father loves the Son, and shows Him all things that He Himself is doing; and *the Father* will show Him greater works than these, so that you will marvel.

John 7:16 NIV Jesus answered, "My teaching is not my own. It comes from the one who sent me.

John 8:28-29 NASB So Jesus said, "When you lift up the Son of Man, then you will know that I am *He*, and I do nothing on

My own initiative, but <u>I speak these things as the Father taught Me</u>. ²⁹ And He who sent Me is with Me; He has not left Me alone, for <u>I always do the things that are pleasing to Him</u>."

John 12:49-50 KJV For I have not spoken of myself; but the Father which sent me, he gave me a commandment, what I should say, and what I should speak. ⁵⁰ And I know that his commandment is life everlasting: <u>whatsoever I speak therefore, even as the Father said unto me, so I speak</u>.

John 14:10 NIV "...The words I say to you I do not speak on my own authority. Rather, <u>it is the Father, living in me, who is doing his work</u>.

John 14:24 NASB He who does not love Me does not keep My words; and <u>the word which you hear is not Mine, but the Father's who sent Me</u>.

Did God provide confirmation that Jesus was the One promised in Deuteronomy 18? He did. When Jesus, James, John and Peter had gone up high unto the mountain [of transfiguration], Moses and Elijah appeared. Then God spoke to the three disciples:

Matthew 17:5 ⁵ While he [Peter] yet spake, behold, a bright cloud overshadowed them: and behold a voice out of the cloud, which said, This is my beloved Son, in whom I am well pleased; <u>hear ye him</u>. (Hear is more than likely the same Hebrew word *shema* meaning to give heed, listen, understand, to take to heart.)

There is another aspect to this prophecy regarding the coming Prophet. <u>Have we missed the possibility that the prophet God would send in the name of God (name of God means the power, authority and presence of God), who would speak ALL of God's words, was God</u>

Himself? (This idea is not preposterous, see Isaiah 7:14 –where a son is born to a virgin and His name called Immanuel which conveys mighty, powerful God who is with us. And Isaiah 9:6 says a son is born who is Mighty God and the Everlasting Father). Could this prophecy be saying that since they were terrified to hear God speak at Mt. Horeb, that God *Himself* would come in the likeness of man (like unto Moses) as one of them (from among their brethren) and in their midst would speak (God's Words) to them directly? Historically Jesus is recognized as a good man, a man of great wisdom, peace and integrity. However, He made some wildly profound statements about Himself; <u>statements that must be truthful or Jesus is guilty of blasphemy</u>. For example, Jesus said that He and the Father are One and if you have seen Him [Jesus], you have seen the Father. In the following verses did Jesus mean the Scriptures were written about Him as the Prophet, Messiah/Christ, Son of God, and King of Israel, or did He mean that *all* the holy Scriptures were written about Him as the One and only God[29] – Creator of the Universe?

John 5:39 and 46 NASB [39] You search the Scriptures because you think that in them you have eternal life; <u>it is these that testify about Me</u>; ... [46] For if you believed Moses, you would believe Me, for <u>he wrote about Me</u>.

Luke 24:44 And he said unto them, These are the words which I spake unto you, while I was yet with you, that all things must be fulfilled, which <u>were written in the law of Moses, and in the prophets, and in the psalms, concerning me</u>.

John 12:49-50 For I have not spoken of myself; but the Father which sent me, he gave me a commandment, what I should say, and what I should speak. [50] And I know that his commandment

---

29 See Isaiah 43:10-11, 45:5, 18, 45:21-22, and Isaiah 46:9-10. These verses speak of being the only God.

is life everlasting: <u>whatsoever I speak therefore, even as the Father said unto me, so I speak</u>.

John 14:10 Believest thou not that <u>I am in the Father, and the Father in me</u>? the words that I speak unto you I speak not of myself: but <u>the Father that dwelleth in me, he doeth the works</u>.

John 14:24 He that loveth me not keepeth not my sayings: and <u>the word which ye hear is not mine, but the Father's which sent me</u>.

During the giving of the Ten Commandments at Mt. Horeb, the people in fear said they did not want to hear or see God. Moses said their fear of God would keep them from sinning (Exodus 20:20). It did not. Yet in Deuteronomy 18:17 when God recalled this event and the people's response, He said He would send the Prophet (like Moses) who would speak God's Words, who would come in the name of God (power, authority and presence of God), and God would hold accountable those who did not listen and take heed. Jesus said His words were not His own, but rather the Father's. Note what else Jesus said about believing or rejecting His words.

John 12:47-48 [47] And if any man hear my words, and believe not, I judge him not: for I came not to judge the world, but to save the world. [48] He that rejecteth me, and receiveth not my words, hath one that judgeth him: the word that I have spoken, the same shall judge him in the last day.

John 14:23 Jesus answered and said unto him, If a man love me, he will keep my words: and my Father will love him, and we will come unto him, and make our abode with him.

Jesus said <u>He and His words are the source of eternal life</u> (John 6:63) and if people do not believe, they would die in their sins (John

8:21). Long ago the Hebrew people were afraid to listen to the Words from God; they were afraid they would die. To become children of God we will experience death. We die to our old lives, die to our fears, our old beliefs, flesh, and our sinful desires so that we may have eternal life and a relationship with God just as God had sought on Mt. Horeb/ Mt. Sinai in Exodus 19.

Finally, in closing Jesus said in John 8:28 after His resurrection we shall know "that <u>I am He</u>." Is it a coincidence that in Isaiah 43:10 God used that same phrase, "<u>that ye may know and believe me, and understand that I am he</u>"? Did Jesus use God's unique name, "I AM"[30]? Did He mean that we shall know that He is not only *the* Prophet of Deuteronomy 18, but He is the God the people were afraid to hear speak who has come as one of them, and has spoken the Words of Life once more?

John 8:28 Then said Jesus unto them, <u>When ye have lifted up the Son of man, then shall ye know that I am he, and that I do nothing of myself; but as my Father hath taught me, I speak these things</u>.

Isaiah 43:10 Ye are my witnesses, saith the LORD, and my servant whom I have chosen: <u>that ye may know and believe me, and understand that I am he</u>: before me there was no God formed, neither shall there be after me.

Who do the scriptures say Jesus is? Time and time again the things Jesus said and did testified and proclaimed that He is God. While many Christians agree that Jesus is God, have we grasped how significant it is that here, before Moses' death, God said He would come in the form of a man? Although Moses and God said of this coming Prophet that the people were to *shema* Him (means to listen, to obey, to regard/believe),

---

30 See Chapter 21 "No other Name" for the full meaning of God's name I AM.

have we grasped that when Jesus came, many rejected Him just as God was rejected at Mt. Horeb? When Jesus made the following statement in John 5, was He referring to Deuteronomy 18:18-19?

John 5:46-47 For had ye believed Moses, ye would have believed me; for he wrote of me. ⁴⁷ But if ye believe not his writings, how shall ye believe my words?

Isaiah 52:6 Therefore my people shall know my name: therefore they shall know in that day that I am he that doth speak: behold, it is I.
He [Jesus] is the image of the invisible God.... Colossians 1:15

This brings us to the next titles related to Jesus – the title of Son of David and Son of God. Jesus was called the Son of David by a variety of people in several places in the gospels. What does this title mean? If David lived nearly one thousand years before Jesus was born, how could Jesus be his son? And if the Messiah is the Son of David, how could He also be the Son of God?

CHAPTER 3

The Son of David and The Son of God

Then said they all, Art thou then the Son of God?
And he [Jesus] said unto them, Ye say that I am.
                                                    – Luke 22:70

Referring to King David, Jesus is called the Son of David several times in the gospels. However, David lived and died hundreds of years before Jesus was born. How could King David be Jesus' father? Christianity recognizes Jesus as the Son of God, but what does that title mean? When and how did Jesus come to exist as the Son of God? Which one has more power – God the Father or God the Son? Which came first? Our terminology of "son" and "father" implies one is younger, one older; there are two entities and the father produced the son. Does this mean the Son has less, more, or the same amount of power and authority as the Father? What does the Bible or more specifically, the Old Testament say about Jesus being the Son of David, and the relationship between God the Father and the Son of God?

The first time the "Son of David" *and* "Son of God" prophecy appears in the Bible is in II Samuel 7:11-16. The royal historical account of this same prophecy appears in I Chronicles 17:10-14. While there are many scriptures in the Old Testament that foretell the coming of someone very special, none allude to *the* Son to God before the II Samuel reference. When did this prophecy occur in Israel's history and does it really identify Jesus? In the continued account of the Hebrew people and events, the previous chapter told of the prophecy regarding the Prophet like unto Moses who would come speaking the words of God. After Moses' death, the next leader was Joshua,[31] the son of Nun. Joshua was the military and spiritual leader of the Hebrew nation who led them into the Promised Land (the sixth book of the Bible - Joshua). After Joshua's death, over the next several hundred years a succession of judges (the Book of Judges) led the people of Israel. The next prominent and pivotal spiritual leader was the prophet and judge Samuel (the first book of Samuel). Samuel was the last of the judges to rule over Israel. When Samuel grew old, the people asked for a king so that they could be like the other nations around them. As God had responded at the time, the people had not rejected Samuel as their leader; they had rejected God as their King. However, the Kingdom of God, nor had God disappeared.

God's desire for a connected Kingdom of God with a kingdom of Israel was evident from the time God brought the people out of Egypt (Exodus 19:6 And ye shall be unto me a kingdom of priests, and an holy nation…). That opportunity was available when God selected Saul as the first ruler (captain) and king of Israel. When Saul showed he was more concerned about the approval of the people than pleasing or obeying God's instructions, God rejected Saul as king (I Samuel 13:13-14, 15:23). The Prophet Samuel told Saul God would have established his kingdom over Israel <u>forever</u>, but now God had rejected Saul as king. Shortly thereafter God selected the next king of Israel based on young David's love for God, his fierce devotion to God, and his rock-hard trust in the goodness of God (I Samuel 13:14). This time the promise of an eternal Kingdom of Heaven and Israel went to the familial line or

---

31 The English adaptation of the Greek name, Jesus, is Joshua. The Classical Biblical Hebrew letters for the English name, Joshua, (yod-hay-waw-shin-ayin) are the Hebrew letters that spell Jesus' name (most likely *Yahusha, Yahushua* or *Yehoshua* from which the more recognized version of the name became – *Yeshua*). Over time the Hebrew pronunciation and spelling of this name changed slightly.

house of David. When David moved to Jerusalem as King, he expressed the desire to build a permanent house for God (a temple) in Jerusalem. God sent a message through the Prophet Nathan to King David that instead of a house of cedar David wanted to build, God Himself would establish a *house* of David and Kingdom that would never end. Here is Nathan's prophecy as recorded in II Samuel, and I Chronicles:

> **II Samuel 7:11-16 NASB** The Lord also declares to you that the Lord will make a house for you. ¹² "When your days are complete and you lie down with your fathers, I will raise up your descendant after you, who will come forth from you, and I will establish his kingdom. ¹³ He shall build a house for My name, and I will establish the throne of his kingdom forever. ¹⁴ I will be a father to him and he will be a son to Me; (KJV "I will be his father, and he shall be my son.") **when he commits iniquity, I will correct him with the rod of men and the strokes of the sons of men**, ¹⁵ but My lovingkindness shall not depart from him, as I took *it* away from Saul, whom I removed from before you. ¹⁶ Your house and your kingdom shall endure before Me forever; your throne shall be established forever."

Note the difference between the prophecy in II Samuel 7 above and I Chronicles 17 below. The phrase when this son commits iniquity, God would correct him with the rod of men is not there. An explanation of this phrase appears in Psalm 89 below.

> **I Chronicles 17:10-14 NASB** Moreover, I tell you that the Lord will build a house for you.¹¹ When your days are fulfilled that you must go *to be* with your fathers, that I will set up *one of* your descendants after you, who will be of your sons; and I will establish his kingdom.¹² He shall build for Me a house, and I will establish his throne forever. ¹³ I will be his father and he shall be My son; and I will not take My lovingkindness away from him, as I took it from him who was before you. ¹⁴ But I will settle

<u>him in My house and in My kingdom forever, and his throne shall be established forever.</u>"

Psalm 89:30-32 NASB [30] "If his sons forsake My law and do not walk in My judgments, [31] If they violate My statutes and do not keep My commandments, [32] Then I will punish their transgression with the rod and their iniquity with stripes.

    This promise and prophecy has a layered meaning as it speaks of events to come in the earthly realm and the eternal spiritual realm because the word "forever" is used three times. God said when David's days were fulfilled (as king in this life on earth), God would raise up a descendant/a son (Solomon, who at the time had not yet been born) whose kingdom God would establish. King Solomon did build a House/Temple for God's name (II Samuel 7:13, II Chronicles 7:16). When Solomon sinned by worshipping the foreign gods of his wives, God's lovingkindness did not depart from him. Although God did not punish Solomon with the loss of his kingdom during his lifetime, his kingdom and descendants as kings would not reign forever in Israel. After Solomon's death, his son Rehoboam became king and was responsible for causing the split in the kingdom. Ten tribes became the Northern Kingdom (Israel) and Rehoboam remained the king of the Southern Kingdom – Judea (consisting of the tribes of Judah and Benjamin). Several future kings and the people of both kingdoms made sacrifices and some worshipped idols. Eventually the kingdoms were defeated by enemies and taken into captivity. In time Solomon's temple was defiled, decimated and eventually destroyed.

    The prophecy of an eternal kingdom of Israel appeared to be at an end, yet a *spiritual* descendent and heir of David was yet to come. God's Heavenly Kingdom of believers is the eternal Kingdom that will last "forever" (Hebrews 1:8, Genesis 49:10, Isaiah 9:7). Over two hundred years after the prophecy to King David, the prophet Isaiah spoke of David's future descendant and eternal kingdom in Isaiah 9:6-7.

Isaiah 9:6-7: ⁶ For unto us a child is born, unto us a son is given: and the government shall be upon his shoulder: and his name shall be called Wonderful, Counsellor, The mighty God, The everlasting Father, The Prince of Peace. ⁷ Of the increase of his government and peace there shall be no end, upon the throne of David, and upon his kingdom, to order it, and to establish it with judgment and with justice from henceforth even for ever. The zeal of the Lord of hosts will perform this.

By the time Jesus' ministry began hundreds of years later, the people understood this prophecy to King David also spoke of the coming Messiah. They understood that King David would have a son (a descendant) born hundreds of years after his death.

Why was the Messiah to be the Son of David?

The coming of the Messiah (Jesus/God) as a royal descendant of King David restored God's right as the King of Israel. In essence, the divine right as King of Israel (which always belonged to God) was temporarily assigned (with limits) to David, to then be returned to God as Jesus. Why David? What made him so special? God referred to David in I Samuel 13:14 as a man after God's own heart (*Strong Concordance's* Hebrew word #H3823 *lebab* meaning mind, soul, heart, understanding and will) for God. David believed and trusted God, loved God's Word and experienced an ongoing devoted relationship with God. When God promised David a future "Son" whose kingdom would never end, God revealed His plan to bring forth the King of kings who would not only be the true King of Israel, but King of all who receive and believe in Him. Every time someone called Jesus "Son of David", they were acknowledging their belief that Jesus was the Messiah, the King of Israel and the Son of God. In addition, beyond people's understanding and recognition, every time Jesus was called the Son of David, they were also acknowledging the one true King, the God of Abraham, the LORD' who had brought the people out of Egypt with miraculous signs and wonders. And once again, God was revealing Himself to those around Him with signs and wonders.

It is heartbreaking to think the title "King of the Jews" was adhered to the cross at the time Jesus was crucified. And once again, the King of the Jews had been rejected.

Isaiah 53:1 and 3 ... to whom has the arm of the LORD been revealed?... He is despised and rejected by men, A Man of sorrows and acquainted with grief. And we hid, as it were, *our* faces from Him; He was despised, and we did not esteem Him.

I Samuel 8:7 NASB The LORD said to Samuel, "Listen to the voice of the people in regard to all that they say to you, for they have not rejected you, but they have rejected Me from being king over them.

The first time Jesus is mentioned in the gospels as the Son of David **and** the Son of God came from the angel Gabriel at the conception of Jesus (Luke 1:32 KJV – "He shall be great, and shall be called the Son of the Highest: and the Lord God shall give unto him the throne of his father David"). Jesus was called the "Son of David" in the passages of the two blind men asking for healing (Matthew 9:27 and Mark 10:47), then among the crowds (Matthew 12:23) and when He entered Jerusalem for the last time (Matthew 21:9). The fact that the Canaanite woman seeking deliverance for her daughter in Matthew 15:22 called Jesus the Son of David means the idea that the Messiah would be the Son of David was well known even among Gentiles (non-Jews) living in the area. Finally, Jesus Himself acknowledges He is the fulfillment of the II Samuel 7 prophecy when He said in Revelation 22:16 NASB, "I, Jesus, have sent My angel to testify to you these things for the churches. I am the root and the descendant of David, the bright morning star."

Jesus – The Son of David and Son of God

What does the "Son" relationship represent in this prophecy from God?

Exodus 4:22 … 'Thus says the LORD: "Israel *is* My son, My firstborn."'"

Jeremiah 31:9 [The LORD speaking] "…For I am a father to Israel, And Ephraim is My firstborn."

Exodus 14:15 And the LORD said to Moses, "Why do you cry to Me? Tell the children of Israel to go forward?

Isaiah 54:5 For your Maker *is* your husband, The LORD of hosts *is* His name; And your Redeemer *is* the Holy One of Israel; He is called the God of the whole earth.

In these scriptures, God identified Himself as the Father to Israel, He called Ephraim and Israel <u>His firstborn,</u> and God is referred to as <u>the Husband</u> of Israel. These verses are not speaking of a blood or marital relation. Rather the common relationships of husband and father refer to an emotional connection, an obligation or responsibility, and/or inherited rights. In other Middle Eastern cultures of this time, the term "son" did not always mean a biological relationship but served to convey inheritance rights.[32] In believing Jesus to be the son of David we accept a son can be born hundreds of years after the death of the named father. Since the Bible says Mary was a virgin when Jesus was born, it must be acknowledged that the genealogical record that connects Jesus to King David through Joseph does not make Jesus a Son to

---

32 Consider Genesis 15:2. Abram told God he was childless and his heir would be Eliezer (heir in the NASB and steward in the KJV. The Hebrew word #H1121 *ben* is translated as son, a builder of the family name). In the book of Ruth 4:13-14 Ruth marries Boaz. Their biological child, Obed is recognized as the child of Ruth's deceased husband, Mahlon to carry Mahlon's name and receive Mahlon's family inheritance rights.

David biologically. Likewise, if it is accepted and believed that Jesus is the Son of God as part of the Christian salvation belief system, subconsciously or intellectually it should be recognized that neither of these Father/Son relationships are biologically based. This statement means there was no mother, nor was there sexual union that produced the son of David or the Son of God. <u>Rather the relationship of Son in this prophecy represents and establishes the right and authority to be recognized as the King of Israel and King of the eternal Kingdom of God.</u>

There are probably specific reasons the Messiah (the anointed one commissioned by God to do a specific task) is identified as the Son of God. One reason is it provided a relationship framework the people of that time and place could understand. In the Middle East, the designation as a son was culturally important. A son represented the father's connection to the future. A son's name spoke of the relationship (for example, males were known as "Jacob ben Isaac"; the *ben* meaning "son of"). In Jewish culture, the firstborn son had a right to that which had belonged to the father and meant he would inherit everything his father had if he were the only son. The son of a king conveyed not only his legitimate relationship to the named father, but his right and authority to rule said kingdom. The birth of Jesus as the *son* of David nearly one thousand years after David's death and John 3:16 which spoke of Jesus as the Son of God identify Jesus as the unique heir (only begotten son - meaning single and only) of both David and the LORD God.

What does "Son of God" tell us about Jesus?

<u>Jesus is not the only son of God</u>. Adam is called a son of God (Luke 3:38). Genesis 6:2 speaks of the actions of some who are identified as the "sons of God." People who come to believe and accept Jesus become sons and daughters of God (John 1:12). However, Jesus as *the* "Son of God" meant something very different and identified something exclusively about Jesus. Some people referred to the God of their

forefathers as "*Our* Father," yet Jesus called him "*My* Father." This distinction did not escape the people who were present. When Jesus said He is the Son of God and He and the Father are one (John 10:30 and 36), they knew Jesus was claiming more than a unique relationship with God. They knew Jesus was proclaiming Himself to be God. John 10:33 KJV says, "The Jews answered him, saying, For a good work we stone thee not; but for blasphemy; and because that thou, being a man, makest thyself God."

When the fallen angels called Jesus the Son of God, they knew exactly who He was. The two demon possessed men called Him the Son of God in Matthew 8:29 NIV - "What do you want with us, Son of God?" they shouted. "Have you come here to torture us before the appointed time?" Mark 3:11 KJV says, "And unclean spirits, when they saw him, fell down before him [involuntary acquiesce?], and cried, saying, Thou art the Son of God." Luke 4:41 reads, "And devils also came out of many, crying out, and saying, Thou art Christ the Son of God. And he rebuking them suffered them not to speak: for they knew that he was Christ." After the forty-day fast, Satan taunted Jesus prodding Him to prove He was the "Son of God" (Matthew 4:3, and 6).

There were others who believed Jesus was the Son of God. Almost as if they could not keep their mouths shut, the disciples worshiped Him and called Him the "Son of God" when Jesus walked on water in Matthew 14:33. "The Son of God" was Peter's answer during the conversation of "Who do you say I am" in Matthew 16:16, and it was Martha's answer just minutes before Lazarus was resurrected in John 11:27. After Jesus healed the man blind from birth in John 9, He asked the man if he believed on the Son of God. The man responds in verse 38, "And he said, Lord, I believe. And he worshipped him." In Mark 14:61-62 (also found in Matthew 26:63-64 and Luke 22:70) on the night before the crucifixion, Jesus was asked in the presence of the council of elders, scribes and chief priests if He was the Christ, the Son of the Blessed (God)? He answered, "I am." After this admission, the trial was over; His fate was decided. Finally, in the early afternoon when the sky darkened, the earth quaked and rocks split after Jesus died on the cross, the centurion and those with him cried out in fear, "Truly this was the Son of God" (Matthew 27:45, 51, and 54 KJV). Did you notice which of these situations in this paragraph revealed Jesus as God?

While people questioned the identity and mission of Jesus, demons knew who He was and where He was from. The admission to the High Priest that He was the "Son of God" was considered "blasphemous,"[33] because they recognized when Jesus admitted He was the *Son* of God, He was also claiming *to be* God. It was based on this admission that Jesus was the Son of God that His death was determined. Mark 14:64 NIV says, "You have heard the blasphemy. What do you think?" They all agreed His sin of blasphemy required death. The situation in question that revealed Jesus is God was when others worshipped Him. The blind man who recovered his eyesight in John 9:38 (KJV- And he said, Lord, I believe. And he worshiped him) and the disciples who saw Jesus walk on water worshiped Him as well (Matthew 14:33 NIV - Then those who were in the boat worshiped him, saying, "Truly you are the Son of God"). According to the Old Testament and Jesus, worship belongs to God alone (Deuteronomy 6:13, Matthew 4:10, and Luke 4:8). Do we recognize the significance of this statement and recall the third of the Ten Commandments (Exodus 20:5 KJV - Thou shalt not bow down thyself to them [means worship], nor serve them [idols]...)? When Jesus <u>*allowed*</u> the blind man and His disciples to worship Him, **HE ACKNOWLEDGED HE IS GOD <u>or according to *Torah*</u> HE WAS GUILTY OF BLASPHEMY FOR WHICH THE PENALTY IS DEATH!**

There was another time Jesus addressed the issue of Son of David/Son of God. After Jesus came to Jerusalem for the last time before His death and resurrection, He spent several days teaching at the temple.[34]

---

33 Blasphemy is the act or offense of speaking sacrilegiously about God or sacred things. In *Strong's Concordance* the word blasphemy in Hebrew means contempt (#5007 *ne'atsah* from the root word #5006 – *na'ats* meaning to spurn, despise or abhor). In the Greek (#988) the word means to slander, speak injurious to divine majesty or to one's good name.

34 The original Passover instructions were to take the lamb into the home for four days, then the lamb was killed (Exodus 12). According to Jewish tradition, the purpose of the four days was to inspect the lamb that he be blemish free (http://www.chabad.org/holidays/

Jesus – The Son of David and Son of God

During those days the people asked Him questions and He, in turn asked some of His own. One of the questions Jesus asked concerned the Messiah being the son of David. This passage is in Mark 12:35-37 and Luke 20:41-44, however the one in Matthew 22:41-46 yields something more. What is so remarkable about this question is that Jesus' follow up question led the people to an undeniable conclusion that left them in a stunned silence; not daring to say or ask anything else. This is the passage:

> **Matthew 22:41-46 NASB** Now while the Pharisees were gathered together, Jesus asked them a question: "What do you think about the Christ, whose son is He?" They said to Him, "*The son* of David." He said to them, "Then how does David in the Spirit call Him 'Lord,' saying,
>
> > 'THE LORD SAID TO MY LORD,[35]
> > "SIT AT MY RIGHT HAND,
> > UNTIL I PUT YOUR ENEMIES BENEATH YOUR FEET"'?
>
> If David then calls Him 'LORD,' how is He his son?" No one was able to answer Him a word, nor did anyone dare from that day on to ask Him another question.

Jesus made a final point very clear: while the Messiah would be known as the "Son of David," in the fullness of truth the Messiah *is more* than the "son of David," more than the "Son of God" – He *is* God. This is Jesus' essential point about Himself as the Son of David: even King David while under the influence of the Spirit of God (the Divine

---

passover/pesach). During the time of the temple, the Passover lambs were brought into Jerusalem a week before Passover and were inspected during the four days prior to Passover. For several (four?) days Jesus went to the Temple, where He taught and answered questions. (See Mark 11:11-15, 20, 27, 14:1). Was this Jesus' time of inspection?

35 When God's name is translated in this verse, it reads, "Yehovah (the I AM) said to my Adonai (means Master refers to God)…."

Presence), called the Messiah *his* Lord (*Adonai* means Lord, and refers to God) – David himself acknowledged that the Messiah was his God!

When entering Jerusalem for the last time before the crucifixion, Jesus spoke of dire events to occur because the people did not recognize the time of their visitation (Luke 19:44). Where does it say in the Old Testament that God will come to earth? Isaiah 35:4-6 says in part:

> …he (God) will come and save you. ⁵ Then the eyes of the blind shall be opened, and the ears of the deaf shall be unstopped. ⁶ Then shall the lame man leap as an hart, and the tongue of the dumb sing.

Recall that Jesus said the works (the miracles) testify (identify) who He is.

Reading between the lines of scripture

One may ask if Jesus is totally and solely God, why was He called the Son of God? Why not just say He was God? He did, but the people at the time of Jesus' ministry struggled with believing He was the promised Prophet of Deuteronomy 18:15. They were outraged by His admission He is the Messiah of Isaiah 61:1 (see Chapter 5 - The Return to Nazareth as told in Luke 4). Matthew 21:15 says the religious leaders were indignant when the people called Jesus the son of David. His identity as the "Son of God" was considered blasphemous and was punished by crucifixion. How would someone then or today respond to the statement that Jesus is God – the God of the Old Testament *and* God of the New Testament?[36] Yet look at statements made by Jesus where He identifies His sameness and oneness with His Father and look at

---

36 Isaiah 42:1-4 describes the mission of the Servant of the LORD. Isaiah 52:13 begins the description of the suffering Servant of Isaiah 53. In Zechariah 3:8-9 God promises His servant, the Branch and says He [God] will remove the sin of the land in one day.

statements from the Old Testament regarding the LORD God as the *only* Savior, the *only* Redeemer and the *only* God. In quoting the prophet Isaiah, Jesus warned in Matthew 13:14 that it is our natural tendency to not understand the things of God: "By hearing ye shall hear, and shall not understand; and seeing ye shall see, and shall not perceive." <u>To understand the message in these verses, we are required to think about what God said He would achieve, to consider what the Hebrew people of the time understood about God, and to determine what the LORD of the Old Testament and Jesus' words were revealing about who He is.</u>

Matthew 11:27 NIV "All things have been committed to me by my Father. No one knows the Son except the Father, and no one knows the Father except the Son…"

John 5:26 NASB For as the Father has life in himself, so he has granted the Son also to have life in himself.

John 6:27 NASB Do not work for food that spoils, but for food that endures to eternal life, which the Son of Man will give you. For on him God the Father has placed his seal of approval."

John 14:1 NIV … You believe in God; believe also in me.

John 14:10 NIV Don't you believe that I am in the Father, and that the Father is in me? The words I say to you I do not speak on my own authority. Rather, it is the <u>Father, living in me, who is doing his work</u>.

John 14:11 NIV <u>Believe me when I say that I am in the Father and the Father is in me</u>; or at least believe on the evidence of the works themselves.

John 17:10 NIV [10] All I have is yours, and all you have is mine. And glory has come to me through them.

John 10:11 "I am the good shepherd…" and **Psalm 23:1** says "The LORD (YHWH[37]) is my shepherd…"

John 8:12 … I am the light of the world… **Isaiah 60:19** … the LORD (YHWH) shall be unto thee an everlasting light …

One more point made from the mouth of Jesus. On the last night before His arrest, Jesus's private conversation with the disciples is in John chapter 13 through 16. At one point in John 14:8 the disciple Philip asks Jesus to show them the Father. This was Jesus' response:

John 14:9 Jesus saith unto him, Have I been so long time with you, and yet hast thou not known me, Philip? <u>he that hath seen me hath seen the Father</u>; and how sayest thou then, Show us the Father?

Jesus' reply says that being with Him over a period of time should clearly have identified who He is: if you have seen Jesus, you have seen the Father. Again - <u>if you have seen Jesus, you have seen the Father.</u> He followed this statement up for those still struggling to understand His very clear point: - John 14:10-11 quoted above, said His words and the things He did identify Him. For those well acquainted with these verses, we fail to see just how audacious the statements are. Try substituting your name in the place of Jesus' name and making these statements about your power and authority.

From the Book of Isaiah, in one passage after another the words of the LORD God Himself says He is the Savior, the Redeemer, the Creator and that <u>there is no one else.</u> <u>He alone is God.</u>

---

37 YHWH or YHVH is a Tetragrammaton, meaning consisting of four letters that represent the Hebrew word for the English name of the Biblical God of Israel – *I AM*.

Isaiah 42:1 NIV "Here is my servant, whom I uphold, my chosen one in whom I delight; I will put my Spirit on him, and he will bring justice to the nations.

Isaiah 42:6-7 NIV "I, the Lord, have called you in righteousness; I will take hold of your hand. I will keep you and will make you to be a covenant for the people and a light for the Gentiles, ⁷ to open eyes that are blind, to free captives from prison and to release from the dungeon those who sit in darkness. (See Luke 4:18-20)

Isaiah 43:10-11 NASB "You are my witnesses," declares the Lord, "and my servant whom I have chosen, so that you may know and believe me and understand that **I am he**. Before me no god was formed, nor will there be one after me. ¹¹ I, even I, am the Lord, and apart from me there is no savior.

Isaiah 43:14 NIV This is what the Lord says—your Redeemer, the Holy One of Israel:

Isaiah 44:6 and 8 NIV "This is what the Lord says— Israel's King and Redeemer, the Lord Almighty: I am the first and I am the last; **apart from me there is no God**... ⁸ Do not tremble, do not be afraid. Did I not proclaim this and foretell it long ago? You are my witnesses. Is there any God besides me? No, there is no other Rock; I know not one."

Isaiah 45:5 and 18 NIV I am the Lord, and there is no other; **apart from me there is no God**... ¹⁸ For this is what the Lord says— he who created the heavens, he is God; he who fashioned and made the earth, he founded it; he did not create it to be empty, but formed it to be inhabited— he says: "I am the Lord, and there is no other.

Isaiah 45:21-22 NIV ...Who foretold this long ago, who declared it from the distant past? Was it not I, the LORD? And **there is no God apart from me, a righteous God and a Savior; there is none but me**. ²² "Turn to me and be saved, all you ends of the earth; for I am God, and there is no other.

Isaiah 46:9-10 NIV Remember the former things, those of long ago; **I am God, and there is no other; I am God, and there is none like me.** ¹⁰ I make known the end from the beginning, from ancient times, what is still to come. I say, 'My purpose will stand, and I will do all that I please.'

Isaiah 59:15-16 NIV The LORD looked and was displeased that there was no justice. ¹⁶ He saw that there was no one, he was appalled that there was no one to intervene; so his own arm achieved salvation for him, and his own righteousness sustained him.

Isaiah 63:4-5 NIV It was for me the day of vengeance; the year for me to redeem had come. ⁵ I looked, but there was no one to help, I was appalled that no one gave support; so my own arm achieved salvation for me...

These verses are almost overkill as again and again God says there is no other God. He alone is the Creator. He alone is the Savior. He alone is the King of Israel, the Redeemer; there is no one but Him. In the following verses as God and Jesus both say they are the first and the last – either one is lying (impossible!) or there is one God. Also, the LORD God of the Old Testament proclaims He is the Creator of the Universe and Earth; that He is the one who causes all to stand up together (Isaiah 48:12-13 and Isaiah 66:1-2). Yet Colossians 1:15-17 of the New Testament says that Jesus is the Creator of all things in heaven and on earth and in Him all things hold together.

Jesus – The Son of David and Son of God

Isaiah 48:12-13 NIV [12] "Listen to me, Jacob, Israel, whom I have called: I am he; I am the first and I am the last. [13] My own hand laid the foundations of the earth, and my right hand spread out the heavens; when I summon them, they all stand up together.

Isaiah 43:10b NASB: Before Me there was no God formed, and there will be none after Me.

Colossians 1:15-17 NIV The Son is the image of the invisible God, the firstborn over all creation. [16] For in him all things were created: things in heaven and on earth, visible and invisible, whether thrones or powers or rulers or authorities; all things have been created through him and for him. [17] He is before all things, and in him all things hold together.

Revelation 1:17-18 NASB [17] When I saw Him, I fell at His feet like a dead man. And He placed His right hand on me, saying, "Do not be afraid; <u>I am the first and the last,</u>[18] and the living One; and I was dead, and behold, I am alive forevermore, and I have the keys of death and of Hades.

Revelation 22:13 NASB [13] I am the Alpha and the Omega, <u>the first and the last, the beginning and the end."</u>

<u>The title "Son of God" had nothing to do with designating the LORD God of the Old Testament as God the Father, and Jesus as God the Son.</u> The previous Isaiah passages said God Himself would be the Servant, the Savior and Redeemer. The LORD God came in the only way mankind's limited intellect could understand – as the Son of God. Long ago Moses told the Hebrew people to prepare for the visitation of their God. This was the same God who had appeared before Abraham, Isaac and Jacob (Genesis 17:1, 18:1, 26:2, and 35:9) and the God who had brought them out of Egypt with a mighty hand. Yet they rejected

Him; they were too afraid. God was too much for them. But they could believe in a calf made of gold fashioned by their own hands was the God who had brought them out of Egypt.

God mentioned that incident on cloud-covered Mount Sinai when He promised to send *The* Prophet like unto Moses (Deuteronomy 18:15-19). This someone with a gentle and humble heart (Matthew 11:29) would be the Prophet like Moses who came 1,500 years later. The promised son of the mighty warrior King David came nearly a thousand years after the death of David stepping through crowds intending to harm Him without ever raising His hand in defense to their attempts at violence (Luke 4:30, John 8:59 and 10:39). He came as the *Son* of God, after the Prophet Isaiah had said a virgin would give birth to a son and called him "God with us" (Immanuel – Isaiah 7:14) and Isaiah 9:6 said He would be <u>born</u> as a <u>Son</u> is also Mighty God and the Everlasting Father. He came as the Son of God with a mission to reveal God, and proclaim redemption and salvation from everlasting destruction is available to everyone who believes.

The people of Jesus' time did not have the advantage people have today to see Jesus' ministry detailed in the Gospels, to see connections of His words, and actions as they relate to and confirm Old Testament prophecies. Jesus' plea to the people to believe Him in John 10:25 and 14:11 is not a plea to Christians today. Christians today do not get to question or ponder the identity of Jesus. Jesus has commanded us to believe who He has revealed, identified and demonstrated Himself to be.

Important points from Chapter 3 - Son of David/Son of God were:

- The Title "Son of David" was recognized as a title for the Messiah
- When people called Jesus "Son of David" they were calling Him the Messiah
- Jesus claimed to be the Son of God, and thereby God
- Many Jewish people recognized that the healings and statements Jesus made proclaimed He was God
- Jesus allowed Himself to be worshipped

* * *

Jesus – The Son of David and Son of God

The three chapters in the *Who is Jesus* section have established that among the people of Israel the topic of the coming Messiah was not a foreign concept. Even the Gentile woman of Tyre (Matthew 15:22 *Son of David*) knew of the coming Jewish Messiah. But more than that, these three chapters have provided scriptures that answer the unspoken question – is Jesus the God of the Old Testament?

The next couple of chapters tell a bit about Jesus' childhood and a homecoming visit to Nazareth. In trying to determine the timing of that visit, it appears that as Jesus left Jerusalem traveling north to the Galilee region, He made a stop in Samaria.

CHAPTER 4

If you knew

"If you knew the gift of God and who it is that asks…"
John 4:10 NIV

Recently I talked to a friend and discovered he is color blind. He said while he can see the green light of the traffic signal, the yellow and red lights look exactly the same. In studying about color blindness, he said all people do not see colors the same way. I was shocked to hear this; I just presumed that when people looked at a sunset, we all saw it the same way. But evidently, we do not. I told him I had seen videos of color-blind men who put on special glasses that allowed them to see color and invariably the men wept as they stood speechless, turning and looking at everything. Perplexed, my friend asked why did they cry. I told him because the men had never known or imagined the beauty and vastness of the colors of everything. Later my friend said he will make a point to find those glasses so he can see what up until now, he has never known or missed.

Gaining full color sight for one who is color blind is similar to what happened to a woman in the Bible. Up until one particular day, she had an understanding, a perception if you will, of God. Like looking through the special glasses, after a conversation with someone, everything she thought she understood about God changed. Her story began with a trip to get water, except on this particular day she met someone who was waiting by the well. He asked her to draw water for Him to drink. She asked why a Jew wanted a Samaritan to get Him water. The above quote was the beginning of His conversation with this woman. And the man at the well who changed everything was Jesus.

Bible readers may know there was a problem between the Jews and the Samaritans, as indicated in John 4:9, "...for the Jews have no dealings with the Samaritans" however, few people know the nature of the problem or its history. Why was Samaria located between Judea and Galilee? Who were the Samaritan people? Why did Jesus make a point of stopping in Samaria? In Luke 10:29-37 an expert in the study of *Torah* asked Jesus who is his neighbor. Why did Jesus answer with a parable involving the kind deeds of the "good Samaritan" helping an injured Jewish man? And in the account of Jesus healing ten men with leprosy when only one returned to say thank you, did you know the one who returned was a Samaritan (Luke 17:16)? To understand what is so profound about the story of the Samaritan woman at the well it helps to know some of the history of Samaria and the people who lived there.

Located in the central region of the nation of Israel Samaria is also the name of the city that later became the capital of the Northern Kingdom of Israel. When the Israelite people moved into the Promised Land after the death of Moses, the twelve tribes settled in different regions of what became the nation of Israel. The tribes of Manasseh, Ephraim (both sons of Joseph) and a large number of Levites settled in the central region of Israel that later became Samaria. Because the people of Samaria were descendants of the early tribes of Manasseh and Ephraim (also referred to as the House of Joseph), later in the Bible they were also referred to as Ephraim (see Isaiah 7:9, 9:9, Hosea 7:1) and later still as Israel.

After the death of Moses and during the leadership of Joshua, his successor, the Tabernacle (the tent-like temple) resided in the town of Shiloh in Samaria. Many years later, when David became king of the unified tribes of Israel, the Tabernacle was moved south to Jerusalem where David lived. The site of the first temple built in Jerusalem was selected by King Solomon and in II Chronicles 7:12 was acknowledged by God as the place for sacrifices and worship. During the reign of King Solomon's son

Rehoboam, the nation of Israel split. Samaria became the southern region of the Northern Kingdom of Israel (consisting of ten tribes), while the southern tribes of Benjamin and Judah became the Southern Kingdom of Judah. After the separation, the kings of Israel reigned in the city of Samaria. Although only a few people of Israel traveled south to the temple in Jerusalem for religious holy days, many in Israel fell to idol worship and eventually most of them were taken into captivity by the Assyrians.

Of the people left in Samaria, some assimilated with Assyrians, however, some remained faithful in worshipping *Yahweh*. Later when the Jews of the Southern Kingdom of Judah returned from the 70-year exile in Babylon, there remained a religious ideological split between the Samaritans and the Jews. Some of the Samaritans felt they were faithful to the original *Torah* given to Moses and believed those of the Southern Kingdom had returned from Babylon with an altered *Torah* and religion. Based on the Samaritan Pentateuch's (*Torah*)[38] instructions in Deuteronomy 27, Mount Gerizim in Samaria was revered as sacred because to the Samaritan people believed it to be the site chosen by *Yahweh* for worship. The Israelites observed a somewhat different version of the *Tanakh*[39] in which Deuteronomy 27 designated Mount Ebal as the place of worship. By the time of Jesus, since the Samarians held to observance of only the first five books of the Bible (*Torah*), they still upheld Mt. Gerizim as the designated place of worship of *Yahweh*.

The story of the Samaritan woman at the well appears in the book (the gospel) of John in chapter 4. It took place while Jesus and His disciples were traveling from Judea in the south, through Samaria on to Galilee in the north. After stopping in Samaria, the disciples set out to get food while Jesus waited at the well. The woman arrived in the middle of the day to draw water and Jesus asked her for a drink. Several speculations have been made about this story. Supposing women go for water in the morning or evening some people have presumed the

---

38 The Samaritans adhered to only the first five books of the Hebrew Bible - *Torah*.
39 The *Tanakh* is an acronym which represents the three sections of the Hebrew Bible or Old Testament. Those three sections are *Torah*, the prophets and the sacred writings.

Samaritan woman was of questionable character because she went to the well during the middle of the day and because the story says she had been married five times and was then living with a man who was not her husband. Also, as proof of the humanity of Jesus, some people cite John 4:6 NIV which says Jesus was too tired to go get food with His disciples. Taking this point as proof of the humanity of Jesus, are we also to believe the disciples were stronger than Jesus? John 4:27 says when the disciples returned with food, they were surprised to find Jesus talking to a woman. It was unusual for men to speak with women unaccompanied by a male (this is probably why Jesus asked the woman to get her husband and return). If Jesus was so hungry, why did He reject the food the disciples brought in preference for the food He said He came to earth to have (John 4:31-34)? As this story has been carefully analyzed, have we missed the point that Jesus was fulfilling Old Testament prophecies of salvation and restoration for the people of Israel? And what if the most important point of this story is who it reveals Jesus to be? Here is the beginning of the story as it appears in John 4:6-26 KJV:

> John 4:6-10 Now Jacob's well was there. Jesus therefore, being wearied (tired – NIV) with his journey, sat thus on the well: and it was about the sixth hour. [7] There cometh a woman of Samaria to draw water: Jesus saith unto her, Give me to drink. [8] (For his disciples were gone away unto the city to buy meat.)

> [9] Then saith the woman of Samaria unto him, How is it that thou, being a Jew, askest drink of me, which am a woman of Samaria? for the Jews have no dealings with the Samaritans.

> [10] Jesus answered and said unto her, If thou knewest the gift of God, and who it is that saith to thee, Give me to drink; thou wouldest have asked of him, and he would have given thee living water…

Ultimately, all life is a gift of God. In this conversation Jesus implies He possesses the gift of God and that it is His to give to others. What is the gift of God? Is the gift of God atonement, and forgiveness from sin? Yes, forgiveness and atonement are gifts from God. They are an automatic response to the sincere request for forgiveness of a repentant heart and soul who has come to believe in the all-powerful God of Israel and seeks to be right with God, the Creator. The word gift in Hebrew (#H5414) is described as a special transference from God to man as something God grants, confers or bestows with honor as a right, a reward. Ecclesiastes 3:13 and 5:19 describes the gift of God as the ability to find acceptance, satisfaction, and enjoyment in the events of one's day to day personal and professional lives; to be satisfied with what one has and not be plagued or possessed by the desire to acquire more or to have what someone else has. There are two verses in the New Testament epistles that relate to the conversation Jesus had with the woman about the gift of God. Ephesians 2:8 says salvation through faith (belief) is a gift of God and Romans 6:23 says eternal life is a gift of God. Note the reference to this eternal relationship in John 4:14:

Ephesians 2:8 For by grace are ye saved through faith; and that not of yourselves: it is the gift of God

Romans 6:23 For the wages of sin is death; but the gift of God is eternal life through Jesus Christ our Lord.

John 4:14 But whosoever drinketh of the water that I shall give him shall never thirst; but the water that I shall give him shall be in him a well of water springing up into everlasting life.

At first the woman did not understand Jesus spoke of a spiritual well of God living inside her, not a physical water well. She asked to drink of this living water. Jesus told her to go and return with her husband. When He mentioned her past relationships and current status, she offered no explanation for her life choices and mentioned Jesus must be a prophet of God. She followed that up stating the difference between the Jews of Judea and the Samaritans regarding where to worship.

¹⁵ The woman saith unto him, Sir, give me this water, that I thirst not, neither come hither to draw.

¹⁶ Jesus saith unto her, Go, call thy husband, and come hither.

¹⁷ The woman answered and said, I have no husband. Jesus said unto her, Thou hast well said, I have no husband: ¹⁸ For thou hast had five husbands; and he whom thou now hast is not thy husband: in that saidst thou truly.

¹⁹ The woman saith unto him, Sir, I perceive that thou art a prophet. ²⁰ Our fathers worshipped in this mountain; and ye say, that in Jerusalem is the place where men ought to worship.

²¹ Jesus saith unto her, Woman, believe me, the hour cometh, when ye shall neither in this mountain, nor yet at Jerusalem, worship the Father. ²² Ye worship ye know not what: we know what we worship: for salvation is of the Jews. ²³ But the hour cometh, and now is, when the true worshippers shall worship the Father in spirit and in truth: for the Father seeketh such to worship him. ²⁴ God is a Spirit: and they that worship him must worship him in spirit and in truth.

²⁵ The woman saith unto him, I know that Messias cometh, which is called Christ: when he is come, he will tell us all things.

²⁶ Jesus saith unto her, I that speak unto thee am he.

To say the Samaritans worship what they don't know is not a statement addressing *where* they worship, but rather *Who*. Since the Samaritans adhered only to the teachings of the Pentateuch would mean there is much about God and His promises the Samaritans did not know. For instance, Jesus mentioned that salvation [to and for others] would come through the Jewish people of which the Samaritans had their part.

While the Samaritans felt they were right about where *Yahweh* wanted to be worshipped, Jesus spoke of the nature of God; and told the woman the time was coming when the *place* to worship God would not be as important as the intimate connected relationship with God. Failing to understand His words, the woman countered saying when Messiah came, He would tell them "all things." Then Jesus told her He was the Messiah in verse 26. And He was indeed telling her things about God.

Jesus said "the hour cometh and now is" in verse 23. This phrase referred to the promises or prophecies of God that some One special would come (Deuteronomy 18:18, II Samuel 7:12-13 and Isaiah 9:6, etc.). Jesus said the fulfillment of those promises and prophecies "is now" (as in the Messiah is here now!). Then He said the Father sought true worshippers to worship Him in spirit and truth. Though the New Testament is written in Greek and many theologians and scholars think the language spoken at the time was Aramaic, the Jewish people's native language was Hebrew. Therefore, it is necessary to see the definitions in both Greek and Hebrew to understand the definitions and concepts behind these same words about a relationship with God and how they relate to Jesus. Here is a brief look of the meaning behind the words Father, worship, spirit and truth:

> Father – Hebrew #H1 *ab* head, founder, originator, chief. In Greek #G3962 *pater* means originator, creator of persons animated by the spirit as himself. One who has infused his own spirit into others
> Worship – Hebrew #H7812 *shachah* to revere; Greek #G4352 *proskyneo* to bow, to show profound reverence, to adore.
> Truth – Hebrew #H571 *emeth* from H539 *aman* means true, right, faithfully assuredly. *Aman* means to believe, establish, uphold, nourish, to make firm, to support. In Greek #G225 *aletheia*, a reality, fact

According to *Strong's Concordance*, the metaphoric meaning of "Father" in Hebrew and Greek speaks not only to God being the creator and the originator, but emphasizes the relationship with those to whom He is their spiritual Father (John 1:12-13). Notice Jesus connected the word spirit as both the nature of God and the manner in which God is to be worshipped. As spiritual children of God, He is the originator and creator of persons animated by the same spirit as Himself (as in He has inhabited them with His Spirit), and one who has infused His own spirit into others, who actuates and governs their minds. Several scriptures throughout the Bible illustrate this definition as they speak of people who are filled with the Spirit of God (see Exodus 31:3, Deuteronomy 34:9, Micah 3:8, and Acts 13:52[40]). The Apostle Paul referenced having or responding to others with the mind of Christ (I Corinthians 2:16 and Philippians 2:4-5) and renewing one's mind in Romans 12:2. This would seem to mean that when one becomes a child of God (and God is their Father), that very relationship causes a change to occur in the "child" as they become connected to the "Father." The word "worship" in John 4:23 ("the Father seeketh such to worship him") means the Father/God seeks those who will express profound reverence, respect and adoration for Him.

This same verse said, "the true worshippers shall worship the Father in spirit and in truth." The word truth is a bit more complex. A review of several scriptures mostly from the book of John, shows when Jesus used the word truth, that word referred to the recognition and acknowledgment that Jesus is God. This is not the case of every reference of the word truth. However, an example of the word indicating the revelation of Jesus' identity is in John 8:32 which says then you will know the truth and the truth will set you free. When a person knows the identity of Jesus as God, that knowledge will set them free. Likewise, Jesus said in John 14:6 "I am the way, the truth and the life." This mean He is the path, the journey, the way to a relationship with God. He doesn't just tell the truth,

---

40   Exodus 31:3 And I have filled him with the spirit of God, in wisdom, and in understanding, and in knowledge, and in all manner of workmanship. Deuteronomy 34:9 And Joshua the son of Nun was full of the spirit of wisdom; for Moses had laid his hands upon him: and the children of Israel hearkened unto him, and did as the LORD commanded Moses. Micah 3:8 But truly I am full of power by the spirit of the LORD, and of judgment, and of might, to declare unto Jacob his transgression, and to Israel his sin. Acts 13:52 NIV says And the disciples were filled with joy and with the Holy Spirit.

He is everything that is truth, faithful, nourishing, our support and it is through Him and in Him that we gain the eternal life that is inseparably a part of God/Jesus. Therefore, it is impossible to worship (express profound reverence, respect and adoration for God) without knowing who God is and being inhabited by the Spirit of God. Look at these verses from Psalms that speak of having this reverent relationship with God.

> Psalm 16:11 NASB You will make known to me the path of life; In Your presence is fullness of joy; In Your right hand there are pleasures forever.

> Psalm 9:1 NASB I will give thanks to the Lord with all my heart; I will tell of all Your wonders.

> Psalm 34:1 NASB I will bless the Lord at all times; His praise shall continually be in my mouth.

> Psalm 34:8 NASB O taste and see that the Lord is good

> Psalm 84:2, 10 NASB My soul longed and even yearned for the courts of the Lord; My heart and my flesh sing for joy to the living God…For a day in Your courts is better than a thousand *outside*. I would rather stand at the threshold of the house of my God than dwell in the tents of wickedness.

This intimate relationship with God happens when individuals have taken God into themselves and are transformed by knowing who God is and seek to live and treat others according to His instructions for right living. From God the person receives the living water of not only eternal life, but also wisdom, spiritual insight, guidance and the peace of God's presence with them. Jesus' conversation with the Samaritan woman about God is a Spirit who will live inside those who believe, must be viewed with Jesus' conversation with Nicodemus where Jesus says a person cannot see or enter the Kingdom of God (which means the rule, reign, power and presence of God) unless the person is born of the Spirit. Being born of the Spirit not only makes one spiritually born, but makes the person a child of God (John 1:12-13), that is, a child of the Father, who is a Spirit. Note the word "verily" in the John 3 quote. This word is actually the Hebrew word for truly, truth, firm and faithfully. Here are the verses from that conversation with Nicodemus in John 3:3-6:

John 3:3-6 ³ Jesus answered and said unto him, **Verily, verily**, I say unto thee, Except a man be born again, he <u>cannot see</u> the kingdom of God.

⁴ Nicodemus saith unto him, How can a man be born when he is old? can he enter the second time into his mother's womb, and be born?

⁵ Jesus answered, **Verily, verily**, I say unto thee, Except <u>a man be born of</u> water and of <u>the Spirit</u>, he <u>cannot enter</u> into the kingdom of God.

⁶ That which is born of the flesh is flesh; and <u>that which is born of the Spirit is spirit</u>.

Now look at these Bible verses that speak of truth as they relate to identifying God.

Psalm 145:18 NIV The LORD is near to all who call on him, to all who call on him in truth. (God is near to those who call on God who is living in them.)

John 8:32 NIV Then you will know the truth, and the truth will set you free."

John 8:44 NIV You belong to your father, the devil, and you want to carry out your father's desires. He was a murderer from the beginning, not holding to the truth, (not holding to God because God is not in him) for there is no truth in him. When he lies, he speaks his native language, for he is a liar and the father of lies.

John 14:6 NIV Jesus answered, "I am the way and the truth and the life. No one comes to the Father except through me.

John 14:16-18,20 NIV [16] And I will ask the Father, and he will give you another advocate to help you and be with you forever— [17] <u>the Spirit of truth</u>. The world cannot accept him, because it neither sees him nor knows him. But you know him, for <u>he lives with you and will be in you</u>. [18] I will not leave you as orphans; I will come to you… [20] On that day you will realize that <u>I am in my Father, and you are in me, and I am in you</u>. (Note – Jesus says the Spirit of truth will be in you, Jesus is in the Father, you are in Jesus, and Jesus is in you.)

John 16:13 NIV But when he, <u>the Spirit of truth</u>, comes, he will guide you into all the truth. He will not speak on his own; he will speak only what he hears, and he will tell you what is yet to come.

John 17:17 NIV Sanctify them by the truth; your word is truth.

John 18:37 NIV "You are a king, then!" said Pilate. Jesus answered, "You say that I am a king. In fact, the reason I was born and came into the world is to testify to the truth. Everyone on the side of truth listens to me."

Romans 1:25 NIV They exchanged the truth about God for a lie, and worshiped and served created things rather than the Creator—who is forever praised. Amen.

II Thessalonians 2:9-11 NIV [9] The coming of the lawless one will be in accordance with how Satan works. He will use all sorts of displays of power through signs and wonders that serve the lie, [10] and all the ways that wickedness deceives those who are perishing. <u>They perish because they refused to love the truth and so be saved</u>. [11] For this reason God sends them a powerful delusion so that they will believe the lie.

II Thessalonians 2: 13 NIV [*Stand Firm*] But we ought always to thank God for you, brothers and sisters loved by the Lord, because God chose you as firstfruits to be saved through the sanctifying work of the Spirit and through belief in the truth.

I Timothy 2:3-5 NIV [3] This is good, and pleases God our Savior, [4] who wants all people to be saved and to come to a knowledge of the truth.

I John 2:19-21 NIV [19] They went out from us, but they did not really belong to us. For if they had belonged to us, they would have remained with us; but their going showed that none of them belonged to us.

[20] But you have an anointing from the Holy One, and all of you know the truth. [21] I do not write to you because you do not know the truth, but because you do know it and because no lie comes from the truth.

Knowing and believing who God is, including His character, faithfulness, perfection, and His love for us is *the truth* that changes us. This assured knowledge of who God is *is* the living and eternal water that springs up in a person. The encounter with the woman at the well was not the only time Jesus likened this special eternal relationship to food or water. He spoke of it after He provided bread and fish for 5,000+ people in John 6:35 and 47, again on the last day of the Feast of Tabernacles in

John 7:37-38, and on the evening prior to His arrest in John 15:5. The Bible also likens the eternal sustaining relationship with God to food and water. From the beginning in Genesis 2:9 with the tree of life that is mentioned again in the last chapter of Revelation (22:2 and 14) and Jeremiah 17:13 where the LORD is referred to as "the fountain of living waters."

John 6:35 and 47 And Jesus said unto them, I am the bread of life: he that cometh to me shall never hunger; and he that believeth on me shall never thirst… ⁴⁷ Verily, verily, I say unto you, He that believeth on me hath everlasting life.

John 7:37-38 In the last day, that great day of the feast, Jesus stood and cried, saying, If any man thirst, <u>let him come unto me, and drink</u>.

³⁸ He that believeth on me, as the scripture hath said, out of his belly shall flow rivers of living water. (Could the scripture he refers to here be Isaiah 58:11 and Psalm 36:8-9 and Jeremiah 17. See these two scriptures listed after John 15:5.)

John 15:5 I am the vine, ye are the branches: He that abideth in me, and I in him, the same bringeth forth much fruit: for without me ye can do nothing.

Isaiah 58:11 And the LORD shall guide thee continually, and satisfy thy soul in drought, and make fat thy bones: and thou shalt be like a watered garden, and like a spring of water, whose waters fail not.

Psalm 36:8-9 They shall be abundantly satisfied with the fatness of thy house; and thou shalt make them drink of the river of thy pleasures. ⁹ For with thee is the fountain of life: in thy light shall we see light.

Jeremiah 17:13 O Lord, the hope of Israel, all that forsake thee shall be ashamed, and they that depart from me shall be written in the earth, because they have forsaken <u>the Lord, the fountain of living waters.</u>

To those who believe, receive and know Jesus, eternal life is automatic (John 1:12). This was the message and the invitation Jesus waited to deliver to the woman at the well. After their conversation, the disciples returned, and the woman spoke to the men in town about Jesus. Here is the conclusion of the story.

John 4:39-42: [39] And many of the Samaritans of that city believed on him for the saying of the woman, which testified, He told me all that ever I did.

[40] So when the Samaritans were come unto him, they besought him that he would tarry with them: and he abode there two days.

[41] And many more believed because of his own word; [42] And said unto the woman, Now we believe, not because of thy saying: for we have heard him ourselves, and know that this is indeed the Christ, the Saviour of the world.

Why did Jesus go to Samaria to reveal Himself as the Messiah? The Samaritans were descendants of tribes of Israel, some of whom had continued to worship the God of Abraham and Moses. Recall that Samaria is referred to as Ephraim in the scriptures and that the Samaritans were a remnant left in the land after the Assyrian invasion and removal of most of the people of the Northern Kingdom of Israel. The people removed were scattered with the goal to destroy them as the nation of Israel. Look at these verses from Ezekiel 37 and Jeremiah 31 that speak to both the remnant of Israel and those scattered and God's promise the bring them back to their land and restore their relationship with God.

Ezekiel 37:11-14 ¹¹ Then he said unto me, Son of man, these bones (those scattered) are the whole house of Israel: behold, they say, Our bones are dried, and our hope is lost: we are cut off for our parts.

¹² Therefore prophesy and say unto them, Thus saith the Lord God; Behold, O my people, I will open your graves, and cause you to come up out of your graves, and bring you into the land of Israel.

¹³ And ye shall know that I am the Lord, when I have opened your graves, O my people, and brought you up out of your graves,

¹⁴ And shall put my spirit in you, and ye shall live, and I shall place you in your own land: then shall ye know that I the Lord have spoken it, and performed it, saith the Lord.

Jeremiah 31:6-7, 10, 17-18 and 33-34 ⁶ For there shall be a day, that the watchmen upon the mount Ephraim shall cry, Arise ye, and let us go up to Zion unto the Lord our God. ⁷ For thus saith the Lord; Sing with gladness for Jacob, and shout among the chief of the nations: publish ye, praise ye, and say, O Lord, save thy people, the remnant of Israel.

¹⁰ Hear the word of the Lord, O ye nations, and declare it in the isles afar off, and say, He that scattered Israel will gather him, and keep him, as a shepherd doth his flock.

¹⁷ And there is hope in thine end, saith the Lord, that thy children shall come again to their own border. ¹⁸ I have surely heard Ephraim bemoaning himself thus; Thou hast chastised me, and I was chastised, as a bullock unaccustomed to the yoke: turn thou me, and I shall be turned; for thou art the Lord my God. ³³ But this shall be the

covenant that I will make with the house of Israel; After those days, saith the Lord, I will put my law in their inward parts, and write it in their hearts; and will be their God, and they shall be my people.

³⁴ And they shall teach no more every man his neighbor, and every man his brother, saying, Know the Lord: for they shall all know me, from the least of them unto the greatest of them, saith the Lord: for I will forgive their iniquity, and I will remember their sin no more.

Jesus' trip to Samaria was not happenstance. His conversation with the woman had nothing to do with Him being tired or thirsty. The visit had everything to do with God fulfilling His promises. In Matthew 15:24 Jesus said He was sent only to the lost sheep of the house of Israel. Look at Jeremiah 50:6 and Ezekiel 34:11:

Jeremiah 50:6 "My people hath been lost sheep: their shepherds have caused them to go astray, they have turned them away on the mountains: they have gone from mountain to hill, they have forgotten their resting place."

Ezekiel 34:11 For thus saith the Lord God; Behold, I, even I, will both search my sheep, and seek them out.

The God of Israel had not forgotten His lost sheep on the mountains. God kept His promise; God came to seek them out. Jesus came and spoke to this woman telling her things about herself that as a man, He couldn't have known. Then He told her He had living water for her from which she would never thirst; waters that would spring forth inside her to everlasting life. After telling His disciples He had a ripe harvest there to be gathered, Jesus stayed two days. Many came to believe Jesus is the Savior of the world. Surprisingly enough, this is not the end of the reconciliation story of the Samaritans in the Bible. In the book of

If you knew

Acts, chapter 8 after the resurrection and ascension of Jesus, Philip, a disciple of Jesus visited Samaria. This is the account of that visit:

Acts 8:5-8, 12,14 and 25 Then Philip went down to the city of Samaria, and preached Christ unto them. ⁶ And the people with one accord gave heed unto those things which Philip spake, hearing and seeing the miracles which he did.

⁷ For unclean spirits, crying with loud voice, came out of many that were possessed with them: and many taken with palsies, and that were lame, were healed. ⁸ And there was great joy in that city…

¹² when they believed Philip preaching the things concerning the kingdom of God, and the name of Jesus Christ, they were baptized, both men and women… ¹⁴ Now when the apostles which were at Jerusalem heard that Samaria had received the word of God, they sent unto them Peter and John… ²⁵when they had testified and preached the word of the Lord, returned to Jerusalem, and preached the gospel in many villages of the Samaritans.

This chapter like the entire book is about discovering who Jesus revealed Himself to be and the reason He came. Most of the Pharisees could not see Messiah in front of them. Knowing the many miracles of Jesus, the High Priest couldn't believe Jesus when He acknowledged He was the Messiah. After three years of traveling with Jesus, having seen the miracles, listened to the teachings, the disciples didn't understand who Jesus was even on His last night with them. Believing Jesus to be the Messiah, Jesus' dear friends, Mary and Martha didn't understand Jesus' power as God and His gift of eternal life. Some Christians speculate that it was possible Jesus' Mother and siblings didn't believe He was the Messiah until after the resurrection (Mark 3:21, 31 and John 7:5). Peter, John and James on the mount of transfiguration didn't understand who Jesus was even when He turned all shiny and bright. In prison John the Baptist doubted. From Adam and Eve forward through time, mankind has been consistent in their failure to see and believe God and quick to doubt and reject Him.

As the focus of Christianity on Jesus has been about the cross and the redemption of mankind, is it possible we too have failed to recognize who Jesus is? Immediately after the resurrection and ascension of Jesus the questions, theories and debates began. Is Jesus God? Is He both human and God? Is He an aspect of the God of the Old Testament, or are they different deities? Should the Jewish God of the Old Testament be set aside and replaced by the new understanding and teachings of Jesus? How does one best describe the relationship between the God of the Old Testament, God the Father Jesus referred to, God the Son and what of the Spirit Jesus mentioned? What did Jesus' crucifixion on Passover mean? Around and around, apostles, new believers (both Jewish and Gentile), church leaders and followers debated. Are we aware that many of the answers to these important questions adopted by the Church of today were determined nearly 300 years after the resurrection when there were no Jewish believers participating in these ecumenical councils? Are we aware that many of the answers to the questions about the purpose and meaning of Jesus death and resurrection are predominately answered from the epistles of the New Testament? Have we been like the woman at the well believing what we have been told passed down from one generation to another? Are we satisfied to look at Jesus perhaps with color blind eyes, or do we dare put on illuminating glasses and look at the Gospels and the Old Testament to find our own answers to these questions of who Jesus is and why He came?

*And I will give them a heart to know me, that I am the L*ORD*: and they shall be my people, and I will be their God: for they shall return unto me with their whole heart.*

Jeremiah 24:7

* * *

After His stay in Samaria, John 4:43-44 says, Jesus preceded on to Galilee. Perhaps He stopped in Capernaum for a while. Then when the time was right, He returned to Nazareth as recorded in Luke 4:14-16 and verse 23. Notice Luke 4:24 mirrors the John 4:44 verse. While at the synagogue of His youth, Jesus said one thing that turned everything upside down – not only for the people at the synagogue that day but for Christianity regarding atonement and redemption from sin.

CHAPTER 5

The Return to Nazareth

"The Spirit of the Lord is upon Me,
Because He anointed Me... He has sent Me ..."
Luke 4:18

The first four books of the New Testament are the gospels which mean "good news." The gospels are good news because they tell of God's love and desire to draw people to Him through Jesus. Of the four gospels, only the books of Matthew and Luke tell of Jesus' birth. Luke records one incident when Jesus was 12 years old and His parents could not find Him because He had remained in Jerusalem talking to scholars at the temple.[41] Other than that the gospels only tell of Jesus' ministry, arrest, death and resurrection. The Bible records no other information about Jesus' early life until the start of His ministry, or does it? Where did He grow up? What did He do? Many have heard Jesus was a carpenter; but where is that in the Bible? Did His family and neighbors suspect anything unusual about Him? What did they think when they heard about the miracles and the crowds following Him? In the

---

[41] The unique stories of Jesus' birth, childhood and probably this particular story are believed to have come from Jesus' mother, Mary. Biblical scholars and historians have concluded that the physician, Luke, who wrote both the books of Luke and Acts knew the disciples and Jesus' mother (Luke 1:3 and Acts 1:1, 14).

journey to understand who Jesus is and why He came, this chapter answers the questions regarding the years before His ministry began.

Until His ministry began, it appears that Jesus spent most of His life in Nazareth. Jesus' parents, Mary and Joseph were living in Nazareth at the time of their engagement and Mary's conception of Jesus (Luke 1:26). They left Nazareth shortly before Jesus was born and traveled to Bethlehem, the birth city of Jesus and King David. Obeying an angel's warning, the little family went to Egypt where they stayed for a brief period (as short as a few months).[42] Upon hearing Herod was dead, the family returned to Nazareth where they continued to live (Matthew 2:23). Mark 6:3 says His sisters were still living in Nazareth when Jesus began His ministry. It may very well have been that most of His family (brothers, nieces, nephews, uncles, aunts and cousins) continued to live there as well.

During Jesus' life on earth, Nazareth was a relatively small town. Its population could have been as small as a couple hundred people or as large as 2,000 people.[43] According to the Bible, the town was small enough that the people at the synagogue knew Jesus' parents and siblings by name (Mark 6:3). They knew Jesus; He had lived there among them and knew the occupation of Jesus and His father, Joseph as carpenters (Matthew 13:55 and Mark 6:3). The Books of Matthew, Mark and Luke tell of Jesus' return to Nazareth. Mark's 6:1-6 account is very similar to the one told in Matthew 13:53-58. The story recorded in the Book of Luke (Chapter 4) gives more details. Based on the placement of this event in the books of Matthew and Luke, it is possible this visit took place early in the ministry of Jesus. It is interesting to note that only in the book of Mark does it say the disciples were with Jesus. Yet in the Luke account there were no recorded comments or reactions of the disciples to the events that unfolded.[44] There are several reasons to

---

42 According to Deuteronomy 16:16, all Hebrew males were required to go before the LORD at a designated place to observe three of the annual feasts. Jesus and His parents would have observed these feasts in Jerusalem, in obedience to *Torah* instructions.

43 These statistics are from American archaeologist James F. Strange, Professor of Religious Studies and Distinguished University Professor at The University of South Florida.

44 While difficult to ascertain if this event occurred before acquiring disciples or not, it is possible if there were disciples, they had returned to their own home towns for the holy day.

think Jesus may have gone to Nazareth alone. The disciples did not yet know the information declared about Jesus and His mission that day in Nazareth. Nor was His identity revealed to the disciples in such a straight forward manner until the "Who do you say I am?" conversation recorded in Matthew 16, Mark 8 and Luke 9 that seemed to take place further along in His ministry.

When Jesus returned to Nazareth, the townspeople were aware of the miraculous healings Jesus had done. They knew He was teaching in synagogues in Capernaum and being praised by many (Luke 4:14-15). His hometown people were probably very curious to see Him and hear what He had to say. Luke's account (4:16) implies that Jesus did not arrive in town on the Sabbath, but it was *on* the Sabbath that He went to the synagogue He had attended hundreds of times. Often, He had read on the Sabbath, but this Sabbath would be different from any other Sabbath before or since. Here is the account of Jesus' visit to Nazareth as told in Luke 4:16-30 NIV.

[16] He went to Nazareth, <u>where he had been brought up</u>, and on the Sabbath day he went into the synagogue, <u>as was his custom</u>. He stood up to read, [17] and the scroll of the prophet Isaiah was handed to him. Unrolling it, he found the place where it is written:

[18] "The Spirit of the LORD is on me, because he has anointed me to proclaim good news to the poor. He has sent me to proclaim freedom for the prisoners and recovery of sight for the blind, to set the oppressed free, [19] to proclaim the year of the LORD's favor."

[20] Then he rolled up the scroll, gave it back to the attendant and sat down. The eyes of everyone in the synagogue were fastened on him. [21] He began by saying to them, "Today this scripture is fulfilled in your hearing." [22] All spoke well of him and were amazed at the gracious words that came from his lips. "Isn't this Joseph's son?" they asked.

²³ Jesus said to them, "Surely you will quote this proverb to me: 'Physician, heal yourself!' And you will tell me, 'Do here in your hometown what we have heard that you did in Capernaum.'"

²⁴ "Truly I tell you," he continued, "no prophet is accepted in his hometown. ²⁵ I assure you that there were many widows in Israel in Elijah's time, when the sky was shut for three and a half years and there was a severe famine throughout the land.²⁶ Yet Elijah was not sent to any of them, but to a widow in Zarephath in the region of Sidon. ²⁷ And there were many in Israel with leprosy in the time of Elisha the prophet, yet not one of them was cleansed—only Naaman the Syrian."

²⁸ All the people in the synagogue were furious when they heard this. ²⁹ They got up, drove him out of the town, and took him to the brow of the hill on which the town was built, in order to throw him off the cliff. ³⁰ But he walked right through the crowd and went on his way.

Luke 4:20 says when Jesus sat down all eyes were on Him. Then Jesus said, "Today this scripture is fulfilled in your hearing" (Luke 4:21 NIV). With this statement the people knew precisely who Jesus was proclaiming Himself to be. The portion of scripture He read could be fulfilled *only* by the Messiah. Messiah (also known as *Christ*) means "anointed."[45] Isaiah 61:1 says that the Spirit of the LORD has *anointed* Him to do certain things – some of the very things the people of Nazareth had heard Jesus had been doing! Yet here He was proclaiming to His neighbors, to His extended family, where some or most of His immediate family still lived that He was the promised and long-awaited Messiah!

---

45 Messiah, which means anointed, is also known as *mashiyach* in Hebrew, *Christos* in Greek and Christ in English. Traditionally a king or High Priest were anointed with holy oil symbolical of the solemn commission to serve God.

This was a significant announcement in the ministry of Jesus, because it was the first time Jesus publicly proclaimed He was the Messiah. This announcement was as important as His announcement at *Sukkot* six months before the cross when He proclaimed He is the source of Eternal Living Water and the Light of the World;[46] just as important as the night before the cross when Jesus acknowledged before the High Priest He is the Messiah, the Son of the Living God (Matthew 26:63-64).[47]

After this shocking proclamation about who and what His mission was, the stunned people at the synagogue recovered and tried to make sense of what He had just said. They rattled off a bunch of questions. Where did He get this power, isn't He the son of, the brother of --? In the account of Luke (4:22 NIV), they asked only one question – "Isn't this Joseph's son?" Note the change in Jesus' tone after this question was asked in Luke 4:23 NIV. The people knew the Messiah would be the Son of David and the Son of God, so this question struck at the heart of Jesus' claim to be the Messiah. The conversation went awry after that. In what seemed like minutes the people of His hometown would try to push Jesus from a cliff edge although it says the people spoke well of Him. Why? Perhaps the answer lies in Luke 4:22 and the interpretation we have. The verse in the KJV and NIV reads:

---

46 According to *The Complete Family Guide to Jewish Holidays,* by Dalia Hardof Renberg, Adama Books, New York, p. 61, the seven-day festival of *Sukkot* (also known as the Feast of Tabernacles) had such large oil lamps in the court of the temple that they illuminated nearly every courtyard in Jerusalem. It was within this context that Jesus proclaimed He is the Light of the World (see John 8:12). According to www.chabad.org. water was poured each day of *Sukkot* as part of the special celebration and rejoicing in recognition that the connection to God is so deep, it is like water to us – a part of our very being and vitally necessary to sustain life. "In addition, the water-drawing was said to be accompanied by a great awareness of G-dliness, to the degree that… along with water, people would 'draw' prophetic revelation." John 7:37-38 says this was when Jesus announced He is the source of Living Water and if any man thirst to come onto Him.

47 According to *Rosh Hashanah and the Messianic Kingdom to Come,* by Joseph Good, Hatikva Ministries, Port Arthur, Texas, p. 37, Jesus was condemned to die after confirming He is the Messiah to the High Priest. His death on the cross on Passover was at the same precise time the Passover lamb was sacrificed. The major Holy Days all relate to God and His plan for the salvation, redemption and restored relationship with mankind.

And all bare him witness, and wondered at the gracious words which proceeded out of his mouth. And they said, Is not this Joseph's son? (KJV)

All spoke well of him and were amazed at the gracious words that came from his lips. "Isn't this Joseph's son?" they asked. (NIV)

According to Robert Lindsay, an American pastor who lived in Israel for over four decades studying Hebrew and translating passages of the New Testament back into Hebrew from the Greek said one of his students had a different take on Luke 4:22. In his book, *Jesus, Rabbi & Lord*, Lindsay told how one of his students reasoned that when this verse was translated back to the corresponding Hebraic words, there was an alternative meaning.[48] The *"gracious"* words could be the Hebrew word *chesed (Strong's Concordance #H2617)*. While *chesed* can mean "kindly, good, or favor," it can also mean "wicked thing, pity or reproach" as found in Leviticus 20:17 (If a man takes his sister, his father's or his mother's daughter, and sees her nakedness and she sees his nakedness, it is a wicked *[chesed]* thing). Again, this same negative meaning appears in Proverbs 14:34 KJV (Righteousness exalteth a nation: but sin is a reproach *[chesed]* to many people). In addition, the phrase translated "and all of them spoke well of him"; can also have a negative connotation as in "they spoke critically" (see I Kings 21:10) or "admonished" or "they spoke words of protest." With this interpretation, the understanding of the verbal exchange at the synagogue in Nazareth changes and makes sense. Look at this adapted translation of Luke 4:22:

All spoke critically of him and were astonished at the wicked words that came from his lips. [In indignation they responded, "After all], isn't this Joseph's son?" they asked.

---

48 *Jesus, Rabbi & Lord*, by Robert Lindsay, Cornerstone Publishing, Oak Creek, WI 1990, pg. 45.

This interpretation now fits with the flow of events that followed. In the other two accounts of Jesus' trip to Nazareth (Mark 6:3 and Matthew 13:57) they say the people took offense. Jesus' next response addressed their thoughts that He was crazy or possessed when He said in Luke 4:23 NIV, "Surely you will quote this proverb to me: 'Physician, heal yourself!'" Then Jesus quoted their request, "'Do here in your hometown what we have heard that you did in Capernaum.'" Does this mean they were testing Him, tempting Him, asking Him to *perform* a miracle like He had done in Capernaum? What did Satan say to Jesus after the forty-day fast? "*If* you are the Son of God," turn the stone into bread, throw yourself down from here … *do something to prove it* (Luke 4:3 and 9). Surely this request by the people of His hometown was an offense to Jesus. His response was God's message of reconciliation and redemption would go beyond the people of Israel and out to the world. Jesus reminded them the prophets Elijah and Elisha's messages from God to Israel had been rejected. Although there were many people who were starving and sick in Israel, God's healing and mercy went beyond Israel's borders and answered the heart's desire of those who sought the God of Israel for salvation and healing (I Kings 17:9-24 and II Kings 5:1-18). When the people heard this, Luke 4:28 KJV says *all* of the people in the synagogue were filled with wrath (the NIV says they were furious), and drove Him out of the city to throw Him over the cliffs. But they did not harm Him. Scripture says He passed in the midst of them and went His way. It was not His time.

Important points from Chapter 5 were:

- Jesus grew up in Nazareth and followed the traditional practices in the local synagogue. His earthly father, Joseph, was a carpenter. Jesus had several brothers and at least two sisters
- Early in His ministry Jesus told His family, friends and neighbors He was the Messiah

CHAPTER 6

Why Return to Nazareth?

He went to Nazareth, where he had been brought up, and on the Sabbath day he went into the synagogue ...
Luke 4:16 NIV

4 But when the fullness of the time was come, God sent forth his Son, made of a woman, made under the law 5 <u>To redeem</u> them that were under the law, that we might receive the adoption of sons.
Galatians 4:4-5

Time and again Jesus did and said things that were perplexing to His disciples, and the people around Him. Yet after His resurrection, when His followers reviewed Jesus' words and actions in context of specific scriptures, they suddenly understood what He was revealing about Himself and why He had come. What if Jesus' visit to Nazareth was not random or without purpose? What if that visit was timed – like an appointment – for a specific day, a specific year, for a very important reason? What if this visit to Nazareth was in fulfillment of a *Torah* command? Galatians 4:4-5 above said there was and is a very specific timing of events that involved Jesus' mission and ministry as if these events were fixed appointments. When Jesus' words are understood in relationship to *when* He said them, <u>the return to Nazareth becomes as</u>

much a part of the story of Jesus' plan of restoration, forgiveness and eternal life for mankind as the cross itself on Passover.

This chapter shows that in accordance with a command in *Torah*, Jesus returned to His hometown and on the holiest day of the year proclaimed who He is and His mission. How is it possible to be sure of what day this happened? Although the books of Matthew and Mark merely mention the return to Nazareth, the book of Luke's account provides enough details to determine why Jesus returned to Nazareth at that time. The story says when Jesus stood to read, He read from the prophet Isaiah. This is one of the first clues that reveals the time of the year this event occurred. When Jesus read Isaiah 61:1-2 and proclaimed that the specific passage spoke of Him, it is not likely that this event occurred on just *any* Sabbath. Only on certain Sabbaths were passages from Isaiah read orally at the temple.

The order in which *Torah* (the books of Genesis through Deuteronomy) and *Haftarah*[49] passages are read trace back several hundred years to the scribe Ezra (as in the Bible's book of Ezra). A specific portion of *Torah* is read along with the complimentary or related *Haftarah* each weekly Sabbath as well as on the holy day Sabbaths. This means that during the year, all of *Torah* is read. The routine was established that someone of the priestly line or the Levitical tribe read the *Torah* portion; another man in the community was invited to read the *Haftarah* portion and the service concluded with prayers and blessings that were sung. It would have been unusual for someone to read a passage which was not designated for that day. Yet that is exactly what Jesus did on the holiest day of the year.

How can we know when Jesus returned to Nazareth based on the passage He read in Isaiah? Traditionally the Hebrew months of the year have themes based on historical events and holy days. Therefore,

---

49 *Haftarah* (means completion) are selected passages from other books of the Hebrew Bible (Old Testament) that complement the *Torah* portion that is read. Therefore, all other parts of the Old Testament are not read as part of the Sabbath services.

Why Return to Nazareth?

the latter passage of Isaiah and the specifics of the verses provide a clue as to when this event happened. Since Jesus was from the tribe of Judah, when He stood to read, He would have read a *Haftarah* passage. A review of the *Haftarah* readings for the year shows that the Isaiah 61:1-2 verses, were *not* part of any of the scheduled *Haftarah* readings. Luke 4:17 NASB says, "…the book of the prophet Isaiah was handed to Him. And He opened the book and found the place where it was written…." It is important to note an error in the KJV and NASB translations: it would not have been a book of Isaiah, but a scroll. For example, the Pentateuch was in one scroll, Isaiah and Psalms would have been two separate scrolls, with the Minor Prophets combined in one scroll. To give some idea of the size of the Isaiah scroll, the Dead Sea scroll of Isaiah measured at 24 feet long and 11 inches high.[50] Thinking of a book in today's Bible, it is easy to imagine turning to a specific passage, but the *Torah* scrolls in the synagogue were quite different. The *Torah* scrolls were (and still are) handled with care and reverence. Traditionally the attendant had the selected passages already located and to limit touching the *Torah* scrolls, used a pointer to follow what was read. Keeping in mind that columns of the scrolls were not numbered, nor were there any chapter or verse designations, it seems reasonable to presume that Jesus would have first read the designated Isaiah passage then located the nearby verses of Isaiah 61:1-2. To illustrate this idea, look at Luke 4:17 from the NIV, "and the scroll of the prophet Isaiah was handed to him. Unrolling it, he found the place where it is written." There is another clue: since the *Torah* scrolls were handled with such care, it is not likely that Jesus would have read a regularly scheduled *Haftarah* portion – from Isaiah 7 or 28 then start adjusting the scroll to find the much later portion of Isaiah 61.

There are 54 weekly *Torah* (Genesis through Deuteronomy) and *Haftarah* readings during the year (see the list of readings in Note 1 –

---

50 "How Came the Bible," by Edgar J. Goodspeed, Abingdon 1979, pp 12-13. Dimensions are from Wikipedia on the "Isaiah Scroll."

Sabbath Readings). Sixteen of these *Haftarah* passages are from the prophet Isaiah. While there are additional Isaiah readings for specific commemorative and fasting days, those passages are not considered for this event with Jesus since they are not Sabbaths. Of the sixteen Sabbath passages, only three occurred on a Sabbath that is within range of limited movement required to adjust the scroll to read Isaiah 61. For example, adjusting the scroll from Isaiah 57 to Isaiah 61 or from Isaiah 61 to 65. Oddly enough these three Sabbath readings (Isaiah 60:1-22, Isaiah 61:10 through 63:9 and Isaiah 57:14 through 58:14) all take place within a one month period in the early fall and only one of the three passages occurs on a Holy day or holiday.[51] Can someone just pick a Sabbath and say it was *that* day? Absolutely not! However, we must take into consideration that Jesus seemed to be acutely aware of the timing of things He did; saying it was not yet His time or the time had come for such and such (see Matthew 26:18, Luke 9:51, John 2:4, 7:6, 7:8, 16:4 and 16:25). Therefore, it is likely that this visit and milestone announcement was timed to align with a very specific Sabbath message. In determining which Sabbath this occurred on, we need to know: 1) Why are there three *Haftarah* readings so close together in Isaiah that also occur within a 21 to 28-day period? 2) Does *Torah* provide any information that will help determine on which Sabbath this event occurred? 3) And does the Isaiah 61:1-2 passage He read give an indication of the day?

As mentioned, during the year there are sixteen readings from the prophet Isaiah. Interestingly enough, seven of these readings come at the end of the Jewish civil year during the months of *Av* and *Elul*. These seven readings in a row are called the Consolation passages commemorating the destruction of Jerusalem and Solomon's temple when many people died, including those brutally murdered, followed by the 70-year

---

51 All occurring within a three to four-week period, the first two passages are on the last two Sabbaths of the civil year during the month of *Elul* (Isaiah 60:1-22 and Isaiah 61:10-63:9). The third passage, Isaiah 57:14-58:14, is read on the holiest day of the year - *Yom Kippur*.

exile in Babylon.⁵² The Consolation readings were taken from the book of Isaiah because it contained passages that related to the Babylonian exile, consoled the nation of Israel with prophecies for the future return to Zion⁵³ and the promises of God to restore the nation. The sixth and seventh Consolation readings that conclude the Hebrew year, are two of the three possible Sabbaths Jesus could have been present in Nazareth. The Hebrew civil New Year begins on the first day of the month, *Tishrei,* which is *Rosh Hashanah* (a Sabbath). The next Sabbath is the first regular Saturday Sabbath of the year. Neither of these two Sabbaths have *Haftarah* readings from the prophet Isaiah. The third Sabbath of the New Year occurs on the tenth day of *Tishrei* which is *Yom Kippur,* the Day of Atonement.⁵⁴ The *Haftarah* reading for that special day is Isaiah 57:14 to Isaiah 58:14, which is within easy range of Isaiah 61. Because the month of *Elul* proceeds the holiest day of the year, *Yom Kippur,* the focus for that entire month is on repentance. The beginning of the month of *Elul* starts the 40-day period of introspection before *Yom Kippur* - a Day of Atonement. It is during this 40-day period that apologies and reparations are made, and extra charitable contributions are given. During the ten days between *Rosh Hashanah* and *Yom Kippur* known as the Days of Awe, additional prayers are made and people are more careful of their deeds. On the day before *Yom Kippur* the people have prepared themselves with the ritual cleansing (*mikveh*- the origins of what would later become known as baptism). Two meals are consumed that day, one in early afternoon and a lighter meal before sundown. Then on the actual day of *Yom Kippur,*

---

52   There are several incidents in Jewish history that align on certain days. For example, the first Consolation reading is after the ninth day of the Hebrew month *Av* called *Tish B' Av*. *Tish B' Av* has a unique history of destruction and trouble for the Jewish people. Both temples were destroyed on *Tish B' Av*, along with the expulsion of the Jews from Spain in 1492 and the outbreak of World War I in 1914.

53   Zion is the name of a hill in Jerusalem and over time came to identify the area where Solomon's temple was built, the city of Jerusalem, the land of Judah and the nation of Israel.

54   *Yom Kippur* is also known as the Day of Atonement. It is the holiest day of the year in Judaism. Its central themes are repentance and atonement.

which begins at sundown, the people fast (no eating or drinking) and the day is spent in prayer at the temple or synagogue seeking forgiveness from God.

The following chart shows the three to four-week period of *Torah* and *Haftarah* readings involving the nearby Isaiah passages. The Sabbaths in bold print represent the passages from Isaiah that are closest to the Isaiah 61:1-2 verses Jesus read.

Sabbath	*Torah* Passage	*Haftarah* Passage
3rd Sabbath of Elul	**Deuteronomy 26:1 – 29:8**	**Isaiah 60:1-22** (**6th Consolation**)
4th Sabbath of Elul	**Deuteronomy 29:9 – 30:20**	**Isaiah 61:10 – 63:9** (**7th Consolation**)
Rosh Hashannah (first day of Tishrei)	Genesis 21:1-34, Numbers 29:1-6	I Samuel 1:1 – 2:10
1st Sabbath of Tishrei	Deuteronomy 32:1-52	2 Samuel 22:1-51
Yom Kippur - **10th of Tishrei**	**Leviticus 16:1-34 Numbers 29:7-11**	**Isaiah 57:14 – 58:14**

Within the seven Consolation passages are these promises:

Isaiah 40:5 And the glory of the LORD shall be revealed, and all flesh shall see it together: for the mouth of the LORD hath spoken it.

Isaiah 40:10 Behold, the Lord GOD will come with strong hand, and his arm shall rule for him: behold, his reward is with him, and his work before him.

Isaiah 52:6 Therefore my people shall know my name: therefore they shall know in that day that I am he that doth speak: behold, it is I.

Isaiah 55:3 Incline your ear, and come unto me: hear, and your soul shall live; and I will make an everlasting covenant with you, even the sure mercies of David.

The last verses of the seventh Consolation are:

Isaiah 63:8-9: For he said, Surely they are my people, children that will not lie: so he was their Saviour. ⁹ In all their affliction he was afflicted, and the angel of his presence saved them: in his love and in his pity he redeemed them; and he bare them, and carried them all the days of old.

Admittedly the seven Consolation passages were sifted through to select verses that speak of God coming to the aid of His people. However, there is an undeniable anticipatory feel within these chapters, a sense of promise that God, their Savior, will come. Of the three *Haftarah* readings that Jesus could have read, only one stands out and for very specific reasons connects profoundly to His ministry. There are several clues that seem to indicate Jesus proclaimed He was the Messiah on the Sabbath of the holiest day of the year (*Yom Kippur*) at the synagogue of His hometown. Look at the last verse from the *Torah* passage that is read on *Yom Kippur*. I have slightly altered the verse removing these three words "every year and" to get the full impact of Jesus' once for all atonement.

Leviticus 16:34 NASB Now you shall have this as a permanent statute, to make atonement for the sons of Israel for all their sins once ... just as the LORD had commanded Moses, *so* he did. **(altered)**

³⁴ Now you shall have this as a permanent statute, to make atonement for the sons of Israel for all their sins once every year." And just as the LORD had commanded Moses, *so* he did. **(unaltered)**

<u>Out of all 54+ Sabbath days of the year that Jesus could have gone to Nazareth, there is only one Sabbath that *Torah* commands men to return to their home.</u> It is the start of a year of Jubilee, which occurs once every fifty years. And when does a year of Jubilee begin? Jubilee begins <u>on *Yom Kippur*, the Day of Atonement when those who have repented and have humbled themselves to draw closer to God are cleansed, purified, forgiven of their sins and therefore are reconciled to God</u>. The *year* of Jubilee dealt with the purchasing back of land, property rights and setting free those who were in bondage due to extenuating circumstances. Look at these verses concerning the year of Jubilee. The first one is from the King James and the second is the same verse from the NASB for an easier read:

Leviticus 25:9-10 Then shalt thou cause the trumpet of the jubilee to sound on the tenth day of the seventh month, in the day of atonement shall ye make the trumpet sound throughout all your land. [10] And ye shall hallow the fiftieth year, and proclaim liberty throughout all the land unto all the inhabitants thereof: it shall be a jubilee unto you; and ye shall return every man unto his possession, and ye shall return every man unto his family.

Leviticus 25:9-10 NASB You shall then sound a ram's horn abroad on the tenth day of the seventh month; on the day of atonement you shall sound a horn all through your land. [10] You shall thus consecrate the fiftieth year and proclaim a release through the land to all its inhabitants. It shall be a jubilee for you, and each of you shall return to his own property, and each of you shall return to his family.

The year of Jubilee in Leviticus chapter 25 is about redemption. The word redemption appears 17 times in this chapter. Related to the words redeem and redeemer, redemption refers to the payment for what is secured and released. In Hebrew, the word redemption has two slightly different emphasis– one translation speaks to the motivation of restoring or preserving the solidarity of the clan and the other speaks of a ransom or purchasing back. However, when the subject of redemption involves God's relationship to mankind, the word takes on an even different meaning since everything belongs to God, the Creator. <u>God's redemption is not motivated by retaining or regaining the right of possession, rather its focus is to liberate, to deliver from the bondage of oppression, death, and sin</u>. God's redemption is to provide "salvation *from* circumstances that destroy the value of human existence."[55] (See Deuteronomy 7:8, Hosea 13:14, Psalm 68:6, 130:8, 119:134, and Isaiah 1:27.) As the Savior and Redeemer, God has a special reason behind His desire to redeem. It is because of God's deep abiding concern and love for mankind that He seeks to reconcile people to Himself. As the scripture says in Matthew 18:14 and II Peter 3:9, God is not willing that any should perish. (Also see Isaiah 44:24, 48:17, and 54:5)[56]

<u>Atonement, pardon, redemption, liberty, and restoration during a year of jubilee is for everyone</u>. Just as Jesus' message of redemption, reconciliation and gift of eternal life was not exclusively for Israel but for all mankind (Isaiah 42:5-7, 49:6, John 3:16 and 10:16). The year of Jubilee is a year of great joy because of God's mercy <u>to the people on earth</u>.[57] As mentioned earlier the only time all Jewish males are required to return to their home land's property and family is for the start of a year of Jubilee. Was it really on Jubilee that Jesus made this declaration about Isaiah 61:1-2? Compare these verses pertaining to the year of Jubilee from

---

55 Wikipedia's article on "Salvation."
56 Definitions and expositions are taken from the *Encyclopaedia Judaica* on the words *ransom* on pg. 1546 and *redemption* on pp. 1 through 5, Volume 14, Keter Publishing House, Jerusalem Ltd., Israel.
57 Leviticus 25:10 KJV says, "proclaim liberty throughout <u>all</u> the land unto <u>all</u> the inhabitants." The Hebrew word for land is *erets* #H776. *Strong's Concordance* says 712 times in the Bible *erets* is translated as "earth." The means this verse could be translated as "proclaim liberty throughout all the earth unto all the inhabitants.

Leviticus 25:10-11 to Isaiah 61:1-2 the passage Jesus read. Based on match ups between these two passages, others have surmised Jesus returned to Nazareth at Jubilee. Then look at the Isaiah 61:1-2 passage as quoted in Luke 4 and notice the phrase added about recovering sight to the blind.

Leviticus 25:10-11 NIV	Isaiah 61:1-2 KJV
"Consecrate the fiftieth year and <u>proclaim liberty</u> throughout the land to <u>all its inhabitants</u> … The fiftieth <u>year</u> shall be a jubilee for you."	The Spirit of the Lord God is upon me; because the LORD hath anointed me to preach good tidings unto the meek; he hath sent me to bind up the brokenhearted, to proclaim liberty to the captives, and the opening of the prison to them that are bound; To proclaim <u>the acceptable year</u> of the LORD"

Luke 4:18-19 KJV The Spirit of the Lord is upon me, because he hath anointed me to preach the gospel to the poor; he hath sent me to heal the brokenhearted, to preach deliverance to the captives, and <u>recovering of sight to the blind</u>, to set at liberty them that are bruised, ⁱ⁹ <u>To preach the acceptable year</u> of the Lord.

What is significant about Isaiah 61:1-2a? As mentioned previously, the verse says the Spirit of the Lord has anointed Him and the word anointed means Messiah or *mashach* in Hebrew. Since there were no chapter or verse designations at that time, Isaiah 60 through 61 should be viewed for context of Jesus' announcement. Notice within these verses <u>God refers to Himself as their Savior and Redeemer</u> who will cause righteousness and praise to spring forth. He speaks of there being a great darkness, of His light coming forth, and of the Gentiles being drawn to the light.

Isaiah 60:1-3 Arise, shine; for thy light is come, and the glory of the LORD is risen upon thee. ² For, behold, the darkness shall cover the earth, and gross darkness (as in can't see – blindness – recovering sight) the people: but the LORD shall arise upon thee, and his glory shall be seen upon thee. ³ And the Gentiles shall come to thy light, and kings to the brightness of thy rising.

Isaiah 60:16 thou shalt know that I the LORD am thy Saviour and thy Redeemer,

Isaiah 61:10-11 ¹⁰ I will greatly rejoice in the LORD, my soul shall be joyful in my God; for he hath clothed me with the garments of salvation, he hath covered me with the robe of righteousness, as a bridegroom decketh himself with ornaments, and as a bride adorneth herself with her jewels.

¹¹ For as the earth bringeth forth her bud, and as the garden causeth the things that are sown in it to spring forth; so the Lord GOD will cause righteousness and praise to spring forth before all the nations.

Occurring only once every fifty years, indeed It was an extraordinary day when Jesus walked into the synagogue on the Sabbath of *Yom Kippur* and Jubilee; then as part of the service, announced He is the Messiah. The Anointed One said He had come in the Spirit of God to preach good news to the downtrodden, and to heal those who have been broken in life. He who later proclaimed He is the Light of the world; said He had come to bring understanding to those blinded to truths about God and to this world covered in darkness. He said He had come to deliver and to set free those held prisoner by the bad things in their lives (adapted from the Hebrew definitions of the words from Isaiah 61:1-2a).

After reading from the scroll of Isaiah during the Sabbath service, Jesus returned to His seat. The verse in Luke 4:20 said every one's eyes were fixed on Him; they were probably in shock. Jesus had just broken Sabbath protocol by reading a couple of verses that were not part of the designated reading. Then in explanation for what He had just done, Luke 4:21 NIV says, "He began by saying to them, 'Today this scripture is fulfilled in your hearing.'" "Today," "This day," (KJV) not yesterday, tomorrow or next week Jesus said the scripture was fulfilled on that specific date – the Day of Atonement and the beginning of the Year of Jubilee. According to our English translations of the Bible, the word "fulfilled" is in the past tense. Redemption and spiritual reconciliation could only be given by God and Jesus had just said that He was the fulfillment of this prophecy. Jesus said He had already been anointed as the Messiah and that He had accomplished what only God can do. When was Jesus anointed? When did atonement, reconciliation and redemption become available?

As discussed in Chapter 1 of this book, John the Baptist did not baptize Jesus; John anointed Jesus. John's baptism of the people was for repentance (Matthew 3:11), and forgiveness of sin (Mark 1:4 and Luke 3:3). John did not understand why Jesus came to him for baptism. Jesus knew it was necessary to fulfill the requirements of *Torah* for commissioning a Prophet, Priest and King (Matthew 3:15 NIV "…it is proper for us to do this to fulfill all righteousness"). Jesus had to be anointed by a priest or prophet of God. John was both. He was the son of a Levitical priest (Luke 1:5/Exodus 28:41) and a prophet in the spirit of Elijah (Malachi 4:5). Why is this point significant? God instructed Moses regarding the anointing of priests for ministry (washed with water - Exodus 29:4). The verse in Isaiah 61:1 says, "The Spirit of the Lord God is upon me; because the Lord hath anointed me…" then Matthew 3:16-17 said the baptism of Jesus (the anointing – the holy consecration and dedication) was confirmed by a voice

Why Return to Nazareth? 105

from heaven and the appearance of the Spirit of God upon Jesus. Next point – atonement, forgiveness, redemption and eternal life were always available to those who knew God, who loved Him, who sought to walk in His ways and follow His instructions. When God described Himself in Exodus 34:6-7, He said He is "merciful and gracious, long-suffering, and abundant in goodness and truth, keeping mercy for thousands, <u>forgiving</u> iniquity and transgression and sin." God who changes not always wanted a relationship with people. When people acknowledge God, seek to know God and do what pleases Him, then their sins are forgiven, they are redeemed and reconciled to Him. Relationship with God and eternal life were always available to God's people, but for the many who did not believe in or know the God of Israel, and those who could not see the goodness of God through His creation, were lost (Ecclesiastes 3:11 and Romans 1:20, and 2:6-16).

Luke 4:22-30 records a brief conversation that followed Jesus' statement. The people questioned His identity; they asked Jesus to prove Himself by performing miracles. Then just as Isaiah 60:3 said God's message would go to the Gentiles, Jesus told the people a prophet is not accepted [or believed] in His own country [Israel]. He said like the prophet Elijah with the widow in Sidon, and Elisha with Naaman of Syria, the message of redemption would go beyond Israel. Luke 4:28 said the people were filled with wrath and rose up to throw Him over the cliff's edge, but Jesus walked through the midst of them. This means that the traditional ending prayers and songs were probably set aside, and the service was over.

Back tracking a bit, assuming Jesus initially came forward to read the *Haftarah* portion for that day, it is of special interest to know what the passage was before He located Isaiah 61. The *Torah* reading for the morning of *Yom Kippur* is Leviticus 16:1-34 and the *Haftarah* portion is Isaiah 57:14 – 58:14. The afternoon *Torah* reading is Leviticus 18:1-30 and the *Haftarah* reading is the book of Jonah and Micah 7:18-20. Sometimes one man or several men would come forward to read the *Haftarah* portion. I have listed below the last eight verses of *Haftarah* reading - Isaiah

58:6-14 NASB. Take note of the call to repent – to reflect and change one's behavior to care for others. Then, verse 9 says the people will call, will cry out to the LORD and He will say, "Here I am."

"Here I am" in Hebrew is *Hineni* and depending on how it is said and in the context of which it is said, it is a way of expressing complete readiness to make one's self available for whatever is needed or required to comply. It was Abraham's response when God called him to offer his son as a sacrifice (Genesis 22:1). It was Moses' response when God called to him from the burning bush (Exodus 3:4), young Samuel's response when God called to him three times (I Samuel 3:4-8), and the prophet Isaiah's answer when God asked who could He send to speak to the people (Isaiah 6:8). When we cry out to God to help us, when we are in pain, or need Him to save us, could "*Hineni*" be God's response? In this *Yom Kippur Haftarah* passage (Isaiah 58:6-14 NASB), verse 9 says it is God's response – along with what God needs us to do.

> ⁶ "Is this not the fast which I choose, to loosen the bonds of wickedness, to undo the bands of the yoke, and to let the oppressed go free and break every yoke? ⁷ "Is it not to divide your bread with the hungry and bring the homeless poor into the house; when you see the naked, to cover him; and not to hide yourself from your own flesh? ⁸ "Then your light will break out like the dawn, and your recovery will speedily spring forth; and your righteousness will go before you; the glory of the LORD will be your rear guard. ⁹ "Then you will call, and the LORD will answer; you will cry, and He will say, 'Here I am.' If you remove the yoke from your midst, the pointing of the finger and speaking wickedness, ¹⁰ And if you give yourself to the hungry and satisfy the desire of the afflicted, then your light will rise in darkness and your gloom *will become* like midday. ¹¹ "And the LORD will continually guide you, and satisfy your desire in scorched places, and give strength to your bones; and you will be like a watered garden, and like a spring of water whose waters do not fail. ¹² "Those from among you will rebuild the ancient ruins; you

will raise up the age-old foundations; and you will be called the repairer of the breach, the restorer of the streets in which to dwell.

¹³ "If because of the sabbath, you turn your foot from doing your *own* pleasure on My holy day, and call the sabbath a delight, the holy *day* of the LORD honorable, and honor it, desisting from your own ways, from seeking your *own* pleasure and speaking *your own* word, ¹⁴ Then you will take delight in the LORD, and I will make you ride on the heights of the earth; and I will feed you *with* the heritage of Jacob your father, for the mouth of the LORD has spoken."

Galatians 4:4 NASB But when the fullness of the time came, God sent forth His Son, born of a woman, born under the Law…

The holy days established by God are not just random days with random meaning. They are appointments to mark and commemorate important messages from God. The previous verse from Galatians 4 opened this chapter. It implies God had a very precise time for the birth of Jesus. The unique timing of Jesus' announcement at Jubilee on *Yom Kippur* in His hometown according to the instructions of *Torah* was not happenstance. Jesus' birth was meant for a specific year so that when He was thirty years old, His ministry began at the same age a priest begins to serve. Jesus told His Mother Mary at the wedding at Cana it was not His time (to begin His ministry). His ministry began instead with His anointing (baptism) at age 30 by the son of a Levitical priest and prophet on *Shavuot* (the feast of weeks – celebrating the gifts of God[58]) to fulfill all righteousness according to *Torah* (Numbers 4:3, Matthew 3:15). Then at the perfect time in history to fulfill the instructions set forth in *Torah*, Jesus returned to His hometown and

---

58 The holy day of *Shavuot* (Pentecost) celebrates and commemorates the giving of *Torah*. It was on *Shavuot* that the gift of the Spirit of God upon believers occurred after the resurrection of Jesus.

announced on the one very special day in fifty years that He is the Messiah; He has provided atonement for the sins of mankind (the Day of Atonement), and the opportunity for redemption is available for everyone (Jubilee) who believes. And since it was the start of a year of Jubilee, it was time to rejoice, because that which had been lost has been restored; those who are held captive in darkness (spiritual confusion and disbelief) and sin, now could be free. Freedom and liberty had been provided for anyone who believes and accepts it. And Jesus actually spoke as the mouth of God saying: "I am here" - "*Hineni*" and "the mouth of the LORD has spoken."

Passover and *Yom Kippur* (The day of Atonement)

Ever wonder why Jesus' death occurred at Passover instead of *Yom Kippur* (the Day of Atonement)? It is vitally important to understand the answer to this question. *Yom Kippur* is about the sins being atoned for and forgiven; the sin slate wiped clean. Passover is about redemption from death.

The first Passover was the culmination of a series of unusual events or as the Bible describes them, signs and wonders that served a double purpose. First the signs and wonders revealed a God who was profoundly different and more powerful than any of the gods of Egypt. Secondly, God's revelation of Himself through these signs and wonders served to draw people to Him. Not only the Hebrew people (descendants of Abraham), but many others who as a result of what they had seen and experienced, came to believe in the reality, power and identity of the Most High God of the Hebrew people. As Pharaoh repeatedly changed his mind about letting the people go, the tenth and final miraculous event of Passover ended his indecision. In preparation for the tenth plague, God instructed Moses to tell the people to take a young lamb into their homes for four days. Then the lamb was killed, and the people consumed part of the animal, taking the lamb into themselves, making the lamb a part of them. Each household was to have the blood of a lamb painted on the doorway of their home.

Those who believed in God enough to follow the instructions were spared from the death of the firstborns in their home. The next day the Hebrew people were led out of bondage; the captives were set free.

The Passover lamb was not killed to atone for sin. The lamb gave his life so that those who believed and obeyed might live. <u>Passover is about belief in the Word of God and obedience to God's instructions to defeat death and gain deliverance</u>. The death at Passover was a sign, a message to everyone that there is only one all-powerful God who has control over death and life. During the first Passover, <u>all</u> the firstborn in Egypt – Egyptians, Hebrews, peoples of other cultures, and their animals died if they were not covered by their belief in God and obedience to God's instructions. The death and blood of a lamb merely represented their belief and obedience. This act of obedience and the death of the unbelievers resulted in setting free those who were held captive physically, culturally and spiritually. The opportunity for a new life and an ongoing relationship with God was available for everyone who believed, trusted and obeyed God's instructions. Passover is observed to remember that through belief and obedience, death passed over the people and they were set free from captivity.

The events and its symbolic meaning from the first Passover are directly related to what happened when Jesus went to the cross. All throughout His ministry Jesus performed miracle after miracle. He said if people could not believe who He said He is, the miracles (signs and wonders) themselves identified Him (John 10:25, and 38). Jesus said that those who believed and trusted in Him (John 11:26), had taken Him into themselves (John 6:53-54), whose homes (their heart, their souls) were covered by His Life (John 17:21, 23), are protected from the last enemy – death (John 3:16). They are set free from the bondage and penalty of sin and unbelief and are given true Life.

John the Baptist called Jesus the *Lamb* of God who takes away the sin of the world (John 1:29). Exquisitely stated, John combined the concepts of both holy days - Passover and *Yom Kippur*. As Passover represents the principle that belief and obedience saves one from spiritual death, *Yom Kippur* (the Day of Atonement) illustrates that repentance produces forgiveness, the removal of sin and a reconciled relationship with God. It was God who ordained *Yom Kippur*, a day in which the people of Israel addressed their sins each year. According to tradition, the people began their preparation for *Yom Kippur* forty days prior to that date (like Catholicism's observance of Lent forty days before Easter). During this almost six-week period, people were introspective, and repentant; they made amends to those they had wronged and increased their charitable contributions to the poor. Based on their past deeds, the Jewish people believed God inscribed their fate for the coming year in the Book of Life (Exodus 32:32-33, Psalm 69:28, Daniel 12:1, Philippians 4:3, Revelation 3:5, 20:12 and 15) on *Rosh Hashanah*, and that it was possible for favorable adjustments before it was sealed on *Yom Kippur*. On the solemn day of *Yom Kippur*, the people fast, reflect and pray, then believing God has forgiven their sins begin a joyous period of celebration and rejoicing during *Sukkot* (the Feast of Tabernacles) five days later.

Leviticus 16 described the actions of the priest on *Yom Kippur*. First, He made atonement for himself and his household with the blood of a bull. Then two goats were selected. Oddly enough, neither the bull nor the two goats were required to be without blemish. One goat was killed as the sin offering for the people. <u>After the priest confessed the iniquities, transgressions and sins of the people upon the scapegoat</u> (the second goat), this goat was led into the wilderness and let go. The two goats conveyed the principle that like the first goat, it is God who chooses people. After reflection, regret and repentance of their deeds and choices in life, it is the old life of the person that is sacrificed – a sin offering that atones for their sin before God. (In Luke 9:24 Jesus said, "whosoever will lose his life for my sake, the same shall save it.") The life offered atones/reconciles the breach between the individual and God. God's forgiveness redeems and restores. The second goat – the scapegoat was symbolic of God's forgiveness. This goat carried the sins, transgression, iniquities of the people and was removed from people never to be seen again, conveying the principle that after the LORD has forgiven people, their sins will never be held against them again. *Yom Kippur* connects to the followers of Jesus because Jesus is the scapegoat who takes on the sins of people and removes it permanently. It is important that we understand our past life is dead, buried, gone – never to be held against us again. Satan, the accuser, will try to keep bringing up sins of our past and we may have trouble forgiving ourselves or others, but God has taken our sins away. Recall John the Baptist's statement about Jesus in John 1:29, "the Lamb of God, <u>which taketh away the sin</u> of the world."

It is through our belief in the Passover Lamb of God that everlasting death passes over us. It is through the scapegoat of *Yom Kippur* that our sins are taken away never to be held against us again. Jubilee on the same day as *Yom Kippur*? Jubilance and solemn remorse on the same day? Yes! Regret, remorse is overtaken by joy, triumph and exhilaration! God's forgiveness and restoration are cause for a permanent Jubilee. That which was lost, traded, sold, and held captive by sin has been redeemed and set free to experience the abundant life with God as we have never known it.

In time the people feared the return of the scapegoat and what that would symbolize so instead of the *Yom Kippur* scapegoat being released, it was led several miles away to cliffs where he was shoved off a cliff. At the onset of this journey a crimson (red) cord was tied to the scapegoat's horns, while part of the cord was retained. At this point the red cord that was retained turned white when the goat died – symbolic that the animal had atoned for the sins of the people and now their sin like blood was removed leaving them pure like snow (Isaiah 1:18).[59] According to some Jewish sources,[60] <u>forty years</u> before

---

59 Mishnah, R. Ishmael in Book 3, Tract Yomah, Chapter 6.

60 One source - http://jewishencyclopedia.com/articles/2203-azazel. Also see the Babylonian Talmud translated by Michael L. Rodkinson [1918], Book 3, Tract Yomah, Chapter 4 - The two goats, pg. 60. "The rabbis taught: Forty years before the Temple was destroyed, the lot never came into the right hand, the red wool did not become white...."

the destruction of the Temple in 70 AD, the cord never turned white again. If the years are accurate, forty years before the 70 AD destruction could place this change *not after or at* the death and resurrection of Jesus, but <u>at the beginning of His ministry</u>.[61] This could mean Jesus' return to the synagogue in Nazareth on the Sabbath of *Yom Kippur*, would have been the last time the cord turned white. The implication is that after the once-for-all atonement was fulfilled by Jesus, there was no further need for the confirmation of atonement involving a scapegoat.

Recall in this story of Jesus' return to Nazareth, the people were filled with rage after hearing Jesus' remarks. They then tried to drive Jesus out of the city and throw Him down the cliff (Luke 4:28-29). What was the fate of the second goat - the *Yom Kippur* scapegoat who took away the sin of the people never to return? He was thrown off the cliff.

* * *

If atonement/reconciliation and forgiveness were always available to the Jewish people who believed and followed God's instructions, what was new because of Jesus' visit to the synagogue in Nazareth? Two things, Jesus announced He is the Messiah. Prophets, priests, wise men and hundreds of thousands of Jewish people had waited for the Messiah. The other thing – Jesus mentioned salvation and relationship with God would go beyond the borders of Israel to include Gentiles (Luke 4:24-27).

Spiritual concepts like sin, atonement, forgiveness, redemption and salvation are frequently used but have rarely been studied to see

---

[61] Jesus' birth year has been linked to the death of Herod (Matthew 2:15) and Josephus' report in Antiquities 17.6.4 indicated Herod's death occurred just after a lunar eclipse. While the minor and partial eclipse of 4 BC is thought to be the correct year of Herod's death, some scholars or theologians think the more visible and memorable eclipse in late 1 BC is possibly the correct year. At any rate, the timing of Jesus' ministry begun at age 30 (possibly in 26AD if born in 4 BC or in 30 AD if born in 1 BC) plus forty years comes very close to the 70 AD year of the destruction of the temple after which there were no more temple sacrifices.

Why Return to Nazareth?

what the Bible has to say. The next chapter looks at the scriptures that answer and explain these questions:

1. Are all sins alike to God?
2. Why and when did animal sacrifice for atonement of sin begin?
3. What does atonement mean?
4. Can God forgive sins without blood atonement?
5. Are we required to forgive someone who continues to hurt us?
6. What does God require to forgive sin?

CHAPTER 7

Sin-Atonement, Forgiveness & Redemption

Do murdered children and children who die go to heaven?
Were Abraham, David, and Ruth saved and did they receive eternal life?
Jesus told two men to keep the commandments
and they would inherit eternal life.
Can sins be forgiven without death atonement?
Jesus told the paralyzed man and the sinful woman
their sins were forgiven.
Today if an observant Jew (obedient to Torah, charitable and kind
to others) does not believe Jesus is the Messiah,
can he be saved and receive eternal life?
If a man prays the sinner's prayer, is baptized yet returns to his old life of
sin, will he receive eternal life if he dies tonight?
Does the Bible say God's holiness & righteousness require death
for sin atonement?
How can we know the answers to these questions with certainty?

He has shown you, O man, what is good. And what
does the LORD require of you?

Micah 6:8 NIV

"...*eventually I saw it as a real commitment to truth and as being willing to open oneself up to the possibility that one's views need to be revised in light of further knowledge and life experience.*"[62]

Bart Ehrman, Distinguished Professor of Religious Studies at the University of North Carolina at Chapel Hill, author of "Misquoting Jesus: The Story behind who changed the Bible and Why"

After watching an infomercial about a pesticide used predominately in the US on most crops, my husband proceeded to tell me this pesticide is believed to increase people's chances for developing high blood pressure, diabetes, dementia and a host of other health problems. As he went on with further details beyond what I wanted to know, I told him to please stop, don't tell me anything else – I would rather not know. This chapter may be like that for some Christians. Most of what is believed in Christianity about the purpose and meaning of the death and resurrection of Jesus will be contradicted by the examination of scriptures and the Hebrew and Greek definitions of certain words. While I don't want to speculate about the possible harm of a pesticide, I do want to know the Truth about my God.

The cross has stood at the pinnacle of Christianity representing forgiveness, atonement, redemption and salvation for those who choose Jesus as their Lord and Savior. Since many people were crucified on crosses by Roman soldiers during the time of Jesus, it wasn't the cross or Jesus' death that called millions of people to a relationship with the one true God. It was Jesus Himself who made everything different. The miraculous healings, Jesus' teachings and His power to defeat death are what made Jesus incomparable. It is Jesus' timeless message, His gentle call and His continued transforming power that has drawn

---

62 From the Introduction of Misquoting Jesus: The story behind who changed the Bible and Why, by Bart Ehrman, HarperOne Publisher, November 2005.

millions to Him. Jesus has transformed lives so profoundly that thousands of people have chosen to die acknowledging Jesus as their Savior rather than live one more day and deny their belief in Him. Yet how much do we know about Jesus today and why He came as answered through the Old Testament and Jesus Himself?

We can reason or guess at the answers to the questions on the previous page or quote what we have heard pastors say, but the most important question is how does the Bible answer these questions? Although we may know what the words sin, atonement, forgiveness, salvation, redemption and reconciliation mean, until their meaning in Hebrew (Old Testament) and Greek (New Testament) are evaluated in the context of the Bible verses in which they are used, we may be surprised at the conclusions these words draw. To begin this quest, it is important to know the character of God, and a bit about the historical practice of animal sacrifices. It is also important to understand the authors of the New Testament epistles' struggle to define this new movement of Judaism with its inclusion of Gentile believers, and their attempt to answer questions about Jesus' identity, and provide meaning to His death and resurrection.

A central point of Christianity today is the belief that people are separated from God because of their sins. A good place to start is to answer what is sin, what makes a person a sinner and why does sin separate people from God?

Sin and the Sinner

Sin can be defined as the failure to do what God has instructed people to do or it is doing what God has commanded people not to do. What we miss in this explanation is how damaging sin is. Deuteronomy 6:18 says to do what is right and good in the LORD's sight so that it may go well with you. This implies that by following God instructions, life will be better than if one does not follow His instructions. Proverbs

16:25 says there is a way that seems right to a person, but leads to death. This means that trusting in one's perceptions of what is right can be misleading and can lead to spiritual and eventually physical death; whereas obedience to God's instructions leads to spiritual and eternal life (Leviticus 18:5, Deuteronomy 30:10-20, and John 5:39).

The more perverse and harmful sins (discussed later) affect both parties involved. These sins create a stain, a debt and a wound in both parties. If the sin is not handled correctly through repentance, amends made, forgiveness, and becoming at peace with God's sovereignty, the one wronged will be negatively impacted and in turn, will himself sin. For the one who sinned, their deed takes them hostage (Proverbs 5:22), it infects their soul (Proverbs 8:36) growing and spreading. They numb their conscience, harden their hearts, and justify their actions while continuing and escalating their deeds of wrongdoing (Romans 1:28-32). As described here, it is easy to understand how sin causes a break in relations with God who is sinless.

It is commonly thought in Christianity there are no degrees in sin and that any sin causes a break with God. It may be surprising to learn that in Hebrew there are twenty different words for sin. According to an article on "Sin" in the *Encyclopaedia Judaica*[63] three of the most commonly used words for sin are the ones that appear in the Bible. Appearing 459 times in the Old Testament is the word **ht** or **het**[64] meaning to miss, or to fail; also a lack of perfection in carrying out a task or duty or to miss the mark as in one shooting an arrow (Leviticus 5:15-16, Numbers 14:40). It is from this Hebrew word that we get the word "sinner" (Hebrew word #H2398 *chata*). However, a person is considered righteous (a **zaddik** – see Deuteronomy 6:25) when they fulfill an expected duty.

Another often-used Hebrew word for sin is **pesha** or **psh.** It appears 136 times in the Old Testament often as the word "transgression" and

---

[63] "Sin" by R. Knierim – *Encyclopaedia Judaica*, Volume 14, page 1589, Keter Publishing House, Jerusalem Ltd, Israel, 1972.

[64] *Het* meaning to miss or fail appears in *Strong's Concordance* as word #H2398 *chata*.

means a breach, a rebellious transgression, or a break in the peaceful relation between two parties including sinful behavior of man toward God (I Kings 8:50, Psalm 25:7, 51:3). The third Hebrew word often used for sin and inequity is **awan/awon/avon** (Hebrew word #H5753). **Awan/awon/avon** appears over 200 times in the Old Testament and means a perverse crookedness and/or bent as in having deliberately done wrong so often, that there is a *bent* toward *crookedness*. This word also conveys the idea of blame, guilt and punishment for acts of depravity and perversion.

Many of God's instructions (commonly referred to as "laws" in English translations of the Bible) involve showing respect for God, and His Sabbaths, practicing fair, responsible and just treatment of others, and following health and dietary regulations. For people who knew of God and His commandments, the perverse and harmful sins identified as *awan/awon/avon* were done deliberately and rebelliously. Yet not knowing God nor His commandments does not lessen the severity of these sins. It is because of these practices, other nations were removed from their land and sometimes, destroyed. These sins defiled (to be or to become unclean, impure or polluted) the perpetrator, the victim(s) and those closest to them causing damage and long-term consequences. Sins of this nature also causes **a break** in one's relationship with God. Left unrepentant, the break is a permanent and eternal breach. The sins identified in *Torah* as *awan/awon/avon* sins are adultery (Leviticus 20:10, Deuteronomy 22:22), blasphemy (Leviticus 24:16), murder, false witness intended to lead to a conviction (Deuteronomy 19:16-19), incestuous or unnatural relations (Leviticus 18:22, 20:11-14), kidnapping (Exodus 21:16 Deuteronomy 24:7), the rape of a betrothed woman (Deuteronomy 22:25-27), striking or cursing a parent (Exodus 21:15, 17, Leviticus 20:9), Sabbath breaking (Exodus 31:14, 35:2), idol worship, and casting spells or incantations (Leviticus 20:27). Sometimes these sins are identified and translated as abominations, wickedness, evil and are said to defile the land (Leviticus 18:24-28). According to *Torah* instructions, each of these offences carry the death penalty. The more serious and damaging type of sin (*avon*) involves the deliberate practice of known wrongdoing. In the Old Testament, most of the verses involving the word "sinned," are related to people having sinned against the LORD. This does not imply that sins against others is less important than the sins against God. All sin (against God or others) represents a violation of and the wandering away from God's instructions to do what is right.

Nearly all Christians will admit they are a sinner. It is a common conception that they continue to sin daily. (Three questions come to mind about this idea of Christians sinning daily: what sin are they committing daily, why do they continue to do it, and why won't they stop?) What does the word "sinner" mean? As mentioned earlier, in the Old Testament, the word "sinner" is derived from the Hebrew word "*het*" or "*chata*" meaning to miss the mark. However, in the Bible when the word "sinner" appears with words like "ungodly, evil, wicked or wickedness," this indicates that the "sinner's" sin is of a more serious nature suggestive of the *awan/avon* types of sin. In several verses "sinner" is used in a doublet, meaning a similar phrase is used that relates, describes or reveals in this case, the serious nature of the sin and the sinner (see examples below).

In the New Testament, **sin** is the Greek word #G268 *harmartolos*. It's meaning is consistent with the Hebrew's more serious term for sin - *awan/avon*. *Harmatolos* is described as devoted to sin, preeminently sinful, and especially wicked. (Wicked in Hebrew means one who is morally wrong, ungodly, an actively bad person.) In the gospels, the word is frequently coupled with publicans (aka tax collectors,) who were known to be harsh, greedy and deceptive. In a couple of places in the epistles of the New Testament, the sinner is described in very strong terms. See I Timothy 1:9-10 listed below, then Romans 3:10-18 in the next section of "None Righteous, All are Sinners".

Genesis 13:13 NASB Now the men of Sodom were wicked exceedingly and sinners against the LORD.

Sin - Atonement, Forgiveness & Redemption

1 Samuel 15:18 and the LORD sent you on a mission, and said, 'Go and utterly destroy the sinners, the Amalekites, and fight against them until they are exterminated.'[65]

Psalm 1:1 [*The Righteous and the Wicked Contrasted*] How blessed is the man who does not walk in the counsel of the wicked, Nor stand in the path of sinners, Nor sit in the seat of scoffers!

Psalm 1:5 Therefore the wicked will not stand in the judgment, Nor sinners in the assembly of the righteous.

Psalm 26:9 Do not take my soul away *along* with sinners, Nor my life with men of bloodshed,

Psalm 104:35 Let sinners be consumed from the earth and let the wicked be no more. Bless the LORD, O my soul. Praise the LORD!

Proverbs 11:31 Behold, the righteous shall be recompensed (to be re-paid, made whole, restored) in the earth: much more the wicked and the sinner.

Proverbs 13:6 Righteousness keepeth him that is upright in the way: but wickedness overthroweth the sinner.

Isaiah 1:28 But transgressors and sinners will be crushed together, and those who forsake the LORD will come to an end.

1 Timothy 1:9-10 and 15 NASB realizing the fact that law is not made for a righteous person, but for those who are lawless

---

[65] Without provocation, the Amalekites attacked the Israelites who were lagging behind (the elderly, mothers with young children, and the handicapped) as they traveled from Egypt during the Exodus. See Exodus 17:8 and Deuteronomy 25:17-18.

and rebellious, for the ungodly and sinners, for the unholy and profane, for those who kill their fathers or mothers, for murderers[10] and immoral men and homosexuals and kidnappers and liars and perjurers, and whatever else is contrary to sound teaching,... [15]It is a trustworthy statement, deserving full acceptance, that Christ Jesus came into the world to save sinners, among whom I am foremost *of all*.

None Righteous; All are Sinners – True or False?
Romans 3 is an important chapter for the Christian doctrine that all are sinners separated from God because of their sins. This chapter is a continuation of a discourse on righteousness and unrighteousness discussed in Romans chapters 1 and 2. While chapter 3 contains the often-quoted verses that none are righteous, all have sinned and fallen short of the glory of God, is this an overall assessment of mankind? Is this idea that all are sinners separated from God because of their sin consistent with the teachings in the Old Testament and conveyed in Jesus' ministry? Few pastors or Bible teachers provide the context of these comments or acknowledged that Paul wrote this letter to a specific audience for the purpose of settling differences of opinions. Therefore, it is not accurate to assume these verses in Romans 3 are an assessment on the nature of mankind.

The letter or epistle[66] called Romans is believed to have been written near the end of Paul's life, 20 to 30 years after the resurrection to believers in Rome who had never heard Jesus teach. In this epistle, the apostle Paul's audience were both Jews (*Torah* observant and those who were not) and Gentiles (non-Jews including those who had previously worshipped other gods). During this time (and over the next 200 to 300 years), there was much debate about this new "religion," what it meant, how it fit with traditional Judaism, and about the identity and

---

66   An epistle is a literary form of communication intended for an audience. A letter is a personal or confidential form of communication written to a specific person.

deity of Jesus. There were Jews who believed Jesus was the Messiah, and those who were unsure; and Gentiles who previously knew little of the God of the Hebrew people and His commandments. At times in this epistle, Paul seems to be addressing Jewish, then Gentile believers and sometimes the church as a whole.

Some Jews believed their relationship with God was secure because they observed the commandments. Paul explained that righteousness is not based on having kept the law; righteousness comes by believing and trusting (faith) in God (Romans 3:28). The goal of the Roman letter was to instruct and advise both Gentile and Jewish believers on several topics that had caused disagreements and division. One of the topics of division was whether Gentiles had equal standing in relationship with God as the Jewish believers, and whether Gentiles needed to convert to Judaism and get circumcised. Paul said that Jews and Gentiles have all sinned (3:9). In verses 10 through 18, he quoted from Psalms, Ecclesiastes and Isaiah an assessment about "sinners." Modern Christianity has considered Romans 3:9-10 to be an overall assessment of the sinful state of mankind. However, examination of the context of original passages indicate these scriptures are not addressing everyone, rather they are speaking of those who are hostile to a relationship with God because of their lust, greed and unbelief. Romans 3:10-18 NASB says, "as it is written,

"THERE IS NONE RIGHTEOUS, NOT EVEN ONE;

[11] THERE IS NONE WHO UNDERSTANDS,

THERE IS NONE WHO SEEKS FOR GOD;

[12] ALL HAVE TURNED ASIDE, TOGETHER THEY HAVE BECOME USELESS;

THERE IS NONE WHO DOES GOOD,

THERE IS NOT EVEN ONE." (Psalms 14:1-3; 53:1-3; Ecclesiastes 7:20)

[13] "THEIR THROAT IS AN OPEN GRAVE,

WITH THEIR TONGUES THEY KEEP DECEIVING,"

"THE POISON OF ASPS IS UNDER THEIR LIPS"; (Psalm 5:9, 140:3)

[14] "WHOSE MOUTH IS FULL OF CURSING AND BITTERNESS"; (Psalm 10:7)

> ¹⁵ "Their feet are swift to shed blood,
> ¹⁶ Destruction and misery are in their paths,
> ¹⁷ And the path of peace they have not known." (Isaiah 59:7-8)
> ¹⁸ "There is no fear of God before their eyes." (Psalm 36:1)

Psalms 14 and 53 say the same thing. Verses 1-3 speak of the fool who is corrupt and vile, who says there is no God. Psalm 5 speaks of evil and wicked people who are liars and rebel against God. Psalm 140 of the evil and violent man and Psalm 10 of the wicked, the evil and murderous man. Isaiah 59 tells of those who revel in their iniquity and Psalm 36 of the wicked who do not fear God. Based on the context of these verses, it is easy to see that people who do not believe in God, who deliberately commit acts of evil, mistreat others and are violent are not called righteous nor would they be considered people who are seeking God. It is people who <u>practice</u> these seriously offensive behaviors that the Bible calls sinners again and again.

Addressing the argument of one's righteousness, Paul says there is no boasting for those who have obtained righteousness by following the law (3:21), because now righteousness can also be obtained by those who believe and trust (faith) in the true identity of Jesus (3:22). He says there is no distinction between the two because all have sinned (at some point) and come short of the glory of God (3:23). Romans 3:23 has often been taken as a pronouncement that all of mankind is inherently a disappointment to God because of their sins and shortcomings. This idea is not consistent with the theme throughout the Bible of God's profound love for people and His desire for people to come to know Him (John 3:16, II Peter 3:9, and Ezekiel 18:4). Jesus said in John 17:22 of those who believe, "And the glory which thou gavest me I have given them; that they may be one, even as we are one." While believers can share in bringing God glory, when we consider that the glory of God is His presence (see Exodus 16:7, 10, 24:17, 40:34, and Numbers 16:19, etc); His immense power, authority, perfection, wisdom and beauty, then Paul's statement declares a simple truth: no human in all of their best qualities can compare to the glory of God. Although we fall short of God's glory, we are not separated from God because of it nor does this mean that God is displeased with us. There is only one place in the Bible that God speaks of His overall displeasure with all of mankind because of their sins. Yet even then there was an exception. Before the destruction by the Flood Genesis 6:5-6 says, "⁵ And God saw that the wickedness of man was great in the earth and that every imagination of the thoughts of his heart was only evil continually. ⁶ And it repented the LORD that he had made man on the earth, and it grieved him at his heart." Then three verses later in Genesis 6:9 amongst the people of that time, Noah is described as: "… a just man and perfect in his generations, and Noah walked with God." In Hebrew the word for perfect is #H8552 *tamiym* which means complete, whole, sound, upright and the Greek word #G5046 *teleios* means complete, to act with virtue and integrity.

The point: It is true that all people have sinned (made mistakes, failed to uphold all of God's instructions either intentionally or unintentionally), yet it is also a fact that all throughout the Old Testament there are many people who are called righteous. The designation of "sinner" is not one who has broken *a* single or even several commands of God. Rather the Bible classifies a sinner as one who does not believe in the God of the Bible, those who repeatedly commit acts of evil, along with those who claim to know and follow God yet have knowingly and consistently acted in a manner harmful to others, dishonest and contrary to God's instructions. And it is the repeated practice of sin and consistent sinful behavior of these people that separate them from God. See Isaiah 58:1 through 59:14.

The Sin and Death Connection

When most people hear the words life and death, they tend to think of life or death in terms of one's life here on earth. Yet that is not how the Eternal God perceives it. In Genesis 2, God told Adam on the day he ate of the tree of knowledge of good and evil, he would surely die, yet

Adam went on living. In Deuteronomy 30:19 Moses tells the people death and life are set before them, and to choose life, yet we know that the many who chose life did one day die. The prophet Ezekiel of chapter 18 records God saying He has no pleasure in the death of those who die, rather turn (repent) and live. Jesus in John 11:25 tells Martha those who believe in Him, though they die, yet shall they live, and those who are alive, shall never die. Clearly these statements are not referring to the natural life cycle of the physical body; but are referring to the eternal spiritual state. Life in this context refers to those who are born again, who have believed, received (to take in, acquire, choose, accept) and chosen to follow God, and live according to His instructions for right living.

For those not in a relationship with God, who have consistently and deliberately done that which they know to be wrong and have rejected God, although having been born spiritually alive,[67] they become spiritually dead. If they never repent, the physical death of their body is the first death. All throughout the Old Testament are references to those who will "perish"[68] (Job 4:8-9, Psalm 1:6, 68:12, 112:10, New Testament - John 3:16). According to Revelation 20:11-15 at the white throne judgment two books are opened – the book of deeds (for those who experienced the first death) and the book of Life (contains the names of those who have been granted eternal life by God). The people who experienced the first death come forth from the sea, the grave or wherever else their remains resided. They are judged by their deeds in the first book. Since their names are not found in the

---

67 The principle established in the following verses show from conception God intimately knows the child He has created with care, and that God has plans and purposes for those lives. Jesus says it is the innocence and purity in children that is remindful of being in the Kingdom of Heaven/God. See Jeremiah 1:5, Psalms 139:13-16, Jonah 4:11 (120,000 babies, young children and mentally handicapped), Matthew 18:3, and 19:14. Ephesians 2:5, Colossians 2:13, and James 2:26 show that through sin a person becomes spiritually dead.

68 In *Strong's Concordance*, the Hebrew word for perish is #H6 *abad*. It means destroy, vanish, to be exterminated, to blot out, to do away with. In Greek the word is #G622 *apollymi* which means to destroy, to put an end to ruin, to abolish.

Book of Life, they are cast in the lake of fire, and <u>perish</u>, experiencing the second death. It is not a harsh God who pushes people away at the judgment. It is people's repeated disobedience, their persistent unbelief, and consistent rejection of God that lead to permanent separation from eternal God and a perishing death.

The apostle Paul called this connection between disobedience and death "the ***law*** of sin and death" (Romans 8:2). Paul's statement in Romans 6:23, "For the wages of sin is death; but the gift of God is eternal life through Jesus Christ our Lord" mirrors Proverbs 10:16 NIV, "The wages of the righteous is life, but the earnings of the wicked are sin and death." This means the automatic cause and effect for disobedience/sin is death. But for the innocent,[69] the righteous (word H#6662 *tsaddiyq* means those who act justly, to be lawful, right and correct), those who are obedient, who treat others honorably (Romans 6:16), the payment, gift or reward is eternal life (Romans 5:21). Therefore, since permanent death is inseparably connected to the sin of unbelief, willful rebellion and disobedience, death should hold no fear for those who have loved, believed and lived a life reflecting the God of the Bible. Their names are written in the Book of Life. When their days of physical life are at an end, they fall asleep and are awakened by God and go on living in their spiritual form (John 11:11, 13, 25-26, 14:2-3, Ezekiel 18:8-9, 20-23, I Corinthians 15:44).

Many have thought that the battle between God and Satan is for the souls of people. This is not true. God wants a personal connected relationship with each person because He created all life (John 3:16, Ezekiel 18:3) and He loves us beyond our comprehension of that type of profound love. Each person is a part of God, and He wants everyone to know Him. Satan, on the other hand, does not want people to serve or worship him, i.e. devil worshippers. Satan wants people kept dead spiritually (unsaved), or/and dead physically (John 8:44 and

---

69 The innocent in Hebrew (word H#5355 *naqiy*) means those who are clean, blameless, exempt, and those who are free from punishment.

10:10). For those who believe in God, Satan wants to deceive and limit their knowledge of God and destroy the effectiveness of the believer in God. Probably Satan's most damaging tactic is he strives to deceive people by besmirching (to soil and damage) the character and identity of God by lying, denying God's existence, causing confusion, division and distorting the meaning of God's Word, motives and instructions. As illustrated in the story of the Garden of Eden (Genesis 3:4-5) when the crafty serpent (Satan) spoke with Eve, Satan would have people doubt the importance and truth of God's words and commandments and characterize God to be harsh, cruel, selfish and lacking compassion and love. Jesus said in John 8:44 that Satan is a liar and a murderer from the beginning.

<u>While it has been thought in Christianity that sacrificial death is required for sin atonement; it is Satan, the murderer who is all about death.</u> I Corinthians 15:26 says the last enemy (of God) to be destroyed is death. Again, and again all throughout the Bible the eternal God calls people to repentance and to choose life (eternal life). While it is true that unrepentant sin will lead to permanent death, Jesus said that a person's own disobedience, unbelief and rejection of God would condemn and judge them (John 3:17-18 and John 12:44-50). Look at the scriptures below. They are a sampling to illustrate the principle that God wants people to choose eternal life (with Him). Interestingly enough Leviticus 18:5 says, "Ye shall therefore keep my statutes, and my judgments: which if a man do, he shall live in them: I am the Lord." He shall live in them means those who live by God's instructions and judgments will have life, remain alive, sustain life, live prosperously, live forever, be alive, be restored to life or health (according to *Strong's Concordance* Hebrew word #H2421 *chayah* meaning life, live, alive). God requires repentance for salvation, not death (Mark 1:4, Luke 5:32, 24:47, Acts 11:18, Romans 2:4 and II Peter 3:9). <u>Death is not God's instrument for achieving atonement of sin. Death is the consequence of unrepentant sin.</u> Permanent, perishing death is not God's goal or

desire for mankind, nor does God require sacrificial/substitutionary death to forgive sin. The last book of the Bible says in the end death shares the same fate as the grave, the devil, the beast, false prophet and those who did not choose eternal life through belief in God. Death is cast into the lake of fire (Revelation 20:10, 14 and 15).

Deuteronomy 30:19 I call heaven and earth to record this day against you, that I have set before you life and death, blessing and cursing: therefore choose life, that both thou and thy seed may live...

Psalm 51:16-17 ¹⁶ For thou desirest not sacrifice; else would I give it: thou delightest not in burnt offering. ¹⁷ The sacrifices of God are a broken spirit: a broken and a contrite heart, O God, thou wilt not despise.

Ezekiel 33:11 Say unto them, As I live, saith the Lord God, I have no pleasure in the death of the wicked; but that the wicked turn from his way and live: turn ye, turn ye from your evil ways; for <u>why will ye die</u>, O house of Israel?

2 Peter 3:9 The Lord is not slack concerning his promise, as some men count slackness; but is longsuffering to us-ward, not willing that any should perish, but that all should come to repentance.

II Timothy 2:10 ... our Saviour Jesus Christ, who hath abolished death, and hath brought life and immortality...

Hebrews 2:14-15 ... through death he [Jesus] might destroy him that had the power of death, that is, the devil and deliver them who through fear of death were all their lifetime subject to bondage.

Revelation 20:14 ... And death and hell (the grave) were cast into the lake of fire.

What is atonement and reconciliation?

Over the years the main road near my home had developed numerous potholes and cracks. Finally, the road was scheduled to be resurfaced. First the old road was removed leaving a dirt road. There was a significant drop to the bumpy dirt road and cars had to be driven slowly. Eventually the new road was laid. It was smooth and a joy to drive on. However, when I turned onto my street, there was a big bump as the two surfaces were not the same. Then one day the repair was finished and the new road had been perfectly joined to the adjacent streets and the change was seamless. Nothing of the old road remained. It had now been repaired, restored, made whole and was new. Now it was compatible to its original connections.

The word **atonement** in Hebrew (word #H3722 *kaphar* in *Strong's Concordance*) means the covering of, or <u>making reconciled</u>, consistent or compatible with something else. This word in Hebrew for atonement and reconciliation has the same definition as the Greek word translated in English as "propitiation" (I John 2:2 - And he is the propitiation for our sins: and not for ours only, but also for *the sins of*[70] the whole world). The word "propitiation" only appears in the New Testament three times (Romans 3:25, I John 2:2, and 4:10). In Greek the word for **propitiation** is #G2434 *hilasmos*. *Hilasmos* means to appease and to atone. In some instances, there is also a sense of redemption and ransom associated with the concept of atonement; an exchange or payment involved to buy or get back.[71] In the Hebrew language atonement

---

70   Italics in the King James Version of the Bible indicates words or phrases added that were not found in the original manuscript.
71   Genesis 20:16 speaks of Abimelech giving Abraham 1,000 pieces of silver to cover his eyes to not see Abimelech's sin. Exodus 30:12 speaks of the males' requirement to pay a ransom for their souls.

Sin - Atonement, Forgiveness & Redemption

is also associated with the concept to put off or "put it off" as found in Isaiah 47:11 (Therefore shall evil come upon thee; thou shalt not know from whence it riseth: and mischief shall fall upon thee; thou shalt <u>not be able to put it off</u>: and desolation shall come upon thee suddenly, which thou shalt not know). The Hebrew word here in Isaiah 47:11 is #H3722 *kaphar*. Again, this is the exact same Hebrew word for "atonement" and "reconcile" (see Leviticus 16:20). What does all this mean? **The fullness of the meaning of atonement encompasses** the active confrontation and defeat of evil and/or disobedience; the ransom or exchange to get back, and the cleansing, restoration or reestablishment of a relationship between a person and God. Later as the verses regarding animal sacrifices for atonement are examined, it becomes obvious that atonement cannot take place without repentance. (**Repentance means** <u>to turn from</u> and stop offensive actions, to reconsider said actions through which one regrets their former choices and <u>turns to</u> God and the path of righteousness.) Only God can reconcile (atone) and make compatible the relationship between man and God *after* a person believes in the One True God and has repented.

The connection between repentance and forgiveness

Forgiveness can be described as the concept and intentional process of letting go of the negative feelings of resentment or/and a desire for revenge. Forgiveness does not deny, justify or minimize a wrong. Forgiveness does not preclude the necessity for reparations or punishment, nor does it require that the deed be forgotten. In the Bible, the meaning of forgiveness is a bit different. According to the *Encyclopaedia Judaica*, the Biblical concept of forgiveness presumes that sin itself is a force that adheres to the sinner. Since it is God's role as the one who forgives; <u>forgiveness is the divine means for removing sin</u>. As God's forgiveness is followed by the removal of sin, it is easy to see forgiveness' connection to the words purify and cleanse.[72]

---

[72] *Encyclopaedia Judaica* on the subject of Forgiveness, pp 1433-1434. Vol. 6, Keter Publishing House, Jerusalem Ltd., Israel, 1972.

Leviticus 16:30 For on that day shall the priest make an atonement for you, to cleanse you, that ye may be clean from all your sins before the LORD.

After reading passages in the book of Leviticus about animal sacrifices for sin atonement, one may be led to think that this was the method for forgiveness of all sins. Yet a closer read shows animal sacrifices were optional (see the section in this chapter on animal sacrifices – and Leviticus 1:2, Jeremiah 7:22-23), and were for inadvertent errors (for example: Leviticus 4:2, 13, 22, 27, and 5:1-6). Deliberate or blatant contempt for God and His commandments were not atoned or forgiven by animal sacrifices (see Numbers 15:30-31, I Samuel 3:14, Exodus 23:21, and Joshua 24:19).

Numbers 15:30-31 ³⁰ But the soul that doeth ought presumptuously, whether he be born in the land, or a stranger, the same reproacheth the LORD; and that soul shall be cut off from among his people. ³¹ Because he hath despised the word of the LORD, and hath broken his commandment, that soul shall utterly be cut off; his iniquity shall be upon him.

I Samuel 3:14 And therefore I have sworn unto the house of Eli, that the iniquity of Eli's house shall not be purged with sacrifice nor offering forever.

Joshua 24:19-20 And Joshua said unto the people, Ye cannot serve the LORD: for he is an holy God; he is a jealous God; he will not forgive your transgressions nor your sins. ²⁰ If ye forsake the LORD, and serve strange gods ....

Some sins, such as those named in Exodus 21:12-17, say the punishment for the guilty party required their death. This conveys the point that certain sins could not be covered by the sacrificial death of an animal. <u>Repentance with contrition, humility, being moved to</u>

compassion for the one wronged and a resolve to change one's actions and follow God are required for God's forgiveness.

We may tend to think God's commandments, their being broken and the need to be forgiven were for all mankind, but *Torah* instructions and commandments were part of the covenant between God and His people.[73] Likewise in the New Testament gospels, Jesus spoke to followers, His disciples, and people of the Jewish community about how they were to forgive and respond to the offenses between family, friends and those living in their community. The idea that any sin separates any and every person from God permanently is a Christian belief that is not scripturally based. The unbelievers are indeed separated from God; not so much because of their sins but because of their unbelief (see John 3:18-20). The only sin that separates one from God permanently is willful disobedience and one's firm stand of unbelief. And the idea that full forgiveness from God for one's sins occurred only after Jesus' redemptive and atoning death is not scripturally based either. God forgave sin in the Old Testament just as Jesus forgave sin before the cross in the gospels. Notice what Jesus said in Luke 5:24:

Luke 5:24 NIV "…I want you to know that the Son of Man has authority on earth to forgive sins."

Look how similar the instructions for forgiveness and restoration are for those who believe in God in both the Old Testament and the New Testament in II Chronicles 7:14 and I John 1:9:

II Chronicles 7:14 If my people, which are called by my name, shall humble themselves, and pray, and seek my face, and turn from their wicked ways; then will I hear from heaven, and will forgive their sin, and will heal their land.

---

[73] God's people of *Torah* were the Hebrew people (later known as the Jews) and the people who had left Egypt with the Hebrew people.

I John 1:9 ⁹ If we confess our sins, he is faithful and just to forgive us our sins, and to cleanse us from all unrighteousness.

Having addressed forgiveness for believers, what then of the unbeliever, those who worshipped other gods, those who practiced evil, who cheat and harm others, the true sinners? First, is the response of the unbeliever to God's call, next a new realization of the reality and character of God (belief in this specific God), followed by confession and repentance. Then it is God who redeems, forgives and atones/reconciles. This is an explanation of being born again/or experiencing a new birth (II Corinthians 5:17 where the old character passes away and is made new). God is always the first call, the initiator for a changed spiritual life. The unbeliever is the one blinded who must see the Hand of God intercepting in their life, and acknowledge it is the one and only God, the Creator. Notice that the Isaiah 42 passage below speaks of the *avon* (bent/crooked) sins.

Luke 6:35 ... he (God) is kind unto the unthankful and to the evil.

Romans 8:29-30 For whom he (God) did foreknow, he also did predestinate .... Moreover whom he did predestinate, them he also called....

John 6:44 No man can come to me, except the Father which hath sent me draw him...

John 14:6 Jesus saith unto him, I am the way, the truth, and the life: no man cometh unto the Father, but by me. (Notice the oneness of God and Jesus in John 6:44 and 14:6)

I John 4:19 We love him, because he (God) first loved us.

Isaiah 42:16-18 And I will bring the blind by a way that they knew not; I will lead them in paths that they have not known: I will make darkness light before them, and crooked things straight. These things will I do unto them, and not forsake them.¹⁷ They shall be turned back, they shall be greatly ashamed, that trust in graven images, that say to the molten images, Ye are our gods. ¹⁸ Hear, ye deaf; and look, ye blind, that ye may see.

John 9:39 And Jesus said, "For judgment I am come into this world, that they which see not might see...."

As part of the process of becoming a believer and follower of Christ, we are told to confess our sins, but what does that mean? The word "confession" comes from the concept of putting out, or casting out like shooting an arrow or extending forth with an open hand regarding what you have done (no hiding, or withholding). The Hebrew word also includes the idea of hands extended to praise God or to bemoan something as in wringing one's hands. Therefore, when someone confesses or reveals the depth of their wrongdoing, God is faithful, merciful, and gracious, forgiving inequity, transgressions and sin and cleanses us (Exodus 34:6-7 and Jeremiah 33:8). After the "salvation" of the sinner, comes the work of discovering who God is, how He expects us to live and treat others as defined in His Word so that the new believer can be transformed by the renewing of their mind, and become conformed to the likeness of God (Romans 8:29 and 12:2).

What is the connection between repentance and forgiveness? In the secular world forgiveness can be necessary for healing or restoring emotional stability for the injured party. Repentance from the one who committed the offense would be good, but is not always an option. In the spiritual realm, <u>repentance is required to obtain forgiveness from God</u>. The Hebrew word for **repentance** is *nacham* #H5162 in *Strong's Concordance*. It is translated mostly as comfort or repent. It conveys the thought to be sorry, to console one's self, to be moved to pity, to bitterly regret, to have compassion. Oddly enough, this definition of repentance explains verses in the Old Testament that say the LORD repented (Genesis 6:5, Exodus 32:12, 14, Judges 2:18 and I Samuel 15:11). In the New Testament, the Greek word for **repentance** is *metanoia* #G3341.

It means a change of mind for the better. The root word - *metanoeo* #G3340 means to think differently, to reconsider. Based on these definitions, repentance conveys a process of reflection or reassessment of one's past actions, and attitudes a person has come to deeply regret. Then this reassessment concludes with the need to <u>turn from</u> past behavior and attitudes and <u>turn toward</u> choices and a life pleasing to God. True repentance changes a person's viewpoint, their choices, and actions.

The Greek word (#G859 *aphesis*) for "**remission**" and "**forgiveness**" is the same word. It means to release, to pardon. *Aphesis* comes from the root Greek word G#863 *aphemi* meaning to send away, to depart, or go away from. "**Forgive**" in Hebrew is *Strong's Concordance* word #H5375 *nasa*. It means to bare, lift, take away as in when one is forgiven; they are pardoned, their wrongdoing is lifted and taken away. Several scriptures describe the *taken way* aspect with such finality that in Psalm 103:12 it says God has removed our sins from us as far as the east is from the west. In Isaiah 43:25 and Jeremiah 31:34, God says He will not remember their sins and iniquities. Through repentance, forgiveness conveys the removal or putting off or putting an end to an offense and is necessary for restoring a right relationship between the person and God.

The goal of forgiveness for both parties is to stop the negative impact of sin on their psyche and health allowing some level of peace and healing. However, the goal of God's forgiveness is twofold: 1) it is to stop the negative impact of sin and 2) to restore a right relationship. Without true repentance, there is no forgiveness from God and the relationship is not restored.

Only God can reconcile (atone – to make compatible) the broken relationship once the person has repented. Then forgiveness follows and God removes the sins.

How does redemption connect to atonement/reconciliation?
There are two different Hebrew words translated in English as **redeem** or **redemption**. Both Hebrew root words describe a divine intercession

in human affairs. **Pdh** or **padah** (#H6299 *Strong's Concordance*) refers to ransom or payment for what is released. It does not imply a relationship between the agent and that which is being redeemed, nor that the payment is of equal value for what is being exchanged. *Pdh* takes on the meaning of a "deliverer." The other root word for **redeem** is *g'l* or *ga'al* (#H150 in *Strong's Concordance*) implies a family connection or obligation to what is being redeemed or bought back.[74] *Padah or pdh* appears in Numbers 3 with the redemption of the first born. *Ga'al or g'l* is identified by the term "kinsman redeemer" in the story of Ruth in the book of Ruth, chapter 4.

Like the concept of atonement and forgiveness in the Old Testament, redemption has an evolving meaning in the Bible. In time redemption also meant to liberate from woes, bondage, and oppression. Generally, redemption means salvation from a state of or circumstance that destroys the value of human existence.[75] In the New Testament redeem or redemption appears in the context of the Messiah redeeming Israel from the oppression of Rome (Luke 2:38). It also appears in connection with the end times redemption (Luke 21:28), and redemption from an old life of sin to a reborn or renewed relationship with God (Romans 3:24-25, 8:21-8:23, and Colossians 1:14, etc). Only a couple of times in the Old Testament is redemption spoken of in the context of people's redemption from eternal death. (Note these verses speak of redemption from perishing, redemption from the power of the grave, and from death; but redemption from hell is not mentioned.) Here they are:

Isaiah 1:27-28 NIV Zion will be delivered (redeemed) with justice, her penitent ones with righteousness. [28] But rebels and sinners will both be broken, and those who forsake the LORD will perish.

---

[74] *Encyclopaedia Judaica* on "redemption," Keter Publishing House, Jerusalem Ltd, Israel. Volume 14, pages 1-2.
[75] Ibid.

Psalm 49:15 But God will redeem my soul from the power of the grave: for he shall receive me. Selah.

Hosea 13:14 I will ransom them from the power of the grave; I will redeem them from death: O death, I will be thy plagues; O grave, I will be thy destruction: repentance shall be hid from mine eyes.

Redemption and atonement in *Torah* are linked to the year of Jubilee which, begins on the Day of Atonement (*Yom Kippur*). Jubilee is about redeeming and restoring what was lost. Atonement is about reconciling or making compatible with something or someone else. Only God can redeem (liberate, free) mankind from the bondage and oppression of sin and make repentant people compatible with how He has called His people to live.

Animal Sacrifices for Atonement

Numbers 35:33 So ye shall not pollute the land wherein ye are: for blood it defileth the land: and the land cannot be cleansed of the blood that is shed therein, but by the blood of him that shed it.

This opening verse is regarding the murder of another person. The verse says that murder pollutes and defiles the land and the land cannot be cleansed of that murder, except by the death of the person who committed the murder in the first place. We get a sense of this when Cain murdered his brother, Abel. Genesis 4:10 says, And the LORD said, "What have you done? The voice of your brother's blood is crying to me from the ground."

Animal sacrifices were a common practice amongst a number of ancient Middle Eastern societies. According to the *Encyclopedia Judaica*, the word "**sacrifice**" in *Torah* is more accurately translated "slaughter." Like today, many animals were slaughtered for food.

Sin - Atonement, Forgiveness & Redemption

Offerings are gifts, presents; something presented or offered to God or a deity. Usually animal sacrifices and offerings were for worshipping or appeasing pagan gods to gain favor for rain, crops, and fertility. Some Jewish sages have thought the Hebrew people (later identified as Jewish people) picked up the practice of sacrificing animals to pagan gods from their stay in Egypt. It is interesting to note that immediately after citing the Ten Commandments in Exodus 20:24 (shown below), God spoke to Moses about building an altar of earth on which the people could make their sacrifices for burnt offerings and peace offerings where His name was acknowledged and God said He would come and bless them, however, sin offerings were not mentioned. Leviticus 1:2 KJV has the word "if" implying that from the beginning of the nation of Israel animal sacrifices were voluntary and not a command of God. This is confirmed in Jeremiah 7:22-23 when God says He did not command the people to make burnt offerings or sacrifices.

Exodus 20:24 An altar of earth thou shalt make unto me, and shalt sacrifice thereon thy burnt offerings, and thy peace offerings, thy sheep, and thine oxen: in all places where I record my name I will come unto thee, and I will bless thee.

Leviticus 1:2 Speak unto the children of Israel, and say unto them, **If** any man of you bring an offering unto the Lord, ye shall bring your offering of the cattle, even of the herd, and of the flock.

Jeremiah 7:22:23 For I spake not unto your fathers, nor commanded them in the day that I brought them out of the land of Egypt, concerning burnt offerings or sacrifices: ²³ But this thing commanded I them, saying, Obey my voice, and I will be your God, and ye shall be my people: and walk ye in all the ways that I have commanded you, that it may be well unto you.

Although the Bible tells of animals killed as an offering to God by Abel, Noah, and Abraham, these were not sin sacrifices. (See Genesis 4:4, 8:20, and 22:13). While it is commonly thought in Christian circles that Adam and Eve's sin was covered by God killing an animal to cover them, that is not what Genesis 3:21[76] says. To contain, minimize and shift this pagan practice, God said in Leviticus 17:1-7[77] that only certain animals (domesticated, non-predatory animals along with certain birds as offerings from the poor) prepared in a specific way, at a specific place could be sacrificed to eliminate worship to "devils" (Leviticus 17:7 and Deuteronomy 32:17).

It is often explained in Christianity that by laying one's hand on the animal prior to its sacrifice was symbolic of the transference of sin onto the animal and the animal was killed instead of or as a substitute for the person who had sinned. Some people have implied and assumed a transference of sin took place,[78] however, the Bible does not say the animal's death was a substitute for the person who sinned. The laying on of a hand or hands is indeed a transference, called *smicha* or *semikhad* in Hebrew meaning leaning and *smichut* meaning ordination. In Deuteronomy 34:9 Moses laid hands on Joshua through which the spirit of wisdom was transferred.

As stated earlier on the topic of forgiveness, there are certain crimes and sins for which no animal's death could cover, atone or substitute. In Leviticus 24, a man blasphemed the name of the Lord. Before he was stoned to death for this sin, everyone who heard the blasphemy was told to lay their hands on the man's head (Leviticus 24:11 and 14).

---

76 Genesis 3:21: Unto Adam also and to his wife did the Lord God make coats of skins, and clothed them.

77 According to www.jewishvirtuallibrary.org/jsource/Judaism/vegsacrifices.html and the *Encyclopaedia Judaica* (p. 606), the revered *Torah* scholar, Rabbi Maimonides, held the position that sacrificial animal atonement was rooted in the customs and cultures of the time rather than a requirement from God as a basis for forgiveness.

78 James 5:14-15 suggest the laying on of hands for healing, does not mean that one person's health transfers to the person who is ill nor does I Timothy 4:14 mean the spiritual gift was transferred from one person to another.

Almost as if by being present to hear the blasphemy had negatively impacted or stained the hearers, and the laying on of hands was symbolic of returning the blasphemy back to the blasphemer before his death. Notice that God said the penalty for this sin required the death of the guilty person. Animal sacrificial atonement was not an option. The same was true of the man stoned to death who had broken the Sabbath by gathering sticks (Numbers 15:33-36).

There is only one time in *Torah* that speaks of the transference of sin from people to an animal. In Leviticus 16:21-22 the High Priest Aaron laid both of his hands upon the live animal, confessed all the iniquities and transgressions of the people, "putting them upon the head of the goat." This took place on *Yom Kippur* with the scapegoat that was sent into the wilderness <u>alive</u>. Here is Leviticus 16:21-22:

[21] And Aaron shall lay both his hands upon the head of the live goat, and confess over him all the iniquities of the children of Israel, and all their transgressions in all their sins, putting them upon the head of the goat, and shall send him away by the hand of a fit man into the wilderness:

[22] And the goat shall bear upon him all their iniquities unto a land not inhabited: and he shall let go the goat in the wilderness.

In time, it became clear that many of the sacrificial sin or guilt offerings had become an empty ritual, reflecting neither remorse for the people's actions nor indicating their love for God. And God was not fooled. David said in Psalms 40 that animal sacrifices were not what God wanted from His people. Proverbs 21:3 says justice and judgment are more acceptable to God than sacrifice. In Amos 5:21-22 and Isaiah 1:11-17 God said He hated and despised their feast days (when sacrifices were made). Some Jewish philosophers have speculated that animal sacrifices were a concession on God's part; allowed to eventually wean His people from these habits altogether.

Psalm 40:6 NIV Sacrifice and offering you did not desire— but my ears you have opened— burnt offerings and sin offerings you did not require.

Psalm 50:13-14, and 23 NASB "Shall I eat the flesh of bulls or drink the blood of male goats? [14] "Offer to God a sacrifice of thanksgiving and pay your vows to the Most High; ...[23] "He who offers a sacrifice of thanksgiving honors Me; And to him who orders *his* way *aright* I shall show the salvation of God."

Psalms 51:16-17 [16] For thou desirest not sacrifice; else would I give it: thou delightest not in burnt offering. [17] The sacrifices of God are a broken spirit: a broken and a contrite heart, O God, thou wilt not despise.

Amos 5:21-22 [God speaking] I hate, I despise your feast days, and I will not smell (accept #H7306) in your solemn assemblies. [22] Though ye offer me burnt offerings and your meat offerings, I will not accept (be pleased with – #H7521) them: neither will I regard the peace offerings of your fat beasts.

Isaiah 1:11-18 To what purpose is the multitude of your sacrifices unto me? saith the Lord: I am full of the burnt offerings of rams, and the fat of fed beasts; and I delight not in the blood of bullocks, or of lambs, or of he goats.

[12] When ye come to appear before me, who hath required this at your hand, to tread my courts? [13] Bring no more vain oblations; incense is an abomination unto me; the new moons and sabbaths, the calling of assemblies, I cannot (endure-NASB) away with; it is iniquity, even the solemn meeting.

[14] Your new moons and your appointed feasts my soul hateth: they are a trouble unto me; I am weary to bear them. [15] And when ye

Sin - Atonement, Forgiveness & Redemption

spread forth your hands, I will hide mine eyes from you: yea, when ye make many prayers, I will not hear: your hands are full of blood.

¹⁶ Wash you, make you clean; put away the evil of your doings from before mine eyes; cease to do evil; ¹⁷ Learn to do well; seek judgment, relieve the oppressed, judge the fatherless, plead for the widow.

¹⁸ Come now, and let us reason together, saith the Lord: though your sins be as scarlet, they shall be as white as snow; though they be red like crimson, they shall be as wool.

Notice the last verse quoted above (Isaiah 1:18). Many Christians have taken this verse as an example of sin being like blood and is washed away by the death atonement of Christ. However, in context that is not what is implied. Rather than animal/death sacrifices or offerings transforming one's sin, God says to make one's self clean is achieved by stop doing evil acts, learning what is correct and living out God's commands for righteous behavior, which is repentance.

Some would mention Leviticus 17:11 and Hebrews 9:22 regarding blood/death atonement for sin. Leviticus 17:11 says, "For the life of the flesh is in the blood: and I have given it to you upon the altar to make an atonement for your souls: for it is the blood that maketh an atonement for the soul." In context this verse is from a chapter that discusses things that should not be done involving animal sacrifices. In Leviticus 17 God says it is forbidden for any of His people to sacrifice an animal in the field and not bring a peace offering to the Lord at the tabernacle (Leviticus 17:4). Leviticus 17:7 says do not offer sacrifices to devils (or other gods). In Leviticus 17:10 God says He will set His face against anyone who consumes blood.[79] It is after this verse that

---

[79] Several ancient cultures including Egyptians, Canaanite and Baal worshippers practiced drinking blood (both animal and human blood) as part of the pagan religious and health rituals. Note Leviticus 17:10-14 does not designate animal versus human blood; only that God forbids the practice because blood is sacred as a life force.

God speaks of blood for atonement of a person's soul. God goes on to say in Leviticus 17:14 that the circulating blood is the life force of all flesh (also see Genesis 9:4). In context Leviticus 17:11 is not referring to the necessity of blood to atone for sin (in fact sin is not mentioned), but rather God is restricting sacrifices to other gods and commanding respect for life by forbidding His people to consume its life force. Apart from the practice of drinking or eating blood, a fairly common practice among many cultures, consuming blood on a regular basis poses a serious health risk. There are a variety of blood-borne pathogens that can be passed on through consumption. In addition, blood is high in iron and the human body has difficulty excreting excessive amounts of iron.

The next perplexing verse comes from the New Testament. Hebrews 9:22 says, "And almost all things are by the law purged with blood; and without shedding of blood is no remission." While this verse is often quoted to prove that there is no forgiveness without sacrificial death to atone, it is almost never mentioned that eight sentences later in Hebrews 10:4-6 the writer also says this:

Hebrews 10:4-6 For it is impossible for the blood of bulls and goats to take away sins. ⁵ Therefore, when He comes into the world, He says,

> "SACRIFICE AND OFFERING YOU HAVE NOT DESIRED,
> BUT A BODY YOU HAVE PREPARED FOR ME;
> ⁶ IN WHOLE BURNT OFFERINGS AND *sacrifices* FOR SIN
> YOU HAVE TAKEN NO PLEASURE.

Hebrews 9:22 is in a passage that compares the first covenant, tabernacle and Moses (Exodus 24) to the new or renewed covenant of Jeremiah 31:31-34 where the author of Hebrews says Jesus is the Great High Priest. In the new covenant when God says He will forgive "the house of Israel" (believers in God) their iniquity and will remember their sin no more, there is no mention of animal sacrifice or the need for a sacrificial death.

Jeremiah 31:33-34 "But this is the covenant which I will make with the house of Israel after those days," declares the Lord, "I will put My law within them and on their heart I will write it; and I will be their God, and they shall be My people. [34] They will not teach again, each man his neighbor and each man his brother, saying, 'Know the Lord,' for they will all know Me, from the least of them to the greatest of them," declares the Lord, "for I will forgive their iniquity, and their sin I will remember no more."

In the Exodus 24:5-8 passage the writer of Hebrews 9:18-21 referred to the offerings made for the covenant of relationship between the Hebrew people and God. Those offerings were burnt and peace offerings, not sin offerings.

Exodus 24:5-8 KJV And he sent young men of the children of Israel, which offered burnt offerings, and sacrificed peace offerings of oxen unto the Lord. [6] And Moses took half of the blood and put it in basons; and half of the blood he sprinkled on the altar. [7] And he took the book of the covenant and read in the audience of the people: and they said, all that the Lord hath said will we do, and be obedient.

[8] And Moses took the blood, and sprinkled it on the people, and said, Behold the blood of the covenant, which the Lord hath made with you concerning all these words.

The Point: After leaving Egypt, God did not institute animal or death sacrifices for atonement of sin. Rather God forbade the cultural practice of sacrificing animals (and sometimes people) to gods for favors. The scriptures listed earlier (Exodus 21:12 -17,

Psalm 40:6, Psalm 50:13-14, and 23, Psalms 51:16-17, Amos 5:21-22 and Isaiah 1:11-18) show animal sacrifices could not atone for sin.

The Story of the Redemption of Manasseh, son of King Hezekiah

Some pastors quote from Ezekiel 18:4 that the soul who sins shall surely die. However, death and life in that chapter speak of spiritual/perishing death and spiritual/eternal life. So, Ezekiel 18:4 refers to those who knowingly, willfully, deliberately and consistently sin will surely die and not obtain eternal life. Look at what God said in verse 21-23 of this same chapter.

Ezekiel 18:21 But if the wicked will turn from all his sins that he hath committed, and keep all my statutes, and do that which is lawful and right, he shall surely live, he shall not die.

²² All his transgressions that he hath committed, they shall not be mentioned unto him: in his righteousness that he hath done he shall live.

²³ Have I any pleasure at all that the wicked should die? saith the Lord God: and not that he should return from his ways, and live?

Why would God say that the wicked one who turns from his sins and does what is right will surely live and not die if God were referring to the normal cycle of life?

King Hezekiah of Judah was succeeded by his son Manasseh as king. Manasseh did great evil in the land – from worshipping false gods, enticing the people of Israel to worship idols to offering his own children as sacrifices to idols. Could God forgive Manasseh? God did. Was the basis for Manasseh's forgiveness the sacrificial death of bulls and lambs to cover his many sins? No. For a God who says in Malachi

3:6 He changes not, is there a different requirement to forgive sin in the Old Testament versus the New Testament?

II Chronicles 33:1-19 Manasseh was twelve years old when he began to reign, and he reigned fifty and five years in Jerusalem: ² But did that which was evil in the sight of the LORD, like unto the abominations of the heathen, whom the LORD had cast out before the children of Israel. ³ For he built again the high places which Hezekiah his father had broken down, and he reared up altars for Baalim, and made groves, and worshipped all the host of heaven, and served them.

⁴ Also he built altars in the house of the LORD, whereof the LORD had said, In Jerusalem shall my name be for ever. ⁵ And he built altars for all the host of heaven in the two courts of the house of the LORD.

⁶ And he caused his children to pass through the fire in the valley of the son of Hinnom: also he observed times, and used enchantments, and used witchcraft, and dealt with a familiar spirit, and with wizards: he wrought much evil in the sight of the LORD, to provoke him to anger.

⁷ And he set a carved image, the idol which he had made, in the house of God, of which God had said to David and to Solomon his son, In this house, and in Jerusalem, which I have chosen before all the tribes of Israel, will I put my name for ever: ⁸ Neither will I any more remove the foot of Israel from out of the land which I have appointed for your fathers; so that they will take heed to do all that I have commanded them, according to the whole law and the statutes and the ordinances by the hand of Moses.

<u>⁹ So Manasseh made Judah and the inhabitants of Jerusalem to err, and to do worse than the heathen, whom the LORD had destroyed before the children of Israel.</u>

¹⁰ And the LORD spake to Manasseh, and to his people: but they would not hearken. ¹¹ Wherefore the LORD brought upon them the captains of the host of the king of Assyria, which took Manasseh among the thorns, and bound him with fetters, and carried him to Babylon.

¹² <u>And when he was in affliction, he (Manasseh) besought the LORD his God, and humbled himself greatly before the God of his fathers, ¹³ And prayed unto him: and he was intreated of him, and (God) heard his supplication, and brought him again to Jerusalem into his kingdom. Then Manasseh knew that the LORD he was God.</u>

¹⁴ Now after this he (Manasseh) built a wall without the city of David, on the west side of Gihon, in the valley, even to the entering in at the fish gate, and compassed about Ophel, and raised it up a very great height, and put captains of war in all the fenced cities of Judah. ¹⁵ And he took away the strange gods, and the idol out of the house of the LORD, and all the altars that he had built in the mount of the house of the LORD, and in Jerusalem, and cast them out of the city. ¹⁶ And he repaired the altar of the LORD, and <u>sacrificed thereon peace offerings and thank offerings</u> (notice they were not sin offerings), and commanded Judah to serve the LORD God of Israel.

¹⁷ Nevertheless the people did sacrifice still in the high places, yet unto the LORD their God only.

¹⁸ Now the rest of the acts of Manasseh, and his prayer unto his God, and the words of the seers that spake to him in the name of

the LORD God of Israel, behold, they are written in the book of the kings of Israel.

[19] His prayer also, and how God was intreated of him, and all his sins, and his trespass, and the places wherein he built high places, and set up groves and graven images, before he was humbled: behold, they are written among the sayings of the seers.

If animal sacrifices do not atone, what does?

II Chronicles 7:14 If my people, which are called by my name, shall humble themselves, and pray, and seek my face, and turn from their wicked ways; then will I hear from heaven, and will forgive their sin, and will heal their land.

By now the answer to this question should be obvious – repentance! The original idea behind atonement was *to* appease the one offended – which is God, however, eventually the sin or offense itself became the object of atonement. When the generation of Hebrew slaves left Egypt, the practice of sacrificing animals came with them (Leviticus 17:5). These practices eventually ended. However, they served to illustrate unrepentant disobedience to God's instructions and teachings result in an erosion to one's relationship with God, and will cause permanent destruction of one's life, and eternal separation from God. Over time what people thought achieved atonement changed. During the Babylonian exile, temple animal sacrifice atonement ended and atonement was then sought by fasting and prayer (Daniel 9:3). In Jeremiah 36:3 and 7 God and the prophet Jeremiah declared sincere repentance and prayer could achieve atonement. Also, there are verses that say it is God who has redeemed (atoned/reconciled) His people (see Isaiah 44:23, Lamentations 3:58 and Deuteronomy 21:8 below).

Isaiah 43:1 But now thus saith the LORD that created thee, O Jacob, and he that formed thee, O Israel, Fear not: for I have redeemed thee, I have called thee by thy name; thou art mine.

Isaiah 44:23 Sing, O ye heavens; for the LORD hath done it: shout, ye lower parts of the earth: break forth into singing, ye mountains, O forest, and every tree therein: for the LORD hath redeemed Jacob and glorified himself in Israel.

Lamentations 3:58 O LORD, thou hast pleaded the causes of my soul; thou hast redeemed my life.

Deuteronomy 21:8 Be merciful, O LORD, unto thy people Israel, whom thou hast redeemed, and lay not innocent blood[80] unto thy people of Israel's charge. And the blood shall be forgiven them.

Just as a covenant or legal agreement is between two parties, spiritual atonement/reconciliation is between the person and God. The person seeks to atone and be reconciled to God through repentance. Spiritual repentance involves introspection that concludes it is God they have offended, feelings of remorse over one's grievous actions, produces change in future responses, along with a desire to make amends. After a person has repented of their sinful actions, it is God who atones or reconciles (makes compatible) the repentant through His love and mercy (grace) and then redeems and restores that which was spiritually stolen, lost, broken, soiled, or marred (see Ezekiel 36:23-27 and II Corinthians 5:17 below). Then forgiveness, which follows atonement, is the permanent removal, the lifting and taking away of sin and iniquity.

Ezekiel 36:23-27 And I will sanctify my great name, which was profaned among the heathen, which ye have profaned in the midst

---

[80] The word "blood" can be a euphemism for the word death as in "his blood is on your hands."

of them; and the heathen shall know that I am the LORD, saith the Lord GOD, when I shall be sanctified in you before their eyes. ²⁴ For I will take you from among the heathen, and gather you out of all countries, and will bring you into your own land. ²⁵ Then will I sprinkle clean water upon you, and ye shall be clean: from all your filthiness, and from all your idols, will I cleanse you. ²⁶ A new heart also will I give you, and a new spirit will I put within you: and I will take away the stony heart out of your flesh, and I will give you an heart of flesh. ²⁷ And I will put my spirit within you, and cause you to walk in my statutes, and ye shall keep my judgments, and do them.

II Corinthians 5:17 Therefore if any man be in Christ, he is a new creature: old things are passed away; behold, all things are become new.

The Point: In the Old Testament atonement and forgiveness were an ongoing part of the Hebrew people's (nation of Israel's) relationship with God. The handling of infractions was a family matter; as in the Hebrew people were God's people, His children. God's instructions and warnings (*Torah* translated as "the law") were not to all the people of the world. They were to the people God had designated as His and had given His promise to – the descendants of Abraham, that is, the nation of Israel. Atonement/reconciliation with God can only be achieved when there is belief in God, and a desire to be right with God.

Proverbs 21:3 and 27 To do justice and judgment is more acceptable to the LORD than sacrifice… ²⁷ The sacrifice of the wicked is abomination: how much more, when he bringeth it with a wicked mind?

Isaiah 66:2-3 NASB "…But to this one I will look, To him who is humble and contrite of spirit, and who trembles at My word.

[3] "*But* he who kills an ox is *like* one who slays a man; he who sacrifices a lamb is *like* the one who breaks a dog's neck; he who offers a grain offering *is like one who offers* swine's blood; he who burns incense is *like* the one who blesses an idol. As they have chosen their *own* ways, and their soul delights in their abominations…

Jeremiah 7:22:23 For I spake not unto your fathers, nor commanded them in the day that I brought them out of the land of Egypt, concerning burnt offerings or sacrifices: [23] But this thing commanded I them, saying, Obey my voice, and I will be your God, and ye shall be my people: and walk ye in all the ways that I have commanded you, that it may be well unto you.

The Bible teaches that we are required to keep all of "The Law" or we are deemed sinners – True or False?

This is false. What is "The Law?" The English word "Law" refers to the Hebrew word "*Torah*" which consists of God's commandments found in the first five books of the Bible. The more accurate translation of "*Torah*" is instructions. Hebrew word #H8451 *towrah*, from the root word #H3384 *yarah* means "to instruct, to teach, to direct."

    An assumption by many Christians has been that failure to keep all 613 Mosaic Laws (commands) causes a permanent break in one's relationship with God, and atonement can be obtained only by sacrificial death. Some Christians believe they are free from having to keep the law, because they have received salvation through God's grace by Jesus' sacrificial payment for their sins (a loose interpretation of Romans 6:14, Ephesians 2:8-9 and much of Galatians 5). Here is an example to help put this idea into perspective. As a parent, you teach or expect your children to do or not do many things, such as potty training, to put their dirty laundry in the proper place, after a certain age to not eat with their fingers, do not cut their siblings hair, do not push or hit their sibling, to clean their room, treat others with respect, etc. While failure to do one or several of these things will not cause a break in your relationship with your child, it may very well have unpleasant consequences. Many of God's instructions are like this. Failure to do them, does not cause a break in relationship, but are likely to trigger unpleasant and possibly long-term, irreversible consequences – for the person and others. Now let's say a child grows to adulthood, becomes addicted to drugs, steals from and repeatedly threatens violence to family members, beats up their sibling or your spouse, and tells you they hate you and you are no longer their parents; their family. Then they murder several people in a robbery. In spite of your love for this child, their actions have caused a permanent break in which your relationship will never be the same without repentance. This example shows that some infractions will not break one's relationship while willful, deliberately devastating deeds will. Although the parent loves the child, and wishes they were different, without repentance, their relationship is broken.

Within God's 613 commandments are the principles for being just, kind, merciful and compassionate toward others, taking care of one's health and respecting all of God's creation. Therefore, the word translated as "law" is <u>God's instructions, percepts, teachings, and directions for His people on how to live, treat others and revere God</u> are never obsolete nor can they be replaced by God's grace. With this understanding of God's *Law*, how could His followers ever be free of observing God's instructions? Near the end of the book of Leviticus in chapter 26 God tells of the blessings for His people (the children of Israel – verse 26:46) who acknowledge, respect and live by His instructions and the negative consequences for His people who despise and abhor God's instructions. God is by no means asking or demanding one's perfection in keeping the commands, but He wants us to acknowledge, respect and try to live by their principles. Notice that the opposite of living by God's instructions is not the failure to have kept all the instructions perfectly. Leviticus' contrast is identified as those who <u>despise and abhor God's instructions</u> which are a reflection of one's feelings for God, and in turn separates them from God. Although Deuteronomy 18:13 and Matthew 5:48 call for God's people to be "perfect," that word is more accurately translated as upright, whole, just, complete, and to act with integrity.[81] Perfection in observing every command is not what is demanded or expected, rather the scriptures show it is one's belief and attitude about God and His instructions that matters. See Deuteronomy 6:18 (do what is right), 30:11-18 (it is not too difficult to do what God has asked), Micah 6:6-8 (what does God require of man), and Matthew 22:36-40 (Jesus sums up the 613 commandments into two commands – love God with everything within you and honor/care/treat all others with love).

The idea that no one is righteous in the eyes of God is false.[82] The Bible is filled with references of the righteous including Abel (Hebrews 11:4), Noah (Genesis 7:1), and Abraham (Romans 4:3). Psalms and Proverbs have over 100 verses about the righteous. God's "judgment" of His children has never been based on their ability to perfectly keep all His instructions, rather His compassion, mercy and grace is based on the individual's heart, their intentions, and their desire to make amends and repent (example – the story of Zacchaeus in Luke 19:5-9). It is not our dogged, self-righteous adherence of the Law that God desires, but rather He wants us to grasp the *spirit* of the Law (Matthew 23:23, Romans 7:6 and Hosea 6:6). Look at these verses along with the new or renewed covenant from Jeremiah 31:33-34 where God speaks of putting His Law in the minds and hearts of people who will be committed to Him. Ezekiel 36:25 and 27 speak of cleansing people from

---

81   "Perfect" in Hebrew word #H8552 *tamiym* means complete, whole, sound, upright. The Greek word #G5046 *teleios* means complete, to act with virtue and integrity. In Genesis 6:9 Noah is described as just and perfect and that He walked with God. Genesis 17:1 calls Abram (Abraham) to walk before God and be perfect. In Psalms 37:18 and 84:11 the same word is translated as "upright" and it is "undefiled" in Psalms 119:1.

82   In Romans 3:10, the apostle Paul says that none are righteous; not one. The context of that remark compares the Jew who has had the Word of God yet does not believe (3:2-3) and the Gentile who has not had a relationship with God (3:9). For more details of these verses read the context of who is being spoken of in Paul's quotes in Romans 3:10-18 discussed earlier in this Chapter under the section "None Righteous: All are Sinners - True or False?"

their sins and God causing the people to walk (live by) His statutes. Ezekiel 36:31 speaks of their repentance; the remembering of their evil deeds and their change of heart. The verse in Romans 7:6 says we will have no need to be taught <u>the letter</u> of the law because believers will have grasped the *spirit* of what God wants of us. Then notice God says He will forgive their iniquity and remember their sin no more.

Jeremiah 31:33-34 ...I will put my law in their inward parts, and write it in their hearts; and will be their God, and they shall be my people.
³⁴ And they shall teach no more every man his neighbour, and every man his brother, saying, Know the Lord: for they shall all know me, from the least of them unto the greatest of them, saith the Lord: for I will forgive their iniquity, and I will remember their sin no more.

Ezekiel 36:25-32 NASB ²⁵ Then I will sprinkle clean water on you, and you will be clean; I will cleanse you from all your filthiness and from all your idols.²⁶ Moreover, I will give you a new heart and put a new spirit within you; and I will remove the heart of stone from your flesh and give you a heart of flesh. ²⁷ I will put My Spirit within you and cause you to walk in My statutes, and you will be careful to observe My ordinances. ²⁸ You will live in the land that I gave to your forefathers; so you will be My people, and I will be your God. ²⁹ Moreover, I will save you from all your uncleanness; and I will call for the grain and multiply it, and I will not bring a famine on you. ³⁰ I will multiply the fruit of the tree and the produce of the field, so that you will not receive again the disgrace of famine among the nations. ³¹ Then you will remember your evil ways and your deeds that were not good, and you will loathe yourselves in your own sight for your iniquities and your abominations. ³² I am not doing *this* for your sake," declares the Lord God, "let it be known to you. Be ashamed and confounded for your ways, O house of Israel!"

Matthew 23:23 Woe unto you, scribes and Pharisees, hypocrites! for ye pay tithe of mint and anise and cummin, and have omitted the <u>weightier matters of the law</u>, judgment, mercy, and faith: these ought ye to have done, and not to leave the other undone.

Romans 7:6 But now we are delivered from the law, that being dead wherein we were held; that we should serve in newness of spirit, and not in the oldness of the letter.

Hosea 6:6 For I desired mercy, and not sacrifice; and the knowledge of God more than burnt offerings.

Jesus spoke of this very point in Matthew 12:1-13 when He conveyed the principle that the intent, the spirit of the Law, our compassion toward another is more important than keeping a legalistic interpretation of the Law (the strict adherence to achieve a sense of self-righteousness). Notice what Jesus said to the Pharisees when they accused Him and His disciples of breaking the Sabbath's command to do no work. He recalled King David taking the shewbread when he and his men were hungry which was lawful only for the priest to eat and then this statement about the priest serving at the tabernacle:

Matthew 12:5 and 7 Or have ye not read in the law, how that on the Sabbath days <u>the priests in the temple profane the Sabbath, and are blameless</u>? ⁷ But if ye had known what this meaneth, I will have mercy, and not sacrifice, (quoting Hosea 6:6) ye would not have condemned the guiltless.

In reading the instructions in the epistles[83] of the New Testament it is helpful to understand the audience to whom those letters addressed.

---

83   The letters attributed to the apostles Paul, James, Peter, John and Jude to churches and/or individuals in the early church.

Sin - Atonement, Forgiveness & Redemption

Written during the beginning of the early Church, there were a small but growing number of Gentiles who were new to belief in the God of Israel. Many of these new Gentile Christians were unsure of what was expected and required of them in their new relationship with the God of Israel and Jesus. In some of the epistles Paul instructed Gentiles on what their response to sin, temptation, persecution and adversity should be. Sometimes Paul addressed Jewish believers regarding what they were teaching Gentile followers. Therefore, well-known verses in the epistles written by Paul or other apostles that appear to be a general exposition for everyone should be examined within the context of who and what issues were being addressed at the time. When the apostles Paul and James spoke of one law broken nullifying all the Law or it being as if all the laws were broken (shown below), they were addressing Jews who were saying their righteousness or right standing with God was based on having kept the law and to the Gentiles who felt they needed circumcision to be right with God. Paul explained that righteousness is not determined solely by what a person does (works). Righteousness is based on believing and trusting in God and the grace of God. In Romans 4 Paul showed this is not a new understanding of relationship with God. He explained prior to the instructions for circumcision and the *law*, the promise for relationship to Abraham and his descendants was based on belief and the grace of God (Romans 4:13).

James 2:10 NIV "whoever keeps the whole law and yet stumbles at just one point is guilty of breaking all of it."

Galatians 5:3 NASB And I testify again to every man who receives circumcision, that <u>he is under obligation to keep the whole Law</u>"

The Point: Those who are righteous are not "sinners." While it is true that the righteous have made and will sometimes make mistakes and sin, the willful, deliberate, continual practicing of sin is not true of those who are righteous (See Ezekiel 18). Righteousness or right standing with God is neither based on the strict observance of *Torah* (the *Law*), nor is it bestowed upon someone because they confess belief in Jesus. A person is righteous when they desire to please God (Jesus) because they believe and trust in God's (Jesus') power, authority and perfection and is reflected in how they live and treat others.

Salvation

Can someone lose their salvation? The answer to this frequently asked and discussed question should be apparent by the end of this section. In modern Christianity salvation is commonly thought to mean God saving someone from the penalty of their sin through Christ by His death on the cross as their substitute, thus saving people from God's wrath[84] against sin. Penal substitution thus presents Jesus saving people from the divine punishment of their past wrongdoings."[85] According to *Wikipedia* under "Salvation in Christianity", this theory for salvation is just one of several. Surprisingly, no part of this theory is based on principles established by Jesus' teachings or the Old Testament. In fact, this substitutional atonement theory is said to have been developed during the 16th century by Protestant reformers influenced by the secular legal system.

To understand how the Bible defines and categorizes salvation, one should start in the Old Testament. **Salvation** is *Strong's Concordance* Hebrew word #H3444 *yeshuw ah* and #H3468 *yesha* from the root word #3467 *yasha*. All the words translated as salvation or save mean

---

84 A review of the scriptures involving the wrath of God relate to Israel evoking God to anger during the 40 years after leaving Egypt and their subsequent period of idol worship (Exodus 32:11, Deuteronomy 9:7, II Kings 22:7, II Chronicles 34:25 Ezra 5:12, Ezekiel 22:31, etc.). The wrath of God in connection with judgment of God appears in Romans 2:5. In Ephesians 5:6 and Colossians 3:6 wrath appears to be a consequence of willful sin, unbelief, i.e. "the children of disobedience." God's wrath appears 3 times in Revelation 16 in the imagery of seven vials poured out on the earth.

85 From Wikipedia on "Salvation in Christianity" under the subsection entitled, "Penal substitution and faith."

some variation of deliverance, victory, to avenge, to defend, save, safe, liberation and rescue. Considering Jesus' name as we known it in Hebrew is Yeshua, it is interesting to see His mission to deliver, save, liberate and rescue people who are lost are a part of His name and identity. When the many verses of the Old Testament containing the word "salvation" are examined, these verses usually involved instances where the people of Israel needed salvation from attacks by others or to restore their position with God.[86] Nearly all of the verses connect the LORD with salvation so much so that God is often referred to as the God of their salvation. <u>Therefore, as established in the Old Testament by its usage and Hebraic definition, salvation is a situational event as in being saved from something or someone; salvation is not a category or designation of spiritual relationship."</u>

It does make sense that those who have fallen away from God and those who have never known God need salvation from the wrong path of life, however, Jesus' death in and of itself does not provide eternal spiritual salvation. As previously reviewed, true atonement for one's soul could never be achieved by death alone; not the death of an animal and not even the death of Jesus. The concept of atonement through belief and repentance conflicts with Romans 5, which contain several statements that are not supported by principles in the Old Testament or from statements made by Jesus. These unsupported statements in Romans 5 are: 1) Verse 6 - the Messiah would die for the ungodly, 2) Verse 9 – believers are justified by the blood of Jesus from the wrath of God, 3) Verse 12-14 that death and sin came through Adam to everyone, and 4) Verse 18 that by the offense of one [person], judgment came upon <u>all men</u> to condemnation, and through the righteousness of one [person] came the free gift to <u>all men</u> unto justification of life.) If this

---

86 For instance, see Exodus 14:13 involving salvation from the attack of the Egyptians, I Samuel 2:1 God answered the prayer of Hannah saving her from shame and the taunts of her adversary (I Samuel 1:6). I Samuel 19:5 salvation from the Philistines, II Chronicles 20:17 attacked by the Moabites and Ammonites. For restored relationship with God, see Psalms 85:4 and 7, 51:12, and Isaiah 12:1-3.

were true, then just as sin death came to everyone by Adam's sin, then through Jesus' sacrificial death, forgiveness, redemption and salvation came to everyone whether they believe or not, whether they repented or not. No, this is not correct. It is belief in God, acknowledgment that the path and choices of one's life have been wrong, choosing to follow God (repentance); and receiving a new Spirit life from God that brings atonement (reconciliation), spiritual re-birth and eternal life. Spiritual salvation is God saving a person from a life that would lead to permanent destruction. They receive salvation through their belief and trust in God, and through repentance (changing their beliefs, attitude, perspective, and their actions). Then it is God who reconciles, redeems, forgives and restores.

Salvation is the initial act of one's relationship with God – God saving them from a previous life without God. However, one's ongoing relationship with God is what constitutes the longevity of the relationship. <u>Therefore, the question is not can someone lose their salvation? Rather the question is can someone stop following and believing in God?</u> Can a person return to their old life of sin, and reject God once again? The answer is yes; many have fallen away. Take a look at these verses in Ezekiel 18:24 and Matthew 7:21-23 which both speak of those who once were righteous and had served God, but fell away and did things that were not consistent with the will of God. Hebrews 5:9 speaks of eternal salvation to those who obey God. After King David slept with a married woman and caused the deaths of several people, he asks God to <u>restore</u> (because he had lost) the joy of his salvation in Psalm 51:12.

> **Ezekiel 18:24 NASB** "But when a righteous man turns away from his righteousness, commits iniquity and does according to all the abominations that a wicked man does, will he live? All his righteous deeds which he has done will not be remembered for his treachery which he has committed and his sin which he has committed; for them he will die.

Matthew 7:21-23 NASB "Not everyone who says to Me, 'Lord, Lord,' will enter the kingdom of heaven, but he who does the will of My Father who is in heaven *will enter.*²² Many will say to Me on that day, 'Lord, Lord, did we not prophesy in Your name, and in Your name cast out demons, and in Your name perform many [a]miracles?' ²³ And then I will declare to them, 'I never knew you; DEPART FROM ME, YOU WHO PRACTICE LAWLESSNESS.' (KJV ye that work iniquity)

Hebrews 5:9 And being made perfect, he became the author of eternal salvation <u>unto all them that obey him</u>;

Psalm 51:12 Restore unto me the joy of thy salvation; and uphold me with thy free spirit.

The bottom line is: It is not God's will that any be lost. No one comes to God without God's calling, direction and intervention. God requires our belief, trust and repentance, then our obedience and choice to walk in His ways with Him. We are therefore "saved" from our path of destruction and given a new spirit life in which we must make efforts to grow in our knowledge of God, His Word and His ways. Look at Micah 6:8 again, Ecclesiastes 12:13 and John 1:12-13.

Micah 6:8 NASB He has told you, O man, what is good; And what does the LORD require of you but to do justice, to love kindness, And to walk humbly with your God?

Ecclesiastes 12:13 Let us hear the conclusion of the whole matter: Fear God and keep his commandments: for this is the whole duty of man.

John 1:12-13 NASB But as many as received Him, to them He gave the right to become children of God, *even* to those who believe in His name, ¹³ who were born, not of blood nor of the will of the flesh nor of the will of man, but of God.

Psalm 119:155 Salvation is far from the wicked: for they seek not thy statutes.

* * *

Has modern Christianity misinterpreted the meaning of what God requires for relationship? Does the Old Testament show the death of animals were not required to atone for sin? Yes. Does the Old Testament say certain sins could not be atoned by animal sacrifice? Yes. Did Jesus forgive the sins of others before His death on the cross? Yes. Does God forgive sin without repentance? No. Does the Bible say God requires perfection for relationship with Him? No. The Gospels provide evidence that reconciliation (atonement), forgiveness, redemption and salvation were available during Jesus' ministry before the cross. Below are statements made by Jesus regarding salvation for the tax collector, Zacchaeus in Luke 19:9; for forgiveness to the man lowered through the roof in Matthew 9, and the sinful woman who wept over Jesus' feet in Luke 7:47. In addition we can miss the message of the Gospels' verses that say John the Baptist's baptism was for repentance and forgiveness (remission) of sin.

Luke 19:9 And Jesus said unto him, This day is salvation come to this house, for so much as he also is a son of Abraham.

Matthew 9:2 And, behold, they brought to him a man sick of the palsy, lying on a bed: and Jesus seeing their faith said unto the sick of the palsy; Son, be of good cheer; thy sins be forgiven thee.

Luke 7:47 Wherefore I say unto thee, Her sins, which are many, are forgiven; for she loved much: but to whom little is forgiven, the same loveth little.

Sin - Atonement, Forgiveness & Redemption

Mark 1:4 John [the Baptist] did baptize in the wilderness, and preach the baptism of repentance for the remission of sins.

Again, and again throughout the Bible God is described as merciful, gracious, abundant in goodness, who forgives iniquity, transgressions and sin (Exodus 34:6-7, Deuteronomy 4:31, II Chronicles 30:9, Nehemiah 9:17, Psalm 103:8, etc.) The purpose of this chapter was to show that God has always made atonement, (reconciliation), redemption, salvation and restored relationship with Himself possible for anyone who believes in Him and chooses to walk and live with Him. The offer and warning were made to Cain before he sinned and murdered his brother, Abel (Genesis 4:6-7). Salvation and relationship were there for Ruth who chose to make the God of Israel her God (Ruth 1:16-17). Salvation was provided for Rahab, the prostitute and her family, and she was granted a prominent place within the genealogy of the Messiah because she believed and trusted God (Joshua 6:25 an Matthew 1:5). To David who intimately knew God, yet committed the *avon* sins (adultery, murder, and causing the name of God to be blasphemed), David was forgiven and restored in his relationship with God through repentance. (See II Samuel 11:4, 15-17, II Samuel 12:14, and Psalm 51.)

Keeping in mind that atonement means reconciliation, it is not the blood or death of animals that atones and reconciles man to God. It is not the death of Jesus that atones and reconciles man to God. <u>Death cannot redeem, save or reconcile mankind to the Creator and Source of all Life</u>. Through belief and repentance, we are redeemed, saved and reconciled to God by God, by God's everlasting love, by His great mercy/grace and compassion. It is God who loves us, who wants us, who has called us. We become children of God when we choose God, when we believe and trust in the one and only God.

Jeremiah 31:3 The LORD hath appeared of old unto me, saying, Yea, I have loved thee with an everlasting love: therefore with lovingkindness have I drawn thee.

John 5:24 Verily, verily, I say unto you, He that heareth my word, and believeth on him that sent me, hath everlasting life, and shall not come into condemnation; but is passed from death unto life…

Somewhere along the path of trying to understand who Jesus is, and what His death and resurrection meant, first the apostle Paul, then other followers and infant Church leaders latched on to the idea that Jesus' death was necessary for the forgiveness of sins. Later in history this idea became the theology that God could not forgive without the penalty of death being paid. Through the ages this theory only grew. However, the concluding words of Torah at the end of Deuteronomy tell a different story about what God requires for a relationship, and how difficult it is to obtain the requirements:

Deuteronomy 30:11-18 [11] Now what I am commanding you today is not too difficult for you or beyond your reach. [12] It is not up in heaven, so that you have to ask, "Who will ascend into heaven to get it and proclaim it to us so we may obey it?" [13] Nor is it beyond the sea, so that you have to ask, "Who will cross the sea to get it and proclaim it to us so we may obey it?" [14] No, the word is very near you; it is in your mouth and in your heart so you may obey it.

[15] See, I set before you today life and prosperity, death and destruction. [16] For I command you today to love the LORD your God, to walk in obedience to him, and to keep his commands, decrees and laws; then you will live and increase, and the LORD your God will bless you in the land you are entering to possess.

[17] But if your heart turns away and you are not obedient, and if you are drawn away to bow down to other gods and worship them, [18] I declare to you this day that you will certainly be destroyed.

Concepts discussed in Chapter 7

Sin – Hebrew has 20 different words for sin. The three most common found in the Old Testament are:
1. *ht* or *het* appears 459 times. The word means to miss, or to fail; also a lack of perfection in carrying out a task or duty or to miss the mark as in one shooting an arrow.
2. *psh* or *pesha* appears 136 times and means a breach, a rebellious transgression, or a break in the peaceful relation between two parties including sinful behavior of man toward God
3. *Awan/awon/avon* appears over 200 times in the Old Testament and means a perverse crookedness and/or bent as in having deliberately done wrong so often, that there is a *bent* toward *crookedness*. This word also conveys the idea of blame, guilt and punishment for acts of depravity and perversion.

Sinner – Sinner is often used in verses to refer to the awan/awon/avon type of sins and behaviors.

Righteous – #H6662 *tsaddiyq* one who is just, correct, lawful, to be in the right.

Perfect – #H8549 *tamiym* means complete, sound, whole, innocent, having integrity.

Atonement – means the covering of, or <u>being reconciled</u>, consistent or compatible with something else. In Hebrew atonement and reconciliation have the same definition as the Greek word translated in English as propitiation. Atonement conveys the active confrontation and defeat of evil and/or disobedience; the ransom or exchange to get back, and the cleansing, restoration or reestablishment of a relationship between a person and God.

Repentance – is translated mostly as comfort or repent conveys the thought to be sorry, to console one's self, to be moved to pity, to bitterly regret, to have compassion. Repentance also means <u>to turn from</u> and stop offensive actions, to reconsider said actions through which one regrets their former choices and <u>turns to</u> God and the path of righteousness.

Forgiveness/forgive - the Biblical concept of forgiveness presumes that sin itself is a force that adheres to the sinner. Since it is God who forgives; <u>forgiveness is the divine means for removing sin</u>. The Greek word (#G859 *aphesis*) for "**remission**" and "**forgiveness**" is the same word. It means to release, to pardon. *Aphesis* comes from the root Greek word G#863 *aphemi* meaning to send away, to depart, or go away from. "Forgive" in Hebrew is *Strong's Concordance* word #H5375 *nasa*. It means to bare, lift, take away as in when one is forgiven; they are pardoned, their wrongdoing is lifted and taken away.

Redeem and **redemption** - There are two different Hebrew words translated in English as redeem or redemption. Both describe a divine intercession in human affairs. ***Pdh*** or ***padah*** (#H6299 *Strong's Concordance*) refers to ransom or payment for what is released. It does not imply a relationship between the agent and that which is being redeemed, nor that the payment is of equal value for what is being exchanged. *Pdh* takes on the meaning of a "deliverer." The other root word for **redeem** is ***g'l*** or ***ga'al*** (#H150 in *Strong's Concordance*) implies a family connection or obligation to what is being redeemed or bought back.

Animal sacrifices were a common practice amongst several ancient Middle Eastern societies. The word "**sacrifice**" is more accurately translated "slaughter." Like today, many animals were slaughtered for food.

Offerings are gifts, presents; something presented or offered to God or a deity. Usually animal sacrifices and offerings were for worshipping or appeasing pagan gods to gain favor for rain, crops, and fertility.

Sin - Atonement, Forgiveness & Redemption

The Law – "Law" refers to the Hebrew word "*Torah*" which consists of God's commandments found in the first five books of the Bible. The more accurate translation from the root word #H3384 *yarah* means "to instruct, to teach, to direct."

Salvation – All the words translated as salvation or save mean some variation of deliverance, victory, to avenge, to defend, save, safe, liberation and rescue. Salvation is a situational event as in being saved from something or someone; salvation is not a category or designation of spiritual relationship.

The Day of Atonement – Also known as Yom Kippur occurs once per year. Through repentance and reparations, God forgives the people's sin.

The Year of Jubilee occurs every 49 years and begins on Yom Kippur. Jubilee is about redeeming and restoring what was lost. Atonement is about reconciling or making compatible with something or someone else. Only God can redeem (liberate, free) mankind from the bondage and oppression of sin and make repentant people compatible with how He has called His people to live.

* * *

Hopefully after looking at what is in the Bible regarding sin, forgiveness and salvation, it is easy to answer the questions stated at the beginning of this chapter. However, if the answers are not clear, here are the scriptural references to consider:

1. *Do murdered children and children who die go to heaven?*
    Unborn, babies, children, and the innocent are covered under God's mercy, grace and abundance of goodness –
    Exodus 34:6-7 And the LORD passed by before him, and proclaimed, The LORD, The LORD God, merciful and gracious, longsuffering, and abundant in goodness and truth,[7] Keeping mercy for thousands, forgiving iniquity and transgression and sin, and that will by no means clear the guilty....

Luke 18:16 ...Suffer little children to come unto me, and forbid them not: for of such is the kingdom of God.

Psalm 127:3 ³ Lo, children are an heritage of the LORD: and the fruit of the womb is his reward.

2. *Were Abraham, David, and Ruth saved and did they receive eternal life?*

3. *Today if an observant Jew (obedient to Torah, charitable and kind to others) does not believe Jesus is the Messiah, can he be saved and receive eternal life?*

   A Jewish person who believes in God and observes God's commands to love God and treat others fairly and with compassion will earn or inherit eternal life: See Mark 10:17-19 and Luke 10:25-28 and John 11:25.

4. *Can sins be forgiven without death atonement?*

   God forgives sins through repentance. Jesus forgave sins: II Chronicles 7:14, Matthew 9:2 and Luke 7:47-48.

5. *If a man prays the sinner's prayer, is baptized yet returns to his old life of sin, will he receive eternal life if he dies tonight?*

   Saying words and performing rituals do not guarantee salvation and eternal life while continuing to willfully and knowingly sin.

   Matthew 7:21-23 Not every one that saith unto me, Lord, Lord, shall enter into the kingdom of heaven; but he that doeth the will of my Father which is in heaven. ²² Many will say to me in that day, Lord, Lord, have we not prophesied in thy name? and in thy name have cast out devils? and in thy name done many wonderful works? ²³ And then will I profess unto them, I never knew you: depart from me, <u>ye that work iniquity</u>.

6. *Does the Bible say God's holiness & righteousness require death for sin atonement?*

   Returning to this Chapter's opening Bible verse from Micah 6:

> **Micah 6:7-8 NIV** Will the Lord be pleased with thousands of rams, with ten thousand rivers of olive oil? Shall I offer my firstborn for my transgression, the fruit of my body for the sin of my soul? ⁸ He has shown you, O mortal, what is good. And what does the Lord require of you? To act justly and to love mercy and to walk humbly with your God.

The next couple of chapters are about several of Jesus' healings and miracles. Considering what the Hebrew Bible (Old Testament) said God does and will do, we start to understand the people's reactions and responses. From their stunned silence, unbridled praises, and their anger that bordered on violence, we see that Jesus is making the most amazing proclamations about Himself. Not only was He proclaiming Himself to be the long awaited and promised Messiah: He said and showed the people that He is God!

As amazing as it is to consider that the one and only God, Creator of the universe came to earth in the form of a human and lived among us, that is exactly what the Bible tells us happened. Why did He come? What did He want us to know? In the following stories Jesus does the most unusual and unexpected things – not for shock value, but from the beginning of His ministry He was telling those around Him and us today who He is. Considering who He reveals Himself to be – it is up to each of us to decide how the information will change us.

CHAPTER 8

The Salvation of Simon Peter

[18] As Jesus was walking beside the Sea of Galilee, he saw two brothers, Simon called Peter and his brother Andrew. They were casting a net into the lake, for they were fishermen. [19] "Come, follow me," Jesus said, "and I will send you out to fish for people." [20] At once they left their nets and followed him.
[21] Going on from there, he saw two other brothers, James son of Zebedee and his brother John. They were in a boat with their father Zebedee, preparing their nets. Jesus called them,[22] and immediately they left the boat and their father and followed him.

Matthew 4:18-22 NIV

When I was a kid, I was terrible at sports. I have memories of two team captains looking at a bunch of kids and alternating in their choice who they wanted on their team. I was torn between not wanting to be chosen at all or being horrified I would be the last person chosen. This is the story of Jesus choosing Peter. According to the Bible, God has chosen all of us. The question is will we chose Him?

At some point after Jesus began His ministry, He began to choose disciples. It is commonly thought there were only twelve disciples, but the Bible does show there were many more – both men and women (see Mark 15:41, Luke 10:1, and Acts 1:15). However, the man who comes to mind as Jesus' main disciple would probably be Peter (formerly

Simon), with John being a close second. The gospel of John is said to have been written by John, the disciple as well as I, II, and III John and the book of Revelation. I and II Peter are the epistles attributed to this same Peter. This story is about when Peter first began to believe Jesus was the Messiah.

The story begins with Jesus walking by the shore and calling Simon Peter,[87] his brother Andrew, John and James, the sons of Zebedee, to follow Him with the promise He would make them fishers of men. Have you ever wondered why they left their work as fishermen? Was it the tone of Jesus' voice or a look that influenced them? Are we missing part of the story? John chapter 1 and Luke chapter 5 add more details to this story. John 1:32-42 describes John the Baptist's testimony that Jesus is God's Chosen One (NIV) or as some translations say – "the Son of God" (KJV). John also told two of his disciples Jesus is the Lamb of God. One of the two disciples was Andrew, who in turn told his brother Simon (Peter) that Jesus is the Messiah. Upon hearing this significant piece of news, Simon did not even go to meet Jesus. As told in Luke 5:1-11 NIV, this would happen later.

> [1] One day as Jesus was standing by the Lake of Gennesaret, the people were crowding around him and listening to the word of God. [2] He saw at the water's edge two boats, left there by the fishermen, who were washing their nets. [3] He got into one of the boats, the one belonging to Simon, and asked him to put out a little from shore. Then he sat down and taught the people from the boat.
>
> [4] When he had finished speaking, he said to Simon, "Put out into deep water, and let down the nets for a catch."
>
> [5] Simon answered, "Master, we've worked hard all night and haven't caught anything. But because you say so, I will let down the nets."

---

87   Jesus gave Simon the name Peter. Mark 3:16

⁶ When they had done so, they caught such a large number of fish that their nets began to break. ⁷ So they signaled their partners in the other boat to come and help them, and they came and filled both boats so full that they began to sink.

⁸ When Simon Peter saw this, he fell at Jesus' knees and said, "Go away from me, Lord; I am a sinful man!" ⁹ For he and all his companions were astonished at the catch of fish they had taken, ¹⁰ and so were James and John, the sons of Zebedee, Simon's partners.

Then Jesus said to Simon, "Don't be afraid; from now on you will fish for people." ¹¹ So they pulled their boats up on shore, left everything and followed him.

Luke 5:1-11 NIV

There are several interesting points made in the Luke account. The story begins with Jesus teaching "the word of God" to a crowd of people on the shore of the Lake of Galilee (also known as the Lake of Gennesaret). The fishermen were probably close enough to hear Jesus' teachings, but continued to wash their nets. There were enough people gathered that Jesus got into Simon's boat, and asked Simon to row out from the shore a bit as He continued to speak. This was probably so the people could see and hear Him better. When Jesus finished speaking to the people, a personal interaction began with Simon that would leave little doubt in Simon's mind about *who* Jesus was. In response to this revelation Simon would fall to his knees before Jesus.

Jesus told Simon to put out into the deep and let out his nets. Simon explained that they had been out all night and had caught nothing. It is possible that after telling Jesus they had already been out all night, Simon saw something when he looked at Jesus that replaced further words with a willingness to comply – "but because you say so, I will let down the nets." The scripture says when they had done so; they caught a large number of fish that the nets began to break. This implies that as soon as they put out the nets, they instantly became overflowing with fish!

In that moment, Simon had an epiphany. What changed was Simon's awareness of who Jesus is. Simon then tells Jesus, "Go away from me, Lord; I am a sinful man!" This reaction is similar to the Prophet Isaiah and righteous Job when they became aware they were in the presence of God and felt conviction. When the Prophet Isaiah experienced being in heaven in Isaiah 6:5 KJV he said, "Woe is me! for I am undone; because I am a man of unclean lips, and I dwell in the midst of a people of unclean lips: for <u>mine eyes have seen the King, the Lord of hosts</u>." The word "undone" in Hebrew (*damah* #H1820 in *Strong's Concordance*) means to cease, to cease to be, to destroy.

Job (from the Bible's book of Job), was a good and upright man who followed God and lived by God's principles. Yet there came a time when he suffered great loss involving property, servants and his family. The Bible says Job felt he had not been treated fairly by God and wished he had an opportunity to plead his case before God. Starting in chapter 38 of the book of Job, God appeared and spoke to Job out of a whirlwind, questioning him. After God's revelation of Himself and questions to Job, Job responded, "My ears had heard of you but now my eyes have seen you. Therefore, I despise myself (abhor – KJV) and repent in dust and ashes" (Job 42:5-6 NIV). Like Isaiah and Job, Simon experienced a new assessment of himself as he fell to his knees before Jesus and asked Jesus to go away from him because he (Peter) was a sinful man.

Perhaps earlier that day Simon would have described himself as a pretty good guy. Yet in the presence of holy God, our shortcomings are abundantly clear. Then the response is one of fear and conviction of what we immediately know we deserve – annihilation; the gulf between perfect, all powerful God and ourselves is too vast. Yet in the wake of our seeing God as He truly is, it is not God's plan or agenda to destroy us. Rather it is the Will of God that we know, trust and believe in Him and ultimately, come to love Him. Jesus told Simon to fear not and then invited Simon to follow Him into what would be the most profound life changing experience for Simon Peter. Consequently, instead of catching fish for a living, Simon Peter's career would be catching people for the Kingdom of God.

The account in the Books of Luke and Mark shows Simon was not in the boat alone with Jesus. Simon's brother Andrew was there. Luke 5:9 says there were companions in the boat. Although it is not known how much of this conversation the brothers John and James heard in the nearby boat, it is easy to guess since they were called out to help Simon with his overflowing catch, they had seen Simon kneel before Jesus. Struggling with the largest catch of their lives, they knew they had experienced something greater than just an amazing day of fishing. When they reached shore, and secured their boats, Simon, Andrew, John and James all accepted Jesus' invitation to follow Him.

This story does not end here. It tells us they left "everything and followed him." They simply and incredibly made the most important decision of their lives: to leave everything and follow Jesus! We get a sense of confirmation of this in the story of the rich man who wanted to know what he needed to do to inherit eternal life (Matthew 19:16-29, Mark 10:17-30 and Luke 18:18-30). Jesus told the wealthy man to obey the commandments. Note that belief, obedience and a desire for pleasing God will achieve eternal life. The man responded he had kept the commandments since his youth. Although obedience is very important, Jesus saw what the man lacked: he didn't really know God (God's great love for him) or trust God (that God would provide for him). The man valued and placed his trust in his wealth above trusting in God for His needs, security and wellbeing. Jesus told the wealthy man to sell everything, give it to the poor; and follow Him, then he would have treasures in heaven. Disheartened, the man left. Jesus remarked it is harder for the rich to enter the kingdom of God. It is easy for the lure of money to overshadow one's awareness that God is more important (Deuteronomy 8:11-18). Simon Peter exclaimed in

Luke 18:28 NIRV, "We have left everything we had in order to follow you!" Jesus said those who have left family and home for the sake of the Kingdom of God, will be rewarded in this life and in the life to come. The point is: when Jesus called them, they left everything of their old lives to follow Him.

From the gospels, we know this was not the entire story involving Simon Peter. He would walk on water with Jesus; and be the first of the disciples to answer correctly when Jesus asked who do *you* say I am? Peter was there on the Mount of Transfiguration seeing Jesus transformed into His true glory along with the Prophets Moses and Elijah. It was Peter who promised even if all others deserted Jesus, he would die for Him. That same night it was Peter who denied knowing Jesus three times. Yet, after the resurrection, he was the first disciple to enter the empty tomb.

In John 21 after the resurrection, Peter had gone fishing once again with several of the disciples. From the beach, a man called out to them and when they had done as instructed, they caught a tremendous number of fishes. John recognized this man as Jesus. Peter jumped from his boat into the water and swam ashore. Jesus prepared and served the disciples breakfast. Then just as Peter had denied knowing Jesus three times, Jesus asks Peter if he loves Him three times. Each time Peter proclaimed his love, and Jesus told him to care for His flock, to feed them, to care for them. John 21:17 says Peter was hurt when Jesus asked him the third time, "Do you love me?" He said, "Lord, you know all things; you know that I love you." Yes, God knows all things, but God wants *us* to know that even when we have made mistakes and fallen short of responding with Godly character, His love for us is unchanged. He can forgive us and utilize us in His plan to reach and care for others. *Saying* we love God is not evidence of our love, nor is the strict observance of keeping the commandments. It is how we live, care for and treat others that show our love for God.

In the first fishing story Jesus invited Simon Peter to follow him. In this later fishing story, after Jesus' resurrection, Jesus *commands* Peter

The Salvation of Simon Peter

to follow Him, "you must follow me." We are invited and called into a committed relationship with God. To learn and grow in that relationship, we must stay; we must follow Him. In the midst of trouble, or when we are hurting or lost, when we have failed God miserably or experienced incredible successes, we must continue to follow God. There can be no turning back to our old lives or going our own way in our walk with Jesus. We have the same task and responsibility as the one given to Peter – we are to care for others and teach others so they may come to know the love and goodness of God and grow in their relationship with God.

<u>Important points from Chapter 8 were:</u>
- Saying we love God is not evidence of our love. It is how we live and treat others that show our love.
- In times of trouble, when we are hurting or lost, or when we feel we have failed God miserably or experienced incredible successes, we must continue to follow God.

CHAPTER 9

Easy to Say, Difficult to Do, Unless …

*"But I want you to know that the Son of Man
has authority on earth to forgive sins."*
Luke 5:24 NIV

During the spring college basketball playoffs of 2013, a young man landed wrong on one foot and fell to the floor with his leg broken in two places. Several inches of bone protruded the skin. People in the nearby audience, his team mates, the coaches from both teams burst into tears, and some nearly wretched at the gruesome scene. Some things are so incredible we are affected instantly and our response is involuntary. This Bible story is like that – something so incredible happened to the body of a man right in front of the people who were present and it profoundly affected everyone there – except Jesus.

Had Jesus only taught, would He have attracted the attention of so many people and become famous? At the beginning of His ministry it was His teachings that amazed the people around Him (Matthew 7:28, Mark 1:22, Luke 4:32); but there had been other great teachers in Israel. However, it was the miracles that put Jesus in a different class from everyone else. Each of the gospels say He healed crowds of people who had come to him (Matthew 14:14, Mark 3:10, Luke 4:40 and John 6:2).

When we read the scriptures, we fail to grasp the variety of ailments the Bible says were instantly cured – bones, muscles, ligaments, organs, internal chemical imbalances, blindness and cataracts corrected, deafness, tumors, seizures, mental illness, demon possession, leprosy – all healed and restored. Skin was made new, crooked bones straightened instantly without pain, eyes, mouths, and ears opened and working. People, who had been deaf and mute, without any speech therapy could now suddenly talk! Take a moment to fully comprehend how miraculous and unprecedented this is.

The few miracles detailed in the Gospels convey specific information about the authority of Jesus and the goodness of God. This story is recorded in all the synoptic gospels (Matthew, Mark and Luke) and is often remembered because of the crippled man being lowered through the roof. The friends or relatives of the crippled man had to believe healing was possible *if* their friend could be seen by Jesus. The home where Jesus was teaching was too crowded to enter by the door. Refusing to accept failure, the friends came up with an unusual idea. They climbed to the roof with the fellow on his mat, dug through the roof, and lowered their friend down in front of Jesus.

What were those inside the crowded house thinking? First the noise on the roof, the digging sound, then dust floating down below. There were those who probably continued to try to focus on what Jesus was saying, yet they were watching the event unfolding above them. When the friends had broken through the roof, they began to slowly lower their friend down right in front of Jesus. The people inside moved out of the way, grabbed onto the new arrival, and lowered him to the floor. Perhaps some onlookers were not amused; but everyone was probably wondering what Jesus would say or do. According to the Bible's account, Jesus' first response was a bit unusual. He did not ask what was wrong with the man, nor did He ask what the man wanted Him to do. Jesus addressed what was lacking in this man's individual relationship with God. For some it was unbelief or doubting the power or goodness of God; for others it was their selfishness or self-righteousness. In some instances, it was Satan who had the person bound with illness. For the man on the mat, he needed his sins forgiven.

Easy to Say, Difficult to Do, Unless …

When Jesus told the young man his sins were forgiven, He was speaking for the benefit of more than just the man on the mat. In the very crowded room Jesus was establishing a vital point central to the reason He came to earth – to reveal the goodness of God to forgive sins and to make reconciliation to God available for everyone who believes. Why did Jesus choose this incident to speak of forgiving sins? The account told in Luke Chapter 5 gives us clues not found in the Matthew 9:1-8 or Mark 2:3-12 account.

[17] One day Jesus was teaching, and Pharisees and teachers of the law were sitting there. They had come from every village of Galilee and from Judea and Jerusalem. And the power of the Lord was with Jesus to heal the sick. [18] Some men came carrying a paralyzed man on a mat and tried to take him into the house to lay him before Jesus. [19] When they could not find a way to do this because of the crowd, they went up on the roof and lowered him on his mat through the tiles into the middle of the crowd, right in front of Jesus.

[20] When Jesus saw their faith, he said, "Friend, your sins are forgiven."

[21] The Pharisees and the teachers of the law began thinking to themselves, "Who is this fellow who speaks blasphemy? Who can forgive sins but God alone?"

[22] Jesus knew what they were thinking and asked, "Why are you thinking these things in your hearts? [23] Which is easier: to say, 'Your sins are forgiven,' or to say, 'Get up and walk'? [24] But I want you to know that the Son of Man has authority on earth to forgive sins." So he said to the paralyzed man, "I tell you, get up, take your mat and go home." [25] Immediately he stood up in front of them, took what he had been lying on and went home praising

God. ²⁶ Everyone was amazed and gave praise to God. They were filled with awe and said, "We have seen remarkable things today."

Luke 5:17-26 NIV

In Luke's account Pharisees and teachers of the law were in the room when this event took place. In the Gospels the Pharisees often questioned and expressed doubt about Jesus, His teachings and healings. At the time of Jesus, the Pharisees were a political and spiritual group. In simple terms the Pharisees believed in the Written Law or the *Tanakh* (the Hebrew Bible containing *Torah*, Prophets and sacred writings) and the Oral Law (known as *Mishna* which later became part of the *Talmud*). On the other hand, the Sadducees, a religious elitist sect within Judaism rejected the Oral Law and believed only in *Torah* (the first five books of the Bible). What is termed "law" in the scriptures are God's instructions, commands, teachings, and percepts for right living. In time the term *Torah* came to refer to the entire Hebrew Bible (Old Testament). Therefore, at the time of Jesus' ministry teachers of the law were studious men who taught about the specifics of *Torah* (as in the first five books of the Bible). Scribes were men who copied documents; in the New Testament the scribes were usually men who copied *Torah* scrolls.

Luke 5:17 says there were Pharisees and teachers of the law who "had come from every village of Galilee and from Judea and Jerusalem." These men probably were sitting closest to Jesus and had not come for healing. They were there to observe Jesus in action for themselves. No doubt they were watching His every movement and scrutinizing His words. Jesus chose this opportunity to reveal something important about Himself to this group of religious people who had come from all over Israel. To this man paralyzed or suffering with palsy (KJV), a debilitating muscular disorder, Jesus said, "your sins are forgiven." Notice the simplicity and lack of rebuke or condemnation in this simple sentence to the man who lay broken before him, and more importantly, notice the man did not ask to be forgiven nor did he confess he was a sinner. Meanwhile, it was the Pharisees and teachers of the law in the room who were offended by Jesus' statement. They were accurate in their assessment that <u>only</u> God can forgive sins; therefore, Jesus statement was more than presumptuous, it was blasphemous. It was commonly known at the time that blasphemy was (and still is) a very serious offense against God. Blasphemy was a sin punishable by death. Jesus' statement that the man's sins were forgiven implied Jesus had the authority of God to forgive him.

While the Bible instructs us to forgive those who have wronged us and make amends when we have sinned against another, only God can forgive *all* sins. One could ask how does our sin against someone involve God and why is that God's business? Because God has ordained correct behavior, there is also wrong behavior. Since the heavens and earth and everything were created by God, then everything belongs to God (Psalm 24:1). God is connected to mankind as their Creator and because of His great Love for them. One child cannot harm another child without it affecting God. Therefore, when we sin against another, ultimately, we have also sinned against God. The consequences and damage of our sin is like a virus spreading outward from us, having an impact on those closest to us and infecting and affecting everyone else involved to some extent. It is because of the effects of sin that God instructs us *not* to do such and such. Therefore, when we sin, it is first and foremost against God.

King David understood this principle. David sinned by committing adultery with Bathsheba who was married to one of David's mighty men, Uriah (II Samuel 23:8, 39). When she became pregnant, David tried to cover up the child's paternity. When he was unsuccessful in that attempt, David choose to have Uriah murdered in battle (II Samuel 11-12). Several other valiant soldiers were killed along with Uriah. Their deaths affected the lives of their families and friends. David's deeds and their consequences had an impact not only on his own family, but also on his servants and colleagues who knew or suspected what he had done. In the future it altered David's confidence to directly confront the sins of his sons. When David had repented and prayed about this incident, he asked God to blot out his transgressions and to cleanse him from his sins. He went on to say in Psalm 51:4 NASB, "Against You, You only, I have sinned and done what is evil in Your sight." David understood when we harm or dishonor another, we have also dishonored God. Likewise, this same point is made when the apostle Paul was persecuting believers of Jesus; Jesus asked Paul, "Why are you persecuting *Me*?" (Acts 9:4)

The Bible contains dozens of scriptures (Exodus 32:32, 34:7, Numbers 14:19, II Chronicles 7:14, Psalm 86:5, Jeremiah 31:34, Ezekiel 16:63, to name a few) about the forgiveness of God for the sins of people. Yet on this day in the house with a hole in its roof, Jesus did not play it safe and say "may God forgive your sins," or "I'll pray for you to be forgiven." No, with authority He said, "Take heart, son; your sins are forgiven" (Matthew 9:2 NIV). Jesus did not allow the boiling thoughts of the others in the room to stew quietly. In rapid succession He confronted not the sinner but the leaders – "Why are you thinking these things?" He did not wait for them to evade the question, or to sin by lying, Jesus promptly asked them another question, "Which is easier to say – Your sins are forgiven or pick up your mat and walk?" Again, He waited for no response before the next sentence which is the most telling of the entire conversation – (24-NIV) "But <u>I want you to know</u> that the Son of Man has authority on earth to forgive sins." In Isaiah 42:8 and 48:11 God said He will not give His glory to another. Jesus was making a profoundly bold statement about who He was, about the power He had, and His authority to effect change. And they *knew* that Jesus had just claimed that He was God because they asked themselves, "Who is this fellow who speaks blasphemy? Who can forgive sins but God alone?" Lest the religious leaders think that He was possessed or out of His mind, Jesus told the man to get up, pick up his mat and go home. And the paralyzed man immediately obeyed! Because this man stood, picked up his mat and walked out, he <u>*proved*</u> Jesus had authority to heal *and* to forgive sins because Jesus *is* God! This is the same God who created all things and has authority over all things according to Colossians 1:16-17.

Do we know the thoughts or words of the Pharisees and teachers after the man stood and walked out? Yes! Luke 5:26 (KJV) says "they were all amazed, and they glorified God." Matthew 9:8 NIV says, "When the crowd saw this, they were filled with awe; and they praised God, who had given such authority to men." Mark 2:12 (NIV) says, This amazed everyone and they praised God, saying, "We have never seen anything like this!" Was their excitement due to watching atrophied legs, ankles and feet straighten and fill out as muscles were restored? Was it the realization that Jesus had authority and power to forgive sins or were some awestruck because they recognized they were indeed in the presence of Mighty God? All three gospels say they praised God – how could they do otherwise? It is likely that when these Pharisees and teachers returned to their perspective homes and villages, all over the Galilee, Judea and Jerusalem, they spoke of what they had seen and heard.

In each of these stories thus far, there is a pattern of Jesus revealing Himself as God within the framework of the situation and persons involved. In each instance, His revelation with such gentleness and constraint, is undeniable. In the story of Jesus' encounter with the woman at the well in Samaria, she felt no condemnation when Jesus revealed her history of relationships with men. When Jesus returned home and neighbors and possibly family members questioned or rejected His bold and clear confession that He is the Messiah, He did not condemn or respond to their disbelief and rejection in anger. With the miraculous catch of fish, Jesus told Peter not to be afraid but to follow Him. And after Peter had denied knowing Jesus, Jesus had no rebuke for Peter, just the admonition to care for His flock. In this story He confronted beliefs held by religious leaders thereby posing a spiritual conundrum that could and would point to His deity, because they themselves had admitted *only* God can forgive sins.

* * *

When the miracles recorded in the gospels (Matthew, Mark, Luke and John) are reviewed, it is possible the number of miracles could have been in the hundreds or thousands. For example, Matthew 4:24, 8:16, and 14:14 say a crowd was there and Jesus healed them all. What may not be apparent is that those miracles (also known as signs and wonders) revealed who Jesus is. As mentioned in Chapter 1 of this book, Isaiah 35:5-6 NASB says that by <u>God</u> "the eyes of the blind will be opened and the ears of the deaf will be unstopped. The lame will leap like a deer, and the tongue of the mute will shout for joy." Psalm 103:3 says <u>God</u> "heals all your diseases," and Jeremiah 33:6 NASB says <u>God</u> will "bring to it [Israel] health and healing, and I will heal them; and I will reveal to them an abundance of peace and truth."

One other point: the scriptures do not say Jesus performed miracles. In John 10 Jesus refers to them as "works." Healing, restoring, and making something whole is the work of God (John 9:3-7). God said the signs and wonders in the Exodus story (Exodus 4-14, Numbers 11, and 20) and the miraculous events of the battles to enter the Promised Land (the book of Joshua) served the purpose of letting people know He is the LORD.

> **Exodus 10:2 NASB** and that you may tell in the hearing of your son, and of your grandson, how I made a mockery of the Egyptians and how I performed My signs among them, that <u>you may know that I am the LORD</u>."

> **Number 14:11 NASB** [11] The LORD said to Moses, "How long will this people spurn Me? And how long <u>will they not believe in Me</u>, despite all the signs which I have performed in their midst?

> **Jeremiah 32:20 NASB** [20] who has set signs and wonders in the land of Egypt, *and* even to this day <u>both in Israel and among mankind; and You have made a name for Yourself</u>, as at this day.

I Samuel 10:7 NASB ⁷ It shall be when these signs come to you, do for yourself what the occasion requires, for <u>God is with you</u>.

<u>These Old Testaments verses said the "miracles," the "signs and wonders" identified God, they distinguished God from any other supposed god, and they proclaimed that God is real, nearby and present</u>. After seeing or experiencing miracles, people are supposed to believe and recognize that God is present. The central point is this: the miracles, signs, or works of Jesus' ministry identified Him as God.

<u>Important points from Chapter 9 were:</u>

- When we sin against anyone, we also sin against God.
- Only God can forgive all sins. Jesus showed He had authority to forgive sin.
- Jesus wanted the people to know that God was present among His people to heal, restore and to forgive.

CHAPTER 10

One Day with Jesus

What would it be like to awaken after lying on the ground all night wrapped in a blanket to open your eyes and see the face of Jesus lying there beside you with His glorious eyes looking at you with such love and a hint of laughter that makes your eyes tear and your breath catch in your throat? He is your very life. Without Him you would cease to exist. What would it be like to scramble to get up and join Him in the activities of the day – to walk beside Him, standing taller and feeling better than you have ever felt, to hear His voice and feel His words go right through your heart and being? What is it like to struggle to say something intelligent or witty and be unable to utter anything simply because you are with Him? You rush to jump in the boat with Him, too shy to sit beside Him, but so glad you are not being left behind. You are excited just to be with Him to see what He is going to do next.

This next story was gleaned from stringing several events together that could be construed to have taken place on the same day. According to the Bible's chapter numbers and verses, the Books of Matthew and Luke place four of these incidents in close proximity that it is possible they occurred on the same day. These incidents are Part 1) the storm involving the boat ride while Jesus sleeps, Part 2) the encounter with the demon possessed man, Part 3) the healing of the woman with the bleeding disorder, and Part 4) the resurrection of the little girl. Matthew's gospel includes the account of healing the paralyzed man (told in the last chapter) and the calling of the disciple, Matthew.

For the sake of this story events told in the gospels of Matthew and Mark from the night before are included. While Mark's account of the storm says it took place during the evening, my arrangement places it in the early morning, because of the storm's placement in the Book of Matthew in relationship to the healing of Simon Peter's mother-in-law, and the early morning encounter in Mark.

The chart below shows the incidents and where they appear in each gospel to reflect the possibility that these events could have occurred in one day. The incidents underlined are the ones that appear in this story of one day with Jesus.

One Day with Jesus

Matthew	Mark	Luke
	1:21-28 Synagogue	
8:14 Jesus at Peter's home	1:29 At Peter's home	
8:18 Cost of following Jesus	1:35 Early next morning	
8:23 Boat in storm	4:35 Boat in storm	8:22 Boat in storm
8:28 Restores possessed men	5:1 Restores possessed man	8:26 Restores man possessed
9:1 Heals paralyzed man		
9:9 The call of Matthew		
9:14 Questioned about fasting		
9:18 Heals bleeding woman and Jairus' daughter	5:21 Bleeding woman and Jairus' daughter	8:40 Bleeding woman & Jairus' daughter

PART 1

Don't you care, Lord? I'm drowning here!

It was on a Sabbath that Jesus was teaching in the synagogue in Capernaum (Mark 1:21-26). The people there that day were amazed at how well He spoke, as one with authority, unlike the usual teachers. Then the service was interrupted by a man who began to shout out to Jesus. His statements made no sense. He asked if Jesus had come to destroy them, and his next statement evoked a prompt response from Jesus. He shouted, "I know who you are – you are the Holy One of God." Jesus quickly silenced him by telling him to be quiet and commanded the demon to come out. The demon left the man at once. Again, the people were amazed that Jesus spoke with authority to unclean spirits who obeyed instantly. That night when the people left the synagogue, they told others what they had seen Jesus do.

While many people questioned who Jesus was and by what authority He performed the miracles, there was no such uncertainty among the demons. Mark 1:34 NIV says, "he would not let the demons speak because they *knew* who he was." Jesus' revelation of His true self followed a pattern. At the beginning of His ministry He kept asking people not to tell what He had done. Likewise, He quickly silenced the ranting of demons. Later in His ministry, He revealed more and more His divinity until the last couple of months when He spoke quite clearly about who He is.

However, on this night it is still early in His ministry. After leaving the synagogue with the two sets of brothers – Simon Peter and Andrew, James, and John, Jesus went to Simon Peter's home (Mark 1:29). There Simon's mother-in-law was sick in bed with a fever. He spoke with her briefly, took hold of her hand, and helped her up. Suddenly her fever was gone! She felt so well she began to serve them food. After the sun set marking the end of the Sabbath, it seemed like the whole town came to Simon Peter's home bringing their sick and demon possessed (Mark 1:33). Scripture says He healed many of their various illnesses and cast out demons. We have no idea how long the crowd was there or how late Jesus stayed up speaking with people.

Very early the next morning while it was still dark, Jesus went out alone. Mark 1:35 says Jesus found a solitary place to pray. Later when He was discovered by Peter and others, Jesus suggested they go someplace else. Already the crowd was waiting for Him. Matthew 8:18 NASB says, "Now when Jesus saw a crowd around Him, He gave orders to depart to the other side *of the sea*." The account in Mark 4:35-41 says that even when they got into the boat, there were other boats that followed along.

Shortly after setting out, Jesus fell asleep on a cushion at the back of the boat. It was while He was asleep that "suddenly a furious storm" came up on the lake[88] with waves that broke over the boat nearly swamping it. Several of the men on the boat were professional fishermen. They had years of experience on boats during all types of weather. But this storm was different and the disciples were frightened. They were afraid not only because of the storm, with the boat being tossed, and waves pummeling them, but it was more than unnerving that Jesus continued sleeping! There was water in the boat, their clothes were drenched and they could hardly see or hear above the roar of the storm. As they held on for dear life, Jesus slept on. How long did they watch

---

88 The Sea of Galilee is also called the Sea of Kinneret, Lake of Gennesaret, or Lake Tiberias. It is a fresh water lake in Israel.

Don't You Care Lord? I'm Drowning Here!

Jesus sleep and look at one another wondering at what point would He wake up?

Finally, one or several of them called out in fear - "Master! Teacher! Lord! Save us, do you not care that we are perishing?" The last part is so heart wrenching - "Don't you care?" Many of us have experienced times when we are hurting, grieving, fearful or worried about a situation or decision to be made. We feel we are walking or crawling through the valley of the shadow of death or our lives seem to be in the middle of a horrific storm. Sometimes it seems our anguished prayers beseeching God to help us ascend no higher than the ceiling of our room. We may wonder "Is God asleep" or "Don't you care? Do you know what is happening to me?"

The truth of the matter is that <u>we cannot imagine how much God loves and cares for us</u>. The Bible says the depth of this realization has not entered our hearts. I Corinthians 2:9 loosely quotes from Isaiah 64:4 NASB which says, "For from days of old they (people) have not heard or perceived by ear, Nor has the eye seen a God besides You, Who acts in behalf of the one who <u>waits</u> for Him." The Corinthians passage alters this verse a bit. It says that it has not entered the hearts of men what God does acting in behalf of those who <u>love</u> him. Waiting on God involves a level of trust; it reveals a level of experience with, knowledge of, and love for God. God speaks in Jeremiah 31:3 NASB saying, "I have loved you with an everlasting love; Therefore, I have drawn you with loving kindness." The last sentence in the Book of Matthew (NASB) Jesus says, "and lo, I am with you always, even to the end of the age." God is with us whether we sense Him or not, whether we hear, see or experience His much-needed intervention. So often it is only when we have gone *through* the tough situation do we gain the perspective to see His loving hand guiding, protecting, shielding, carrying us through our dark days.

Jesus handled their problem effortlessly. He simply spoke. Scripture does not say or imply that He shouted above the roar of the waves and wind or that He waved His hands in any magically way, He just spoke.

"Hush, be still," is the translation from the New American Standard, like a mother would say to her wiggling and talkative little one at church. While the King James Version says, "Peace, be still," according to *Strong's Concordance*, the word peace is from the Greek root word *"siope"* which means among other things - silence as in involuntary stillness. "Still" means to muzzle as in to reduce to silence. So, with a simple command Jesus stilled the tumultuous waves into involuntary stillness and muzzled the winds of the storm into silence.

Jesus asked the men on the boat why they were so afraid (Mark 4:40). It is easy to understand why they were anxious; they were afraid death was imminent. But what can make you *more* afraid than the fear of imminent death? After Jesus got up and rebuked (meaning He commanded as one with authority) the wind and raging water which calmed instantly (Mark 4:41), the NIV says the disciples were terrified. They were *afraid* during the storm and raging waters, but to see Jesus stop the waves and wind now *terrified* them! In Matthew (NASB) and Luke scripture says in fear and amazement they asked, "What kind of man is this that even the winds and the sea obey Him?"

When we read through this story and on to the next, we are likely to miss the answer to these very important questions of who is this, and what kind of man is this? Within this story of the sudden end to a fierce storm we miss the opportunity to glimpse into the scope of time and the vast universe and fail to see Almighty God as He was during creation in Genesis Chapter 1. Colossians speaks of Jesus in 1:16 and 17 NASB and says:

> [16] For by Him all things were created, *both* in the heavens and on earth, visible and invisible, whether thrones or dominions or rulers or authorities—all things have been created through Him and for Him. [17] He is before all things, and in Him all things hold together.

Jesus, who *created* all things both in the heavens and on earth, has *control* over all things in the heavens and on earth. This account of an actual event tells of *The Creator* who spoke the universe into being, telling the wind and waves to be quiet. The raging wind and swelling sea obeyed The Creator just as The Creator so long ago said "Let there be light"; and there was light (Genesis 1:3). The men in the boat that day had witnessed the involuntary compliance of the elements of nature to the command of God Almighty! (When God is referred to as God Almighty [*El Shaddai* in Hebrew] it is when God has revealed Himself as One who compels nature to do what is contrary to itself. See the last chapter of this book – No other Name.)

When the men awoke Jesus and asked whether He cared that they were perishing, He asked them in return why they were so afraid; did they still have no faith (which means belief and/or trust)? What Jesus was asking them is this: "Do you still have no trust in me and my ability to protect and care for you?" When we discover how powerful the Creator of the Universe is, how vast the knowledge is of the One who knows the future as well as the past, how great His love for us is, then our love for Him grows, and our trust in His guidance becomes tangible and transforms our lives.

There must have been stunned silence for the remainder of the journey. Had I been on the boat, I imagine I would have been replaying the scene over and over in my mind trying to make sense of what I had just witnessed. But their thoughts couldn't linger very long on what had just occurred for now their boat reached the shore and they had another surprise waiting for them.

<u>*Important points from Part 1 were:*</u>
- When Jesus quieted the wind and the waves, He revealed the same power and authority He had in the beginning when He created the heavens and the earth.
- We have no idea how much God loves and cares for us.

PART 2

The Divine Appointment

As soon as those traveling with Jesus arrived on the shore of the Gentile region of Gerasenes,[89] they could hear an eerie howling, screaming sound. The disciples looked around trying to get a fix on where the sound was coming from. Some thought they could make out words in the screams, but they couldn't be sure. Again, as on the boat, several of the disciples were casting glances at one another. The main unspoken question was, "Why did we come here?"

Then from the shadows of the trees along the shore, one disciple thought he glimpsed movement. Suddenly, a man came out of the woods running straight for them. The man looked part animal. He wore no clothes, the hair on his head was long and matted giving him a wild and dirty appearance. At first, it looked as though he was about to attack them because he carried a long chain. He wasn't carrying the chain; rather it was still attached to one of his wrists. In the other hand he carried a sharp-edged rock which he kept slashing at his other arm and across his chest. As he got closer, it was clear his eyes were riveted on Jesus. The possessed man was screaming as he ran directly toward Jesus, who stood still, then commanded the demons to come out of him.

---

89 In Mark 5:1 and Luke 8:26 the town is referred to as Gerasenes, while Matthew 8:28 says the town or region is Gadarenes. In explanation one source says the Matthew account may have a translational error or Gadara may have been known as the region. At any rate, neither town is in close vicinity to the Sea of Galilee.

At this point the man slammed to a halt and dropped to his knees in front of Jesus almost as if he had hit an invisible barrier. His body kept heaving and writhing. He continued to make very weird and guttural sounds. "What business do we have with each other, Jesus, Son of the Most High God? I implore You by God, do not torment me!" (Mark 5:7 NASB. Matthew 8:29 NASB says, "Have You come here to torment us before the time?). The disciples looked at each other in shock. Why did this man think that Jesus had come to torment him?

Jesus did not acknowledge the question but asked the man his name. "My name is Legion; for we are many" (Mark 5:9 KJV). Then he began to implore Jesus earnestly not to send them out of the country. The demons that possessed the man asked permission to be sent into a nearby herd of pigs. As soon as they were cast out of the man, they entered the pigs. Notice Jesus only told the demons to come out of the man. He did not tell them nor give permission for the demons to enter the pigs. Even in obeying the command of Jesus, the demons sought to cause trouble for Jesus and prevent those in the town from being drawn to Jesus.

The herdsmen stood transfixed as the large herd of pigs turned and ran straight down the hill into the lake and drowned! As one herdsman turned and ran, the others quickly joined him running in abject terror through the countryside to the city. They told everyone what they had seen, their words tumbling out telling the strange tale. The townspeople came out in droves to see if it were true.

The man who had been a menace for years, who frightened women and children and made grown men uncomfortable now sat quietly beside Jesus. He was fully clothed and had washed himself there by the shore. He hardly looked like himself, but clearly it was him. The people from the town looked at the man, then they looked out to the sea where the bodies of hundreds of pigs still floated. They were no longer curious; now they were afraid. The herdsmen pointed to Jesus and clamored that it was Jesus who had done it. Looking at Jesus and the men with him, the townspeople knew they were Jews by the way they dressed.

What did they want? Had they come to attack them? What kind of person and what kind of power or magic did this man have to control that demon possessed man and had power to kill the entire herd of pigs without touching them? The townspeople were growing more and more terrified. A significant source of income and food was destroyed. The towns' leaders grouped together talking quietly, then turned and asked Jesus to please leave their area – they wanted no trouble.

Why did some people see the miracles of Jesus and draw near, while others became frightened and rejected him? This kind of response was not unusual. At the time of the Exodus story in Egypt, some Gentiles experienced the signs and wonders, believed and joined the Hebrew people. Yet others saw and experienced the same incredible events and rebelled. Just as today, nearly every American of accountable age has experienced or knows of someone who has witnessed a miraculous encounter, yet millions ignore, or assign credit to coincidence, a recently passed loved one, the gods, angels, the stars, or luck. The book of Revelation says that during the end times, there will be many who will look at the horrific wonders, and still not repent.

Why did Jesus sail to Gerasenes in the first place? Gerasenes was predominately a Greek town. Did this demon possessed man have something in common with Rahab, Ruth, and the widow from Zarephath who lived long ago? Each of these women were Gentiles who lived close enough to the Jewish people, or Israel and had heard of the God of the Israelite people. Rahab was the prostitute who was saved from doomed Jericho (Joshua 2:11). Ruth was the destitute, but faithful widow from Moab (Ruth 1:4). During a severe drought God sent the prophet Elijah to Zarephath to help a starving widow and mother (I Kings 17). As each of these women were facing life threatening situations, did their hearts cry out for the help of Almighty God, and He responded? The God and Creator of us all knows the deepest cry of our hearts. He reaches out to everyone, providing the right and supreme privilege to become a child of God to those whose hearts seek Him and will accept Him as their God.

> Behold, all souls are Mine ... Do I have any pleasure in the death of the wicked," declares the Lord God, "rather than that he should turn from his ways and live?
>
> Ezekiel 18:4 and 23 NASB

After being asked to leave, Jesus and the disciples got back in the boats to sail across the lake to the crowds awaiting them in Capernaum. The scriptures say that the restored man *begged* (Mark 5:18) to go with Jesus. I can think of no other passage of scripture where someone wanted to follow Jesus and Jesus told them no.[90] However, Jesus instructed the man to go home and tell them what the *Lord* had done for him. Luke says he told everyone in his town what *Jesus* had done. The account in Mark says he began to tell the ten cities (the Decapolis) what Jesus had done for him. It says all the people were amazed by these events.

Did Jesus make this "new son of God" a disciple and send him out to spread the good news among the Gentiles just as He would send His disciples out a short time later to the children of Israel? Perhaps this answer will not be known until we are in heaven. We have no idea how many seeds of salvation were sown by this new child of God.

Below is the account as told in Mark 5 NASB:

> They came to the other side of the sea, into the country of the Gerasenes. ² When He got out of the boat, immediately a man from the tombs with an unclean spirit met Him, ³ and he had his dwelling among the tombs. And no one was able to bind him anymore, even with a chain; ⁴ because he had often been bound with shackles and chains, and the chains had been torn apart by him and the shackles broken in pieces, and no one was strong enough

---

[90] Matthew 8:19-20 has a scribe telling Jesus he will follow him anywhere. Jesus' response seems to imply the scribe's true motive was not to follow Jesus.

to subdue him. ⁵ Constantly, night and day, he was screaming among the tombs and in the mountains, and gashing himself with stones. ⁶ Seeing Jesus from a distance, he ran up and bowed down before Him; ⁷ and shouting with a loud voice, he said, "What business do we have with each other, Jesus, Son of the Most High God? I implore You by God, do not torment me!" ⁸ For He had been saying to him, "Come out of the man, you unclean spirit!" ⁹ And He was asking him, "What is your name?" And he said to Him, "My name is Legion; for we are many." ¹⁰ And he began to implore Him earnestly not to send them out of the country. ¹¹ Now there was a large herd of swine feeding nearby on the mountain. ¹² The demons implored Him, saying, "Send us into the swine so that we may enter them."¹³ Jesus gave them permission. And coming out, the unclean spirits entered the swine; and the herd rushed down the steep bank into the sea, about two thousand of them; and they were drowned in the sea.

¹⁴ Their herdsmen ran away and reported it in the city and in the country. And *the people* came to see what it was that had happened. ¹⁵ They came to Jesus and *observed the man who had been demon-possessed sitting down, clothed and in his right mind, the very man who had had the "legion"; and they became frightened. ¹⁶ Those who had seen it described to them how it had happened to the demon-possessed man, and all about the swine. ¹⁷ And they began to implore Him to leave their region. ¹⁸ As He was getting into the boat, the man who had been demon-possessed was imploring Him that he might accompany Him. ¹⁹ And He did not let him, but He said to him, "Go home to your people and report to them what great things the Lord has done for you, and how He had mercy on you." ²⁰ And he went away and began to proclaim in Decapolis (ten cities) what great things Jesus had done for him; and everyone was amazed.

Mark 5:1-20 NASB

PART 3

Daughter!

But as many as received Him, to them He gave the right to become children of God, even to those who believe in His name, who were born, not of blood nor of the will of the flesh nor of the will of man, but of God.

John 1:12-13 NASB

After being asked to leave the region of Gerasenes, Jesus and the disciples simply left. Is this what it is like today when Jesus comes knocking on the doors of our hearts (Revelation 3:20) and asks if there is room for Him? We attribute the call as our depression, a sense of something missing, guilt or our conscience. We push past those feelings; we push past Jesus and His help and Jesus simply leaves[91] – for the time being.

Scripture says they sailed back to a waiting crowd. Luke 8:42 says the crowds nearly crushed them. I can imagine the crowd calling out to Jesus like He was a rock star, hundreds of people screaming His name, shouting out requests, pushing, reaching out to touch Him. What I cannot imagine is *not* becoming afraid of being the object of such attention.

---

[91] God promises He will never leave, fail or forsake His people (who believe and follow Him). See Deuteronomy 31:6, Joshua 1:5, and Hebrews 13:5. However, for those who reject God persisting in wickedness, and pursue other gods, God says He will leave and forsake them. See Deuteronomy 31:17, II Kings 21:14, Ezekiel 22:20 and 29:5.

I can't imagine not wanting to shove back or just scream, "Leave me alone!" I can't imagine looking at all the people and my emotional response being one of love; caring about them and having "compassion" for them. Yet scripture tells us that was precisely Jesus' response (see Matthew 9:36, 14:14, and 15:32). Jesus gave us a clue of how much God knows us unlike any other verses in the Bible. He said God has numbered every hair on our heads (Matthew 10:30 and Luke 12:7), and He knows what we need before we ask (Matthew 6:8). It is reasonable to assume that as He looked at the crowd, He saw individuals – each person He knew by name, their problems, fears, worries and what they needed. This keen knowledge of each one brought up such love and compassion for them, it can be difficult to imagine. He describes us as sheep without a shepherd in Matthew 9:36; sheep with injuries, lost, hungry and unaware. We are vulnerable to attack and Jesus said He is the Good Shepherd who longs to care for us if we will let Him.

There was a unique woman among this vast throng of people who had come out to see Jesus. Surely, she had heard that He healed people. Maybe she had heard Jesus teaching, and had witnessed some of the healings. She had heard the Holy Scriptures read and discussed most of her life. So many discussions about the coming Messiah – what He would do, and how they would recognize Him. But this day she had no more questions about Him. She knew who He was as surely as she knew she was sick.

She had been suffering from a prolonged loss of blood for twelve years. She was probably anemic from excessive blood loss. Anemia can cause fatigue, loss of energy, shortness of breath, headaches, difficulty concentrating, dizziness, leg cramps and insomnia. Prolonged bleeding in women can be associated with either gastrointestinal tumors, the need for a hysterectomy, or cancer. Abdominal pain and intestinal obstruction often accompany these conditions. Mark 5:26 NIV says, "She had suffered a great deal under the care of many doctors and had spent all she had, yet instead of getting better she grew worse." So indeed, on that day she was probably desperate to see Jesus.

The serious medical condition involved more than pain and discomfit. Because of her continued flow of blood, she had been considered "unclean" for twelve years. Blood is a very big deal in the Jewish culture. Blood is associated with life and death (you can't live without blood flowing). There were instructions in *Torah* about remaining pure by not touching someone with an issue of blood and not eating meat with the blood still in it. Unclean meant she was restricted on where she sat, slept and what she touched within Jewish society of that day. She could neither enter the sanctuary, nor sit with others. She was unable to have an intimate life with a spouse or have anyone touch her since they too would be considered unclean (see Leviticus 15 and 12). To join the crowd seeking Jesus, she was jeopardizing others' ritual purity. Yet she knew the promise from the prophet Malachi that the Sun[92] of Righteousness would bring healing in His wings (Malachi 4:2). She had said to herself, "If I only touch his cloak, I will be healed (Matthew 9:21 NIV)." This information was not something just this woman knew about the coming Messiah. Matthew 14:35-36 NIV says, "People brought all their sick to him and begged him to let the sick just touch the edge of his cloak, and all who touched it were healed."

What was so important about Jesus' cloak? Numbers 15:38–40[93] says:

> *Speak to the children of Israel, and say to them that they shall make for themselves fringes on the corners of their garments, throughout their generations, and that they shall affix a thread of sky-blue [wool] on the fringe of each corner.*

---

92 *Strong's Concordance* defines this Hebrew word #H8121 *shemesh* as brilliant – like the Sun. Malachi 4:2 Sun of Righteousness refers to God as a Brilliant (bright like the Sun) just judge, ruler, and king. Note that at the mount of transfiguration Matthew 17:2 says "And [Jesus] was transfigured before them: and his face did shine as the sun, and his raiment was white as the light."

93 Quoted from the website: http://www.chabad.org/library/article_cdo/aid/537949/jewish/ What-is-the-Tzitzit-and-Tallit.html

> *This shall be* tzitzit *[fringes] for you, and when you see it, you will remember all the commandments of G-d to perform them, and you shall not wander after your hearts and after your eyes after which you are going astray.*
>
> *So that you shall remember and perform all My commandments, and you shall be holy to your L-rd.*

More specifically, it was not a cloak, or a robe but a *tallit,* a large sheet-like prayer shawl. The fringes or tassels are known as tzitzit. To Jews the *tallit* with the *tzitzit* represent all of God's commands and instructions; serving to remind the wearer of their commitment and obligation to God and others and to do what is right. When one prays, the *tallit* is wrapped around the wearer symbolizing enclosing themselves with God and shutting out all that can distract them.

Among those who have lived on a farm, many have seen a hen gather her young chicks under her wings when a hawk is circling in the sky. This type of devotion and refuge says the protector is willing to risk their life for those who are smaller, weaker and are dearly loved. The Bible uses this very same analogy to show how much God cares for us. The tallit of God is called the "wings" of God. In Ruth 2:12 it is under the God of Israel's wings (*tallit*) that Boaz prays Ruth will seek refuge or safety. In Psalm 17:8 David prays to be hidden in the shadow of God's wings. Jesus, revealing His identity as God says in Luke 13:34 NASB, "O Jerusalem, Jerusalem, *the city* that kills the prophets and stones those sent to her! How often I wanted to gather your children together, just as a hen *gathers* her brood under her wings, and you would not *have it*!" So there was a general understanding among the people that under the "wings" or *tallit* of Messiah (God) they find refuge and healing.

Did this woman believe that Jesus was the promised Messiah? Can we be sure of the answer? The story itself provides the answer to this question. She did not say "*If* He is the Messiah, I will be healed."

Instead the story tells us she knew who He was: the if was not doubting Jesus' identity, the if was doubting her ability to make her way through the crowd of shouting and pressing multitude to be close enough to touch the hem of His *tallit*. The story says that once she touched His garment, the healing was immediate. After twelve years, many doctors, and trying so many different remedies, she was set free immediately! As mentioned earlier, a host of other health problems that accompanies this condition – headaches, muscle weakness, abdominal pains all stopped instantly!

The story says Jesus stopped, turned and asked who had touched Him. Luke 8:45 NASB says, When they all denied it, Peter said, "Master, the people are crowding and pressing against you." Yet Jesus knew something significant had occurred and He would not dismiss what had happened. Jesus knew someone had recognized, acknowledged and acted upon His true nature, authority and power. However, do we really think Jesus didn't know who touched him? He who stopped demon possessed men, stilled a raging storm, and knew the thoughts of the people in the room when He healed the paralyzed man – didn't know who had touched him? Invariably, when God asks someone a question, the purpose is not for God to gain understanding or knowledge. It is for us to gain understanding, knowledge or wisdom!

God knows when we come to Him. We *cannot* sneak up on God. Jesus says in Matthew 10:32 NIV "Whoever acknowledges me before others, I will also acknowledge before My Father in heaven." The Books of Mark and Luke both say the woman came forward trembling and fell at Jesus' feet and confessed what had happened to her. Why had she been reluctant to come forward and tell what had happened? Could it be that she was so used to being shunned and separated from others because of her illness? Had she considered herself defective as well as unclean? How does one reconcile themselves to the fact that when they touch someone, they have defiled them? Yet, she had dared to touch the Messiah! And she was afraid of confessing what she had done. We need never be afraid to come to Jesus in any circumstances.

In Matthew 11:28-30 NIV He says, "Come to me, all you who are weary and burdened, and I will give you rest. Take my yoke upon you and learn from me, for I am gentle and humble in heart, and you will find rest for your souls. For my yoke is easy and my burden is light." In John 6:37 NIV He says, "All those the Father gives me will come to me, and whoever comes to me I will <u>never</u> drive away."

    Reluctantly the woman who had been healed after twelve years of misery came forward to Jesus in fear and trembling. How did the Messiah respond? The only time in the gospels that Jesus called *any* woman "daughter" occurred in the accounts of this story. In Matthew, Mark and Luke, He calls her Daughter! I can think of no more precious name for our Lord to call a female. In Matthew He tells her to take heart. In all accounts He tells her it is her faith[94] (belief/trust in Him) that has healed her. This implies the healing is not so much from Him, nor touching His cloak, it is *her* belief without doubts, her unwavering trust in Jesus as the Messiah, as God that brought healing and wholeness. It is the recognition and acknowledgment of who God is that transforms lives. It is her acting upon this truth that made her *His Daughter*. John 1:12 says to those who believe in His name (His reputation, His revealed identify and character), He gives the right to become children born of God. She who had probably felt unclean, unworthy, sick and broken for years was acknowledged by the Messiah as His Daughter!

* * *

The passage of scripture that told of this Daughter of the Living God who had suffered with a bleeding disorder for twelve years also told of another beloved daughter who in this instance was twelve years old. And just as the first Daughter had a Loving Father who cared deeply for her wellbeing, this little girl was blessed with a loving father named Jairus who was deeply concerned for his daughter's wellbeing. The

---

[94] Greek word "pistis" meaning the steadfast conviction in believing something to be true.

story of these two females and how Jesus changed their lives are told in Luke 8:40-56 NASB.

> [40] And as Jesus returned, the people welcomed Him, for they had all been waiting for Him. [41] And there came a man named Jairus, and he was an official of the synagogue; and he fell at Jesus' feet, and *began* to implore Him to come to his house; [42] for he had an only daughter, about twelve years old, and she was dying. But as He went, the crowds were pressing against Him.
>
> [43] And a woman who had a hemorrhage for twelve years, and could not be healed by anyone, [44] came up behind Him and touched the fringe of His cloak, and immediately her hemorrhage stopped. [45] And Jesus said, "Who is the one who touched Me?" And while they were all denying it, Peter said, "Master, the people are crowding and pressing in on You."[46] But Jesus said, "Someone did touch Me, for I was aware that power had gone out of Me." [47] When the woman saw that she had not escaped notice, she came trembling and fell down before Him, and declared in the presence of all the people the reason why she had touched Him, and how she had been immediately healed. [48] And He said to her, "Daughter, your faith has made you well; go in peace."
>
> [49] While He was still speaking, someone came from *the house of* the synagogue official, saying, "Your daughter has died; do not trouble the Teacher anymore." [50] But when Jesus heard *this*, He answered him, "Do not be afraid *any longer*; only believe, and she will be made well." [51] When He came to the house, He did not allow anyone to enter with Him, except Peter and John and James, and the girl's father and mother. [52] Now they were all weeping and lamenting for her; but He said, "Stop weeping, for she has not died, but is asleep." [53] And they *began* laughing at Him, knowing that she had died. [54] He, however, took her by the hand

and called, saying, "Child, arise!" ⁵⁵ And her spirit returned, and she got up immediately; and He gave orders for *something* to be given her to eat. ⁵⁶ Her parents were amazed; but He instructed them to tell no one what had happened.

- *<u>An important point from Part 2 and 3 is:</u>*
- *Scripture says we will find God when we search for Him with all our heart (Jeremiah 29:13). Therefore, we can never be too crazy, too ill, too unclean, too broken, too lost, or too far away for God to love us, to find us, to heal us, to cleanse us, to make us brand new and call us His beloved.*

PART 4

But it's My Child, Jesus!

If you then, being evil, know how to give good gifts to your children, how much more will your Father who is in heaven give what is good to those who ask Him!
Matthew 7:11 NASB

For the sake of exploring each story and how it relates to the person involved, the last story of the woman with the bleeding disorder was told a little out of order. Shortly after the boat returned from Gerasenes, Jesus and the disciples were welcomed by the waiting crowd. It is here that a leader in the synagogue made his way through the throng of people to make a request of Jesus. While the book of Matthew's account (Matthew 9:18-26) says Jairus knelt before Jesus, the books of Mark and Luke (Mark 5:22-43 and Luke 8:41-56) says he fell at the feet of Jesus and pleaded with Him to come to his home. Matthew's account says that Jairus' daughter is already dead; Mark and Luke's accounts say she is dying. In the few sentences of this story we learn a couple of important things about Jairus: he is a leader in the synagogue, and he is aware of Jesus' power and authority over illness and death. Mark 5:23 NASB says, "… [Jairus] implored Him earnestly, saying, "My little daughter is at the point of death; *please* come and lay Your hands on her, so that she will get well and live."

This is no small statement of belief and trust in Jesus. Recall Jesus said after meeting the Roman Centurion how rare it was to encounter the Centurion's level of faith(belief) that Jesus had power and authority to heal from afar (in Matthew 8:5-13 and Luke 7:1-10). Yet Jairus possessed the same level of faith in Jesus' ability to heal his only child who was at the brink of death. Did Jesus ask if Jairus knew who He is? Did He tell Jairus first he must believe in Him as the Messiah? No, Jesus just went with him. On the way they encountered the woman with the bleeding illness. Wonder what was going through Jairus' mind. Was he thinking, "Hurry, hurry, my daughter doesn't have much time." Was he as amazed as everyone else at the healing he witnessed? Scripture says that shortly after the woman's healing, they were told Jairus' daughter was dead and that Jesus was not needed. Again, we don't know Jairus' thoughts, but it is easy to imagine. He has just been told that his beloved daughter who had been desperately ill and getting worse with each hour was now dead. How long had he been waiting for Jesus? How insistently had he made his way through the pressing crowds to get to Jesus? And now it was too late; his baby was dead.

The next words from our Lord, our ever-present help, Jesus/God shows how well He knows our broken and trembling hearts. It is easy to imagine that Jesus took hold of Jairus' arm and looked into his eyes when Luke 8:50 NIV says: Hearing this, Jesus said to Jairus, "Don't be afraid; just believe, and she will be healed." This sentence tells us Jesus *knew* the father's feelings of fear and grief; He encouraged him to believe. Believe what? To believe the amazing event Jairus was about to witness. <u>The profound truth that is at the root of the reason why Jesus came to earth is He wants us to know that He knows us, He cares about us, that He holds the power of death and life (John 11:26, Deuteronomy 32:39 and I Samuel 2:6) and He wants us to not be afraid and to believe and trust Him (Matthew 11:28-29).</u>

In all three accounts of Matthew, Mark and Luke, the mourners were there already when Jesus and His disciples entered the house. When Jesus told them the child was asleep not dead, He was laughed at.

The Creator of the Universe who made all life was laughed at! Deuteronomy 32:39 NASB says, "And there is no god besides Me; It is I who put to death and give life. I have wounded and it is I who heal, and there is no one who can deliver from My hand." How does Jesus respond to their laughing at Him? He who is called long-suffering simply told them to leave. Shortly thereafter the parents, a few disciples and Jesus were alone in the room with the girl who was quickly "awakened" from her deathly slumber. Then Jesus asked them not to tell anyone.

I wonder if later every time they looked at their daughter, they remembered she had died that day, and remembered how easily Jesus called her back to life. I wonder if a day ever went by that they did not recall the power of God. A few years later I bet they were not surprised when they heard Jesus came back to life after being crucified. I bet they never looked at death the same way for the rest of their lives.

The Gospels tell of Jesus raising two other people from the dead – a widow's son (story shown on next page) and Jesus' friend Lazarus (see Chapter 17 – The Resurrection and the Life). In each of these other incidents scripture reveals Jesus' empathy and compassion for the bereaved. Why is this important for us to know? Throughout the history of mankind, people have questioned God's love, power, and character because of the deaths of their loved ones. This is the story of the oldest book of the Bible – the book of Job. Job is described as a perfect and upright man (Job 1:1 KJV). Yet after the loss of his livestock, servants, his own health and the deaths of all his children, in grief and pain Job struggled with doubt about the fairness and goodness of God. Sometimes our questions to God take on an accusatory tone, as if we assume God is wrong and at fault in causing or allowing tragedy and the death of our loved ones. However, as explained in the book of Job, the lack of understanding is on our part. After a great deal of discussion with his friends, and Job voicing his questions, anger and pain, God appeared and spoke. In Chapter 38 God asks Job how vast is his knowledge of all creation? Can our wisdom compare to the Infinite Creator on what, when and how is best in the totality of all life and history? When Job was asked many questions of his knowledge and wisdom, Job said he spoke of things he did not know; things too wonderful for him to understand (42:3).

Like the story involving the resurrection of Jairus' daughter, the account of the resurrection of the woman's son in Nain reveals the tender heart of God. In Jewish society at the time of the Bible, life could be very harsh for a single or widowed woman facing the future with no husband or son. In Luke 7 we read of Jesus' encounter with a woman whose son is about to be buried. The scripture makes a point of telling us that she is a widow and the dead man is her only son. This story told in ten sentences, conveys so much. Luke 7:11-15 NIV says:

> [11] Soon afterward, Jesus went to a town called Nain, and his disciples and a large crowd went along with him. [12] As he approached the town gate, a dead person was being carried out—the only son of his mother, and she was a widow. And a large crowd from the town was with her. [13] <u>When the Lord saw her, his heart went out to her and he said, "Don't cry."</u>
>
> [14] Then he went up and touched the bier they were carrying him on, and the bearers stood still. He said, "Young man, I say to you, get up!" [15] The dead man sat up and began to talk, and <u>*Jesus gave him back to his mother.*</u> [16] They were all filled with awe (fear-KJV) and praised God. "A great prophet has appeared among us," they said. "<u>God has come to help his people.</u>" [17] This news about Jesus spread throughout Judea and the surrounding country.

An interesting point: notice the scripture says that after the young man was restored to the living, the people *praised God* and they said "<u>God has come</u> to help his people." Here we see that the people of the town of Nain (along with the crowd who followed Jesus) acknowledged that the resurrection of this man could only be done by the hand of God.

Jesus knows the condition of those who have passed from this life. Just as Jesus told Jairus not to be afraid, scripture says His heart went out to the widow and told her not to cry. If Jesus knew He would restore their loved ones' lives in just minutes, why was He gentle and compassionate to the parents? Why did His heart go out to the grieving family members? He was touched and troubled for those who were left here afraid and grief stricken. Those who are hurting touch the heart of God. We *cannot* suffer and hurt without God being troubled and moved by our pain. Just as we are connected to our children and deeply concerned for their welfare, can we ever outdo God, whom we call our Father? No!

The two stories of the widow's only son and the young daughter of Jairus show Jesus' empathy and compassion for the bereaved, and it showed us something more. In each story of a resurrection, Jesus spoke to the deceased as if they were asleep. He who spoke the universe into being, spoke to the deceased and they heard Him as easily as a person standing next to Jesus. What then do these scriptures reveal about those who have passed from this life? In Matthew 22:32 KJV Jesus said, "God is not the God of the dead, but of the living." The apostle Paul speaks of an almost instantaneous transformation for believers from our earthly flesh and blood body (weak and perishable body– NASB) into our celestial, and spiritual body raised in glory and power in heaven (I Corinthians 15:42-50). II Corinthians 5:8 KJV says, "We are confident, I say, and willing rather to be absent from the body, and to be present with the Lord." Jesus *knew* that Jairus' daughter, the widow's only son and His friend Lazarus were perfectly fine. Revelation 21:4 tells what it is like when children of God have taken on their glorious and imperishable spiritual bodies. There are no more tears, sorrow, death, or pain; it says the former things have passed away. What former things? All the sin and its resulting corruption that brings sorrow, regret, worry, illness, heartache, sadness and fear are gone. Few grasp the reality of the spiritual realm. Our minds and hearts are too imprinted with decadence and the degradation of life on earth to truly imagine the beauty, perfection and peace of heaven. Isaiah 64:4 and

I Corinthians 2:9 say that mankind's eyes have not seen, their ears have not heard, nor their hearts comprehended what God has prepared for those who love and wait for Him. The apostle Paul says in I Corinthians 13:12 KJV that comprehending the spiritual realm is like looking through a dark glass now, but when we are there, we will know fully, see clearly.

When our children or loved ones have believed and trusted in the God of the Bible, whether they are here on earth now or in heaven with God, God is with them. Psalm 139:7-10 NASB says, "Where can I go from Your Spirit? Or where can I flee from Your presence? If I ascend to heaven, You are there; If I make my bed in Sheol (in the ground), behold, You are there. If I take the wings of the dawn, If I dwell in the remotest part of the sea, even there Your hand will lead me, And Your right hand (power and strength) will lay hold of me."

When we are unsure of the salvation of our children or loved ones now gone, we can trust that God is fairer and more merciful than we can imagine. Scripture tells us that if we call upon Him, we will be saved (Joel 2:32, Acts 2:21 and Romans 10:13). The difficult truth is that only those who have rejected God time and time again will not be with Him for eternity. (If someone did not believe, trust or want to be with God while they were here on earth, why would they want to spend eternity with Him after this life is done?) I believe that He who said He is not willing that any should be lost (Matthew 18:14, Ezekiel 18:23 and 32), calls us to Him until the last moments of our lives. Only the deliberate, hardened heart and lifetime of decisions, choices and actions will overrule someone's opportunity for eternal life.

Each of these resurrection stories that dealt with the death of a loved one, and the sorrow and heartache of the mourning family, shows Jesus understands and cares. He is moved by our pain. We can trust and be reassured in the love and perfection of a God who is concerned, compassionate and caring with us when we are hurting for those gone, and when we are worried for our children still here, because *they* are His children first.

The LORD appeared to him from afar, saying, "I have loved you with an everlasting love; Therefore I have drawn you with loving kindness.
Jeremiah 31:3 NASB

* * *

This story concludes the "One Day with Jesus" – from the teaching at the synagogue the day before, the crowd at the home of Simon Peter, Jesus' early morning time of solitude, the boat ride to the other side of the Galilee in the sudden storm. We saw His encounter with the possessed man near Gerasenes, the return to Capernaum to the waiting crowd; witnessed the healing of the woman with the bleeding disease, and the resurrection of the synagogue leader's only daughter. We have seen Jesus infinitely patient and compassionate with the crowds of the broken and sick, straight forward and direct with demons as well as the wind. He answered the silent cry of one held hostage by many demons, restored the ostracized daughter, and watched Him turn the mourning of the bereaved into joy.

What was it like for Peter, James or John? Were they in shock; stunned silent? Did they struggle trying to make sense of all they had witnessed that day? Surely everything they thought they understood about how things worked in this world were turned upside down. Did scriptures from the sacred writings and *Torah* come to mind? The realization that these events were the fulfillment of passages out of Deuteronomy, Job, Psalms and the prophet Isaiah would probably come much later. Do we gain a deeper understanding of the verse that says, "The fear of the LORD is the beginning of wisdom" (Psalm 111:10)? Had I been there, I think I would have gained a healthy dose of fear and respect. And I would have a growing certainty of the answer to the question asked earlier – "Who is this?"

Personally, I am not sure my heart could stand spending everyday with Him; nor am I sure I could live another minute without Him.

CHAPTER 11

Anointing The Anointed

Disclaimer: This story appears in the Book of Luke and has been dear to my heart since reading it the first time. I closely relate to the woman of many sins who was forgiven much. I took liberty in fictionalizing her story, then it is brought back to the original story as told in Luke 7:36-50 NIV.

Surely, this woman had heard of Jesus. She had heard that He was healing people. Moreover, she had heard He was forgiving people of their sins. Everyone was talking about Him – what He said and what He had done. She had a neighbor who had been healed. Each time she looked at the man, or overheard people talking about Him, her heart weighed heavier. She, who had not shed tears in years, now found herself crying every night. She didn't know what was wrong or what to do. Her thoughts were filled with good and bad memories long buried that now popped up like germinating seeds in freshly prepared soil. She had no peace.

Then one day she heard Jesus was in town. She knew it was not a rumor. She had seen the crowds pressed together like sheep bleating for their shepherd as they followed Him clamoring their requests, shouting His name. His disciples walked near Him, like they were trying to protect Him, but Jesus kept reaching out touching first one then another, leaving many shouting out praises. She watched with her cloak covering part of her face, hiding her falling tears. After the crowd had passed her window, she sat still thinking. She was unworthy, but everyone came to Him, and He turned no one away. All were healed. Maybe, just maybe she could be healed too.

Quickly she jumped up from the little bench and moved to the other room. She looked over her shoulder to be sure no one was watching and she retrieved her savings from its hiding place. She tucked the bag under her sash tied around her waist and reached for her garment, covered her head, and walked to the door. She paused once more, before unlatching the door and hurrying out to the marketplace. There was something she needed to buy.

One merchant sensed her anxiety and quoted her a high price. But she did not hesitate, she did not negotiate. She figured the price the merchant quoted was the price required for what she needed. She pulled out the bag with gold pieces in it and placed it on the table. The merchant counted out his price, leaving her only a few coins. He eyed her with unspoken questions as he put the money away and carefully wrapped the alabaster jar in cloth. The woman took the wrapped jar and left as quickly as she had come. Along the way, she stopped and asked an old man and woman if they knew where Jesus was. They ignored her and kept walking. A smiling younger man reached for her arm and said he could take her to Jesus. This time she shrugged away and kept walking. A young boy had overheard her question and ran after her. He told her Jesus had been invited to Simon, the Pharisee's house.

She thought of going home and changing her clothes, but she moved steadily toward Simon's house – no detours, no delays, carrying the expensive jar close to her heart. When she arrived, she paused at Simon's courtyard for just a moment, then walked boldly to and then through the door as if she lived there. Once inside she listened for the voices and walked toward the sound. Suddenly, there He was – reclining at the low table eating and talking. She would have recognized Him in a crowd. While He didn't look unusual, there was something undeniably different about Him. Nothing on this earth could have stopped her next movement.

She walked toward Him and stopped behind Him at His feet. She could not look up; then she began to shake. She could not speak and she did not dare touch Him; all she could do was weep. The tears ran down her face and from her chin they fell onto His feet. Drop after drop, she was so ashamed. She was unworthy to touch Him. She was unclean and He ... was perfect. She could no longer remain standing; slowly she began to bow down. She sank to her knees and began to slightly rock backwards and forward. Still her tears continued to fall on His feet. She was so embarrassed. Not because of the other men there watching but because Jesus was there and between them was a gulf made by her many sins. She wanted to wipe away her tears that had fallen on Him, but she didn't dare touch Him. She sat the precious alabaster jar down and using her own hair, she began to wipe her tears from His feet. The moment she touched Him something moved through her body breaking away the calloused shell around her heart causing her to sob. Like rinsing away the dirt from a garment, the longer she cried the cleaner she felt.

Silence filled the room except for her weeping. Some of the other men sitting around the table looked uncomfortable and embarrassed to witness this scene. Others seemed disgusted to see *this* kind of woman fawning over the Rabbi. There was an audible gasp when she bent lower still and began kissing Jesus' feet. Then she opened the alabaster jar and sweet aromatic perfume filled the air as she poured out the expensive contents onto Jesus' feet.

Still she could not look at Jesus' face. Jesus turned from her to Simon and looked at him. Slowly the slight smirk disappeared from Simon's face as he noticed Jesus was looking at him. Jesus told him He had something to tell him.

Simon said, "Tell me teacher."

"Two people owed money to a certain moneylender. One owed him five hundred denarii, and the other fifty. Neither of them had the money to pay him back, so he forgave the debts of both. Now which of them will love him more?"

Simon replied, "I suppose the one who had the bigger debt forgiven."

"You have judged correctly," Jesus said.

Then he turned toward the woman and said to Simon, "Do you see this woman? I came into your house. You did not give me any water for my feet, but she wet my feet with her tears and wiped them with her hair. You did not give me a kiss, but this woman, from the time I [she] entered, has not stopped kissing my feet. You did not put oil on my head, but she has poured perfume on my feet.

Therefore, I tell you, her many sins have been forgiven—as her great love has shown. But whoever has been forgiven little loves little."

Now – she had turned to look at Jesus. As He looked at her, His eyes told it all. He understood. He knew. He knew her. He knew her shame, her sin, her illness, her debt she could never hope to pay. There was no condemnation, only profound love.

Then Jesus said to her, "Your sins are forgiven."

The other guests began to say among themselves, "Who is this who even forgives sins?"

She felt the change coursing through her soul and body like new life. She didn't hear them, she only heard her Redeemer, her Savior, her Lord who had set her free.

Jesus said to the woman, "Your faith has saved you; go in peace."

* * *

Anointing The Anointed

Jesus being anointed by a woman is one of the few stories aside from His last day, and resurrection aftermath which appears in all four gospels. Matthew 26:6-13 and Mark 14:3-9 are virtually the same. Their accounts involve a Simon and the encounter takes place shortly before Jesus' death. John's account (12:1-8) involves Mary, the sister of Lazarus and shares much of the same conversation and comments as told in Matthew and Mark's account. While Luke's (7:36-50) account involves a Simon, nearly everything else is different.

CHAPTER 12

The Three Gentiles &
What They Reveal About Jesus

"You believe at last!" Jesus answered.
– John 16:31 NIV

When Jesus began His ministry, His focus was on teaching and preaching the good news that God cares about how we live and treat one another and revealing who He is and why He had come. The miracles were not the focus of His ministry, but they did serve a specific purpose. They served as a witness to His identity.[95] His earliest healings often involved people who suffered with demon possession, because while He taught, those with unclean spirits interrupted Him, proclaiming He was the Holy One of God or the Son of God. Only a few people saw His involvement in the other early miracles – the water into wine, the man healed of leprosy, the miraculous catch of fish, Peter's mother-in-law healed of a fever, and the resurrection of Jairus' daughter. Several of the early miracles came with the admonition to tell no one what He had done. However, it did not take long before word spread about Jesus' ability to heal. Then the crowds who followed Him everywhere came and with them, the sick.

---

95 John 5:36, and John 10:25 – the works bore witness of Him.

Several times Jesus made a point of saying His coming and message was to the Jews or the lost sheep of Israel (Matthew 10:6 and 15:24). However, He did encounter Gentiles (non-Jews) – both within Judea and Israel, and in Tyre and Gerasenes. Why would His coming and message be mainly for the Jews? There must be many reasons. The Jews were the people God had cultivated for His purposes. God's covenant was with this people. Through the Jewish people came the Law (instructions for right living – *Torah*, or as we know it, the first five books of the Bible), the Prophets and the sacred writings, all of which constitute the Old Testament. From their ancestor – Abraham on to the messages from the prophets came the promises of the coming Anointed One of God, who would be called God's Son. Of all the people on planet earth, only the Jews were looking and waiting for the arrival of the Messiah. The Jews knew specifics about the Messiah from the messages of their Prophets. Yet while many Jews suspected Jesus was the Messiah, far too many looked right at Him, quoted scriptures about the Messiah, and could not recognize those very scriptures spoke of Jesus.

This story involves three different people. Scripture is clear that two of them were Gentiles (non-Jews), and the third gives no clue that he was Jewish. In each story the individual did not come to Jesus for themselves but came for a loved one. These three stories share something in common that is unique – a glimpse and confirmation of the deity of Jesus. The first story involves the Roman Centurion told in Matthew 8:5-13 and in Luke 7:1-10. In the Matthew account the conversation takes place between the Centurion and Jesus. In the Luke story the Centurion is not present; however, his request is conveyed through his Jewish friends.

A Roman Centurion was an officer in charge of 60 to 100 soldiers. Luke's story tells us something unique about the heart of this Centurion. It is the illness of the servant of whom the "master valued highly" that moved the Centurion to seek Jesus' help. This Centurion felt he was unworthy to speak with Jesus face to face, so Jewish elders came to Jesus in his behalf to make his request. The elders "pleaded earnestly" with Jesus telling Him this man was worthy of Jesus' help "because he loves our nation and has built our synagogue."[96] These are significant words; this meant that like Ruth (from the book of Ruth 1:16) the Jewish people had become dear to him; he had come to understand, respect and believe in their God and in following their ways. The Centurion was so deeply moved by his belief in their God that out of his own resources this Roman built them a synagogue.

The fact that the Centurion did not come to Jesus himself and speak of what he had done for the Jews reveals his humility and it also shows he knew the Jewish tradition that Jews did not enter the homes of Gentiles (non-Jews) lest they become or be considered "unclean" (John 18:28 and Acts 10:26). Therefore, it was the Jewish leaders who sought Jesus for him. What did Jesus do when the elders came with this request? The scripture tells us He went with them to the Centurion's home. However, before they reached their destination, the Centurion sent some of his friends out to meet Jesus and to give Him this message, "Lord, don't trouble yourself, for I do not deserve to have you come under my roof. That is why I did not even consider myself worthy to come to you. But say the word, and my servant will be healed. For I myself am a man under authority, with soldiers under me. I tell this one, 'Go,' and he goes; and that one, 'Come,' and he comes. I say to my servant, 'Do this,' and he does it." (Luke 7:6-9 NIV)

How did Jesus respond to this statement? The scripture says, When Jesus heard this, He was amazed, and turning to the people following him, He said, "I tell you, I have not found such great faith (belief and trust) even in [the people of] Israel." Matthew 8:13 NIV says, Then Jesus said to the centurion, "Go! Let it be done just as you believed it would." And his servant was healed at that moment.

---

96 Many Gentiles believed in the God of the Jews and worshipped with them. They were called "God- fearers." More than likely this Centurion was a "God-fearer." See Acts 13:16 and 26.

The next story is told only in the Book of John (John 4:46-53) involving a royal official whose son was close to death. The official lived in Capernaum and had heard Jesus was in Cana. As a "royal official," it is debatable whether he was a Jew or not. When the official begged Jesus to come and heal his son, verse 48 NIV records Jesus' response, "Unless you people see signs and wonders," Jesus told him, "you will never believe." Some translations do not have the word *people* in this verse. It is possible that interpreters could not be sure whether the "*you*" is singular referring only to the royal official or plural referring to a group or type of people. When the official made his request a second time, Jesus replied "Go, your son will live."

Comparing this story to the Centurion story one might wonder why Jesus spoke so abruptly or harshly to this man. Where is the loving and gentle Jesus? What if Jesus did not speak harshly? What if loving and gentle Jesus is simply speaking the truth lovingly and gently? Jesus' statement that the royal official is like others who do not believe unless they see signs and wonders almost implies that had this official's son not been ill unto death, the official would have had no reason to come to Jesus and would never have believed. In times of great worry and fear we, who have no need of God in our day to day lives, will come asking, begging, and willing to negotiate for what we desperately want. It is scary and sad to think of Jesus' statement of truth that unless there is a need, unless we see the hand of God do what we want, we will *NEVER* believe. Yet what did Jesus do with this heart that did not believe in the reality and power of God, who perhaps up until this day, and this incident previously had no need for God? Jesus engaged him in the briefest salvation conversation of two sentences. Why? Because He wants all to become saved; He is not willing that any be lost.

This father had watched his son's illness grow worse and he knew this would likely end in his son's death. He had heard about Jesus, and heard Jesus was in the nearby town of Cana. Capernaum is approximately 20 to 25 miles from Cana. We do not know how long the journey took to find Jesus, but surely the father worried that it might be too late. He had no way of knowing whether his son was alive or dead. Nevertheless, he had come with the sole intention of getting his son's only hope of survival – Jesus – to return to Capernaum and heal him. After Jesus' stinging remark about miracles and belief, in a minimum of words Jesus told this father, "go home, your boy is okay; he is alive and alright."

When the father was told this, scripture says he believed. This encounter involves a miracle of two beliefs. The first belief came when Jesus told him his son was healed. The verse (John 4:50 NASB) says, "The man believed the word that Jesus spoke to him and started off." On the way home, he received the message that his son was well and discovered it was at the very moment of his conversation with Jesus that the healing took place. The second belief came when he returned home and saw his son, spoke to his family and servants then all of them came to understand that only God could do what they had witnessed and experienced. This royal official came to Jesus for the life of his son and in the end would gain his own eternal life and eternal life for his family in the process.

The third story is of a Gentile woman who came to find Jesus because her daughter was possessed. This story appears in Matthew 15:21-28 and in Mark 7:24-30. Jesus had gone to Tyre, a city along the coast of Lebanon and was trying to keep his presence secret (Mark 7:24). However, this woman found Him and would not stop requesting that Jesus heal her daughter. Matthew 15:22 said she called Jesus "Son of David." These statements indicate she had heard about Jesus, heard of the miracles, and had heard He was the suspected Messiah. Matthew 15:23 tells us Jesus' response to this woman: He did not say a word.

At another time Jesus told a parable of a persistent widow who kept demanding justice until the judge granted her request because he had grown weary of her (Luke 18:1-7). The Canaanite woman was like the persistent widow. The disciples asked Jesus to tell her to go away because she kept calling out to Jesus to help her daughter. At this point in the story, He told her He was sent only to the lost sheep of Israel and "It is not right to take the children's bread and toss it to their dogs (Matthew 15:26 NIV)." While this sounds harsh to our ears, the woman was not put off by Jesus' remark. She staked her claim as a dog, moreover as a pet at the table of the Jews. She told Jesus she deserved the crumbs, a morsel from their table laden with God's bountiful blessings; just a little bit of God's mercy was more than enough. She did not ask Jesus to come with her, she did not say she would bring her daughter – she just begged Jesus to have mercy; to heal her child. Matthew 15:28 NIV says: Then Jesus answered, "Woman, you have great faith! Your request is granted." And her daughter was healed from that very hour.

The Centurion in the first story felt he was unworthy to come before Jesus with his request for his servant. We are all unworthy to come before the Creator of the Universe, but He bids us to come unto Him! How can we receive if we do not ask? (You do not have, because you do not ask God - James 4:2 NIV.) So, the Centurion asked and believed Jesus had full authority to alter reality – even impending death from a distance.

The nobleman of whom Jesus said would never believe without signs and wonder, did come to believe. First, he believed the very word of God when Jesus told him his son was healed ("The work of God is this: to believe in the one he has sent" John 6:29 NIV). Then understanding what had really happened, the nobleman and his family believed Jesus is God after experiencing the signs and wonders from the Hand of God.

Although the Canaanite woman acknowledged she was not worthy to receive a favorable answer to her request, her belief and trust was in the compassionate and merciful God of all creation (The LORD is compassionate and gracious, slow to anger, abounding in love - Psalm 103:8 NIV). She would not give up. She recognized her situation was hopeless without God. Oh, why can't we realize the same thing in our lives; that apart from Him we can do nothing (John 15:5)?

These three stories share something amazing and awe-inspiring. Did you see it? In each case the sick person was not present when their loved one made their appeal before Jesus. In each story the closing lines indicated the sick person was healed at the exact time Jesus said they were healed. So, what was the glimpse of God Almighty? These people did not need to tell Jesus where or what their homes looked like. They did not need to tell Jesus their loved one's age, coloring or name or even what was wrong with them. Jesus did not need a GPS (global positioning system), a computer or even a blood sniffing dog! In these three stories, Jesus is revealed as fully God. Omniscient in that He showed Himself to be all knowing – He knew what was wrong with their loved one and where they were. Omnipotent in that His power to effect complete healing was effortless, precise and undiminished by distance! Omnipresent in that He was with their loved ones and knew they were alive and healed at the moment He spoke their healing into being with the full power and authority as God. He knew them just as He knows us today; as only Almighty God can know us! He knows what we are going through and what our needs are ("for your Father knows what you need before you ask him" - Matthew 6:8 NIV). Yesterday, today and forever He is as touched by our belief and trust in His compassionate mercy and vast power as He is touched by our pain and fear.

CHAPTER 13

Beelzebub & The Sin Not Forgiven

²² Then a demon-possessed man who was blind and mute was brought to Jesus, and He healed him, so that the mute man spoke and saw. ²³ All the crowds were amazed, and were saying, "This man cannot be the Son of David, can he?" ²⁴ But when the Pharisees heard this, they said, "This man casts out demons only by Beelzebub the ruler of the demons."

²⁵ And knowing their thoughts Jesus said to them, "Any kingdom divided against itself is laid waste; and any city or house divided against itself will not stand. ²⁶ If Satan casts out Satan, he is divided against himself; how then will his kingdom stand? ²⁷ If I by Beelzebub cast out demons, by whom do your sons cast them out? For this reason they will be your judges. ²⁸ But if I cast out demons by the Spirit of God, then the kingdom of God has come upon you. ²⁹ Or how can anyone enter the strong man's house and carry off his property, unless he first binds the strong man? And then he will plunder his house. ³⁰ He who is not with Me is against Me; and he who does not gather with Me scatters. ³¹ "Therefore I say to you, any sin and blasphemy shall be forgiven people, but blasphemy against the Spirit shall not be forgiven. ³² Whoever speaks a word against the Son of Man, it shall be forgiven him; but whoever speaks against the Holy Spirit, it shall not be forgiven him, either in this age or in the age to come.

Matthew 12:22-32 NASB

The above scripture about the unforgiven sin should cause justifiable concern. Does this really mean that a person who is guilty of this sin can *never* have a relationship with God; and that heaven and eternal life are out of the question? Most Christians know about the unforgivable sin, but how many of us can tell someone precisely what it is and why it is such a big deal? The stories of the unforgiven sin appear in Matthew 12:22-32, Mark 3:20-30 and Luke 11:14-28 and 12:8-10. For the sake of this story, I will mainly focus on the account told in Matthew shown at the beginning of this chapter. At first glance the stories in the three gospels may appear to be the same, but there are substantial differences in the setting, and what took place before, during and after this conversation. In two of these accounts (Matthew and Mark) someone attributes Jesus' miracles to Beelzebub.[97] In the book of Matthew it is a group of Pharisees who make the comment in question after Jesus heals a demon-possessed man who was blind and mute. In the book of Mark Jesus and the disciples were surrounded by crowds so that they could hardly eat bread. Jesus had been healing people of various ailments and some scribes from Jerusalem made the offensive remark. The account in Luke says Jesus cast a demon out of a man who was mute. When the demon left, the man spoke and the crowd was amazed. Then some people in the crowd made the offensive comment about Beelzebub. It is possible that aside from the subtle differences recorded in these three books, they are speaking of the same incident. It could be possible that the statement about the unforgiveable sin in Luke 12:10 is out of order and really belongs with the passage in Luke 11 making it consistent with the other two versions told in Matthew and Mark. Notice the three (underlined) seemingly different topics covered in these four verses in Luke 12:8-10 NASB:

> [8] "And I say to you, <u>everyone who confesses Me before men</u>, the Son of Man will confess him also before the angels of God;[9] but he

---

[97] Some Bible translations have "Beelzebul" (NIV and NASB) instead of "Beelzebub" (KJV).

who denies Me before men will be denied before the angels of God. ¹⁰ And everyone <u>who speaks a word against the Son of Man, it will be forgiven him</u>; but he who <u>blasphemes against the Holy Spirit</u>, it will not be forgiven him."

Blasphemy

A closer reading of the Matthew passage shows this incident is not just a case of an unforgiveable sin, but more specifically the sin is an unforgivable *blasphemy* against the Spirit of God (also referred to in the Bible as the Spirit and Holy Spirit). Several questions come to mind. What is blasphemy? How could blasphemy against Jesus (the Son of Man) be forgiven yet blasphemy against the Holy Spirit not be forgiven? Who is Beelzebub and why is the mention of Beelzebub so offensive? What is the big deal?

In *Strong's Concordance* the word blasphemy in Hebrew means contempt (#H5007 *ne'atsah*, from the root word #H5006 – *na'ats* meaning to spurn, despise or abhor). In the Greek (G#988) the word means to slander (a false and damaging statement to one's reputation); to speak injurious to divine majesty or to one's good name. However, it is the Merriam-Webster dictionary's definition that captures its more precise meaning for this incident. It is defined as: the act or offense of speaking sacrilegiously about God or sacred things. In the Old Testament each time the words blasphemy, blasphemes, blaspheming, or blasphemer appear, it is always mentioned in connection with an insult to God (see II Kings 19:22 and Ezekiel 20:26-27). Therefore, based on these applications in the Bible, when one blasphemes, it doesn't appear to be an accidental slip of the tongue. Rather it is an intentional and rebellious comment or action that seems to be a reflection of the individual's belief and therefore, a deliberate statement with the intent to attack, demean and cause insult to the character of God. As mentioned in Chapter 7 of this book, blasphemy is one of the perverse and harmful sins (*awon*/

avon) that defiles the perpetrator and can cause a permanent and eternal break in one's relationship with God. According to *Torah* instructions in Leviticus 24:16, this sin carries the death penalty. Jesus says in Matthew 12:34, "O generation of vipers, how can ye, being evil, speak good things? For out of the abundance of the heart the mouth speaketh."

A story is told in Leviticus 24 of a man who "blasphemed the Name [of God][98] and cursed" (Leviticus 24:11 NASB). So that the people of God's community (the Hebrew nation) would understand the importance of reverence for God, God commanded, "If anyone curses his God, then he will bear his sin. Moreover, the one who blasphemes the name of the Lord shall surely be put to death" (Leviticus 24:15-16 NASB). Shortly thereafter, the man was stoned to death.

Why did Jesus say that a blasphemy against Himself would be forgiven? In the Mark 3:28 KJV account instead of "the Son of Man," it reads "all sins shall be forgiven unto the sons of men...." The possibility should be considered that the almost same words in Matthew may not be translated correctly – meaning that sins committed by men ("the sons of men" - mankind) could be forgiven versus blasphemy against Jesus (the Son of Man) can be forgiven. However, if the statement was about Jesus as the Son of Man, at this point of Jesus' ministry, most of the people in the crowds wondered if Jesus was a prophet of God (Matthew 16:13-14). While a great number of people speculated that He *might be* the Messiah, few would feel comfortable saying it in front of a crowd. Jesus, recognizing that blasphemy is against God, said that any "blasphemy" against Him (the Son of Man) could be forgiven, basically because the person saying it did not know exactly who Jesus truly is. However, blasphemy against the Spirit, (the Holy Spirit/Holy Ghost, the Holy Spirit of God) was another matter.

At this point knowing what the Old Testament says about the Holy Spirit, and the nation of Israel's history with idol worship and Baal (Beelzebub) is helpful.

---

98 The Name of God is viewed the same as God Himself. See Chapter 21 – *No other Name*.

The Holy Spirit

Some Christians may think the Holy Spirit did not appear until Pentecost as recorded in Acts 2:2-3 in fulfillment of Jesus' promise in John 14:16-17. However, the Holy Spirit is referred to often throughout the Hebrew Bible (the Old Testament) in a variety of ways, more specifically as "the Spirit," "the Spirit of God," and "the Spirit of the LORD." A word search of the Old Testament shows the Spirit of God is mentioned as early as Genesis 1:2. We see the promise and the fulfillment of the indwelling of the Spirit in Saul in I Samuel 10:6 and 9 NASB when the Prophet Samuel told the newly anointed King Saul "… the Spirit of the LORD will come upon you mightily, and you shall prophesy with them and be changed into another man. [9] God changed his heart; and all those signs came about on that day." Years later, King David cried out to God in repentance regarding his sin with Bathsheba. In Psalm 51:10-12 NASB David begged, "Create in me a clean heart, O God, and renew a steadfast spirit within me. [11] Do not cast me away from Your presence and do not take Your Holy Spirit from me. [12] Restore to me the joy of Your salvation and sustain me with a willing spirit." The two instances above involving Saul and King David show that people in the Old Testament received salvation, exhibited repentance and the indwelling of the Holy Spirit. (Also see Proverbs 1:23, Isaiah 44:1-5, Isaiah 59:16-21, Ezekiel 36:22-28, and Ezekiel 37:11-14.)

In Judaism *Ruach Ha-Kodesh* (Hebrew for the Holy Spirit) and more specifically the *Ruach* (Spirit) can be translated to mean breath, wind, or some invisible moving force. The *Ruach Ha-Kodesh* generally refers to the divine aspect of prophecy and wisdom. "<u>It also refers to the divine force, quality and influence of the Most High God, over the universe or over His creatures,</u> in given contexts breath, can mean either wind or some invisible moving force."[99] This means that the Spirit of God or the Spirit of the LORD, or Holy Spirit refers to its influence in

---

99 Alan Unterman and Rivka Horowitz, "Ruach ha-Kodesh," Encyclopaedia Judaica (CD-ROM Edition, Jerusalem: Judaica Multimedia/Keter, 1997).

giving prophecy (the writing of scripture – see Mark 12:36, Acts 28:24-26, and II Peter 1:21), and imparting wisdom (as in the books of Job, Psalms, Proverbs and Ecclesiastes). According to the definition cited in the *Encyclopedia Judaica*,[100] the *Ruach Ha-Kodesh* (Holy Spirit) is also the divine creative aspect cited in Genesis 1:2 and Exodus 31:1-5. It is the divine influence or force to: change the universe or creatures as in healing people (Acts 10:38, Hebrews 2:4), to cause resurrection from the dead (Romans 1:4), to discern truth or deception (Luke 1:41, Acts 5:3), and to change minds and hearts for salvation (Romans 8:5-11, Romans 15:18-19, and Titus 3:5).

While Christianity generally identifies the God of the Old Testament as part of the Trinity (God the father, Jesus the Son of God and the Holy Spirit), few Christians seem to know the origins of this belief originated over 250 years <u>after</u> the resurrection, and over 150+ years after the last book of the New Testament was written. It is also generally unknown or acknowledged that this doctrine was never mentioned by any writer of the New Testament. This theory originated in Rome and was adopted by what would become the Catholic Church through the Niceno-Constantinopolitan Creed in 381 AD when there was no longer any Jewish/Hebraic influence or exposition.

Beelzebub and idol worship

Since the accusation that the healing was done by the power of Beelzebub, the next logical question could be who is Beelzebub, the ruler of demons (Matthew 12:24) and why is this name such a big deal? Clearly the text indicates that attributing the miraculous healings of Jesus to this demon was an insult. Beelzebub, Beelzebul, and Baal-zebub are all variations of the same name, though Bible readers will probably recognize only the name of Baal. One must have some sense

---

[100] Ibid.

of the history of Baal and worship of Baal to grasp why this remark evoking the name of Baal would be so offensive and was not a slip of the tongue. In the ancient Near East *Baal* is translated as Lord and *zebub* as flies. Baal-zebub/Beelzebub would mean Lord of flies.

In certain ancient cultures flies or creatures that flew were thought to be related to plagues. This is an astute concept because it shows that some people thought illness came through the air. It is common knowledge today that the cold virus, flu, flea and mosquito-caused illnesses (malaria, the black plague and various deadly fevers) and tuberculous are contracted through airborne "bugs." It is understandable that ancient cultures could perceive these same flying creatures as a deity with power to bring about harm or to punish. Even the Bible shows God has used flying creatures to bring about His desired results. In Exodus 23:28 God said He would use hornets to chase the Hivites, the Canaanites, and the Hittites out of the land. The fourth plague of Egypt was the plague of flies. The Jews generally regarded flies as unclean and felt they had a demonic association. We see that demonic association in the passage covered in this story involving Jesus. To add a twist on the name, as flies are drawn to and seen to hover around excrement, the JewishEncyclopedia.com says: The word "Zebul" (from "zebel," dung) is a cacophonic corruption of "Zebub," to give the name Beelzebub the meaning of "god of the dung."[101]

In the Bible God forbade the Hebrew people from worshipping and serving pagan gods (Exodus 20:3-5). However, they continued to be lured into idol worship and many of the later kings did not tear down the places of pagan worship set in the high places (Leviticus 26:30, Numbers 33:52, I Kings 3:3, II Kings 12:3, and II Kings 17:9). Ever wonder why people were drawn to the Canaanite false gods of Ba'al, Molech, Tammuz, Asherah, Ashtaroth and Inanna/Ishtar (the queen of heaven)? Several of the ancient Middle Eastern cultures believed certain gods had power over storms, rain, fertility, health and death. In addition to these supposed

---

[101] JewishEncyclopedia.com on "Beelzebub."

powers, part of the allure was the role sex played in their worship. To show devotion and entice their gods to grant their requests, increase fertility (for man and their animals) and provide good crop production, the followers participated in animal and human sacrifices, and practiced sexual activities often involving temple prostitutes of both sexes. Bible scriptures provide an indication of this when the Hebrew people were commanded to *not* offer up their daughters and sons to prostitution, nor cause them to become harlots in service to these gods (Exodus 34:16 and Hosea 4:13). It appears that forced prostitution was not the worse part of idol worship. It is impossible to guess how many infants and children were offered as sacrifices to these gods (Molech in II Kings 23:10; Jeremiah 32:35; to Baal in Jeremiah 19:5; 32:35).

Reverence for idols is mentioned as early as the wives of Jacob (Genesis 35:2). Baal worship's connection with sex shows up in the Bible in Numbers 22-25 when Balak, king of Moab afraid of being attacked and destroyed by the passing Hebrew people solicited the prophet Balaam's help to curse them. When Balaam could not curse them, he told Balak to entice them to worship Baal (Number 25:1-5 and 9). The Hebrew people joined in the worship of Baal offering sacrifices and eating and drinking in honor to Baal. The Bible described this event as the Hebrew men went with the women of Moab (who played the harlot) and joined themselves to Baal. Twenty-four thousand Israelites died because of this incident. Years later after the death of Joshua, the Hebrew people would continue their on and off sin of worshipping idols. In Judges 2:11-12 NASB the Hebrew people provoked God with Baal worship.

> [11] Then the sons of Israel did evil in the sight of the LORD and served the Baals, [12] and they forsook the LORD, the God of their fathers, who had brought them out of the land of Egypt, and followed other gods from *among* the gods of the peoples who were around them, and bowed themselves down to them; thus they provoked the LORD to anger.

Several hundreds of years after Joshua, the twelve tribes of the nation of Israel split during the reign of King Solomon's son, Rehoboam. Ten tribes became the Northern Kingdom (Israel) and almost immediately became full-time idol worshippers (they worshipped Baal and Asherah among other Near Eastern gods). I Kings 16:31 tells of Israel's Northern Kingdom King Ahab marrying Jezebel and instituting Baal worship. It was against the wide scale Baal worship that the prophet Elijah proclaimed a three-year period of no rain. Three years later in I Kings 18:21 NASB we read that Elijah came near to all the people and said, "How long *will* you hesitate between two opinions? If the LORD is God, follow Him; but if Baal, follow him." The people did not answer him. On Mount Carmel that day there was a jaw-dropping demonstration of who is the one and only God, and the people ended up on their knees proclaiming, "The LORD, he is God!"

Later in II Kings 1 King Ahaziah of Israel had a bad fall and sent his messengers to inquire of <u>Baal-zebub</u>, the god of Ekron about his chances for recovery. The LORD sent the prophet Elijah to intercept them with this message "Is it because there is no God in Israel you are going to inquire of Baal-zebub, the god of Ekron?" The prophet Elijah tells them in verse 4 (NASB): Now therefore thus says the LORD, 'You shall not come down from the bed where you have gone up, but you shall surely die.' The prophecy proved true; the King did indeed die according to the word of the LORD.

Prophet after prophet warned the people of God's coming punishment if they would not stop idol worship.[102] Yet they would not reject Baal (or the other gods) and return with a whole heart to God. After nearly 200 years, the Northern Kingdom was taken into captivity by the Assyrians. They would later be referred to as the Ten Lost Tribes of Israel. Their sin of idol worship was the main reason for their exile to Assyria. The Southern Kingdom was not much better. The tribes of

---

102 Idolatry is the worship of a man-made idol or a physical object that represents a specific god.

Judah and Benjamin comprised the Southern Kingdom (Judah) after the split under King Rehoboam the son of King Solomon. They would go back and forth in faithfulness to God or idol worship depending on who was king at the time. Then certain kings brought this behavior to the temple grounds establishing temples for these false gods next to God's holy temple. However, it was King Manasseh, son of King Hezekiah who exceeded all the other kings when he had the idol worship brought <u>into</u> the temple of God.

> [4] And <u>he built altars in the house of the Lord</u>, of which the Lord said, In Jerusalem will I put my name. [5] And <u>he built altars for all the host of heaven in the two courts of the house of the Lord</u>. [6] And <u>he made his son pass through the fire</u>, and observed times, and used enchantments, and dealt with familiar spirits and wizards: he wrought much wickedness in the sight of the Lord, to provoke him to anger. [7] And he set a graven image of the grove that he had made in the house, of which the Lord said to David, and to Solomon his son, In this house, and in Jerusalem, which I have chosen out of all tribes of Israel, will I put my name for ever... <u>Manasseh seduced them to do more evil</u> than did the nations whom the Lord destroyed before the children of Israel.
>
> 2 Kings 21:4-9 NASB

The Southern Kingdom lasted about 350 years. Because of their continued detestable practices, through the prophet Jeremiah, God told of their coming defeat and seventy-year long exile to Babylon. It seems only after this exile were the Jewish people finally freed of worshipping other gods.

> [4] Because they have forsaken Me and have made this an alien place and have burned sacrifices in it to other gods, that neither they nor their forefathers nor the kings of Judah had *ever* known, and

because they have <u>filled this place with the blood of the innocent</u> (infants and children) ⁵ and have built the high places of Baal <u>to burn their sons in the fire as burnt offerings to Baal</u>, a thing which I never commanded or spoke of, nor did it *ever* enter My mind;⁶ therefore, behold, days are coming," declares the LORD, "when this place will no longer be called Topheth or the valley of Ben-hinnom, but rather the valley of Slaughter.

Jeremiah 19:4-6 NASB

The first two commandments of the Ten Commandments are to have no other gods nor make any idol or worship or serve them (Exodus 20:3-5). This was and is a very big deal with God. Throughout Israel's long history, their two consistent problems were disobedience to God and forsaking God for other gods (which is disobedience to God's first commandment). However, the seriousness of this command goes beyond the God of the Bible wanting His people to remain faithful to Him and connects directly to the central point of this story. Since there is only One God,[103] when people believe in, serve and worship false gods, not only have they denied the only true God, in reality, they are worshipping Satan, who according to the Bible, is quite real (see I Chronicles 21:1, Job 1:6, Zechariah 3:1, Matthew 4:10, Luke 10:18, and 13:16).

<u>Who is Satan and what does he want?</u>

Satan is referred to in the Bible as the devil, the Serpent, and Lucifer. It is generally thought that Ezekiel 28:13-20 and Isaiah 14:12-15 speak of Satan. These verses say Satan was perfect from the day he was created by God, but he became corrupted by his own beauty (Ezekiel 28:15).

---

[103] Isaiah 45:5 NASB says, "I am the LORD, and there is no other; Besides Me there is no God." Also see Deuteronomy 4:35, 4:39, Isaiah 45:21-22, 46:9, and Joel 2:27.

At some point, Satan was tossed out of heaven (Ezekiel 28:17). The verses confirm that Satan was in the Garden of Eden (Ezekiel 28:13), and on Mount Horeb presumably during the giving of the commandments (Ezekiel 28:14 and 16). Isaiah 14:13-14 says that Satan wants to ascend to heaven to be like the Most High God. God says that through Satan the world has been made as a wilderness; that he has destroyed the cities (Isaiah 14:17), defiled sanctuaries by sin (Ezekiel 28:18), and through people has filled the earth with violence (Ezekiel 28:16). Yet God says He will cast him to the ground, lay him before kings that they may behold him (Ezekiel 28:17). God says He will destroy Satan by fire (Ezekiel 28:16) that will devour him and bring him to ashes upon the earth (Ezekiel 28:18).

Jesus said of Satan that He saw him fall to earth (Luke 10:18), that he is a liar, a thief and a murderer from the beginning. He also said that when people do the deeds of Satan they are his children and Satan, their father (John 8:44).

It can be easy to think that Satan is the arch enemy of God and that the true battle between God and Satan is for the souls of mankind. However, this is not true. (Discussed in Chapter 7 of this book) First, Satan is not comparable to God; they are not equal adversaries. God is incomparable, unmatchable, unbeatable. Satan and God's goals are very different. While God wants a personal, connected relationship with each person because He created all life and loves everyone beyond our comprehension (John 3:16, Ezekiel 18:3), Satan does not want people to know, serve or worship him, (i.e. devil worshippers). Satan wants people kept dead spiritually (unsaved), or dead physically (John 8:44 and 10:10), and he wants to diminish, subvert and destroy the believer and their effectiveness for God. Satan's most damaging tactic is he strives to deceive mankind by besmirching (to soil and damage) God, His character and identity by lying, denying His existence, causing confusion and division. As in the story of the Garden of Eden (Genesis 3:4-5), Satan questioned Eve causing her to doubt the meaning of God's words. Then he implied and characterized God as harsh, cruel, selfish and lacking compassion. While some Christians think God requires death for sacrificial sin atonement, this is another lie of Satan that God cannot forgive people without the death of an animal or Jesus. God – who is love, is the source of creation, and everything that is good. He is the Creator of life and the Giver of eternal life. Satan is the deceiver, the liar, thief and murderer from the beginning. (See I John 4:8, James 1:17, Psalm 89:47, John 10:28, and 10:10.)

Satan disguises himself and his motives (II Corinthians 11:14). He causes delusions and confusion, and he accuses, entices and tempts people. People have the power to reject and refuse to participate in Satan's tactics, and to flee. There are things people do that encourages Satan's participation in their lives (altering their inhibitions by using drugs or alcohol, pursuing the occult, doing what they know to be wrong, being rebellious). However, Satan is restricted in what he can do regarding believers and followers of God. In Job 1:10, Satan says that God has a hedge of protection around His children; Satan had to seek permission to cause restricted harm to Job. And hours before His arrest, Jesus tells Peter that Satan asked to sift him like flour (Luke 22:31). The bottom line is Satan has no power of his own. He tricks, deceives, lies and tempts people and is amazingly effective – <u>but the only power given to him is given by people</u>. God's people are warned to be prepared for the antics of Satan. The Bible reveals Satan's most effective tricks, and how to overcome them. Again, Satan is limited in what he can do to God's people if they do not give Satan power through their deliberate or ignorant-based (Hosea 4:6) disobedience to God's instructions.

While Satan has no real power of his own, this does not mean there is no ongoing battle. The battle is for salvation of the unsaved and unbelieving people of the world and keeping those who are saved as ineffective as possible. (What makes a believer ineffective? Not knowing the truth about God and His Word, and the damage and snare of sin.) Part of the conversation of this story of the unforgiveable sin in

Luke 11:23 NASB, Jesus says, "He who is not with Me is against Me; and he who does not gather with Me, scatters." Jesus was warning the blasphemers that not only were they siding *against* God, but whether they knew it or not, they were hindering the work of God and advancing the goals of Satan. In addition, when people forsake the God of the Bible and deny Him, they are not only a danger to themselves; they are a danger to others around them. Look at the examples cited here of Israel's history; the damage of idol worship and belief in a false god was never isolated or restricted to one person but spread like a plague infecting thousands of others with detrimental consequences.

One might ask how are Beelzebub and Satan connected? Jesus knew they were one in the same. While those in question used the name Beelzebub, Jesus responds explaining about Satan. Note these verses again from this story in Matthew 12:24-26 NASB:

²⁴ But when the Pharisees heard this, they said, "This man casts out demons only by Beelzebub the ruler of the demons."

²⁵ And knowing their thoughts Jesus said to them, "Any kingdom divided against itself is laid waste; and any city or house divided against itself will not stand. ²⁶ <u>If Satan casts out Satan</u>, he is divided against himself; how then will his kingdom stand?

A variation of the name of Baal recognizes Baal as the head or master of the household. Jesus' parables involved a strong man's house, a house divided, and their connection to Satan. Jesus explains a house divided cannot stand. In other words, there is no advantage to Satan acting in opposition to his own self. Meaning, there is no advantage to Satan causing healing when he works to destroy. His parable of a strong man (Satan) protecting his possessions, then being overpowered and rendered helpless by one stronger (Jesus) shows that Satan is powerless against the power of Jesus/God. Jesus reveals an important piece of information here: the family home is a battlefield for Satan unless the family has protected themselves by their relationship with the God of the Bible.

The Insult and blasphemy

While it is understandable now why the very mention of Baal was so insulting, this still has not addressed what was so horrible about the blasphemy against the Spirit and exactly what was the blasphemy? The statement that unlocks the mystery goes almost unrecognized in the magnitude of its meaning. While Matthew 12:28 NIV says, "But if it is <u>by the Spirit of God</u> that I drive out demons, <u>then the kingdom of God has come upon you.</u>" Luke 11:20 NIV says something a little different – "But if I drive out demons <u>by the finger of God</u>, then the kingdom of God has come upon you." What is so significant about this? First, the kingdom of God or kingdom of heaven means the rule, domain, the power, and <u>the presence of God</u>. How was that determination made? In upholding the sacredness of the name of God, Jews would refer to the Kingdom of God as the Kingdom of Heaven. The word kingdom is *malkuwth* in Hebrew (#4438 in *Strong's Concordance* as used in I Chronicles 22:10) means royal power, dominion, reign, realm and sovereign power. A kingdom is the place where the king rules, has complete power and <u>is present</u>. (How can you have an all-powerful king in complete charge of the kingdom and the king *not* be there?) When you look at the many verses that speak of what the Kingdom of God/heaven is or is like, they speak to the rule, or power or presence of God.

As stated earlier, the term the "Spirit of God" can refer to the divine force and influence of God over the universe or creatures (see Genesis 1:2, Exodus 35:21, and Judges 14:6 to name a few). What Jesus is saying here is that if this miracle and the other miracles were done by the finger (i.e. hand) and divine power of God, <u>then God is present in front of you</u>! Being humble, Jesus would not say, "I, as God am here in front of you"; rather He would say "the kingdom of God has come upon you." This explains the distinction made in the comment in Matthew 12:32 NASB when Jesus says, "Whoever speaks a word against the Son of Man, it shall be forgiven him; but whoever speaks against the Holy Spirit, it shall not be forgiven him...." While the people there that day may not have been sure of who Jesus (or the Son of Man) was, the miracles they had just witnessed was evidence of the presence of the power of God (the Holy Spirit- John 5:36). So, while a slanderous comment against someone of whom you are not sure of *may* be forgivable, the same odious comment in the midst of evidence of the presence and power of God enters into a whole different category.

Are we now grasping what was so terrible about the Beelzebub comment? Their comment was an insult directly to God and would have eternal consequences for them on the Day of Judgment. In this same conversation Jesus told them they would have to give an account of their careless words on the Day of Judgment and that they would be either justified or condemned by their words (Matthew 12:36-37). Can we see a connection between those people whose names are not written in the Book of Life being held accountable (justified or condemned) for their words on the Day of Judgment (Revelation 20:12-13)?

In the presence of crowds of people, Jesus was healing the sick, blind, deaf, the crippled and demon possessed. Isaiah 35:5-6 NASB says that by <u>God</u> "the eyes of the blind will be opened and the ears of the deaf will be unstopped. Then the lame will leap like a deer, and the tongue of the mute will shout for joy." Psalm 103:3 says <u>God</u> heals all our diseases, and Jeremiah 33:6 NASB says <u>God</u> will "bring to it (Israel) health and healing, and I will heal them; and I will reveal to them an abundance of peace and truth." The people present *knew* that the prophets had said God was the One who healed, therefore their response as recorded in Matthew 12:23 NIV: All the people were astonished and said, "Could this be the Son of David?"[104] The Son of

---

104 The people generally understood that the Messiah would be the "Son of David" in fulfillment of the prophecy given to King David in II Samuel 7:8-17.

Beelzebub & The Sin Not Forgiven

David is another way of asking "Could this be the Messiah – the Son of God?" Verse 24 says, But when the Pharisees and scribes heard the others calling Jesus by a name for the promised Messiah, they *denied* His true identity and attributed His miraculous power to the prince of demons. "It is <u>only</u> by Beelzebub, the prince of demons that this fellow drives out demons." When miracles occur by the divine power of God that scriptures said would be done <u>only</u> by God and are attributed instead to Satan "<u>only</u> by Beelzebub, the prince of demons" (NASB) – a false god who has been the downfall and death of millions of people, a demon, the "prince of demons" – Satan, a lord of flies, a lord of *dung* then this is blasphemy of the worse kind!

Our God is a forgiving God. Are there sins that can be deemed as unforgiveable? The answer is yes. Actually, there are two unforgivable sins. One is the sin of unbelief. The other is when someone professes to love and follow God, yet deliberately and knowingly ignores and breaks God's commandments. This incident involving the name of Beelzebub was a combination of the two: those who professed to know and serve God, yet in their unbelief claimed the miracles were produced by the power of Beelzebub. This was the sin of unbelief spoken with a deliberate insult. How did Jesus respond? Did He slay them where they stood? No. Did He strike them with illness? No. In His great love, mercy and compassion He issued them the sternest warning possible – that they were in jeopardy of the unpardonable sin! Did Jesus say anything new or different from what is written in *Torah*? No.

> [30] "'But anyone who sins defiantly, whether native-born or foreigner, <u>blasphemes</u> the LORD and must be cut off from the people of Israel. [31] Because they have despised the LORD's word and broken his commands, they must surely be cut off; their guilt remains on them.'"
>
> *Numbers 15: 30-31 NIV*

CHAPTER 14

Teach Us to Pray

...The prayer of a righteous person is powerful and effective.
James 5:16 NIV

Prayer is not a conversation between us and God. When we pray, we are communicating with God; making requests. When God responds, He is not praying to or with us. Prayers can be as emotional as a heartfelt thanksgiving or a scream for help; as sacred as a plea for mercy and forgiveness, or just a whispered statement expressing our joy, fear, heartbreak, confusion or desolation to God. Does God hear all prayers? Yes, He does. Jesus said in Matthew 10:30 NASB "the very hairs of your head are all numbered," and in Matthew 6:8 NASB, "for your Father knows what you need before you ask him." If God knows all the hairs on our heads and what we need before we ask, then surely God hears all our prayers.

Some would interject that the Bible says God does not hear certain people – certain prayers. Isaiah 59:2 NASB says, "But your iniquities have separated you from your God; your sins have hidden his face from you, so that he will not hear." God even says in Isaiah 1:15 NASB, "So when you spread out your hands in prayer, I will hide My eyes from you; Yes, even though you multiply prayers, I will not listen (listen does not mean God did not hear the prayers). Your hands are covered with blood." These verses convey a specific point more than a reality. As discussed in Chapter 7 of this "Behold" book, Isaiah 59:2 speaks to those who have done evil acts, *then* offered sacrifices and prayers without repentance. These scriptures show God is not fooled, nor does He participate in mankind's duplicity. He covers His eyes (not actually) and does not hear their prayers (respond variably) until they have a change of heart and repent. Does Jesus say anything along these lines? Yes, in Matthew 5:23-24 NASB Jesus says, "…if you are presenting your offering at the altar, and there remember that your brother has something against you, [24] leave your offering there before the altar and go; first be reconciled to your brother, and then come and present your offering." In other words, don't come to ask God to bless your business at work, when you cannot make peace with your brother.

In speaking of prayer, it is interesting to note that the Jewish people have a prayer book called the *Siddur*. This prayer book contains a set order of prayers; with prayers for nearly all occasions. Some of the prayers trace back to the time of the writing of the book of Deuteronomy and their usage continue even today. After several of the miracles recorded in the gospels, scripture says the people glorified God. More than likely the people spoke or chanted some of the specific praise prayers listed in the *Siddur* (for example, see Matthew 9:8, 15:31, Luke 6:26 and 7:16). While the Bible contains many prayers of all types that are worthy of study, this chapter will focus on what Jesus said about praying. Here are the principle points and verses of what He said regarding prayer both at the Sermon on the Mount and at other times during His ministry.

1. **Do not pray for the benefit of others seeing you pray. Be humble when you come before God.** In Matthew 6:5-6 NASB Jesus says, "When you pray, do not be like the hypocrites, for they love to pray standing in the synagogues and on the street corners to be seen by others. Truly I tell you, they have received their reward in full. But when you pray, go into

your room, close the door and pray to your Father, who is unseen. Then your Father, who sees what is done in secret, will reward[105] you."

The point is when we are talking to God, our conversation should be private. Jesus said the hypocrite <u>loved to be seen</u> praying in public. Does this mean do not pray in public? No, but it does mean examine our motivation when praying publicly. Jesus illustrated another principle about humility in prayer when He told this parable of two men praying in Luke 18:9-14 NASB in the Temple.

> [9] And He also told this parable to some people who trusted in themselves that they were righteous and viewed others with contempt: [10] "Two men went up into the temple to pray, one a Pharisee and the other a tax collector. [11] The Pharisee stood and was praying this to himself: 'God, I thank You that I am not like other people: swindlers, unjust, adulterers, or even like this tax collector. [12] I fast twice a week; I pay tithes of all that I get.' [13] But the tax collector, standing some distance away, was even unwilling to lift up his eyes to heaven, but was beating his breast, saying, 'God, be merciful to me, the sinner!'
>
> [14] I tell you, this man went to his house justified rather than the other; for everyone who exalts himself will be humbled, but he who humbles himself will be exalted."

These verses tell us it is better to come before God in humility with the awareness that our perception of ourselves and/or the situation may be wrong or limited. God does not need a commercial from us about how

---

105 The word "reward" in Greek means that which are wages or what is due when hired for work or a reward bestowed for good or evil deeds. In this context, God rewards people when their charitable deeds (tithes), fasting, and prayers are earnest and private. See Matthew 6:1-6.

great we are. Rather we come before God because of how great God is and because we need God's help, His mercy, wisdom and discernment.

2. **Keep it simple** – Jesus in Matthew 6:7 NIV says, "And when you pray, do not keep on babbling like pagans, for they think they will be heard because of their many words." Ecclesiastes 5:2 NIV says, Do not be quick with your mouth, do not be hasty in your heart to utter anything before God. God is in heaven and you are on earth, so let your words be few.
3. **Pray for what you need**. Matthew 6:8 NIV says, "… for your Father knows what you need before you ask him."

When the Hebrew nation spent 40 years in the desert before entering the Promised Land, they grasped what was essential in life. Our true needs and that of others are basic: health, shelter, sustenance to maintain life, protection, spiritual wisdom and discernment to know what is right and the God-given courage to be obedient. Does this mean we should not pray for someone in trouble or something we have misplaced, lost or just want? No, the Bible says to cast our cares on the Lord for He cares for us. None of our problems are too big or too small for God's help. Years ago, our TV remote control disappeared somewhere in the house (or trash). After searching for several days, I asked God to forgive me for asking Him to help me find the remote my husband kept fussing about, but I needed help. Within the hour, I found the old VCR remote control missing for several years and seconds later I found the remote I'd prayed for! I was reminded no problem is too small for God and with Him nothing is lost. God knows where everything is, even the things we have hidden away and forgotten.

4. **Believe that your request is within God's Will and your prayer will be answered.** In Mark 11:24 NASB Jesus says, "Therefore I say to you, all things for which you pray and ask, believe that you have received them, and they will be granted you." James

1:6-8 NASB says, "But he must ask in faith without any doubting, for the one who doubts is like the surf of the sea, driven and tossed by the wind. ⁷ For that man ought not to expect that he will receive anything from the Lord, ⁸ *being* a double-minded man, unstable in all his ways." James goes on to explain why some prayers are not answered. James 4:3 NASB says, "You ask and do not receive, because you ask with wrong motives, so that you may spend *it* on your pleasures."

God is not our fairy Godfather, where He grants our every wish just because we really believe. God says in Isaiah 55:8 NASB, "For My thoughts are not your thoughts, nor are your ways My ways," declares the Lord. We must acknowledge that "No" is sometimes the best answer; and even when "Yes" is the answer, it may be years, or decades before we see the fulfillment; which leads us to the next two points.

5. **Asking in the name of Jesus.** Many prayers are ended with this phrase, probably because John 14:13-14 KJV says: "And whatsoever ye shall ask in my name, that will I do, that the Father may be glorified in the Son. ¹⁴ If ye shall ask any thing in my name, I will do it."

This extraordinary statement borders on blasphemy **if** Jesus isn't God. Several times in the Old Testament God speaks of the power, authority and His presence associated with His Name (see Exodus 9:16, Leviticus 19:12, Numbers 6:27, and I Kings 9:3). Jesus said the same power and authority as God is in His own name! In making this statement Jesus said that to those who love Him and understand who He is this power is available to glorify God (see Chapter 21 of this book – *No other Name*). However, the words "in the name of Jesus" is not a magical phrase to tack on to the end of prayer requests to coerce God to give us what we want. Rather Jesus was telling His followers that when they have formed their prayer requests with the awareness of who God is, what God's desire is for everyone, recalling the LORD's perfect knowledge and wisdom, then proclaiming their trust in the LORD, they will find that whatever they ask in His powerful name will be granted. The next point is similar:

6. **God's will be done.** Matthew 6:10 of the Lord's prayers says, "Thy kingdom come, Thy will be done in earth, as it is in heaven."

This phrase is similar to praying "in the name of Jesus." It is not a mystical incantation spoken to gain a guarantee that one's prayers are heard and will be answered. Rather it is a declaration of yielding, trusting, and accepting God's choice. We acknowledge that God's ways and thoughts are not our ways and the way we think things should be done. When there is trust in the goodness and love of God to resolve outcomes beyond our understanding (Proverbs 3:5-6 and Romans 8:28), we can be at peace when we pray and ask for God's will.

During several intensive moments of King David's life, he showed he understood this principle of accepting the will of God because he knew he could trust in God's timing, His love, goodness and mercy. The first instance involved King Saul in his attempts to kill David. On two occasions David had the opportunity to kill Saul, yet he refused because he respected that Saul was God's anointed (I Samuel 24:6 and 10). David trusted in God's timing to fulfill His promise to make David the next King of Israel.

On two other occasions, David showed his trust in God's mercy and will. King David sinned when he insisted on counting the fighting men of his country. God told David to select the punishment for his sin – seven years of famine, or three months of pursuit by his enemies, or three days of pestilence (II Samuel 24:10-14). He chose the last option because he trusted God would be merciful. The other incident happened after David committed adultery with Bathsheba, the wife of one of his loyal soldiers, Uriah. After finding out Bathsheba was pregnant with his child, David attempted to cover his deed by arranging the death of Uriah in battle, then marrying Bathsheba (II Samuel 11-12).

Later the priest Nathan confronted David and told him the child would die as part of the consequences for his sin. David fasted, and prostrated himself. Then upon hearing of the child's death, he arose, washed, went to worship God, and resumed eating. When asked about his behavior, David said, "While the child was *still* alive, I fasted and wept; for I said, 'Who knows, the LORD may be gracious to me, that the child may live' (II Samuel 12:16-22 NASB). David not only knew and trusted in God's great mercy and compassion but He accepted God's will even in the death of his son. David went on to reveal just how much he knew of the mercy of God and the gift of eternal life with God when he said of his deceased son, "…I will go to him, but he will not return to me" (II Samuel 12:23 NASB).

It is Jesus' sentence in the Lord's Prayer that elevates God's will to its true status as our best choice and reveals its significance as supreme power – "*Your kingdom* come. *Your Will* be done on earth as it is in Heaven." Here we are reminded that in God's kingdom in heaven His Will is *always* done instantly and unhesitatingly. We cannot see all the good that God's Will produces across this earth until God's Will is done on Earth as it is in heaven. <u>Therefore, our prayers are most effective when they reflect our understanding of who God is, His nature, and what He desires for mankind.</u> We are unable to fully trust, believe and yearn for the Will of God to be done or trust Him in the heartbreaking events of our lives, until we reached the understanding that God is perfect in all of His ways (Deuteronomy 32:4) and that nothing can happen apart from what God can use to bring about His greater good and glory (Romans 8:28).

In the Jewish culture at the time of the New Testament there were specific prayers prayed each morning, afternoon and evening. It was not unusual for a person to ask a popular rabbi or teacher to compose or adapt a prayer. We can then understand why the disciples in the book of Luke (11:2-4) asked Jesus to teach them how to pray "just as John also taught his disciples." The prayer He taught them is almost identical to the one that appears in Matthew 6:9-13 during the Sermon on the Mount. After the discussion of the "right and wrong" aspects of prayer, Jesus said to pray in this way:

> Our Father which art in heaven, Hallowed be thy name.
> [10] Thy kingdom come, Thy will be done in earth, as it is in heaven.
> [11] Give us this day our daily bread.
> [12] And forgive us our debts, as we forgive our debtors.
> [13] And lead us not into temptation, but deliver us from evil:
> [For thine is the kingdom, and the power, and the glory, forever. Amen.][106]
>
> *Matthew 6:9-13 KJV*

As this prayer is examined, we notice it begins with recognition that God is our Heavenly Father. That God, His Name, His Character is holy and special. Next, God's rule, reign and instructions should be acknowledged and obeyed among all mankind on earth as it is in heaven. The prayer addresses our need for food each day, then addresses two main spiritual problems – how we relate with others and with God (our temptation to sin and the need to forgive and to be forgiven). The prayer closes with the acknowledgement of who God is – that everything belongs to an all-powerful God, who is worthy of all the glory forever. Does this prayer follow the guidelines Jesus gave about praying - a simple prayer, request your needs and that of others, a clean slate of forgiveness, power over temptation, acknowledging your belief that God hears you by how you addressed Him and He worded the request in six sentences? Most definitely, this prayer met the criteria Jesus spoke of about prayer.

After this same prayer appeared in Luke, Jesus told the disciples the parable that follows (Luke 11:5-13 NIV) of a neighbor in need of bread for his guests. The point of this parable was to show we can

---

[106] Some early manuscripts of Matthew do not include this last line.

depend on God to help us in time of need just as one would expect assistance from a parent or a friend.

> ⁵ Then Jesus said to them, "Suppose you have a friend, and you go to him at midnight and say, 'Friend, lend me three loaves of bread; ⁶ a friend of mine on a journey has come to me, and I have no food to offer him.' ⁷ And suppose the one inside answers, 'Don't bother me. The door is already locked, and my children and I are in bed. I can't get up and give you anything.' ⁸ I tell you, even though he will not get up and give you the bread because of friendship, yet because of your shameless audacity he will surely get up and give you as much as you need.
>
> ⁹ "So I say to you: Ask and it will be given to you; seek and you will find; knock and the door will be opened to you. ¹⁰ For everyone who asks receives; the one who seeks finds; and to the one who knocks, the door will be opened.
>
> ¹¹ "Which of you fathers, if your son asks for a fish, will give him a snake instead? ¹² Or if he asks for an egg, will give him a scorpion? ¹³ If you then, though you are evil, know how to give good gifts to your children, how much more will your Father in heaven give the Holy Spirit to those who ask him!"

Jesus' audience would have been perplexed by the parable of the friend requesting bread. It was and still is a part of the Middle Eastern culture to provide provisions to a stranger or guest. There certainly would have been no hesitation to give a friend the bread requested. They likely would have offered wine, fruit or any other food products available without request. Jesus told this parable to illustrate how deeply we misunderstand God to think we must beg and plead with God for our basic needs. Jesus tells us it is as simple as asking, seeking and requesting like a knock on the door. He further makes His point by telling us that if we in all our flawed humanity know how to provide and care for our own children and give them good gifts why would we think we have to beg God to treat us fairly or to provide for our basic needs to sustain life or think that harmful things are from God?

As this chapter on prayer concludes there are still some important points worth mentioning. Below are some excerpts of prayers in the epistles written to believers at Ephesus, Philippi, Colossi and Thessalonica. Being aware of new believers' need for ongoing growth in their knowledge of and relationship with God, notice the common theme in these prayers for wisdom, knowledge, understanding, and discernment. When the focus of prayer is God's will, we can indeed pray with confidence and assurance that God will answer our prayers.

Ephesians 1:17-19 NASB "… that the God of our Lord Jesus Christ, the Father of glory, may give to you a spirit of wisdom and of revelation in the knowledge of Him. *I pray that* the eyes of your heart may be enlightened, so that you will know what is the hope of His calling, what are the riches of the glory of His inheritance in the saints, and what is the surpassing greatness of His power toward us who believe.

Philippians 1:9-10 NASB And this I pray, that your love may abound still more and more in real knowledge and all discernment, so that you may approve the things that are excellent, in order to be sincere and blameless until the day of Christ;

Philippians 4:5-7 NASB Let your gentle *spirit* be known to all men. The Lord is near. Be anxious for nothing, but in everything by prayer and supplication with thanksgiving let your requests be made known to God. And the peace of God, which surpasses all comprehension, will guard your hearts and your minds in Christ Jesus.

Colossians 1:9-12 NASB For this reason also, since the day we heard *of it*, we have not ceased to pray for you and to ask that you may be filled with the knowledge of His will in all spiritual wisdom and understanding, so that you will walk in a manner worthy of the Lord, to please *Him* in all respects, bearing fruit in every good work and increasing in the knowledge of God; strengthened with all power, according to His glorious might, for the attaining of all steadfastness and patience; joyously giving thanks to the Father, who has qualified us to share in the inheritance of the saints in Light.

I Thessalonians 5:16-18 NASB Rejoice always; pray without ceasing; in everything give thanks; for this is God's will for you in Christ Jesus.

2 Thessalonians 3:1 NASB Finally, brethren, pray for us that the word of the Lord will spread rapidly and be glorified, just as it did also with you;

First, it is important to point out that these prayers were for the benefit of someone else. In addition, at the time these letters were written the church was in its infancy and the followers of Christ were facing persecution for their beliefs. Some followers were arrested (sometimes facing death), imprisoned, beaten, facing the loss of homes, jobs, separation from families, and being exiled from the synagogue/temple for acknowledging their beliefs (Acts 8:1, 3, 9:1-2, Acts 7:54-59 and John 12:42). Notice the prayers do not mention the persecution aspect. God is not asked to stop the persecution, nor remove them from danger. Many times, our prayers are asking God to get us or our loved ones out of a specific situation, when the request should be to ask God to grant us (and our loved ones) knowledge, strength, wisdom and discernment while we are *in* the situation. Perhaps this is when we grow the most and see the hand of God best when we experience His grace in our lives as we are strengthened by God and gain wisdom and understanding to endure our trouble and adversity and later see the glory that resulted.

The prolific and revered *Torah* scholar and philosopher Rabbi Maimonides complied the list of 613 commandments found in *Torah*. Yet, the command to pray is not one of them. However, Talmud[107] says the command to serve God (Exodus 23:25 and Deuteronomy 6:13) is the same as a command to pray. Could this mean that when we do what we can to help others (protect, feed, clothe, teach, and care for the sick/poor/the elderly), then pray for them, we are serving God, we are doing the will of God that Jesus spoke of in Matthew 6:6 and this is what brings the reward from God?

Jesus was asked to identify the most important commandment. He answered it is to love God with all our heart, mind, strength and soul and to love our neighbor as ourselves. Before we utter our first words in prayer for someone or for ourselves, we should consider what is truly needed, acknowledge that we may have a limited perception of the situation and be willing to accept God's Will. Our most effective prayers are answered when we love God with everything within us and treat fellow human beings and all other life with respect and honor, because then our prayers are in alignment with God's will.

---

[107] Talmud contains both Mishnah (the written form of the Oral *Torah* of oral traditions dating back to the time of Moses) and Gemara (added rabbinical commentary or discussions of Mishnah).

This interlude describes what the experience of writing this book has been for me.

CHAPTER 15

My Secret Stream of Life

I discovered the Wonderful Stream of Life hidden in Paradise. I slip away with my small cup and begin the crawl to get to Paradise. Why do I crawl? The worries, chores, responsibilities, problems, and duties will see me trying to get away. They reach out, entangling me, holding me captive. "Just for a moment, please. It'll only take a minute," I beg. And I am caught back up in this world of obligations, exercising, fixing things, talking to this one or that one. And the Stream in Paradise is further way than before.

So early in the morning, or late at night or any other time I can, I turn and look – stealing away, crawling through my own thoughts, plans, carrying my precious cup. Soon I am past the things that grab hold of me. I hear His Laughter, sense His Presence and I am thrilled. Suddenly I am there – where everything is more beautiful than I could have dreamed or imagined. I tremble with joy. I can't wait to taste the Goodness of Him. I dip my little cup into the whispering Stream in Paradise. I can hardly get the cup to my mouth fast enough. I taste the Life-giving liquid. He fills my heart, my being, my lungs, even my eyes leak with the glory of Him! I am intoxicated in His Presence by Him! His Words of Love and Soothing Touch heal me and I sing the Song of Life. The Lyrics come from knowing and loving the Creator of All things.

But all too soon, the phone rings, someone asks a question and I am back here in an instant. It does not take long before I am seeking to go back to the Sacred Secret Stream in Paradise to be with the One who gives Living Water. I crave Him. The longer I am away, the more I need Him. But if I am not careful, I will get used to doing without Him. I can stand on my own weak, aching, clumsy feet. The colors are dimmer, my eyes are filmy. I have no song. I am hungry all the time, but no food satisfies my need. Then I remember what it was like… when I try really hard, I can close my eyes and sometimes I get a hint of His Presence, and I want to go back.

One day, when this life draws to a close, I will stand with the legs of youth, I will run with the speed of an Olympic runner, and dance with the grace of a ballerina. And I will see the beauty of all that is around me glowing with rainbows of glorious color. I will hear the voices of heaven's saints and angels singing the praises of My Love! And I will drink my fill of the Living Water forever!

> *Nevertheless I am continually with You;*
> *You have taken hold of my right hand.*
> *With Your counsel You will guide me,*
> *And afterward receive me to glory.*
> *Whom have I in heaven but You?*
> *And besides You, I desire nothing on earth.*
> *My flesh and my heart may fail,*
> *But God is the strength of my heart and my portion forever.*
> *Psalm 73:23-26 NIV*

CHAPTER 16

More than Bread – The Feeding of the 5,000

The headlines of a newspaper of the time could have read, "Free food feeds thousands! Unlimited fish and bread prepared to perfection by Jesus!" The amazing story of the feeding of the 5,000+ is in Matthew 14, Mark 6, Luke 9 and John 6. One could read this story and think this is about an incredible miracle where Jesus supplied food for hungry people. However, this story has little to do with feeding a few thousand people who would be hungry again the next day. Throughout Jesus' ministry, He kept making the same point again and again about mankind's need for God and revealing who He, Himself is. This story has everything to do with fulfilling something in us that we can spend a lifetime searching for. People speak of "finding themselves," searching for purpose in their lives, "looking to make a difference" for someone. At the heart of the soul of most people is a desire to find meaning in life and be at peace with themselves. Jesus echoes what God and the Bible has told us all along: there is only one thing that will fulfill us and satisfy our hunger and thirst.

Although there are differences in the four gospel books about what happened prior to this miracle, there are enough similarities that we can surmise this is the telling of the same event. In Matthew and Mark's accounts the miraculous feeding took place shortly after the brutal execution of John the Baptist. John and Jesus were related by their mothers Elizabeth and Mary (Luke 1:36) and linked by connecting spiritual missions. John's birth had been foretold by the very same angel who visited Jesus' mother, Mary. Before John's conception, Luke 1:17 linked John's mission to the prophecy in Malachi 4:4-5 saying an Elijah type prophet would turn the hearts of children and fathers back to one another. Mark 1:4 says that John preached the baptism of repentance for the remission of sins (thereby turning hearts back to loved ones). Isaiah 40:3 prophesied the coming of one crying in the wilderness prepare the way for the LORD when the glory of the LORD would be revealed.[108] In John 1:23 (Matthew 3:3 and Mark 1:3) John the Baptist acknowledged this was his mission to prepare the way for the [coming of the] LORD. But now John was dead. The book of John indicates the feeding of 5,000 people happened near Passover, which was probably one year before the cross (see John 2:13, John 6:4, John 13:1 for notations of Passover). How much did John's murder and the approaching last Passover before the cross factor into the timing of this miracle? It had everything to do with it. The miracle and the timing of the event were not a coincidence. There is another interesting verse in Isaiah 40 that talks about the coming of the LORD.

Isaiah 40:11 He shall feed his flock like a shepherd: he shall gather the lambs with his arm, and carry them in his bosom, and shall gently lead those that are with young.

Upon hearing of John's death, Jesus departed to a secluded place (Matthew 14:13). It is natural for us to assume Jesus felt sorrow and grief. Yet nothing in the scriptures indicates Jesus grieved John's death. While we read that Jesus was moved by the death of others, for example, in the account of the widow of Nain's only son (Luke 7:13), and Jesus offered comfort to Jairus upon hearing of his young daughter's

---

108 After reading Chapter 21 No Other Name you will recognize the significance of Isaiah's prophecy about the coming of the LORD and the glory of the LORD being revealed. The word LORD represents God's name as Yahweh, also known as the I AM name of God. The glory of the LORD is His presence.

death (Mark 5:36), Jesus proclaimed that God is not a God of the dead, but a God of the Living (Matthew 22:32, Mark 12:27). Why would Jesus' reaction to John's death be different from the death of the widow's son, Jairus' young daughter, or Lazarus, brother of Martha and Mary? The difference is Jesus was touched by the pain, sorrow and grief of those still living. God does not see the death of those who love Him the way we do. God, who is Spirit, is eternal. Mankind's life on earth is short compared to the span of eternity. For those who know and love God their earthly "deaths" are transformations into their spiritual form where they enjoy a far greater relationship with God than this fragile and flawed flesh life affords.

In this story when Jesus returned, thousands were waiting for Him. Scripture tells us how He responded to the ever-present crowds that seemed to seek and follow Him everywhere. Matthew 14:13-14 NASB describes the scene:

> ¹³ Now when Jesus heard *about John*, He withdrew from there in a boat to a secluded place by Himself; and when the people heard *of this*, they followed Him on foot from the cities. ¹⁴ When He went ashore, He saw a large crowd, and felt compassion for them and healed their sick.

When pressed and followed by the crowd of thousands of people with their sick seeking healing and answers, Jesus felt compassion. Luke 9:11 says He welcomed them. Mark 6:34 NASB adds Jesus felt compassion "because they were like sheep without a shepherd; and He began to teach them many things." For a day or two (or more) thousands of people had been following Jesus – waiting for healing, hungering for His teaching like a starving person until they were physically very hungry. Can we see the correlation of Jesus' compassion for the people, then providing food is the fulfillment of the Isaiah 40:11 prophecy (shown on the previous page) of what the LORD would do when He came? Mark 6:34 even uses the same analogy (a shepherd with His sheep) as the Isaiah 40:11 verse (a shepherd with His flock/lambs).

The books of Mark and Luke say this miracle happened shortly after the disciples returned from visiting various towns in Israel. Jesus told them to spread the word that the Kingdom of Heaven was near (another way of saying "the Ruler-King of Heaven is here!"). He gave the disciples authority (power) to heal the people, cleanse the lepers, and drive out demons. When the disciples returned, they were excited about what *they had done* (Mark 6:30 and Luke 9:10). As they explained what they had done, seen and said, Jesus asked them to feed the people there in front of them. The disciples were stunned. Instead of looking to God for the answer, they resorted back to their own feeble power to problem solve and saw only their lack of finances. In John 6:7 Philip answered saying eight months wages would not be enough for each person to get a bite! There are two important reminders to us – 1) it is so easy to take credit for what God has done and 2) it is easy to forget that apart from the power of God, we can accomplish very little. Essentially, we can produce a bite when a full grocery store is needed.

Only one disciple was on the right track for solving this problem. In John 6:8-9 Andrew said he had found a boy with five barley loaves and two small fish. Jesus told the disciples to have the people sit in groups of fifties. He took the loaves and fish, gave thanks, and started to distribute the food to His disciples to give to the people. Scripture says the people ate until they were filled; some translations say satisfied. Sufficient food for satisfaction or fullness was not usually the norm for most people at that time. The story tells us there were 5,000 men there. This number could indicate how many total people were there or be an estimate of how many men not including the women and children were present. Yet all were fed and Jesus wanted the remaining food gathered. We can only guess the reasons for this. What God gives should not be squandered or left to be discarded as waste? Or perhaps the people needed to see how bountifully God provides – more than enough, more than what brings satisfaction, more than fulfilling our needs, with plenty left over. There were twelve baskets of leftovers! I heard a pastor mention that there were enough baskets of leftovers for each disciple to have a basket. Could this have been a lesson to the disciples and to us that while our income and abilities will never be enough, no problem or need is ever too big for God?

Aware of the Deuteronomy 18:14-22 prophecy that God would send a Prophet like Moses, John 6:14 says, After the people saw the sign Jesus performed, they began to say, "Surely this is <u>the Prophet</u> who is to come into the world." Now the people were ready to make Him King – not because they recognized Him as King of the Jews or King of the Universe, nor King of their hearts. They were ready to make Him king of providing for their needs, king of doing what they wanted. John 6:15 says that Jesus knew what they wanted to do and He withdrew from the people. Later when Jesus still had not returned, the disciples got into boats and set sail for Capernaum. This is when they saw Jesus walking on the water that night. The next morning a crowd of people followed them to Capernaum and finding Jesus they asked how He had crossed the Sea of Galilee.

Jesus told them it was not because of the signs they saw that they sought Him out, rather it was because of the loaves and their stomachs being filled. In this remarkable conversation Jesus told them He has come from heaven and that He is the source of Eternal Life. He told them to work for food that endures to eternal life which the Son of Man gives. Yet at each point of the conversation someone countered with a request for free food, or for Jesus to perform a "sign" so that they could believe, or uttered a reason not to believe that Jesus is who He said He is. Look at John 6:27-40 below.

[27] Labour not for the meat which perisheth, but for that meat which endureth unto everlasting life, which the Son of man shall give unto you: for him hath God the Father sealed.

[28] Then said they unto him, What shall we do, that we might work the works of God?

[29] Jesus answered and said unto them, This is the work of God, that ye believe on him whom he hath sent.

³⁰ They said therefore unto him, What sign shewest thou then, that we may see, and believe thee? what dost thou work? ³¹ Our fathers did eat manna in the desert; as it is written, He gave them bread from heaven to eat.

³² Then Jesus said unto them, Verily, verily, I say unto you, Moses gave you not that bread from heaven; but my Father giveth you the true bread from heaven.

³³ For the bread of God is he which cometh down from heaven, and giveth life unto the world.

³⁴ Then said they unto him, Lord, evermore give us this bread.

³⁵ And Jesus said unto them, I am the bread of life: he that cometh to me shall never hunger; and he that believeth on me shall never thirst. ³⁶ But I said unto you, That ye also have seen me, and believe not. ³⁷ All that the Father giveth me shall come to me; and him that cometh to me I will in no wise cast out. ³⁸ For I came down from heaven, not to do mine own will, but the will of him that sent me. ³⁹ And this is the Father's will which hath sent me, that of all which he hath given me I should lose nothing, but should raise it up again at the last day. ⁴⁰ And this is the will of him that sent me, that every one which seeth the Son, and believeth on him, may have everlasting life: and I will raise him up at the last day.

⁴¹ The Jews then murmured at him, because he said, I am the bread which came down from heaven. ⁴² And they said, Is not this Jesus, the son of Joseph, whose father and mother we know? how is it then that he saith, I came down from heaven?

⁴³ Jesus therefore answered and said unto them, Murmur not among yourselves. ⁴⁴ No man can come to me, except the Father which hath sent me draw him: and I will raise him up at the last day.

More than Bread – The Feeding of the 5,000

They did not believe Jesus when He said He had come down from heaven; they said they knew His parents. They did not remember that in the days of Moses God said He would dwell among them in Exodus 25:8 or that in Isaiah 7:14 the LORD God said that He Himself would give a sign of a son born of a virgin who would be called Immanuel, which means God with us (Matthew 1:23). Jesus reminded them the Prophets said people would be taught by God (John 6:45, Isaiah 2:3 and Micah 4:2). Still they did not understand nor believe whom He was revealing Himself to be. Finally, to end their single-minded focus of getting bread for their stomachs, Jesus said they would have to eat His flesh and drink His blood to have Life in them.

John 6:51-55 NIV I am the living bread that came down from heaven. Whoever eats this bread will live forever. This bread is my flesh, which I will give for the life of the world."

[52] Then the Jews began to argue sharply among themselves, "How can this man give us his flesh to eat?"

[53] Jesus said to them, "Very truly I tell you, unless you eat the flesh of the Son of Man and drink his blood, you have no life in you. [54] Whoever eats my flesh and drinks my blood has eternal life."

Keep in mind this event was shortly before Passover. When the people of the original Passover had eaten the lamb as part of their meal and covered their doorways with the blood of the animal, death "passed over" them. Every year during the Passover meal, the unleavened bread (matzoh), and wine are served as part of the commemorative meal. Yet no one in this story seems to make that connection.

This figure of speech meant for someone to have eternal Spiritual Life, one would need to hunger and thirst for knowing God and making God part of themselves much like one needs food and water to survive. While the audience took His words literally, it was a figure of speech that later would became the symbolic act of communion representing the eternal spiritual connection between believers and Jesus. This was not the first time Jesus described a desire for knowing God and God's ways in terms of consuming food and drink. In Matthew 5:6 He spoke of those who hungered and thirst for righteousness. In John 4 and John 7:37-38 He spoke of living water inside us that produced eternal life. Writers of Psalms likened their desire for God in a similar way:

Psalm 42:1-2a NASB As the deer pants for the water brooks, So my soul pants for You, O God.[2] My soul thirsts for God, for the living God;

Psalm 34:8 O taste and see that the LORD is good: blessed is the man that trusteth in him.

In this conversation Jesus revealed something more. Four times Jesus alluded to the promise that on the last day He would raise up those who had come to believe. Take a look at these verses:

John 6:39 And this is the will of him who sent me, that I shall lose none of all those he has given me, but raise them up at the last day.

John 6:40 For my Father's will is that everyone who looks to the Son and believes in him shall have eternal life, and I will raise them up at the last day."

John 6:44 "No one can come to me unless the Father who sent me draws them, and I will raise them up at the last day.

John 6:54 Whoever eats my flesh and drinks my blood has eternal life, and I will raise them up at the last day.

Examination of these four verses and the passage they come from reveals answers to some important questions about Jesus. **Why did Jesus come to earth?** Answer: to do the will of God (verse 6:38 NIV - *For I have come down from heaven not to do my will but to do the will of him who sent me*). **What is the will of God?** Answer: It is the will of God that everyone comes to believe who Jesus revealed Himself to be. As a result of this belief, they shall have eternal life and none will be lost (verse 6:40 NIV - *For my Father's will is that everyone who looks to the Son and believes in him shall have eternal life*; verse 6:39 NIV - *And this is the will of him who sent me, that I shall lose none of all those he has given me…*). **What does belief in Jesus mean?** Many say they believe in God, but know nothing of Him. Satan believes in God, yet opposes the will of God. God calls us to be transformed by our belief in Him (Romans 12:2). We are called to learn of Him (Matthew 11:29), and as a result of what we come to believe, our thoughts, perceptions, actions, and relationships with others change to reflect God's compassion, mercy, and love.

What did Jesus mean when He said, "I will raise them up on the last day"? He meant that for all who have chosen Him, have come to believe who He is and have trusted in Him on their last day of life on earth, He will raise them up transformed to their eternal spiritual life. How can we be sure this is what He meant? I Corinthians 15:26 states the last enemy to be destroyed is death and in II Corinthians 5:8 mentions the instantaneous movement from the body into the presence of the Lord. In John 11:26 NASB Jesus said, "everyone who lives and believes in Me <u>will never die</u>…). John 14:2-3 Jesus speaks of preparing a place for us, "I will come again, and receive you unto myself; that where I am, there ye may be also." From the cross, one of the thieves asked that Jesus remember him when Jesus comes into His kingdom. Jesus responded in Luke 23:43, "Verily I say unto thee, <u>Today</u> shalt thou <u>be with me</u> in paradise." Did the people understand? Do we? In John 6:63 NASB Jesus said, "It is the Spirit who gives life; the flesh profits nothing; the words that I have spoken to you are spirit and are life."

After this conversation and the statement that they must eat His flesh and drink His blood, many followers departed. John 6:66 NIV says, "From this time *many* of his disciples turned back and no longer followed him." In John 6:67 Jesus utters the most hauntingly painful question posed by God and if Peter could respond for every believer in God throughout time, his answer was absolutely perfect. Here is John 6:67-69 (NIV):

⁶⁷ "You do not want to leave too, do you?" Jesus asked the Twelve.

⁶⁸ Simon Peter answered him, "Lord, to whom shall we go? You have the words of eternal life. ⁶⁹ We have come to believe and to know that you are the Holy One of God."

The feeding of the 5,000 took place one year before the cross, just before Passover (John 6:4), and just after the execution of John the Baptist, murdered by those who had held him captive. It was not a coincidence that this particular miracle took place at this time. The underlying message of Passover is to commemorate the time when people held captive were set free because they had believed God and had chosen obedience to the Word of God which then brought them protection from certain death. The purpose of this miracle was to provide enough information so the people there could determine who He is and as a result of believing and trusting in Him, would get eternal life. He had effortlessly provided bread and fish for 5,000+ people, thereby identifying Himself as the same God who had provided manna for so many people a long time ago. As some were still shocked by the death of John the Baptist, Jesus basically told the people that when they believed in Him, death would pass over them and He would be there on their last day.

Then why did some disciples and followers leave and stop following Jesus? Could it have been that Jesus was not living up to their expectations of what the Messiah (God) would and should do for them here on earth? Or was it too much to comprehend that the LORD God Almighty was in their midst? And they couldn't or didn't grasp His message about eternal life.

In the next chapter months have gone by and Passover is drawing near once again. The message vital to Jesus to convey in the next chapter is the same message conveyed in this story –believing in Jesus as God and recognizing that those who have spiritual and eternal Life need never fear death.

CHAPTER 17

The Resurrection and The Life

Mankind has viewed death as the end of life. Many have hoped and believed there is an afterlife. At the loss of a loved one, we are comforted to think they have gone to heaven or paradise. One could rightfully say the Bible's story of God and mankind begins with a life and death decision. However, according to the Bible, mankind's story is really a death or life ultimatum. This story of Lazarus speaks to the heart of the question of the finality of death and reveals the love of eternal God.

* * *

Restoring life with medical assistance to someone who has stopped breathing is not a big deal today. It is safe to say it happens every day. Historically there are numerous accounts of people thought to be dead, who suddenly awoke after an hour or even a day or two later. When we hear of these "resurrection" stories, we tend to think the person was not dead in the first place. The Bible has several accounts of life being restored. In the Old Testament God restored life to two boys after the Prophets Elijah and Elisha prayed (I Kings 17:17-23 and 2 Kings 4:32-35). In the New Testament God restored life to a young man who had fallen from a third story window while the apostle Paul preached (Acts 20:9-12). The gospels record two instances where Jesus restored life; once involving the young daughter of Jairus (Luke 8:40-56), and again to the only son of a widow (Luke 7:14). Sceptics of the Bible may think none of these people were really dead, but that assumption fails to address the fact that the trauma from the injury or cause of their deadly illnesses also disappeared.[109] Although it appears Jesus may have restored life to the widow's son and Jairus' daughter out of compassion for their grieving loved ones, when Jesus raised Lazarus' from the dead, He said this incident would serve a very specific purpose.

Readers of the Bible familiar with the story of Lazarus may not be aware of when it happened within the three-year ministry of Jesus. The resurrection of Lazarus appears only in the book of John, chapter 11 and took place near the end of Jesus' three-year ministry. By that time, Jesus had already had the "Who do you say I am" talk with His disciples where Peter confessed his belief that Jesus is the Messiah, the Son of God (Matthew 16, Mark 8, and Luke 9). Jesus had told the stunned and confused disciples several times He would be arrested, killed and would rise again. The transfiguration had taken place where Peter, James and his brother John (the author of the book of John) had seen Jesus changed in an instant, witnessed His visitation with the Old Testament Prophets Moses and Elijah, and heard God acknowledge Jesus as His Son (Matthew 17, Mark 9 and Luke 9).

The year before this incident with Lazarus (the last Passover), after being followed by thousands of people for several days, Jesus had miraculously produced fish and bread to feed them with baskets of food left over (John 6). This miracle caused many of the people present to want to make Him King. Six months later before tens of thousands of observant Jews, at the autumn eight-day Feast of Tabernacles Jesus "stood and cried out," "If anyone is thirsty, let him come to Me and drink. He who believes in Me, as the Scripture said, 'From his innermost being will flow rivers of living water'" (John 7:37-38 NASB).

---

109 The *Zohar* (meaning radiance or splendor) are books that are part of the *Kabbalah*, the Jewish mystical commentary of *Torah* (not to be confused with *Mishnah* or Oral *Torah*). Believed to have been written down by Rabbi Simeon during the second century, the *Kabbalah* did not surface until the 13th century in Spain. The *Zohar* contains mystical discussions of the nature of God, the origins of the universe, and the nature of souls among other topics. The *Zohar* is a source out of Judaism for the belief that the soul lingers three days in which it may return to the decease's body.

The Resurrection and The Life

This statement spoke to a promise made by God in Isaiah 41:17 and to specific symbolic rituals related to this holy day. On the last day of this fall festival, the people traditionally pray to God to sustain their lives by providing water and rain for the coming agricultural year. Also, this same week-long feast commemorates God providing and guiding the Hebrew people as they wandered through the desert for 40 years where God went before them as a pillar of cloud by day and a pillar of fire to light their way by night (Exodus 13:21). Few understood Jesus' claim as God, when He cried out during this holiday, "I am the Light of the World, he who follows Me will not walk in the darkness but will have the Light of life" (John 8:12 NASB).

According to its placement in the book of John, the illness and death of Lazarus happened after the Feast of Dedication mentioned in John 10:22. The Feast of Dedication, more commonly known as Hanukkah, occurs on the 25th of Kislev which could have been anywhere from late November to late December that year. After the story of Lazarus, verse 11:55 indicates the Passover is near. This would be the Passover when Jesus is crucified. If the stories are told in chronological order in the book of John, we can place Lazarus' illness and death after December and before the March or early April Passover; occurring sometime during Jesus' last 100 days. My guess is that it occurred closer to Passover. Did Jesus know when His death would occur? Of course, He did (Matthew 26:18, John 7:6 and 7:8). Why then is it so important to understand *when* the Lazarus incident happened? All along Jesus had been making statements that left clues as to who He is. With the cross being days or weeks away, this last demonstration of power before a group of people would leave very little doubt regarding His identity.

It was no coincidence that this event involved friends of Jesus. Lazarus and his sisters Martha and Mary had an ongoing relationship with Jesus. He had been in their home before (Luke 10:38-42). Jesus was their friend and they *knew* He loved them. Did they believe Jesus could help anyone? Yes, they did. Therefore, they would be the ones most likely to be receptive to His important message and understand what He was revealing about Himself. While they believed Jesus was the long-awaited Messiah, did they believe and understand that Jesus is God, that He is all powerful and has all authority in heaven and on earth? On this point, they would have wavered in their answer to this question, just as many devout Christians today would waver on this same question. Like Martha in John 11:24 our mouths may say one thing, but when we are facing a crisis and are asked if we trust God in every situation, we may find that at the end of our "faith," we have question marks and doubt.

Here is the opening of the story told in John 11:1-16 NASB:

Now a certain man was sick, Lazarus of Bethany, the village of Mary and her sister Martha. ² It was the Mary who anointed the Lord with ointment, and wiped His feet with her hair, whose brother Lazarus was sick. ³ So the sisters sent *word* to Him, saying, "Lord, behold, he whom You love is sick."

⁴ But when Jesus heard *this*, He said, "This sickness is not to end in death, but for the glory of God, so that the Son of God may be glorified by it." ⁵ Now Jesus loved Martha and her sister and Lazarus. ⁶ So when He heard that he was sick He then stayed two days *longer* in the place where He was. ⁷ Then after this He said to the disciples, "Let us go to Judea again."

⁸ The disciples said to Him, "Rabbi, the Jews were just now seeking to stone You, and are You going there again?"

⁹ Jesus answered, "Are there not twelve hours in the day? If anyone walks in the day, he does not stumble, because he sees the light of this world. ¹⁰ But if anyone walks in the night, he stumbles, because the light is not in him."

The Resurrection and The Life

We get a wealth of information here. It is Lazarus's sister Mary who will be the woman who anoints Jesus shortly before His death. Although there were those who were plotting to kill Jesus and He was on the move, the sisters had a good idea where He was staying as they sent a messenger to Him. It is interesting how they referred to their brother as "he whom you love is sick." They knew Jesus well enough that they did not follow this message up with a request to come to them, to heal their brother. Jesus' relationship was so close, that they knew all they had to say was, "He whom you love is sick" and He would come. Jesus did love Martha, Mary and Lazarus, and yet it appears that at the time of their greatest need, Jesus deliberately delayed His coming to them by more than 48 hours. The story reveals that although Jesus was physically away from the sisters and Lazarus, He knew precisely what they were going through and every breath Lazarus took.

When Jesus determined it was time to return to Judea, some of the disciples expressed concern about those who wanted to kill Jesus there. Showing no fear or concern Jesus told them they stumble in darkness not with the light. The term "light" has varied meanings including that which makes visible or stimulates sight or produces illumination. (Note Genesis 1:3 and Revelation 21:23-24.) Here, light speaks of knowledge of spiritual truth and darkness as the lack of the same. Jesus is the Source of spiritual wisdom, knowledge and understanding and therefore, is the Light of the World. Recall Jesus said He is the Light of the World (John 8:12, 9:5, 12:46) and the Light would be with them for a little while longer. He was telling them He is the source of the God-guided illumination that led the nation of Hebrews during the 40 years in the desert and those who believe in Him need not be afraid while He was with them (Psalm 82:5 and Ecclesiastes 2:14).[110]

---

[110] When people come to believe in Jesus as God, they become "children of light" (Luke 16:8). Believers are considered to be the bearers of Jesus' light in the world (Matthew 5:14). Isaiah 42:6 speaks of the Servant of the LORD who would be "a covenant for the people and a light for the Gentiles."

In the next verses Jesus spoke clearly about Lazarus' condition in John 11:11-16 NASB:

> [11] This He said, and after that He said to them, "Our friend Lazarus has fallen asleep; but I go, so that I may awaken him out of sleep."
>
> [12] The disciples then said to Him, "Lord, if he has fallen asleep, he will recover."
>
> [13] Now Jesus had spoken of his death, but they thought that He was speaking of literal sleep. [14] So Jesus then said to them plainly, "Lazarus is dead, [15] and I am glad for your sakes that I was not there, so that you may believe; but let us go to him."
>
> [16] Therefore Thomas, who is called Didymus, said to *his* fellow disciples, "Let us also go, so that we may die with Him."

Note that Jesus uses the euphemism "sleep" for death. This is not an isolated occurrence. There are several other verses that liken death to sleep for believers. Jesus said the same thing regarding the twelve-year-old daughter of Jairus (Matthew 9:24). This same term in used in describing the death of saints (believers) in I Corinthians 15:31 and in I Thessalonians 4:13. Jesus explained to His confused disciples that Lazarus was dead and that He was going <u>to awaken him</u>. Then Jesus says something perplexing. He said He was glad for the sake of His disciples that He was not there so that they may believe. Believe what?

By the time they arrived at Bethany, Lazarus had been in the tomb for four days and many people had arrived from Jerusalem to comfort the two sisters. When Martha heard Jesus had come, she immediately went to Him, and Mary stayed at home. Upon greeting Jesus, Martha said what others who were close to Lazarus and knew Jesus must have thought, "Lord, if You had been here, my brother would not have died." Almost everyone had heard of the miracles Jesus performed. The sisters may have even witnessed some of the incredible healings, so they believed that if Jesus had been there, He could have saved their brother. Was it the look on Jesus' face that prompted Martha's next response? This time she said what she knew she *should* say, but soon it is obvious this is not really what she believes. "Even now I know that whatever You ask of God, God will give You" (John 11:22 NIV). Martha had just stated her continued belief in the relationship between Jesus and God. Jesus answered, but Martha missed the importance of what Jesus said in response. Here is the next part of the story (John 11:23-28 NIV).

²³ Jesus said to her, "Your brother will rise again."

²⁴ Martha said to Him, "I know that he will rise again in the resurrection on the last day."

²⁵ Jesus said to her, "I am the resurrection and the life; he who believes in Me will live even if he dies, ²⁶ and everyone who lives and believes in Me will never die. Do you believe this?"

²⁷ She said to Him, "Yes, Lord; I have believed that You are the Christ, the Son of God, *even* He who comes into the world."

²⁸ When she had said this, she went away ....

Martha stated clearly what she believed – that Jesus is the Messiah (the Christ), the Son of God – He who had come into the world (the one promised to come). Then she left. She did not understand what Jesus meant when He said He is the resurrection and the life. Do we? Martha said she believed her brother would rise at the resurrection of the dead. Like many Jews, she believed when people died, they laid asleep in *Sheol* (the ground) then at the resurrection would arise to either everlasting life or everlasting destruction as stated in Daniel 12:2. This is what followed as recorded in John 11:28-33 NIV:

²⁸ After she had said this, she went back and called her sister Mary aside. "The Teacher is here," she said, "and is asking for you."

²⁹ When Mary heard this, she got up quickly and went to him. ³⁰ Now Jesus had not yet entered the village but was still at the place where Martha had met him. ³¹ When the Jews who had been with Mary in the house, comforting her, noticed how quickly she got up and went out, they followed her, supposing she was going to the tomb to mourn there.

³² When Mary reached the place where Jesus was and saw him, she fell at his feet and said, "Lord, if you had been here, my brother would not have died."

³³ When Jesus saw her weeping, and the Jews who had come along with her also weeping, he was deeply moved in spirit and troubled (KJV says he groaned in the spirit and was troubled).

Mary did not go to the tomb to mourn; she went to ask Jesus why He had not come. As she fell to her knees, she too said the words utmost on her heart, "…if you had been here, my brother would not have died." Then she wept. Their friends and other family members wept also. I believe Mary was hurt not only because her brother had died, but because on some level she felt Jesus had fallen short of her expectation. Mary was not the only one there who felt that way. Others said, "Could not he who opened the eyes of the blind man have kept this man from dying?" Look at Jesus' response in John 11:34-40 NIV:

³⁴ "Where have you laid him?" he asked.

"Come and see, Lord," they replied.

³⁵ Jesus wept.

The Resurrection and The Life

³⁶ Then the Jews said, "See how he loved him!"

³⁷ But some of them said, "Could not he who opened the eyes of the blind man have kept this man from dying?"

³⁸ Jesus, once more deeply moved (again groaning in himself – KJV), came to the tomb. It was a cave with a stone laid across the entrance. ³⁹ "Take away the stone," he said.

"But, Lord," said Martha, the sister of the dead man, "by this time there is a bad odor, for he has been there four days."

⁴⁰ Then Jesus said, "Did I not tell you that if you believe, you will see the glory of God?"

After going to the tomb of Lazarus, surely Jesus knew He was about to call Lazarus to restored life. Then why did Jesus weep? He did not weep the night before the cross. He did not weep during His trial, not during His beating, nor when He was nailed to the cross, or with His last breath from the cross. Why did Jesus weep just before the resurrection of Lazarus? If the Greek definitions of the words used to describe how Jesus reacted are accurate, verse 33 tells us something unique. *Strong's Concordance* says the word "groaned" as in the spirit implies an admonition or murmur against and "troubled" as in agitation or to make restless. Could it be that His admonition, His agitation and sense of inner restlessness was because those who loved Him and knew Him, still did not know Him for who He truly is? Luke 19:41-42 (and 13:34) says Jesus wept as He entered Jerusalem for the last time and mourned the fact that the people did not recognize Him. Did Jesus' groan signify a giving up on the specific point He had hoped they would grasp, and choosing to just move on with the situation in front of Him? Clearly, He was troubled and saddened. As His life on earth drew to a close, there was still a vitally important point He needed to make. However, it appeared that even among His close friends and disciples the point had been missed. This is how the story concludes from John 11:21-45 NIV:

> [41] So they took away the stone. Then Jesus looked up and said, "Father, I thank you that you have heard me. [42] I knew that you always hear me, but I said this for the benefit of the people standing here, that they may believe that you sent me."
>
> [43] When he had said this, Jesus called in a loud voice, "Lazarus, come out!" [44] The dead man came out, his hands and feet wrapped with strips of linen, and a cloth around his face.
>
> Jesus said to them, "Take off the grave clothes and let him go."
>
> [45] Therefore many of the Jews who had come to visit Mary, and had seen what Jesus did, believed in him.

Notice in Jesus' brief conversation with God in verse 41 and 42 above, He did not ask for permission or for the power to restore life. He did not ask if it was God's will. Why not? The reason is because <u>as God, Jesus has all authority and power</u>, and whatsoever Jesus did or does **is** the Will of God. Why did Jesus even speak to God the Father? As Jesus said, it was for the benefit of those present that they may understand that Jesus is *the* Source of the authority and power that controls death and life. After Lazarus was restored to life, many people believed in Jesus because Lazarus had been dead, and now he was alive.

To many people death is the final opponent to be defeated. The first command of God – (do not eat of the tree of knowledge of good and evil [OBEY ME]) came with the warning and consequence that disobedience would mean certain death (Genesis 2:17).[111] In the very

---

111 Adam and Eve were spiritual beings in the Garden of Eden. Through their disobedience, they experienced a spiritual death.

next chapter of Genesis Satan lied when he told Eve she would surely NOT die if she ate of the forbidden tree (Genesis 3:4). Continued disobedience, sin and unbelief cause spiritual death and if left unrepentant, will lead to the physical death of our bodies. The fear of (physical) death has held millions of people hostage through the ages (Hebrews 2:15). However, we have a misunderstanding of life and death. Many have believed that this life is all there is; that death is the finale and should be avoided or forestalled for as long as possible. This is what Martha, Mary and so many others have thought although they believed in the resurrection. And while they no doubt rejoiced and praised God when Lazarus walked out of the tomb, they had still missed the greater point Jesus made that day.

What had they missed? Recall Jesus made three unusual statements involving the death of Lazarus. The first was when Jesus heard that Lazarus was ill. He said that Lazarus' illness would not be unto death but would be <u>for God's glory so that God's Son may be glorified through it</u> (11:4). The second statement was to the disciples after telling them Lazarus had died, He said, "It is for your sake <u>I am glad I was not there, so that you may believe</u>" (John 11:14 NIV). Then to Martha just before He called Lazarus out of the tomb, He said "Did I not tell you that <u>if you believe, you will see the glory of God</u> (11:40)?" Recall God said He would not give His glory to another (Isaiah 42:8, and 48:11). What did Jesus want His disciples and friends to know and what was the glory of God?

Deuteronomy 5:24 And ye said, Behold, the LORD our God hath shewed us his glory and his greatness, and we have heard his voice out of the midst of the fire: we have seen this day that God doth talk with man, and he liveth.

Ezekiel 8:4 And, behold, the glory of the God of Israel was there, according to the vision that I saw in the plain.

The Glory of God is God's presence and power (Deuteronomy 5:24, Ezekiel 8:4). Jesus had shown His power over nature, over illnesses and deformities of the body, and in His authority to forgive sin. Now Jesus wanted His disciples and beloved friends to know He held all power not only over physical death and life, but most importantly, as He had said several times – He is the source of eternal life (John 3:36, 4:14, 6:47, 6:54, and 10:28). Martha and many others through the ages have missed the importance of what Jesus revealed about Himself when He told Martha "I am the Resurrection and the Life" (John 11:25). This does not mean that Jesus has the power to restore the dead to life. It means that Jesus is the Life that restores the dead. Although Acts 5:30, Romans 6:4, and Galatians 1:1 say it was the Father who raised Jesus from the dead, Jesus said in John 10:18, "…No man taketh it from me, but I lay it down of myself. I have power to lay it down, and I have power to take it again." That very power proclaimed His identity as God.

We tend to think our existence here on earth is life and that life is severed by death. But that is not the truth at all. God, our Creator who is eternal knows that after our time on earth, death comes to our physical bodies. However, for those who love and know Him (and therefore, have eternal life) physical death does not end eternal life. Jesus said in John 6:53 NIV "The Spirit gives life; the flesh counts for nothing." What matters is the spiritual life. All of us will experience death here. The question is will we experience eternal spiritual life? Jesus knew that in the months and years to come many of the disciples and His followers would face persecution, be arrested, beaten, imprisoned and executed in His name. It was important for them to know God's power over death and understand His gift of eternal spiritual life. It was important for them to have seen the power and glory (the presence) of God in the face of physical death.

Much of what Jesus said and did in His ministry involved revealing His identity as God and conveying the importance of being a child of God. The feeding of the 5,000+ men, women and children had less to do with food and more to do with recognizing Jesus as our Source of eternal life (John 6:35-40). It was also a message to His disciples that when faced with the impossible, all is possible with God (John 6). The healing of the man born blind had less to do with gaining his physical eyesight and more to do with the spiritual blindness of those who say they love God yet could not recognize the hand of God right in front of them (John 9). The resurrection of Lazarus from the dead had little to with restoring the physical life of Lazarus who would one day die again. The goal in life is not how long we live here on earth. This miraculous event shortly before the cross had everything to do with overcoming our fear of death because we know and trust in the power of Jesus, the Eternal God, who has all power and authority over death and life and is the source of eternal life.

Jesus was not giving a new teaching on eternal life in Bethany days or weeks before the cross. God is and has always been consistent in His love for mankind and His desire that all come to know Him and have eternal life. Look at these verses from Ezekiel 18:21-23 NIV and compare them to John 11:25. The Ezekiel message was given by God to the prophet Ezekiel after he had been taken into captivity in Babylon. God is speaking of those who have turned from Him and sought after other gods and have done and continue to do wicked things. God tells the Jews to stop sinning and come back to Him; to turn from death and to live by changing their behavior. We cannot tell ourselves that God was referring to mankind's brief life here on earth – God knows in the face of eternity our lives are like the life of a flower or grass. God's interest is in people's eternal spiritual life. Is the Christian message of salvation any different from what God requires here: for the wicked to repent (turn from his sins), accept God (observe God's statues), and love others as himself (practice justice and righteousness) that they shall surely live and not die? This is the same thing Jesus said to Martha in John 11:25.

Ezekiel 18: 21-23 NIV "But if the wicked man turns from all his sins which he has committed and observes all My statutes and practices justice and righteousness, he shall surely live; he shall not die. ²² All his transgressions which he has committed will not be remembered against him; because of his righteousness which he has practiced, he will live. ²³ Do I have any pleasure in the death of the wicked," declares the Lord God, "rather than that he should turn from his ways and live?

John 11:25 NASB Jesus said to her, "I am the resurrection and the life; <u>he who believes in Me will live even if he dies,</u> ²⁶ and everyone who lives and believes in Me <u>will never die</u>....

    This incident of restoring life to Lazarus so close to the time of the cross revealed a great deal about who Jesus is. Jesus said He is the Resurrection and the Life. By this statement Jesus revealed Himself to be the One and only God. He did not say that by the power of God (or by the power of His Father) He resurrects; or that through God He gives eternal life. No, He said *He* is the Source of Power over death and restoration ("<u>I am</u> the Resurrection and the Life), and He is the Source of power and cause of Life, i.e. eternal life. Apart from God, our lives here on earth are temporary. God is eternal and is concerned about our Spiritual Eternal Life.

    Soon after the resurrection of Lazarus, Jesus would be arrested, tried, found guilty of blasphemy, beaten, and nailed to a Roman cross for admitting He is God. While death held no power over Him and He would leave the tomb victorious in three days, it was vitally important that those who love Him, who have chosen to believe and follow Him to KNOW that death has no hold on them either because Jesus said:

John 11:25-26 NIV "I am the resurrection and the life. The one who believes in me will live, even though they die; ²⁶ and whoever lives by believing in me will never die. Do you believe this?"

    True Life begins as a by-product of becoming children of the LORD through belief and trust. Then for children of the LORD, death should hold no fear, because death has no sustaining power. Jesus said in John 12:25 if we seek to save our fleshly life, we will lose it (at death), but if we lose it for His sake (dying to our flesh life to become born again spiritually), we gain Life eternal. The night before the cross Jesus told His disciples in John 14:2-3 He went to prepare a place for them, for us. He said He will come again and receive us unto Himself, so we may be with Him. Then He said, "If it were not so, I would have told you...."

Then why would we fear death? Where is death's sting? Where is death's victory?

CHAPTER 18

"My God, Why Have You Forsaken Me?"

*"My heart is troubled. What should I say?
'Father, save me from this hour'?
No. This is the very reason I came to this hour."*
John 12:27 NIV

The last chapter's story of the resurrection of Lazarus took place just days or a few weeks before Jesus' arrest, trial, and crucifixion. This chapter brings us to the strange comment made from the cross and the explanation of it. Over the years several pastors have spoken of God turning away from Jesus while He was on the cross. This well-known theory is now accepted as fact among many in the Christian community: that God rejected, abandoned, forsook, or turned away from Jesus on the cross because He bore the sin of the world. But is this true? Are there scriptures that support this idea or do the scriptures reveal something different? For God whose very reputation is His faithfulness, His compassion, His Love and His promise to never leave or forsake us, this is a serious charge because it speaks directly to the character and nature of God.

The idea that God turned away from Jesus is based predominately and almost solely on one statement Jesus made from the cross, "My God, my God, why have you forsaken me?" Without this statement, I am not sure this idea would have ever come to anyone's mind. The account of the crucifixion of Jesus is told in all four gospels, but this statement appears only in the books of Matthew (27:46) and Mark (15:34). Some pastors explain this statement saying once all of the sin of the world for all time was heaped on Jesus, the Father could not look upon Him. The next conclusion is invariably added: that for the first time in all eternity the inseparable union between God and Jesus was severed thus causing Jesus unimaginable anguish and pain through which this statement was made. While Romans 8:3-4, II Corinthians 5:21 and I Peter 2:24 speak of Jesus taking on the sin of mankind so that righteousness may be obtained, none of these passages say anything about Jesus being forsaken by God during this process. A verse in Isaiah does speak of sin separating one from God. Isaiah 59:2 NASB says, "But your iniquities have made a separation between you and your God, and your sins have hidden *His* face from you so that He does not hear." However, the next verse clearly indicates this passage *cannot* be speaking of Jesus. Isaiah 59:3 NASB says, "For your hands are defiled with blood and your fingers with iniquity; Your lips have spoken falsehood, your tongue mutters wickedness."

Habakkuk 1:13 NASB does say, "*Your* eyes are too pure to approve ("behold" in the KJV; "look at" in the NIV) evil, and You cannot look on wickedness." However, the full verse says "*Your* eyes are too pure to approve evil, and You cannot look on wickedness *with favor*. Why do You look with favor on those who deal treacherously? Why are You silent when the wicked swallow up those more righteous than they?" The main theme of this book is the prophet Habakkuk's concern that God will use the Babylonians to bring correction upon Israel. Clearly this verse has no connection to the Messiah. There are other scriptures that provide insight regarding whether God can look upon the sin of mankind or not. Before the Flood of Noah's time Genesis 6:5-6 KJV says:

> ⁵ And God saw that the wickedness of man was great in the earth, and that every imagination of the thoughts of his heart was only

evil continually. ⁶And (the LORD was sorry – NASB) it repented the LORD that he had made man on the earth, and it grieved him at his heart.

In Genesis 18:20-21 KJV God speaks about the sin of Sodom and Gomorrah:

²⁰ And the LORD said, Because the cry of Sodom and Gomorrah is great, and because their sin is very grievous; ²¹ I will go down now, and see whether they have done altogether according to the cry of it, which is come unto me; and if not, I will know.

While the above verses address a specific region or city of people whose sin gained God's attention, Psalm 33:13-15 say God watches all mankind and considers everything we do. Psalm 90:8 and Jeremiah 16:17 says God is aware of our secret sins and we are told they are not hidden from Him. Clearly according to these verses God has looked upon, considered, and evaluated the sin of mankind.

Psalm 33:13:15 NIV From heaven the LORD looks down and sees <u>all mankind</u>; ¹⁴ from his dwelling place he watches all who live on earth—¹⁵ he who forms the hearts of all, who <u>considers everything they do</u>.

Psalm 90:8 NIV You have set our iniquities before you, our secret sins in the light of your presence.

Jeremiah 16:17 NIV <u>My eyes are on all their ways</u>; they are not hidden from me, nor is their sin concealed from my eyes.

Many Christians believe Isaiah 53 is referring to Jesus. In there someone is said to have hidden their face, and someone is cut off, but these verses clearly say it was *people* who hid their face and that it was the suffering servant who was "cut off" from the land of the living. Isaiah 53:3 and verse 8 KJV state:

> ³ He is despised and rejected of men; a man of sorrows, and acquainted with grief: and we hid as it were our faces from him; he was despised, and we esteemed him not.

> ⁸ He was taken from prison and from judgment: and who shall declare his generation? For he was cut off out of the land of the living: for the transgression of my people was he stricken.

Is it a matter of the quantity of sin? I found no scriptures or principles that support the idea that when *all* the sins of the world are accumulated then it becomes too much for God. Does this rationale lose some of its logic? Are we to believe we have found God's blind or weak spot? Enough sin and Almighty God can't see it; can't look upon it? The idea that holy God turns away because He is too holy to look upon sin would mean that when there are so many horrors and catastrophes are so great then truly we are alone; God could not bear to be with us when these tragedies occurred. That idea goes against a great number of Bible verses that say otherwise. Therefore, since the Bible doesn't speak of God turning away from Jesus because of sin, then why did Jesus ask this question?

The question "My God, My God, why have you forsaken me?" was not a prayer cried out in anguish of being separated from God the Father. Rather Jesus used a rabbinic technique of quoting part of a scripture to evoke the rest of the passage. To be precise, Jesus quoted Psalm 22:1, and by doing so He evoked the rest of Psalm 22. This is like a debate of whether it is okay to pray for one's own needs, and someone cites, "Our Father, who art in heaven…." By using that quote, it is recognized that the rest of the Lord's Prayer which includes the prayer request for food needed each day and to be forgiven supports that point. This technique of Biblical reference, called

"My God, Why Have You Forsaken Me?"

Gezerah Shaveh[112] was developed approximate a century before Jesus' ministry and would have been known among many of the priests, scribes and the elders in Jerusalem. With this one line reference Jesus conveyed the point that the reality before them that day at Golgotha directly related to the description of events recorded in King David's Psalm 22. Looking at what had happened when Jesus was on the cross before He made this statement, both Matthew 27:39-43 and Mark 15:29-32 say nearly the same thing. Here is Matthew's account:

> **Matthew 27:39-43 NASB** ³⁹ And those passing by were hurling abuse at Him, wagging their heads⁴⁰ and saying, "You who *are going to* destroy the temple and rebuild it in three days, save Yourself! If You are the Son of God, come down from the cross." In the same way the chief priests also, along with the scribes and elders, were mocking *Him* and saying, ⁴² "He saved others; He cannot save Himself. He is the King of Israel; let Him now come down from the cross, and we will believe in Him. ⁴³ HE TRUSTS IN GOD; LET GOD RESCUE *HIM* now, IF HE DELIGHTS IN HIM; for He said, 'I am the Son of God.'"

We cannot be sure of how much time passed between the taunts of the priests, scribes and elders and Jesus' quote in Matthew 27:46. However, when Jesus spoke the "My God, my God" line, the chief priests, scribes and elders' skin should have crawled. They should have recognized this quote and known exactly what Jesus was alluding to. They would have preferred to think Jesus was calling for Elijah rather

---

112 *Gezerah Shaveh* is a Talmudic hermeneutic term described in the theory of biblical text interpretation. *Gezerah Shavah* refers to the verbal parallel inference of two cases of similar words or phrases. This means that when a phrase is exact or similar to another phrase, the rest of the quotation of the original passage is invoked. In other words, Jesus quoted Psalm 22:1 and thereby evoked the remaining verses of this passage to provide insight into the events occurring during His crucifixion.

than acknowledge He was telling them that Psalm 22 was playing out before them and they had played their part and spoken their lines as if it had been written for them. Notice the almost word for word statement in Matthew 27:43 KJV and Psalm 22:8 NASB below says:

Matthew 27:43 ⁴³ He trusts in God; <u>let God rescue *Him*</u> now, if <u>He delights in Him</u>; for He said, 'I am the Son of God.'"

Psalm 22:8 NASB ⁸ "Commit *yourself* to the Lord; <u>let Him deliver him</u>; Let Him rescue him, because <u>He delights in him</u>."

    King David wrote Psalm 22 more than 600 years (BCE) before Jesus was born. The sentiment expressed in Psalm 22 is almost as if while in the Spirit, David was one of the witnesses there on Golgotha. Clearly this chapter is prophetic in that the verses recount events that would take place hundreds of years later outside of Jerusalem on a hill. In this Psalm there are verses that describe what it is like to be crucified. Keep in mind that crucifixion history traces back to the possible execution of pirates in the 6th century BCE and was not practiced in the Roman Empire until the first century CE. (Jesus was executed during the first century CE by the Roman Empire representative, Pontius Pilate.)

    The similarities between the descriptions recorded in all four gospels with Psalm 22 are undeniable. Psalm 22:6 speaks of him being despised by people, just as Isaiah 53:3 (NASB) says, "He was despised and <u>forsaken</u> of men." Psalm 22:7 says they sneered at Him, while Matthew 27:29, 31 and 41 (Mark 15:29-32) speaks of those who mocked Him. Matthew 27:35 NASB (Mark 15:24, Luke 23:34, and John 19:24) says, "they divided up His garments among themselves by casting lots." This matches Psalm 22:18. Psalm 22:16 says they have pierced his hands and feet. Psalm 22:17 NASB says, "They look, they stare at me" and Matthew 27:36 NASB says, "And sitting down, they *began* to keep watch over Him there."

"My God, Why Have You Forsaken Me?"

<u>Psalm 22: 6-10 NASB</u>

⁶But I am a worm and not a man,
 A reproach of men and despised by the people.
⁷ All who see me sneer at me;
 They separate with the lip, they wag the head, *saying*,
⁸ "Commit *yourself* to the Lord; let Him deliver him;
 Let Him rescue him, because He delights in him."
⁹ Yet You are He who brought me forth from the womb;
 You made me trust *when* upon my mother's breasts.
¹⁰ Upon You I was cast from birth;
 You have been my God from my mother's womb.

Psalm 22:14-18 NASB speaks from the point of view of being on the cross.

¹⁴I am poured out like water, and all my bones are
 out of joint; my heart is like wax; it is melted within me.
 ¹⁵ My strength is dried up like a potsherd,
and my tongue cleaves to my jaws; and You lay
 me in the dust of death.
¹⁶ For dogs have surrounded me; a band of
 evildoers has encompassed me;
they pierced my hands and my feet.
 ¹⁷ I can count all my bones. They look, they stare at me;
 ¹⁸ They divide my garments among them,
and for my clothing they cast lots.

The descriptions here did not happen to David, so why did David write this heart-wrenching passage? We could ask the same thing of Isaiah 53. The only answer to why any of the prophets, and sacred writings took place was their writers were under the power, influence and direction of the Spirit of God. Bible scholars are not sure at which point of his life King David wrote this Psalm. David experienced years when he was being pursued by King Saul's army whose assignment was to kill David. There are multiple Psalms of David crying out to God for help. Below are several verses written by David from the Psalms that show there were times he felt such despair he felt God had rejected him and wondered if God had forsaken and abandoned him. It is therefore quite possible that the "My God, my God, why have you forsaken me" cry spoke more of David's anguish rather than indicating the future Messiah's sentiment at the crucifixion.

Psalm 27:9-10 NASB

> 9 Do not hide your face from me, do not turn your
>> servant away in anger; you have been my helper.
> Do not abandon me or forsake me, O God of my Salvation.
>> 10 For my father and my mother have forsaken me,
> But the LORD will take me up

Psalm 38:21 NASB

> Do not forsake me, O LORD;
>> O my God, do not be far from me!

Psalm 42:9-10 NASB (Not David)

> 9 I will say to God my rock, "Why have You forgotten me?
>> Why do I go mourning because of the oppression
> of the enemy?"
>> 10 As a shattering of my bones, my adversaries revile me,
>> While they say to me all day long, "Where is your God?"

Psalm 44:23-24 NASB (Not David)

> 23 Arouse Yourself, why do You sleep, O Lord?
>> Awake, do not reject us forever.
> 24 Why do You hide Your face
>> *And* forget our affliction and our oppression?

"My God, Why Have You Forsaken Me?" 301

<u>While our pain and despair are quite real, and we may feel that God has abandoned us or is silent to our pleas, our perceptions are not reflections of the reality that God is compassionate, merciful, slow to anger, loving and faithful and that He keeps His promise to never leave nor forsake us.</u> We have seen several verses that oppose the idea that God cannot look upon the sin of mankind. Psalm 22 provides support to the theory that Jesus was prodding the intellect and memory of the chief priest, scribes and elders to recognize that they were fulfilling a prophecy. Another clue that Jesus was quoting from Psalms 22:1 resides in this quote itself. A word search of the scriptures shows King David referred to God as his LORD, and his God, but <u>never</u> as his Father. Jesus referred to God as "My Father," "The Father" or "Father," but the gospels record He referred to God as "My God" only twice. The first time Jesus referred to God as "My God" was quoting Psalm 22 from the cross as discussed here. Then in John 20:17 NASB just after the resurrection Jesus said this to Mary Magdalena:

> [17] Jesus *said to her, "Stop clinging to Me, for I have not yet ascended to the Father; but go to My brethren and say to them, 'I ascend to My Father and your Father, and My God and your God.'"

According to the Greek Interlinear which records the Greek words precisely without smoothing the words for easier understanding define the words "My Father and your Father" and "My God and your God" as the "Father of me and the Father of you" and the "God of me and the God of you" as in indicating the unique relationship that God has with each of us. This is similar to God identifying Himself to Moses in Exodus 3:6 as "I am the God of your father, the God of Abraham, the God of Isaac and the God of Jacob."

When Jesus quoted the Psalm 22:1 verse from the cross, this was not the first time He gave clues to His audience about what would happen on that day. There are clues in the Old Testament as well as in the gospels that help us discover the answer of whether God, ever rejected or abandoned Jesus while He was on the cross. Several times Jesus spoke of the coming day of the cross and made statements about God's response.

John 8:28-29 NASB says, "When you lift up the Son of Man, then you will know that I am *He*, and I do nothing on My own initiative, but I speak these things as the Father taught Me.²⁹ <u>And He who sent Me is with Me</u>; <u>He has not left Me alone</u>, for I always do the things that are pleasing to Him."

The day before the cross, Jesus stated that God is and will be with Him during the upcoming events.

John 16:32 NASB says, ³²Behold, an hour is coming, and has *already* come, for you to be scattered, each to his own *home*, and to leave Me alone; and *yet* I am not alone, because <u>the Father is with Me</u>.

In a prophecy to King David regarding a future son of David, I Chronicles 17:12-14 NASB God says, "I will establish his throne forever. I will be his father and he shall be My son; and <u>I will not take My loving kindness away from him,</u> as I took it from him who was before you. But I will settle him in My house and in My kingdom forever, and his throne shall be established forever."

Psalm 22 prophetically spoke of that dark day of the cross on Golgotha of Jesus' pain, when His hands and feet would be pierced, that there would be mocking comments by those around Him, and even the gambling for His clothes. Then Psalm 22:24 NASB tells of God's response.

For He has not despised nor abhorred the affliction of the afflicted;
<u>Nor has He hidden His face from him</u>;
But when he cried to Him for help, He heard.

If we are still unsure whether Jesus was forsaken or abandoned by God, there are more clues. This controversial question was not the last thing Jesus spoke on the cross. In the book of John (19:26-27) He tells His mother to behold her son John, and His disciple John to behold his Mother. Verse 28 records His proclamation before death that it is finished. In the Book of Luke Jesus tells the thief on the cross that he will be with Him in paradise. The other two statements are of particular interest because they record Jesus' comments to God, as His Father. These comments would seem to overrule and outweigh the questionable cry of why had God forsaken Him, because here Jesus calls God, "Father" and gives no indication there is or was a breach between them. In the following verses shown from Luke 23, verse 34 appears to be the first thing Jesus said on the cross and verse 46 the last thing He said before death.

Luke 23:34 and 46 NASB [34] But Jesus was saying, "Father, forgive them; for they do not know what they are doing."

[46] And Jesus, crying out with a loud voice, said, "Father, INTO YOUR HANDS I COMMIT MY SPIRIT." Having said this, He breathed His last.

To presume that God turned away and abandoned Jesus while on the cross, would mean God was there for the "Father, forgive them, for they do not know what they are doing" statement, then abandoned Jesus for "My God, why have you forsaken me?" statement, then came back for the "Father, into your hands I commit my spirit." The gospels said God loves and delights in His Son (Matthew 3:17 [Mark 1:11] and Matthew 17:5 [Mark 9:7]), and Jesus said the Father had not left Him alone and was with Him (John 8:29, 16:32). How then can one presume God forsook Jesus when there is no scripture to support that idea, except Jesus' exact quote of Psalm 22:1?

To look at all possibilities in resolving whether God forsook Jesus while He was on the cross, the statement by Jesus that He and God are one should also be evaluated. Jesus told Philip in John 14:9 that <u>if you have seen Me, you have seen the Father</u>. In Isaiah 44:6 God says He is the first and the last and beside Him there is no God. If Jesus is the One and Only God, then He cannot deny, reject or forsake Himself. Since there are no scriptures anywhere in the Bible that indicate God turned away from Jesus because of Jesus taking on the sin of the world, then that theory has no scriptural basis and it disparages the character of faithful, omnipresent, and compassionate God.

<u>*Important points from this Chapter were:*</u>
- *There are no scriptures that imply God abandoned, or turned away from Jesus or that Jesus was forsaken by God while on the cross.*
- *The statement spoken while on the cross "My God, my God, why have you forsaken me?" was a direct quote from Psalm 22 which prophetically detailed events on the day Jesus was crucified.*

This chapter looked at Jesus on the cross and some of the statements He made. Up to this point the stories reviewed in this book have shown Jesus' extraordinary power to heal people, to control the wind and waves, to provide food bountifully for thousands and His effortless power over death. Throughout the stories, Jesus made bold statements about Himself that could only be true if He is God. The next chapter asks a very important question in understanding who Jesus is – can God be a man?

CHAPTER 19

Was Jesus Fully Human?

"<u>God is not a man</u>, that He should lie;
neither the son of man [a human], that He should repent."[113]

Numbers 23:19

²⁷ The men were amazed and asked, "What kind of man is this? Even the winds and the waves obey him!"

Matthew 8:27 NIV

³³ The Jews answered Him, "For a good work we do not stone You, but for blasphemy; and because <u>You, being a man, make Yourself out *to be* God</u>."

³⁶ Do you say of Him, whom the Father sanctified and sent into the world, 'You are blaspheming,' because I said, 'I am the Son of God'?

John 10:33 and 36 NASB

Do you suppose that as a young boy Jesus ever took a raisin cake (a cookie) and lied to his mother when asked if he had taken it? As a toddler

---

[113] According to Hebrew words in **Strong's Concordance** this verse means that God is not a human being that He should be found to be a liar, proved lying or deceiving, neither is he a human subject to mistakes that it be necessary to grieve or regret errors He has made.

do you think he ever threw a toy at another child striking them in anger? Do you think he ever measured wrong or ruined an object he was working on with his father, Joseph? Any of these incidents would have been normal.

In Christianity, it is generally thought that Jesus is fully God and fully man. Yet few Christians know the origins of this doctrinal stand. During the first few hundred years after the ascension of Jesus, the question of whether Jesus was human or God (Son of God) was a source of conflict in the early church. In 325 AD under the Roman Emperor Constantine, the first council of bishops formed a statement of beliefs known as the Nicene Creed which included the acknowledgement that Jesus was of the essence of God the Father "true God from true God" and "was made man."

The question "was Jesus fully human and fully God?" goes directly to the heart of the Christian faith. To not know the answer to something so fundamentally important about one's faith seems to question one's relationship with God. The question of the humanity of Jesus does not deny that Jesus was born, had a body that ate, drank, slept, moved and aged. <u>Rather the question asks if Jesus shared the same mental, physical and emotional aspects and shortcomings that are common and typical of all humans</u>? If He did not, then could He have been fully human? The correct answer to this question cannot be based on one's personal thoughts, revelation, intuition, or faith because the truth is what the Bible scriptures say.

Up to now every chapter in this book has shown how God (and Jesus) was revealing to His prophets that the Messiah to come would be God. From the titles of Messiah (Christ), King, Priest, Son of God, Son of David, and *the* Prophet (spoken of in Deuteronomy 18) all provided clues to His identity as God. Each time Jesus healed the blind and deaf, restored the lame, restored life, and forgave sins, He was revealing His nature, power and identity as God in accordance with what God says He does in the Old Testament scriptures.[114] Likewise, the passages

---

114 See Isaiah 35:5-6, Psalm 103:3, Jeremiah 33:6, Isaiah 42:6, 44:6 and 48:11.

that said He knew what others were thinking; when He healed someone from afar (the Centurion's servant, and the Phoenician woman's daughter), and knew when Lazarus had died, He was revealing Himself to be omniscient (having unlimited knowledge and understanding) and omnipresent (present everywhere at all times). When He turned water to wine, mass produced bread and fish to feed thousands, commanded the wind to cease during a storm, walked on water, and raised the dead, He was revealing Himself to be *El Shaddai* (Almighty God) with unlimited power to cause the laws of nature to respond differently than the norm, that is, omnipotent. Therefore, this chapter does not address whether Jesus is God, but rather asks if Almighty God, Creator of the Universe can be <u>fully</u> man even though He retains all His power, knowledge, character and authority as God? And where is that in the Bible?

Before the scriptures are reviewed, a consensus of what "human" means should be addressed. <u>From a genetic point, a human is the result of conception involving the fertilization of the female egg by a male sperm</u>. The fetus has a functioning neurological (brain activity), and physiological system (circulatory and respiratory system and the ability to receive nourishment). <u>Being "human" can also be defined as sharing characteristics common to all humans</u>. Physical and emotional needs help define a healthy human; as well as mental reasoning and problem solving. It is our mental reasoning and perceptions that makes us prone to making mistakes. Psychological tendencies such as fears, self-perception, depression, motivation and behavior all affect and influence our interpersonal relations. <u>Physical imperfections such as scars, birthmarks, or deformities (however minor) are common to all humans</u>.

Psychological shortcomings and physical imperfections common to all people, are not recorded in the gospels regarding Jesus. Some could say Jesus expressed emotions; yet the Old Testament is filled with examples of God expressing mercy, love, anger, sorrow, forgiveness, compassion and being grieved. We are now aware that animals express anger, shame, grief, happiness and the need to be loved and comforted. Therefore, the expression of emotions is not exclusive to humans. In the theory that Jesus was fully human, did He struggle with guilt, doubt, temptation, have a birthmark, get a cavity or have a scar from working as a carpenter? These emotions and physical conditions would be considered normal for the human experience. However, guilt implies the response to a violation of some moral standard and doubt is an uncertainty or struggle with belief or trust. Temptation is a strong urge or desire that can later produce regret if indulged, and a cavity in a tooth is the result of decay. Birth marks and scars are blemishes (word #H3971 in *Strong's Concordance* meaning spot or defect). Since Jesus is known as the sinless Passover Lamb without blemish, made perfect (John 1:29, I Corinthians 5:7, Hebrews 5:9 and 9:14 NASB) then one could conclude He did not experience guilt, and He never had a cavity, a scar; not even a birthmark! (This statement does not include what was done to Jesus during the last 24 hours before His execution.)

Perhaps one may think this level of perfection is a misrepresentation of what the word "perfect" means. From the Hebrew (#8549 *tamiym* in *Strong's Concordance*) the word "perfect" is defined as complete, whole, unimpaired, innocent and having integrity. This same word was used in the scriptures to identify that which is without blemish and without spot. The animals offered for sacrifice were carefully examined for any indication of deformity, birthmark (spot) or scar because only the ones that were "perfect" were to be accepted for sacrifice. Jesus could not have been less than what scriptures said He was – perfect and without spot (Hebrews 5:9 KJV says, "being made perfect" and 9:14 KJV – "without spot"). In Leviticus 21:16-23 God tells Moses that any person with certain defects cannot offer bread, enter the veil, or come near to the altar in the tabernacle before God.

Some people familiar with Hebrews 4:15 could say, "but Jesus was tempted, He knew what it was like to have our problems and feelings." Hebrews 4:15 KJV says, "For we have not a high priest which cannot be touched with the feeling of our infirmities; but was in all points tempted like as we are, yet without sin." The word "tempted" (#G3985 in *Strong's Concordance*) can mean to try, make trial of, or test for the purpose of ascertaining his quality, or what he thinks, or how he will behave. It can also mean by impious or wicked conduct to test God's justice and patience and to challenge him, as to give proof of his perfections. The same word's definition is implied in Matthew 4:1 when Jesus was in the wilderness and "tempted" by the devil, and in Jesus' response to the devil in Matthew 4:7 (thou shall not *tempt* the Lord thy God). Matthew 16:1 tells of when the Pharisees and Sadducees came tempting Jesus to show them a sign. Was Jesus really tempted to comply with the devil's or Pharisees' requests? The more accurate interpretation is that the devil, the Pharisees and Sadducees attempted to *try* or *test* Jesus to see His response. Therefore Hebrews 4:15 could be translated to say: For we do not have a high priest which cannot be touched with the feeling of our infirmities; but was in all points tested like as we are, yet without sin. Regarding the first part of this verse - do we really think that God is incapable of relating to our feelings, and our infirmities without becoming a human? Does this imply that until Jesus came, God was clueless in this area about His creation? This verse doesn't reveal how much Jesus has in common with us, but rather shows His deity once again – that even when touched with the feelings of our infirmities and being tested, tried, or tempted, He was still God and unlike us, responded without sinning.

What about doubt? Did Jesus experience doubt about going to the cross? Some people may feel there are passages in Matthew, Mark and Luke which indicate Jesus felt fear or trepidation about the coming crucifixion. We cannot be positive of what spiritual circumstances hung in the balance for mankind when these scriptures described Jesus as sorrowful (Matthew 26:38) and in agony (Luke 22:44) or when He prayed asking if "the cup" could pass from Him. But any assessment of fear and doubt the night before the cross as cited in the synoptic gospels must be balanced with the account in John which does not reflect a demeanor of fear or anxiety at all on the part of Jesus. Instead in His last talk with His disciples covered in four chapters of John (13-16), Jesus is gentle, kind, reassuring, straight forward in His language and loving. He tells them to believe in Him, that He will come to them, that He leaves His peace with them. Then He speaks of His joy in John 15:11 "These things have I spoken unto you, that my joy might remain in you, and that your joy might be full." The cross and crucifixion were no surprise to Jesus. Several times Jesus told His disciples what would happen (Matthew 16:21, 20:18 and Mark 10:33). Revelation 13:8 speaks of Jesus as the Lamb who was slain from the creation of the world. He spoke of returning to the Father, that He was not alone. Look at these verses:

> **John 8:29 NIV** "The one who sent me is with me; he has not left me alone, for I always do what pleases him."
>
> **John 12:27** Now is my soul troubled; and what shall I say? Father, save me from this hour: but for this cause came I unto this hour.
>
> **John 13:1 and 3 NIV** It was just before the Passover Festival. Jesus knew that the hour had come for him to leave this world and go to the Father… ³ Jesus knew that the Father had put all things under his power, and that he had come from God and was returning to God;

After reviewing some basics of how science classifies mankind on a physiological and psychological basis to note Jesus' differences, there is another witness that should be heard on the question of whether Jesus was fully man. It is the evaluation of the Jewish people regarding their understanding of the character of God and their assessment of the nature of mankind as defined by *Torah*. Several places in the gospels say when Jesus forgave someone of their sin, Jesus was accused of blasphemy because the people knew that only God could forgive sin. Approximately four months before the cross, this conversation in John 10:22-38 took place. Some people questioned Jesus asking Him to confirm or deny His identity as the Messiah. Here is part of that encounter.

> ²² At that time the Feast of the Dedication (Hanukkah) took place at Jerusalem; ²³ it was winter, and Jesus was walking in the temple in the portico of Solomon. ²⁴ The Jews then gathered around Him, and were saying to Him, "How long will You keep us in suspense? If You are the Christ [Messiah], tell us plainly."²⁵ Jesus answered them, "<u>I told you</u>, and you do not believe; the works that I do in My Father's name, these testify of Me. ²⁶ But you do not believe because you are not of My sheep.²⁷ My sheep hear My voice, and I know them, and they follow Me; ²⁸ and I give eternal life to them, and they will never perish; and no one will snatch them out of My hand. ²⁹ My Father, who has given *them* to Me, is greater than all; and no one is able to snatch *them* out of the Father's hand. ³⁰ <u>I and the Father are one</u>."
>
> ³¹ The Jews picked up stones again to stone Him. ³² Jesus answered them, "I showed you many good works from the Father; for which of them are you stoning Me?" ³³ The Jews answered Him, "For a good work we do not stone You, but for blasphemy; and because <u>You, being a man, make Yourself out *to be God.*</u>"³⁴ Jesus answered them, "Has it not been written in your Law, 'I SAID, YOU ARE GODS'? ³⁵ If he called them gods, to whom the word of God came (and the Scripture cannot be broken), ³⁶ do you say of Him, whom the Father sanctified and sent into the world, 'You are blaspheming,' because I said, 'I am the Son of God'? ³⁷ If I do not do the works of My Father, do not believe Me; ³⁸ but if I do them, though you do not believe Me, believe the works, so that you may know and understand that the Father is in Me, and I in the Father."
>
> *John 10:22-38 NASB*

This is quite possibly one of the most important conversations involving the identity of Jesus in the Bible. The people gathered around Him after He healed the sick, blind, deaf, the crippled and demon possessed. Isaiah 35:5-6 NASB says that by <u>God</u> "the eyes of the blind will be opened and the ears of the deaf will be unstopped. Then the lame will leap like a deer, and the tongue of the mute will shout for joy." Psalm 103:3 says <u>God</u> heals all our diseases. Jeremiah 33:6 NASB says <u>God</u> will "bring to it (Israel) health and healing, and I will heal them; and I will reveal to them an abundance of peace and truth." The people present *knew* the prophets said God was the One who healed.

When the Jews asked Jesus to tell them plainly if He was the Messiah, He responded He had already told them and they did not believe Him. Jesus said His statements and miracles identified Him, but the people there could not believe the implications. Jesus said He was the Good Shepherd (John 10:11) and no one snatched His sheep from His hands. This statement proclaimed His identity as God. (Also see Psalm 23:1, Ezekiel 34:11-16, Isaiah 40:10-11 and 43:12-13 below.)

Psalm 23:1 The Lord is my shepherd….

Ezekiel 34:11-16 [11] For thus saith the Lord God; Behold, I, even I, will both search my sheep, and seek them out. [12] As a shepherd seeketh out his flock in the day that he is among his sheep that are scattered; so will I seek out my sheep, and will deliver them out of all places where they have been scattered in the cloudy and dark day. [13] And I will bring them out from the people, and gather them from the countries, and will bring them to their own land, and feed them upon the mountains of Israel by the rivers, and in all the inhabited places of the country. [14] I will feed them in a good pasture, and upon the high mountains of Israel shall their fold be: there shall they lie in a good fold, and in a fat pasture shall they feed upon the mountains of Israel. [15] I will feed my flock, and

I will cause them to lie down, saith the Lord God. ¹⁶ I will seek that which was lost, and bring again that which was driven away, and will bind up that which was broken, and will strengthen that which was sick: but I will destroy the fat and the strong; I will feed them with judgment.

Isaiah 40:10-11 ¹⁰ Behold, the Lord God will come with strong hand, and his arm shall rule for him: behold, his reward is with him, and his work before him. ¹¹ He shall feed his flock like a shepherd: he shall gather the lambs with his arm, and carry them in his bosom, and shall gently lead those that are with young.

Isaiah 43:12-13 ¹² I have declared, and have saved, and I have shewed, when there was no strange god among you: therefore ye are my witnesses, saith the Lord, that I am God. ¹³ Yea, before the day was I am he; and there is none that can deliver out of my hand: I will work, and who shall let it?

Jesus told the people to believe the works (miracles) He did "in the name of the Father";[115] things that only God could do. Jesus said in John 10:28 He gave eternal life (something only God can do) to those who believed He is God. As clearly as He could make it, when Jesus said He and the Father were *one,* this meant Jesus is God! His audience understood what He said and knew what He meant. Their response was to reach for stones to kill Him. When Jesus asked why, they answered, "Because You, being a man, make Yourself out *to be* God." Their assessment was typical of Jewish thought: that man cannot be God. They thought the coming Messiah would be an anointed Warrior/King in

---

115 In "The Name" of God/Jesus/the LORD – see chapter 21 of this book "No other Name." The Name of God reveals His eternal nature, His power to effect change, and His holiness. It also proclaims He is the source of eternal life and has a unique relationship to each of His people. Jesus' name is the name of the LORD combined with the word save/salvation.

the line and likeness of King David who would save them from their enemies. Instead, Jesus' answer proclaimed He had the full power and authority of God.

While Christians today may be familiar with and lay people are unfamiliar with the idea that Jesus is both man and God, Jewish thought was clear on the distinction and incompatibility of flawed mankind's nature and holy God's character being perfect. This point is addressed in Numbers 23:19, "<u>God is not a man</u>, that He should lie; neither the son of man [a human], that He should repent." Psalm 49:7 NASB says, No man can by any means redeem *his* brother or give to God a ransom for him. Jesus' response was – "do you say of Me who God has sanctified (set apart as holy, hallowed – word #G37 in *Strong's Concordance*) and sent into the world that I am "'blaspheming,' because <u>I said, 'I am the Son of God'</u>?" When did Jesus say He was the Son of God in this conversation? Each time Jesus called God "My Father" or "the Father" He was implying that He was the Son of God! The people understood the implied meaning of these comments to be that Jesus was God in nature. "I and the Father are one" and "the Father is in Me, and I in the Father" are statements that said Jesus is God. The Jewish people had the firm understanding that man cannot be God and God cannot be man. Therefore, when the Jewish people sought to stone Jesus or accused Him of blasphemy, it was because of their recognition that Jesus' words declared Himself to be God, went they felt He was *just* a man. Therefore, when Jesus did the extraordinary, people asked "What manner (or kind) of man is this?" (Matthew 8:27).

As the question of Jesus' humanity is pondered, there is one point that truly ends the theory that Jesus was <u>fully</u> human. That point involves His conception. As mentioned earlier, human conception occurs with the fertilization of a female egg by a male sperm. The child is the product of half their father and half their mother's DNA genetic makeup. Yet the Bible says that Jesus' mother Mary was a virgin at conception. Look at these verses regarding the conception of Jesus.

Luke 1:35 KJV: And the angel answered and said unto her, <u>The Holy Ghost shall come upon thee, and the power of the Highest shall overshadow thee</u>: therefore also that holy <u>thing</u> which shall be born of thee shall be called the Son of God.

Matthew 1:20 KJV ... behold, the angel of the LORD appeared[116] unto him in a dream, saying, Joseph, thou son of David, fear not to take unto thee Mary thy wife: for <u>that which is conceived in her is of the Holy Ghost.</u>

Isaiah 7:14 KJV Therefore the Lord himself shall give you a sign; Behold, <u>a virgin shall conceive</u>, and bear a son, and shall call his name Immanuel (from Matthew 1:23 KVJ "which being interpreted is, God with us").

<u>Since the scriptures indicate no human male sperm was involved in the conception, then Jesus could not be</u> **fully** <u>human</u>. The next logical question is: how was Jesus conceived in Mary (Matthew 1:20)? Luke 1:35 said the Holy Ghost/Holy Spirit (also referred to as The Spirit of the Lord) and the power of the Most High would "overshadow" Mary and for the reason of this overshadowing, the Holy Child (thing in the King James) would be called the Son of God. The words of interest in this verse are "overshadow" and "thing." In *Strong's Concordance* the word overshadow is Greek word #G1982 *episkiazo* which means to envelop as in "a haze of brilliancy; figuratively, to invest with preternatural influence" (preternatural means existing outside of nature, exceeding what is natural or regular). The "Holy thing" is Greek word #G40 *hagios;* comes from two root words: 1) *hagnos* which means pure

---

116 Some Bible commentators believe the appearance of **the** Angel of the LORD is an appearance of Jesus, the Messiah. *Wikipedia* on the topic of "The Angel of the LORD," says "The term *malakh YHWH*, in English translation usually accompanied with the definite article, King James Version "**the** angel of the LORD", occurs 65 times in the text of the Hebrew Bible. In some instances, it is clear the reference is to a theophany, i.e. an appearance of YHWH himself rather than a separate entity acting on his behalf."

(from every fault), chaste, sacred and 2) *thalpo* meaning to cherish and foster with tender love and care, to keep warm. "How was Jesus conceived in Mary?" If the answer resides in Luke 1:35, Matthew 1:20 and Isaiah 7:14, could it be: Jesus, who would be called "God is with us" and the Son of God to be cherished with tender love was placed in Mary through the enveloping supernatural Spirit of the Most High God. This assessment leads to the next question. While believers readily accept the account of Mary being a virgin, when she conceived Jesus through the Holy Spirit and power of God, is it possible that Mary was a surrogate? Is it possible that Jesus/God conceived in Mary required neither human sperm nor human egg?

Does scripture indicate the body of Jesus was different? And if Jesus is God from conception without human sperm, does scripture explain how God could physically be a man? The answer is yes to both questions. Hebrews 10:5 NASB[117] says that God prepared a "body" for Jesus. Philippians 2:7 NASB says although Jesus existed in the <u>form</u> of God, He emptied Himself (according to *Strong's Concordance* word #G2758 can mean Jesus laid aside the form of God) to be made into the <u>likeness</u> of men. Romans 8:3 says that God sent His Son (Jesus) in the <u>likeness</u> of human flesh.

> **Hebrews 10:5 NASB** Therefore, when He comes into the world, He says, "Sacrifice and offering You have not desired, But a body You have prepared for Me;
>
> **Philippians 2:6-7 NASB** [Jesus] ⁶ who, although He existed in the form of God, did not regard equality with God a thing to be grasped, ⁷ but emptied Himself, taking the form of a bond servant, *and* being made in the likeness of men.
>
> **Romans 8:3 KJV** "…God sending his own Son <u>in the likeness</u> of sinful flesh …."

---

117   Hebrews 10:5 is a loosely quoted passage of Psalm 40:6 which does not include the line about "a body prepared for me."

The Philippians and Romans verses cited speak of Jesus being made in the *likeness* of men and Genesis 1:26 KJV spoke of God creating man in the image, after the *likeness* of God. While the word "likeness" (Hebrew root word #H1819 *damah*) means the two shares things that are similar, they resemble each other. They are not the same. Just as man created in the likeness of God does not make man God, then God inhabiting an exclusively unique body in the *likeness* of man did not make God a man. The apostle Peter in Acts 2:29-31 quotes King David from Psalms 16:10 and says this unique body would not decay.

Psalm 16:10 NASB Nor will You allow Your Holy One to undergo decay.

Acts 2:29-31 NASB "Brethren, I may confidently say to you regarding the patriarch David that he both died and was buried, and his tomb is with us to this day. ³⁰ And so, because he was a prophet and knew that GOD HAD SWORN TO HIM WITH AN OATH TO SEAT *one* OF HIS DESCENDANTS ON HIS THRONE, ³¹ he looked ahead and spoke of the resurrection of the Christ, that He was neither abandoned to Hades, nor did His flesh suffer decay.

Throughout this book several extraordinary things Jesus did and said have been examined. Was there something extraordinary or unusual about Jesus' body? Yes, the Bible tells of His ability to alter His own His physical appearance. On three occasions the Gospels tell of people who were familiar with Jesus but did not recognize Him until Jesus chose to make them aware it was Him. These accounts are usually not discussed in sermons or Bible studies but are accepted and presumed to be part of the powers Jesus acquired after His resurrection and in His glorified body, though nothing in the scriptures indicate He did not have these capabilities *before* His death.

The first change of appearance recorded in Mark 16 speaks of an incident that is flushed out in greater detail as Luke 24. This passage tells of the encounter with two disciples of Jesus' on the road to

Emmaus after the resurrection. Mark 16:12 KJV says, "After that <u>he appeared in another form</u> unto two of them, as they walked, and went into the country." Luke 24:31 KJV says, "And their eyes were opened, and they knew him; and <u>he vanished</u> out of their sight." The second incident is in John 20:14 tells of the day of Jesus' resurrection when Mary Magdalene was outside of the empty tomb. The NASB says, "¹⁴ When she had said this, she turned around and saw Jesus standing *there*, and did not know that it was Jesus." So, although she knew Jesus, she did not recognize Him standing in front of her.

The third incident of Jesus' changed appearance is in John 21 involving the second miraculous catch of fish (the first miraculous catch of fish is in Luke 5) when Jesus asks Peter does He love Him three times. Are we aware that in this encounter Jesus did not look like the Jesus these disciples had lived with for the previous three years? John 21:12 NASB says, Jesus said to them, "Come and have breakfast." None of the disciples ventured to question Him, "Who are You?" knowing that it was the Lord. Beyond altering His appearance, Jesus appears and disappears. On the road to Emmaus after Jesus revealed Himself to two of His disciples, He vanished! And as if vanishing were not enough, John 20:19 says that Jesus suddenly appeared in the room although the doors were closed. John 20:19 NASB says, "So when it was evening on that day, the first *day* of the week, and when the doors were shut where the disciples were, for fear of the Jews, Jesus came and stood in their midst and said to them, "Peace *be* with you." Only a magician or illusionist *can appear* to change their appearance, disappear and suddenly appear in a closed room. The use of illusion, curtains, help by assistants, or trap-doors in the floor were not used by Jesus.

These incidents showed Jesus' ability to alter His appearance or the people's perception of His appearance, however, the transfiguration seems to show Jesus' ability to change His form from human to that of a spiritual being. Notice the same description made by John in the book of Revelation of Jesus thirty plus years later in His glorified appearance in heaven.

Matthew 17:2-3 NASB And He was transfigured before them; and <u>His face shone like the sun</u>, and His garments became as white as light. ³ And behold, Moses and Elijah appeared to them, talking with Him.

Revelation 1:13 and 16 NASB *I saw* one like a son of man ... <u>His face was like the sun</u> shining in its strength.

In the blink of an eye while three disciples were with Jesus on a mountain, they entered a spiritual realm where they saw Jesus in His altered state, along with Moses and Elijah whose time on earth had long ceased and they heard God speak. This was not the first time God met with people on a mountain. Moses, Aaron, two sons of Aaron and 70 elders met with God on a mountain as told in Exodus 24:9-11 NIV.

⁹ Moses and Aaron, Nadab and Abihu, and the seventy elders of Israel went up ¹⁰ and saw the God of Israel. Under his feet was something like a pavement made of lapis lazuli, as bright blue as the sky. ¹¹ But God did not raise his hand against these leaders of the Israelites; they saw God, and they ate and drank.

Scripture says Moses, Aaron and company *saw* the God of Israel. Colossians 1:15 says that Jesus is the image of the invisible God. If God is Spirit (John 4:24) and invisible and Jesus is the image of the invisible God, then who did Moses, Aaron and the 70 elders of Israel see? (Based on deductive reasoning, Moses, Aaron and the elders saw Jesus!) With this information about God and the amazing things Jesus did and said, we should have a growing sense of just how different from man Jesus is.

As the Bible classifies all mankind in some specific terms, the gap between mankind and Jesus widens more. Psalms 103:15 and Isaiah 40:6 compare the shortness of life for humans to grass and flowers. The apostle Paul says in Romans 3 that <u>all</u> of mankind have sinned, and in Genesis 6:12 God spoke of <u>all</u> mankind as being corrupt. Can any believer say these statements are true of Jesus? That He had a short life, He's a sinner and corrupt? Did Jesus believe He was different from us? Did He give us indications that He is not like us? The answer is yes, He did.

John 8:23 NASB But he continued, "You are from below; I am from above. You are of this world; I am not of this world.

John 6:38 For I have come down from heaven...

One more thing, Jesus made a couple of statements about His past encounters. These statements do not indicate a typical human life span.

John 8:56-58 NASB [56] Your father Abraham rejoiced to see My day, and he saw *it* and was glad." [57] So the Jews said to Him, "You are not yet fifty years old, and have You seen Abraham?" [58] Jesus said to them, "Truly, truly, I say to you, before Abraham was born, I am."

Luke 10:18 KJV [18] And he said unto them, I beheld Satan as lightning fall from heaven.

Jesus also made this statement about knowing the longings and prayers of righteous men and prophets throughout the history of Israel. What did righteous men and prophets long to see and hear other than God?

Matthew 13:17 [17] For verily I say unto you, That many prophets and righteous men have desired to see those things which ye see, and have not seen them; and to hear those things which ye hear, and have not heard them.

The Bible verses say a virgin conceived Jesus by the Holy Spirit of God, born into a body prepared for Him by God, that He laid aside

His form as God to take on the form of man, and that this unique body would not undergo the decay of death. Jesus' own words said He is not like us, nor from the same place. He tells of His presence at events that exceeds human life spans and acknowledged His presence in heaven! How can these claims describe a human?

Jesus as God, who came in a uniquely prepared body, prompts us to ask the inevitable question: how did, how could God die? The answer to this question is the same as how could God be a fetus inside the body of a human virgin? How does God create the world or foretell events a thousand years before they happen? In Genesis 18:12-14 God Himself answered Sarah's question of doubt about how can the impossible be possible by asking another question, "Is anything too difficult for the Lord?" Matthew 19:26 records this statement, "And looking at *them* Jesus said to them, "With people this is impossible, but with God all things are possible." No doubt on that fateful day of His crucifixion the heart of Jesus stopped beating, His brain activity ceased and had He been examined by the best physicians of today, He would have been declared dead. However, the One who says He is the giver of eternal life (John 6:47-51), that if anyone believes in Him they will never die (John 11:26), the One who promised the dying thief on the cross (from the cross) that day He would be with Him in paradise, surely was not dead as we understand death. Acts 2:24 says it was *impossible* for the power of death to hold Jesus. All throughout John 13-16 Jesus spoke to His disciples of leaving them for a little while, of them not seeing Him then they would see Him, and of returning to the Father. Just as His life and the things He did were unlike any other human, His death would not be a death as we understand death but would accomplish things of which none of His disciples had the faintest idea.

From the Old Testament, the Gospels and the New Testament dozens of scriptures speak of the one of a kind Jesus. Hundreds of years before His birth scriptures told of His nature, power and authority, that He would heal the blind, restore wholeness in the bodies of mankind as well as their spirits. We read that His genetic makeup and His conception (is of the power of the Most High and of the Holy Spirit - Matthew 1:20 and Luke 1:35) would not be like any human ever born on this planet. The miracles He performed in an instant put Jesus in a class that only fictional superheroes of today attempt to mimic with the aid of imagination or special effects.

The question "Was Jesus Fully Human?" and its possible answers are controversial. Does it matter if Christians believe or not that Jesus was fully human as well as the Son of God or that He was fully God? Would it matter if someone believed Jesus was *just* a carpenter; or a wise prophet? Does it matter if we call Him Beelzebub or a prophet of Allah? Yes, it matters, identity matters. From the time of Adam and Eve, and throughout the history of the nation of Israel, and the world, the Bible shows that <u>the central problem and cause of untold trouble is the failure of mankind to recognize who God is</u>.

In the Garden of Eden God gave Adam one command along with the consequences if Adam disobeyed (Genesis 2:16-17). The deceiver (also known as the Devil or Satan), questioned Eve about God's instruction causing her to think, to reason, to doubt. Genesis 3:6 says "When the woman saw that the fruit of the tree was good for food and pleasing to the eye, and also desirable for gaining wisdom, she took some and ate it." Her reasoning led her to break God's command and led Adam to do the same. Why did they disobey God's command so easily? Their lack of understanding who God is, allowed them to think that not only was obedience optional but being like God was possible.

The two central problems of the nation of Israel through the Old Testament were their failure to obey the instructions of God and idolatry. These problems stemmed from the people's inability to comprehend the power and identity of God. Therefore, the scriptures are filled with stories of people who chose paths which brought about devastating consequences; as well as those who chose other gods and lustful desires that brought spiritual starvation, blindness and death. The desire to be in charge of one's destiny has plagued mankind, blinding us to how little we know and to the reality of how powerless we are. In this state, we cannot help but be blind to the character, nature and power of God.

Satan's number one weapon against mankind is causing them to doubt the true identity and nature of God. Notice what Jesus said to those who refused to believe He is the Messiah in John 8:44 and 8:24 NIV. Just like Adam and Eve's dilemma, Jesus makes the same connection that Satan's lies cause death to those who do not know God, nor believe the truth about the power and character of God.

John 8:44 NIV You belong to your father, the devil, and you want to carry out your father's desires. He was a murderer from the beginning, not holding to the truth, for there is no truth in him. When he lies, he speaks his native language, for he is a liar and the father of lies.

John 8:24 NIV [24] I told you that you would die in your sins; if you do not believe that I am he, you will indeed die in your sins."

It is belief in Jesus as God that brings salvation and eternal life (John 1:12, 3:16 and 6:47) and it is vitally important to Satan that people be unsure of the true identity of Jesus as God. Even today, among the unsaved, Jesus was a man. He is not known to them at all as fully human *and* fully God as the early church determined and proclaimed.[118] When people do not recognize Jesus as fully and truly God, they will think He is just a man, or choose to doubt whether He lived at all or did the things the gospels say He did. They can classify Him as a philosopher, a prophet, a teacher, or a wise, gentle, loving and all accepting good man. He can become classified as someone who had a profound effect on history like Gandhi, Mohammed, Martin

---

118   The Chalcedon Creed adopted at the Council of Chalcedon in 451 AD was the fourth (of seven) of the Ecumenical Councils to develop a unified consensus of beliefs determined Jesus Christ had two natures in one person.

Luther King or Buddha. Or people can choose to speculate that Jesus was secretly married to and had children with the formerly demon possessed Mary Magdalene which was the basis of the 2003 bestselling book - *The DaVinci Code* that sold 80 million books in 44 languages by 2009. Does this level of interest and enthusiasm say that millions of people believed Jesus to be God or human? It does speak of a passion of people to know that Jesus was flawed, that He lied, kept secrets, and that He wasn't what He appeared to be. The bottom line is millions would prefer to believe anything other than Jesus was totally and completely God.

Even for those who acknowledge Jesus as the Son of God, they are uncertain of whether this title means that He was also fully God. Often, they are also unsure what the title "Son of God" means in regards to Jesus' authority, power, and relationship to us and with God the Father and the Holy Spirit of God. Some people who consider themselves Christians are unsure whether they can or should pray to God the Father, Jesus, the Holy Spirit, angels, saints or Mary. The essential point is this: <u>when we accept that Jesus was fully man *and* fully God, we cannot help but diminish His deity</u>, and question His total authority and power in and over our lives. When we do not understand who the God of the Bible is, we can mistakenly feel all people believe in the same God, and that they just use different names for the one God. We can mistakenly think we can advise Almighty God or dismiss Him when we don't get *our way*. We can mistakenly believe that God needs us to defend Him or to act in His behalf as we see fit. Like Adam and Eve, many people feel they have options regarding obedience on how they are to live. In reality we have all eaten of the tree of knowledge of good and evil and are lost, afraid, confused, wounded and sick in this world. Until Jesus' true identity is recognized as God, and we come to know that He is perfect in all of His ways (Deuteronomy 32:4), compassionate and merciful to us, and abounding in love for us (Exodus 34:6), we will *never* experience here on earth the abundant eternal life and intimate relationship with God that He created us to have.

Since the scriptures, actions and words of Jesus proclaimed Him to be fully God, then why did He refer to Himself again and again as the Son of Man?

CHAPTER 20

The Son of Man

... Whom do men say that I the Son of man am?
Matthew 16:13 KJV

Ask now about the former days, long before your time, from the day God created human beings on the earth; ask from one end of the heavens to the other. Has anything so great as this ever happened, or has anything like it ever been heard of?
Deuteronomy 4:32 NIV

This book began with the question *Who is Jesus?* The first chapter explained why Jesus is known as Jesus Christ. The title Christ and Messiah both mean the same thing – anointed, which is a sacred consecration and process for making someone a priest or king. From the scriptures, we learned that indeed Jesus was anointed from heaven and here on earth to be both King and Priest of Israel and Heaven. Therefore, whether we understand it or not, when we refer to Jesus as Christ, we are really saying He is the one consecrated King and Priest of Heaven and Earth.

Chapter 2 showed Jesus to be the long-awaited Prophet God promised just before the death of Moses in Deuteronomy 18. God recalled long ago when He had given the Ten Commandments on Mount Sinai, the people were too afraid to hear His voice, His words or even see evidence of His presence. Now this future Prophet would have a physical presence and special mission; He would be like Moses (human, a Jew), a Shepherd and leader. He would speak the Words of God; providing depth of understanding of the *Torah* instructions for how His people are to live, revealing the character of God, His concern for their welfare, and desire for relationship with people.

Today Christians everywhere know Jesus as the Son of God, but several times in the gospels Jesus was also called the Son of David because some of the people at the time of Jesus believed He was the fulfillment of the prophecy about a future son of David who would also be the Son of God (II Samuel 7). Chapter 3 of this book explained that the designation as Son was not a designation of familial relationship but rather a title that conveyed the rights and authority of the named father. In this case, Jesus claimed a right to be the King of Israel as the Son of King David and as the Son of the Most High God, Jesus claimed the right to speak as God. Scriptures revealed this Son of David and God would be the Messiah, the High Priest without beginning or end, the one born King of Israel and King of Heaven whose kingdom would never end.

Throughout the four gospels, Jesus referred to Himself dozens of times not as God or the Son of God, not even as the Messiah, but as the Son of Man. Why the Son of Man? The fact that He did, means this title has a specific and special meaning. When the meaning of the title Son of Man is uncovered, more will be understood about who Jesus is, and why He came to planet earth.

Is the Son of Man the Messiah?

It was relatively easy to see Jesus' connection to the titles Messiah, King, Prophet, Son of God and Son of David, but the title Son of Man is obscure. While the term "son of man" appears dozens of times in the Old Testament, most of them do not refer to Messiah. Rather it

The Son of Man

is a term used to designate mankind. The search to discover what this title meant prompted more questions than it initially answered; yet it has revealed the most about who God is to us and who we are to God. The first question could be: is there anything in the Old Testament that tells us the title "Son of Man" refers to Messiah? The answer is yes. On Jesus' last night before the cross He stood before the High Priest who questioned His identity (Matthew 26:63-66). Jesus' response strung together information from three Old Testament passages (Psalm 80:17, Isaiah 56:1-2, and Daniel 7:13-14) about the "Son of Man" that directly led to Him being condemned for blasphemy and made the High Priest call for His death. Why? Because the High Priest knew that when Jesus proclaimed Himself to be the Son of Man in this context, Jesus was declaring Himself to be the Messiah and God. This is that passage:

Matthew 26:63-64 But Jesus held his peace, And the high priest answered and said unto him, I adjure thee by the living God, that thou tell us whether thou be the Christ, the Son of God.

⁶⁴ Jesus saith unto him, Thou hast said: nevertheless I say unto you, Hereafter shall ye see <u>the Son of man sitting on the right hand of power, and coming in the clouds of heaven</u>.

The first of the three passages about the Son of Man appears in Psalm 80:17. The Psalmist in this chapter tells God the people of Israel are like a vine God had taken out of Egypt and planted in the land. This vine has grown strong and filled the land, but now is being broken down, plucked and devoured. He calls out to God <u>to return to them and visit this vine</u> (verse 14), the vineyard and "the branch that thou madest strong for thyself (v. 15). (Interestingly enough Jesus is thought to be the *Branch* out of Jesse referred to in Isaiah 11:1). What is of particular interest in verse 17 is *where* the son of man God has made strong for Himself is in relationship to God.

Psalm 80:17 Let thy hand be upon the man <u>of thy right hand</u>, upon <u>the son of man</u> whom thou madest strong for thyself.

In Jewish culture, being at the right hand of someone is symbolic of designating <u>equal</u> position and honor.[119] In this verse it conveys the point that the Son of man has equal privilege, dignity, strength, power and authority as God (see John 1:1-3, I Peter 3:22). Psalm 80:17 implies that God has established the Son of Man in the highest place of honor and power for His own purposes.

The second passage about the Son of Man appears in Isaiah 56:1-2. It speaks of the mission of the Messiah as being righteous (see Jeremiah 33:14-18 and Psalm 110:4[120]), bringing the salvation of God and refers to him as "the son of man."

Isaiah 56:1-2 and 4-5 NASB Thus says the Lord, "Preserve justice and do righteousness, for <u>My salvation is about to come and My righteousness to be revealed</u>. ² "How blessed is the man who does this, and the <u>son of man</u> who takes hold of it; who keeps from profaning the Sabbath, and keeps his hand from doing any evil… [and to those who] choose what pleases Me, and hold fast My covenant, ⁵ to them I will give in My house and within My walls a memorial, and a name better than that of sons and daughters; I will give them an everlasting name which will not be cut off."

This passage leaves little doubt that it speaks to the mission of the Messiah. It contains a play on words that can be seen easier in Hebrew.

---

119 This term is an anthropomorphism, which are terms used to attribute human characteristics and behaviors to a deity. God addressed Himself to the Jewish people in terms they could understand, such as "the eyes of the Lord" and "the arm of the Lord."

120 It was generally known that the Messiah would be Righteous. Hebrews 5:6, 10 and 6:20 explains that Jesus' claim to the Priesthood was in the order of Melchizedek as mentioned in Psalm 110:4. Melchizedek means "my king (is) righteous." Jeremiah 33:14-18 speaks of one coming who would be a branch of David and be called: the Lord is our righteousness.'

"My salvation" is *yeshaw ah* (word #3444 in *Strong's Concordance*) and in Hebrew is pronounced *yeshua*. Jesus' name in Hebrew which has generally been thought to be Yeshua, means "Yahweh (the LORD) saves (Matthew 1:21), delivers or rescues." Therefore, this verse *could be* construed to say – "...My Yeshua (salvation for people) is about to come and My righteousness to be revealed." Verse two goes on to say that the person and the Son of man who preserve justice, righteousness, do not profane the Sabbath, nor do what is evil, and uphold God's covenant is blessed. They gain a unique relationship with God and will dwell in the eternal House of God as family.

It is interesting to note that during His years of public ministry, Jesus was accused several times of breaking the rules of Sabbath observance (Matthew 12:1-14 and Luke 13:10-17) which in turn would have been a sin. According to John 7:21-23 performing miracles on the Sabbath was a major point of contention between the Pharisees, other religious groups and Jesus. It is as if this Isaiah 56 verse addressed the future accusations saying that the Son of Man would not profane the Sabbath nor would He do *any* evil. Look at these verses from Mark 2 and John 5 where Jesus speaks of His authority as the Son of Man.

> **Mark 2:10 NASB** "But so that you may know that the Son of Man has authority on earth to forgive sins..." (to provide salvation and make righteous through forgiveness of sin)

> **Mark 2:28 NASB** "So the Son of Man is Lord even of the Sabbath." (keeps from profaning the Sabbath)

> **John 5:26-27 NASB** For just as the Father has life in Himself, even so He gave to the Son also to have life in Himself; [27] and He gave Him authority to execute judgment (preserve justice and do righteousness), because He is *the* Son of Man.

These verses directly relate to the Isaiah 56:1-2 prophecy about the Son of Man. The passages from the book of Mark speak of attributes of God – only God can forgive sins (Mark 2:7) and God designated the Sabbath as holy in Genesis 2:3. A word study of "Lord" from Mark 2:28 shows that Jesus' comment claimed ownership of the Sabbath. He was saying He is the master and rightful creator of the Sabbath. Therefore, He has authority to determine the true holiness of the Sabbath regarding restrictions and proper observance. In addition, in the John 5:26-27 passage Jesus claims He has divine authority to execute judgment. He is equating His authority and power with that of God. This verse is profound in the argument about the deity of Jesus. Either He has the authority and power of Almighty God to grant eternal life and execute judgment of mankind or He <u>is committing blasphemy!</u> Probably the most stunning part of the Isaiah 56 passage is it says through the Son of Man's salvation those who choose a covenant relationship with God will become <u>more</u> than the named relationship of sons and daughters of God and this relationship will never end or be severed (John 1:12).

The third passage about the Son of Man from the Old Testament found in the seventh chapter of Daniel is significant. The book of Daniel spans the life of the prophet Daniel who was taken into exile from Jerusalem to Babylon when he was probably a teen. During his lifetime, he served as an advisor to three foreign Kings and records troubling dreams and visions he had from "the most High" (God) about future events. Chapter 7 of Daniel tells of the first of those dreams/visions. Verses 13-14 specifically speak of the coming Messiah as the "Son of man." These verses in Daniel directly connect to the prophecy given to King David approximately 500 years earlier in II Samuel 7:12-14. They spoke of a descendent of David who would also be the Son to God whose power and kingdom would last forever. Between the two passages in the books of Daniel and II Samuel they say that this someone would be known as the Son of David, the Son of God *and* <u>the Son of Man</u>.

Daniel 7:12-13 NASB "I kept looking in the night visions, and behold, <u>with the clouds of heaven</u>, <u>One like a Son of Man was coming</u>, and He came up to the Ancient of Days and was presented before Him. ¹⁴ "And to Him was given dominion, glory and a kingdom, that all the peoples, nations and *men of every* language might serve Him. His dominion is an everlasting dominion which will not pass away; and His kingdom is one which will not be destroyed.

II Samuel 7:12-14 NASB (the LORD speaking through the prophet Nathan to King David) I will raise up your descendant after you, who will come forth from you, and I will establish his kingdom. ¹³ He shall build a house for My name, and I will establish the throne of his kingdom forever. ¹⁴ I will be a father to him and he will be a son to Me ....

In reading the passage from Daniel, one could miss the part where Daniel says he saw the Son of Man coming with the clouds of heaven. It is interesting to note that when Jesus ascended into heaven He disappeared in a cloud. Acts 1:11 NASB tells of two men dressed in white clothing who said, "This Jesus, who has been taken up from you into heaven, will come in just the same way as you have watched Him go into heaven." Similar phrases from Exodus to Revelation speak of the LORD coming, appearing or descending out of heaven or in the clouds. To illustrate this point, here are just two verses from the Old Testament and two from Jesus in the book of John:

Exodus 19:9 NASB The LORD said to Moses, "Behold, I will come to you in a thick <u>cloud</u>, so that the people may hear when I speak with you and may also believe in you forever." (On Mt. Sinai before the Commandments are given.)

Ezekiel 1:28 NASB As the appearance of the rainbow in the <u>clouds</u> on a rainy day, so *was* the appearance of the surrounding radiance. Such *was* the appearance of the likeness of the <u>glory of the Lord</u>. And when I saw *it*, I fell on my face and heard a voice speaking.

John 1:51 NASB And He said to him, "Truly, truly, I say to you, you will see the heavens opened and the angels of God ascending and descending on the Son of Man."

John 3:13 KJV And no man hath ascended up to heaven, but he that came down from heaven, even the Son of man which is in heaven.

As stated earlier, Jesus referred to Himself as the Son of Man more than any other title. Yet a read through of the gospels shows the people of His time had no idea what that term meant. During the week before His crucifixion, John 12:34 NASB says, the crowd then answered Him, "We have heard out of the Law that the Christ [Messiah] is to remain forever; and how can You say, 'The Son of Man must be lifted up'? <u>Who is this Son of Man</u>?" Although the people would have been aware the prophet Ezekiel was called "son of man" by God dozens of times in the scroll of Ezekiel, why Jesus referred to Himself in this manner made no sense. Yet as noted there are two incidents recorded in the New Testament that when the terms "Son of man," "right hand of God" and "coming on a cloud" (all from Psalm 80:17, and Daniel 7:12-13 and Isaiah 56:1-2) were spoken together, these words triggered a volatile eruption among the religious sect. Their reaction indicated that while the general public did not recognize the significance of this title, apparently some priests, scribes, Pharisees and elders knew that "Son of Man" identified the Messiah especially when put in the context of being at the right hand of God and as the One coming on a cloud. As mentioned earlier, the first time these three phrases were declared together that triggered a volatile response occurred on the night Jesus was arrested and taken before the Jewish priests, scribes and elders.

Matthew 26:63-66 NASB: *And the high priest said to Him, "I adjure You by the living God, that You tell us whether You are the Christ, the Son of God." *⁶⁴* Jesus said to him, "You have said it yourself; nevertheless I tell you, hereafter you will see <u>the Son of Man sitting at the right hand of Power</u>, and <u>coming on the clouds of heaven</u>."*

⁶⁵ Then the high priest tore his robes and said, "He has blasphemed! What further need do we have of witnesses? Behold, you have now heard the blasphemy; ⁶⁶ what do you think?" They answered, "He deserves death!"

When the high priest heard these three phrases strung together, he knew in an instant Jesus had just admitted He was the Messiah; the Holy One of God prophesied to come. Unable to entertain the possibility Jesus' admission could be true, the high priest quickly arrived at the only other conclusion – blasphemy (the act of showing contempt or insulting God), of which the penalty was death. The High Priest determined Jesus was guilty of blasphemy because He claimed He was the Messiah, the Son of God, the Son of Man of whom the scriptures had said His kingdom would never end. Note the irony here – it was the high priest himself who showed contempt for God (blasphemy) when he claimed that God (Jesus) had blasphemed by acknowledging He is God!

The second time in which these three phrases (Son of Man, at the right hand of God, coming on a cloud/in heaven) triggered a volatile reaction is recorded in the book of Acts involving a disciple and follower of Jesus named Stephen. This incident took place after the resurrection and ascension of Jesus (I Corinthians 15:6 and Acts 1:3). After performing great wonders and speaking eloquently with the power of the Spirit of God, Stephen was falsely accused of blasphemy and taken before the religious council. He gave a brief overview of Israel's history and ended with a stinging accusation that it was those in front of him who were responsible for betraying and murdering Jesus (Acts 7:52). Then at that point, Stephen said something so stunning that the enormity of his statement caused them to call out in loud voices (like screaming) to drown out his words. They covered their ears like children and rushed at Stephen in a mob like frenzy, driving him out of town where they stoned him to death. Here is part of that account told in Acts 7:55-58 NASB:

> [55] But being full of the Holy Spirit, he gazed intently into heaven and saw the glory of God, and <u>Jesus standing at the right hand of God</u>; [56] and he said, "Behold, I see <u>the heavens</u> opened up and the <u>Son of Man standing at the right hand of God</u>." [57] But they cried out with a loud voice, and covered their ears and rushed at him with one impulse. [58] When they had driven him out of the city, they *began* stoning *him*....

These two incidents present a strong case that the Old Testament does establish the concept that the title Son of Man designates the Promised One of God who would come to execute justice, bring salvation and righteousness, have the authority and power of God and is the one whose kingdom will never end. However, while we can see that the title "Son of Man" speaks of the promised Messiah, none of the previous verses tell *what* "Son of Man" means.

What does "Son of Man" mean?

He is the Kinsman redeemer

The answer of what Son of Man means is not one single answer - it is multifaceted and complicated. Some people have speculated that the title Son of Man refers to Jesus meeting the requirements of a **"kinsman redeemer"** for all mankind. A kinsman redeemer is a Hebrew term meaning a male relative who redeems that which was lost in behalf of a family member. The concept of the kinsman redeemer was illustrated in the book of Ruth, when Boaz, a relative of Ruth's deceased husband offered to marry her and thereby sire a son to reclaim their family land and inheritance (Leviticus 25:25 and Ruth 3:9). <u>Yes, Jesus as the Son of Man is the "Kinsman Redeemer."</u> Like the story of Joseph whose brothers rejected him, and sold him into slavery, they thought their actions had resulted in his death. Years later during a prolonged famine in their region, the brothers traveled to Egypt and without recognizing their rejected brother were tested to determine their character, given provisions for their families and eventually reunited in a grand way with their brother who had forgiven them. Like Joseph, Jesus is the brother who having been rejected and denied has already forgiven us and provided salvation from spiritual starvation that leads to eternal death for all who believe and accept the gift of relationship with God. Look at John 1:10-13 and Hebrews 2:17 KJV:

> **John 1:10-11 KJV** [10] He was in the world, and the world was made by him, and the world knew him not. [11] He came unto his own, and his own received him not. [12] But as many as received him, to them gave he power to become the sons of God, even to them that believe on his name: [13] Which were born, not of blood, nor of the will of the flesh, nor of the will of man, but of God.

> **Hebrews 2:17 KJV** Wherefore in all things it behoved him to be made like unto his brethren, that he might be a merciful and faithful high priest in things pertaining to God, to make reconciliation for the sins of the people.

He is the Avenger of Blood/Death

The **"avenger of blood"** shares some similarities with the "kinsman redeemer." The Hebrew name – *go'el ha-dam* specifies a clansman or kinsman, who in behalf of the family of the murdered victim, has the duty to avenge and kill the murderer (Numbers 35:27, Psalm 9:12 and II Samuel 1:10-16).[121] According to Jewish tradition tracing back to Genesis, chapter 4, God spoke of the ground crying out [for vengeance] because of the murder of Abel at his brother Cain's hands (Genesis 4:10-11). The Avenger of Blood is regarded not only as a representative of the murdered person's family, but as a representative of God as well. This concept of the Avenger of Blood acting as God's representative is illustrated in II Kings 9:4-8ff and II Chronicles 22:7. In this account God sent a prophet to anoint Jehu and commission him to "avenge the blood" of God's people murdered at the hands of King Ahab and his evil wife, Jezebel.

Many may think the term "life and death" refers to the cycle of life of living organisms. As discussed in Chapter 17 *The Resurrection and the Life* of this book, in the Bible the term "life and death" refers to a spiritual/eternal life of people versus the spiritually dead and eventually the permanently dead. Chapter 7 *Atonement, Forgiveness and Redemption* of this book explained sin and death are inseparably connected. From the beginning of the Bible, Satan revealed His goals and tactics to destroy mankind. He engaged Eve in conversation making her doubt what God had said, accusing God of deception and questioning His goodness toward Adam and Eve (Genesis 3:1-5). At the end of this encounter, both disobeyed God and ate of the forbidden fruit. For all practical purposes, Satan murdered Adam and Eve that day. Jesus said Satan was a murderer from the beginning, and this was it. Millions of people have believed and trusted in Jesus as their Savior.

---

121   *Go'el ha-dam* is translated as "blood-avenger). The term "blood" is a euphemism for the word "death." See Genesis 9:4. Leviticus 17:11 says, "For the life of the flesh is in the blood...." (Examples: His blood is on your head. It is the blood of Jesus that sets us free.)

As the Son of Man, Jesus is also the Avenger of Blood/Death because millions of people have chosen their own destructive spiritual paths, beliefs, and gods (Matthew 7:13-14). The choice to believe, accept and answer God's call to relationship results in the person being born again spiritually and spiritual death being defeated. Jesus, who defeats Satan continually, has destroyed death for those who believe, trust and love God. In the end the book of Revelation says death is destroyed permanently. Revelation 20:14 says that death will be thrown in the lake of Fire along with Hades (Hades is sometimes translated as the grave and hell) and Satan (Revelation 20:10). Death will be defeated - Revelation 21:4 says there will be no more death. Look at I Corinthians 15:26 and II Timothy 1:9-10:

> **I Corinthians 15:26 NIV**: The last enemy to be destroyed is death.

> **II Timothy 1:9-10 NIV**: [9] He has saved us and called us to a holy life—not because of anything we have done but because of his own purpose and grace. This grace was given us in Christ Jesus before the beginning of time, [10] but it has now been revealed through the appearing of our Savior, Christ Jesus, who has destroyed death and has brought life and immortality to light through the gospel.

His Humanity & Deity

Many have wondered if this title – Son of Man - speaks of **the humanity of Jesus**. Rather than identifying Him as part of humanity, **the scriptures identify the Son of Man - Jesus as God** and His purpose of coming to Earth in the form of a man. The humanity of Jesus does not mean that Jesus was a man like all other men or that He shared a dual nature – fully or truly man and God, nor does it imply that He did not have a physical body that grew, ate, slept or could be touched (this subject was addressed in the last chapter). Isaiah 9:6-7 answers more fully the question of the identity, the humanity and deity of the Messiah and the Son of Man. It tells us the Messiah would be born, He would be a male and <u>He is a son to us (mankind) -Son of Man</u>.

Isaiah 9:6-7 ⁶ For unto us a child is born, unto us a son is given: and the government shall be upon his shoulder: and his name shall be called Wonderful, Counsellor, The mighty God, The everlasting Father, The Prince of Peace. ⁷ Of the increase of his government and peace there shall be no end, upon the throne of David, and upon his kingdom, to order it, and to establish it with judgment and with justice from henceforth even for ever. The zeal of the LORD of hosts will perform this.

The Hebrew definitions of the names listed in verse six provide additional information about the promised Messiah. The One to come would be born a male child (versus a sudden unexplainable appearance). His identity would be evident by these Names (*Ha Shem*, in Hebrew means *The* Name of God) as Wonderful (in Hebrew this means extraordinary, surpassing, difficult to understand), Counselor (one who advises resolves, determines, guides [Exodus 15:13, John 16:13], teaches [John 14:26])[122] mighty God (strong and powerful), the Everlasting Father (in perpetuity, forever – Father as the founder, head, originator of benevolence and protection), and the Prince of Peace (One who will reign, rule and have power to make peace, and produce wholeness, completeness).[123] Verse seven also identified the Messiah's two kingdoms - king on earth as David's Son of the nation of Israel as well as in heaven.

The life of Jesus is not so distant in time that His existence can be denied. The title "Son of Man" reveals God's purpose in Jesus being born, living amongst us, and what God wants us to know about Him

---

[122] The attributes of God as Counselor are often recognized in Christianity as the Holy Spirit (aka Holy Ghost, Spirit of God)

[123] Additional definitions and synonyms are taken from *Strong's Concordance*.

and us. From the beginning of the creation God has desired an intimate relationship with mankind. What enfolds in the Bible are accounts of God's personal relationships with people along the journey to establish a nation through which He would come to deliver His message for everyone. The account of Adam and Eve tells us that God is the Creator of mankind. The story also shows that although people are warned of consequences for their actions, they are free to make choices even if their choices produce long-term negative outcomes and separates them from God. To Abraham, chosen because he could teach his children to believe and follow God (Genesis 18:19), God promised to establish the means through which all peoples could come to know Him (Genesis 12:3 and 18:18). Years later, Jacob (Abraham's grandson) entered Egypt with his family (67 members) to avoid the ravages of a long-term famine.

Four hundred thirty years later the 1.5 million plus descendants of Abraham emerged from slavery as the nation of Israel led by God's redeemer and prophet, Moses. They journeyed to Mt. Sinai/Mt. Horeb also known as the "mountain of God" where God would establish a covenant relationship. He would be their God and they His people. God began telling them who He is and they are to have no other god. But the people were terrified by the physical presence and voice of God speaking to them (Exodus 20:18). They asked God not to speak, instead they would listen to Moses speak for God (Exodus 20:19). Some people rejected God; some replaced Him with an idol, they disobeyed God's commands, and rejected His leadership. Later they refused to enter the promised land and accused God of risking their lives and that of their children. God waited out that generation as they wandered in the desert for forty years. After all who had doubted and rejected God died, it was time to enter the promised land. This was when God brought up what had happened forty years earlier at Mt. Horeb when He personally tried to establish a relationship with the people (Deuteronomy 18:16-20).

The people had chosen to listen to Moses instead of God Himself. Now God promised a future prophet (one who delivers God's message) like Moses (with a physical body, and human voice) would come, and again speak to the people. God said this prophet would convey <u>all His words</u> and the people would be held accountable for their response. <u>This is the central point of Jesus coming as a man: God wants us to know Him.</u> He wants us to see and know that He is real and all powerful; that He is merciful, gracious, longsuffering and abundant in goodness and truth; that He loves us more than we can imagine or comprehend and has never wavered in the desire to be our God and have us be His people.

<u>Salvation, forgiveness of sin, eternal life and the opportunity for relationship with God has always been available</u> to those living in the region of Israel because they knew of the God of Israel. However, for the many cultures, and growing nations who revered and worshiped rocks, carved objects, trees, animal and ancestors' spirits, myths, the sun, stars and moon in the sky -- salvation, the gift of eternal life and an opportunity to know the one true God was at stake. Jesus' unusual birth, the miracles, and teachings revealed His identity as God for those who could discern His messages. The resurrection of Lazarus after being dead four days revealed Jesus as God with power and authority even over death.

<u>What was different because of the cross?</u> Jesus' death and resurrection now allowed the announcement/introduction of the One true God, His declaration that God is real and the opportunity for spiritual relationship with God goes beyond the Jews, out to the world, across country lines, through the barrier of languages, transcends time (Isaiah 43:5-9, Ephesians 3:3-11, Acts 11:1, 17-18, and Galatians 3:8-9) to save those who had never heard of the LORD – the Most High God of Israel. God's revelation, salvation message and call had now gone global. When Jesus uttered His last words on the cross, "It is finished" He was not speaking of fulfilling all the points of prophecy about the Messiah from the Old Testament (for there are many prophecies that will be fulfilled with the Second Coming). He was not speaking of

having mastered obedience to every command of *Torah*. Could anything less be expected? No, for the first time an invitation to all mankind had been extended in the most incredible and undeniable way.

The Spiritual Scales for Life and death had been reset and it was time for the whole world to know. The message was launched that there is one God, the Creator of all things, through Whom abundant eternal life is available to everyone who believes, repents and receives His gift of connected relationship. The Most High God did this because He loves us. Because He loves us so, God had taken on the *form* of a man becoming **the Son of Man**. Jesus is our Kinsman Redeemer attaining mankind's redemption. The Son of Man is our Avenger of Spiritual Death who has always dominated control over Satan and broken the stronghold of sin and death for anyone who believes in Him. Through the Son of Man – Jesus – we have received the Promise of Eternal Life with God and victory over physical death. The Son of Man – our Kinsman Redeemer, Avenger of Death, Savior and God had done what no other entity could do. Each time Jesus referred to Himself as the *Son of Man* He was telling us He is the God who loves us; that He has come for us, He wants us! Believe and Live!

Blessed be His Holy Name!

Acts 17:26-27 NIV *From one man he made all the nations, that they should inhabit the whole earth; and he marked out their appointed times in history and the boundaries of their lands.*

[27] *God did this so that they would seek him and perhaps reach out for him and find him, though he is not far from any one of us.*

LORD Jehovah **Savior** Redeemer

MASTER *The Most High God* Christ

Name above all Names I AM THAT I AM Yahweh

I AM **Adonai** Elohim *King of kings*

The Angel of the Lord LORD God LORD of Lords

The God who Provides Ha Shem Everlasting Father

The Lord of Hosts The Holy One of Israel

El Shaddai MIGHTY GOD *JESUS* Abba

The Ancient of Days Immanuel *Creator of the Universe*

CHAPTER 21

No other Name

Salvation is found in no one else, for there is no other name under heaven given to mankind by which we must be saved."
Acts 4:12 NIV

revere this glorious and awesome name—the L<small>ORD</small> your God—
Deuteronomy 28:58 NIV

Wherefore God also hath highly exalted him, and given him a name which is above every name.
Philippians 2:9 KJV

⁹ And the L<small>ORD</small> shall be king over all the earth: in that day shall there be one L<small>ORD</small>, and his name one.
Zechariah 14: 9 KJV

When we say of God, He exists, we mean that His non-existence is impossible; He is living means He is not dead. To say God is the first; His existence is not due to any cause; He has power, wisdom, and will, means that God cannot be feeble or ignorant; He is One means there are no other gods.
  Adapted quote from <u>The Guide for the Perplexed</u> by Maimonides

When we try to define the eternal God with Whom there is no beginning or end, we must begin in humility and acknowledge that God is undefinable by those He created. We speak of what we have heard from others or deduced from Scriptures that do not and cannot reveal everything about God. Therefore, God is knowable and unknowable. Yet God has revealed information and aspects of Himself so that we may have a sense of who God is. The vastness of the universe and the unduplicatable beauty of Earth proclaim God's existence and power. We call God Lord, Father and God, but that is not God's name. In the quest to know the God of the Bible, the name God has provided should be examined to understand what the Name of God can tell us about Him.

Names of things have been around since the beginning of creation. The first chapter of Genesis says that in the beginning when God created the heavens and the earth, He identified what He made by giving it a name – "And God called the light Day, and the darkness he called Night" (Genesis 1:5). Even after God created Adam, the first thing He did was to bring the animals of the field and birds of the air to Adam to see what Adam would name them (Genesis 2:19). In the ancient Hebrew language names of people meant something. They identified something of the person's appearance, their personality, a characteristic, or a legacy wished for; the name conveyed a message.

Jesus – name above all names. There is no other name under heaven by which we may be saved. These are powerful statements about the name of Jesus. What does the name of Jesus mean? What does it tell us about Him? Surely His name must identify Him. Have we missed something? The answer is important. It matters.

For the sake of accuracy neither Jesus nor Christ are the correct names. <u>The name "Jesus Christ" is an English pronunciation and spelling of the Greek adaptation of a Hebraic name and title</u>. Many English-speaking Christians have thought the name "Joshua" is the English version of the name Jesus. Yet interestingly enough, the letter J has only been around approximately 500 to 600 years. The "yă", "yō" and "you"

Hebrew sound became the J sound of "jā", "jō", and "gee" in English. In Hebrew Jesus' name is most likely *Yahusha, Yahushua* or *Yehoshua* from which the more recognized version of the name came – *Yeshua*.[124] The name "Christ" is really a title meaning Anointed– Messiah. Anointed as in consecrated, commissioned for the specific role and duty of either a Priest, a Prophet or a King. In the case of Jesus, He was all three (for more information, see Chapters 1 through 3 of this book). Jesus' Hebrew name was not randomly selected. His name, ordained before He was born as a baby in Bethlehem, conveyed important information about who He is and what His mission would be.

Jesus' name was revealed to Mary (*Miryam* in Hebrew) by the angel Gabriel before the conception (Luke 1:31), and later to Joseph (*Yosef* in Hebrew) by an angel of the LORD who said, "for he shall save his people from their sins" (Matthew 1:21). <u>It is generally thought that Jesus' name means "*Yahweh* is salvation.</u>" This means that the Hebrew name for Jesus consists of two parts – the name of God *and* the part that means to deliver, save, or to rescue. Since the name Joshua is thought to be the same as the name Jesus, it is probably not coincidental that Joshua (as in the sixth book of the Bible), the helper and successor of Moses, was also Israel's first military <u>deliverer</u> and <u>rescuer</u> as they were attacked repeatedly on their way to the Promised Land. Joshua is also the same name in our English translation Bibles as the High Priest in Haggai 2:4 and Zechariah 3 when God said that Joshua and the others with him were symbolic of things to come as the LORD revealed He would remove the iniquity (sin) from the land in one day (Zechariah 3:9).[125]

The name of Jesus' was not haphazardly selected, nor were the profound statements about the power of His name random. In Matthew

---

124 For the sake of conformity throughout this book and easy recognition, the name "Jesus" and "Christ" have been used. The Classical Biblical Hebrew letters for the English name, Joshua, (yod-hay-waw-shin-ayin) are the same letters to spell Jesus' name, however, over time the Hebrew pronunciation and spelling of this name changed slightly.

125 Hebrews 1:3 says Jesus "purged our sins" (cleansed). In 2:17 it says He made reconciliation (atonement) for the sins of the people.

18:20 Jesus said when two or three are gathered in His name, He is there with them. Luke 10:17 states demons submitted to the disciples in the name of Jesus. Jesus said whatever we asked in His name, the Father would give (John 15:16). He warned that there would be others who would come in His name claiming to be the Messiah (Matthew 24:5). Later after His resurrection, the book of Acts reports Peter healed a man (Acts 3:6) and Paul drove out an evil spirit (Acts 16:18) in the name of Jesus. However, the more stunning statements about the name of Jesus are connected to eternal life and becoming children of God. The following verses indicate salvation and relationship with God because of belief in the Name of Jesus (not belief in the cross, or His death and resurrection, but belief in Him and who His Name reveals Him to be!)

Matthew 19:29 KJV And every one that hath forsaken houses, or brethren, or sisters, or father, or mother, or wife, or children, or lands, <u>for my name's sake</u>, shall receive an hundredfold, and <u>shall inherit everlasting life</u>.

John 1:12 NIV Yet to all who did receive him, <u>to those who believed in his name</u>, <u>he gave the right to become children of God</u>—

Look at the following statement of John 17:11-12. While the King James and Amplified Bible translations seem to say that the followers are kept by the name of God, the NASB, and NIV appear to say it is by Jesus' name or perhaps the name of His Father given to Jesus that protects His followers. John 10:25 stated that the works (miracles) Jesus did in His Father's name testified and bore witness that Jesus is the Messiah.

John 17:11-12 KJV [11] And now I am no more in the world, but these are in the world, and I come to thee. Holy Father, keep through thine own name those whom thou hast given me, that they may be one, as we are. ¹² While I was with them in the world, I kept them in thy name:

John 17:11-12 NIV "... Holy Father, <u>protect them by the power of *your name*</u>--the name you gave me--so that they may be one as we are one. While I was with them, <u>I protected them and kept them safe by *that name* you gave me</u>.

John 10:25 KJV ²⁵ Jesus answered them, I told you, and ye believed not: <u>the works that I do in my Father's name, they bear witness of me.</u>

The works were the miracles Jesus performed – forgiving sin, casting out demons, healing the sick, the blind, the crippled, and deaf were miracles or signs and wonders that the Old Testament said God does.[126] Yet Jesus said the miracles He did bore witness and testified as to who He is. So Who did the miracles say He is? Strangely enough God said the same thing in Exodus 10:2 – that the signs and wonders identified Him. However, this verse says we are to understand something when we see or read about these types of miracles. We are to KNOW that it is the LORD.

Exodus 10:2 NASB and that you may tell in the hearing of your son, and of your grandson, how I made a mockery of the Egyptians and how I performed My signs among them, that <u>you may know that I am the Lord.</u>"

---

126 Isaiah 35:5-6 NASB says that by <u>God</u> "the eyes of the blind will be opened and the ears of the deaf will be unstopped. Then the lame will leap like a deer, and the tongue of the mute will shout for joy." Psalm 103:3 says <u>God</u> "heals all your diseases," and Jeremiah 33:6 NASB says <u>God</u> will "bring to it (Israel) health and healing, and I will heal them; and I will reveal to them an abundance of peace and truth."

Recall that the traditional translation of Jesus' name is "Yahweh is salvation?" <u>This means that the Hebrew name for Jesus consists of two parts – the name of the God of the Old Testament and the part that means to deliver, save, and/or to rescue.</u> Do we grasp that the first part of Jesus name *is* God's name and the second part tells what He would do? Angels from Heaven whose assignment is to deliver messages,[127] told Mary and Joseph what the child's name <u>is</u> – not what it would be (Luke 2:21). Jesus (Yeshua/ *Yehoshua*) was not given a common name in His culture about what God does. Rather, Jesus <u>kept</u> the name He has always had. At the perfect and precise time for His plans, God chose to come to earth. He did not change His name but added His purpose to His name to identify Himself. Within the context and awareness of the promises God made in the Old Testament, Jesus made direct and profound statements that He is God, the God of Abraham (John 8:56-58), the God of *Torah* and the Old Testament, and the One of Whom the scriptures speak (Luke 24:27, John 5:39, Matthew 13:17). Look at the following statements made by Jesus to His disciples just hours before His arrest. Then look at the passage from Isaiah 43 where God says He is the only One, the only Savior, the Redeemer (Isaiah 60:16 and 63:16). If Jesus and God are not one and the same, then Jesus lied about who He is.

John 12:45 NIV The one who looks at me is seeing the one who sent me.

John 14:7 NIV ⁷ If you really know me, you will know my Father as well. From now on, you do know him and <u>have seen him</u>."

John 14:9 NIV ... Anyone who has seen me has seen the Father...

John 14:11 NIV Believe me when I say that I am in the Father and the Father is in me; or at least believe on the evidence of the

---

127 Angel in Hebrew means messenger.

works themselves. (For the sake of clarity, remove the word "in" and read this verse again.)

John 16:15 NIV All that belongs to the Father is mine…

Isaiah 43:10-13a: ¹⁰ Ye are my witnesses, saith the LORD, and my servant whom I have chosen: that ye may know and believe me, and understand that <u>I am he</u>: before me there was no God formed, neither shall there be after me. ¹¹ I, even I, am the LORD; and beside me there is no saviour. ¹² I have declared, and have saved, and I have shewed, when there was no strange god among you: therefore ye are my witnesses, saith the LORD, that I am God. ¹³ Yea, before the day was I am he;

Isaiah 60:16 Thou shalt also suck the milk of the Gentiles, and shalt suck the breast of kings: and thou shalt know that I the LORD am thy Saviour and thy Redeemer, the mighty One of Jacob.

Isaiah 63:16 Doubtless thou art our father, though Abraham be ignorant of us, and Israel acknowledge us not: thou, O LORD, art our father, our redeemer; thy name is from everlasting.

Most Christian believers agree that God is omnipotent (all powerful), omnipresent (is present everywhere at the same time), and omniscient (possesses unlimited knowledge, awareness and understanding). Yet many find it difficult to grasp that God can be in heaven, and on earth in a bodily form, and be present spiritually with the falling sparrow, and dying children in thirty countries on the other side of the planet all at the same time. Some Jews asked Jesus if He was the Messiah, why didn't He just say so? For many Christians the question would be similar: if Jesus is the one and only God, why didn't He say that? Jesus' answer to both questions would be the same:

John 10:25 Jesus answered them, I told you, and ye believed not: the works that I do in my Father's name, they bear witness of me.

Since Jesus did the miracles the Old Testament scriptures say that God does, and He proclaimed His oneness/sameness with God, and has the same name as God, what other conclusion could one reach? Next is an examination of the meaning of God's name.

The name of God revealed at the burning bush

The words "God" and "Lord" identify God in the English language, but as mentioned earlier these titles are not God's name. Some people have wondered if all religions believe in the same God, or if the same God has been known by different names in different cultures throughout history. The God of the Bible answered these two important questions. Although God is referred to as the Lord, God, Almighty God, etc. in the Hebrew Bible (Old Testament) many times, it is in Exodus 3:14-15 that God first declares His Name and proclaims that His name uniquely identifies Him. This incident occurred when Moses encountered God (to be precise – it was the Angel of the LORD [Exodus 3:2 KJV]) in the midst of a burning bush on the "mountain of God" – Mt. Horeb (also known as Mt. Sinai). At that time God told Moses to return to Egypt to free the Hebrew people and bring them to the land of milk and honey. Moses asked what name of God should he use when speaking to the Hebrew people. God answered in Exodus 3:14-15 (these verses are referred to several times in this chapter). Many theologians and linguists researching the Bible have studied and parsed Exodus 3:14-15- verses. It reads this way in the King James Version:

Exodus 3:13-15 KJV [13] And Moses said unto God, Behold, when I come unto the children of Israel, and shall say unto them, The

God of your fathers hath sent me unto you; and they shall say to me, <u>What is his name</u>? what shall I say unto them?

¹⁴ And God said unto Moses, <u>I Am That I Am</u>: and he said, Thus shalt thou say unto the children of Israel, <u>I Am</u> hath sent me unto you.

¹⁵ And God said moreover unto Moses, Thus shalt thou say unto the children of Israel, the LORD God of your fathers, the God of Abraham, the God of Isaac, and the God of Jacob, hath sent me unto you: this is my name for ever, and this is my memorial unto all generations.

A closer look at this passage indicates that God gave four names: (1) *I AM THAT I AM*. This is the name God gave Moses personally. (2) The name *I AM*, is the name the children of Israel should know Him as. (3) Then He identified Himself as the <u>LORD God</u> of their fathers, and finally (4) <u>the God of Abraham, the God of Isaac and the God of Jacob</u>. Each of these names identify and distinguish God from any other god in the world. With the last two names (the LORD God and the God of Abraham, the God of Isaac, and the God of Jacob) God says something more – He says this is His name forever to all people for all time ("unto all generations"). "This is my memorial" means we are to remember His name (as in to record it), commemorate it (as in to honor the name). We are to be remindful of the name of God and what it means. <u>Therefore, it is out of the question to presume that the God of the Bible would be known by any other name among any other peoples or religions</u>.

Understanding God's name is no easy or simple feat, nor does it lend itself to a simple one sentence definition. In the first name given in the Exodus passage (*I AM THAT I AM* is *Ehyeh asher Ehyeh* in Hebrew) the word "that" can be replaced with "who", "which", or "where" conveying a meaning of: I AM WHO and WHERE I AM, I AM WHO I

WAS, I AM WHO I WILL BE, conveying a sense of unchanging and consistency in character[128] and His ability to be everywhere at once. The Hebrew word for the English name of God (*I AM*) is *Ehyeh* (word #H3068 in *Strong's Concordance* means the existing One). The consonants of this name in English is YHVH or YHWH (a Tetragrammaton, meaning consisting of four letters). These four letters in Hebrew is pronounced as **yod-hey-vav-hey** or **yod-hey-uu-hey**. We cannot be certain of the pronunciation of God's name because it is generally thought the early Hebrew alphabet of 22 consonants did not have vowel notations. Since vowels have been a conjecture and the Hebrew people abstained from pronouncing or even writing God's name as reverence to God and to protect it from blasphemy, the pronunciation has remained debatable. When vowels are added, it is thought that God's name could possibly be pronounced as either *Yehovah*, *Yahweh*, or in more modern times with a J replacing the Y sound - *Jehovah*. The Hebrew word representing the name of God - *Ehyeh* (I am) appears in most English versions of the Bible as the word "LORD" spelled with all capital letters.

God told Moses in Exodus 6:3 that in His relationship with Abraham, Isaac and Jacob He appeared as *El Shaddai*, which is God Almighty in English. There are several different names for God in the Old Testament that speak of God's character, power and relationship to mankind or His creation. The translated words in English as God, Lord, and Almighty do not convey the depth of their Hebraic meaning. Here are a few of the main names for God, what they reveal about the character and array of power of God, and how they are translated in English translations of the Bible.

Elohim – Appearing more than 2,500 times in the Hebrew Bible, the Hebrew name for God as the <u>creator and judge of the Universe</u>

---

[128] Malachi 3:6 says, "For I, the LORD, do not change…." Hebrews 13:8 refers to Jesus as "Jesus Christ the same yesterday, and today, and forever." Revelation 1:8 and 4:8 where God is referred to as LORD God Almighty, which was, and is, and is to come.

implies strength, power and justice. The "El" portion of the name is considered a Semitic word meaning "god" or "deity." In Hebrew the root "El" means "might" or "power." Although the "im" suffix implies this word is plural, when referring to the Hebrew God it is singular and takes a singular verb in the Hebrew.[129] *Elohim* appears in the English Bibles as "God" and is translated as such 31 times just in chapter 1 in the book of Genesis. (In English translations of the Bible it is the mistranslation of this plural name using plural pronouns in Genesis 1:26: "And God said, Let us make man in our image, after our likeness…" that some people assume is an appearance or acknowledgment of the Trinity. Yet the very next verse Genesis 1:27 uses God [Elohim] with singular pronouns regarding the creation of man: "So God created man in his own image, in the image of God created he him; male and female created he them.")

Adonai appears as either My Lord, Lord, owner or Master in the English Bible. It carries the meaning of master, owner or lord and usually appears as a compound name. Like Elohim, the word "Adonai" is plural meaning "lords," however, when it is used exclusively for the God of the Bible, it is singular and is used with singular verbs or modifiers.

Adonai Elohim appears in the Bible as the Lord God. Based on the definition of the individual names, Lord God conveys the idea of a strong and powerful Creator and Judge of the Universe who is also the Master and Owner.

---

129 *Wikipedia* on "Elohim" says *Elohim* is a Semitic and Canaanite word referring to a pantheon of gods (meaning a group or all of the gods) later adapted by the Hebrew people to identify the One God of Israel. Also https://outreachjudaism.org/elohim-plural/ by Rabbi Tovia Singer: "The word *Elohim* possesses a plural intensive syntax and is singular in meaning. In Hebrew, the suffix ים (*im*), mainly indicates a masculine plural. However, with *Elohim* the construction is grammatically singular, (i.e. it governs a singular verb or adjective) when referring to the God of Israel, but grammatically plural *elohim* (i.e. taking a plural verb or adjective) when used of pagan divinities (Psalms 96:5; 97:7)."

El Elyon appears 12 times in the Old Testament and is translated as "the Most High God." The first appearance of this name involves the mysterious priest of Salem, Melchizedek who brought forth bread and wine to Abram (Abraham) and accepted Abram's tithe. The root word in Hebrew means to go up or to ascend. *Elyon* is an adjective and <u>means the highest or uppermost</u>. When speaking of God – El, God is identified as the Most High God.

Avinu appears as Our Father

Ha Shem or Hashem appears as "<u>the name</u>." In the Hebrew tradition of keeping the true name of God sacred, many times God was and is referred to as the Name.

El Shaddai – means the all Sufficient One and is conventionally translated as "<u>God Almighty</u>." *El Shaddai* appears over 70 times in the Old Testament. The *dai* portion of *Shaddai* is reported to mean to pour out or heap up benefits, provisions, substance, or blessings. The root word *Shadad* (word #H7703) conveys the meaning to overpower or destroy – suggesting absolute power. "While *Elohim* is the God who creates, in the name of *Shaddai* God reveals Himself [as one] who compels nature to do what is contrary to itself. He is able to triumph over every obstacle and opposition; He is able to subdue all things to Himself."[130] *El Shaddai* appears a couple of dozen times in the Old Testament (See Genesis 17:1, 43:14, Numbers 24:4, Ruth 1:20-21, Job 5:17, 33:4, 34:12, Isaiah 60:15-16 and Joel 1:15.) *Shaddai* (word #H7706) appears 41 times with 29 of them in the book of Job. (See Genesis 49:25, Job 5:17, 6:4, 14, 34:10,12 and Psalm 64:14.)

---

130 From an analysis of The Names and Attributes of God http://www.myredeemerlives.com/namesofgod/el-shaddai.html

This definition of *El Shaddai* brings to mind the Old Testament 's splitting of the Red Sea (Exodus 14:21), and the water from a rock in the desert (Exodus 14:6). In the New Testament Jesus demonstrates His power as *El Shaddai* when He produced enough food to feed thousands with baskets of leftovers and triggered the large catch of fish. He also compelled nature to respond contrary to itself with the stilling of the storm, and walking on water (Matthew 14:25, Mark 6:49, and John 6:19). Not to mention healings and restoration of life after death.

YHVH-Tzva ot –appears 235 times (predominately in Isaiah, Jeremiah, Zachariah and Malachi) and is translated as the Lord of Hosts. The Hebrew word *Tzva ot* means armies. Since the Hebrew word is plural, Hosts/Armies represent an unparalleled and vast army with the singular focus to work together toward a common goal of *Yahweh*.

Generally, Christianity recognizes the deity of God in the Old Testament, Jesus and the Holy Spirit of the New Testament, however, the Angel of the LORD tends to receives limited attention or study. The Angel of the LORD – appears in both the Old and in the New Testament over 30 times. This is not an ordinary angel. There are verses where this Angel appears and speaks as God, and is identified in the subsequent verses as the LORD. For example, in the offering of Isaac (Genesis 21:11-18), and in the encounter with Moses at the burning bush (Exodus 3:2-6). Some theologians think the physical appearances of the Angel of the LORD in Judges 13:2-25 involving the preconception of Samson and in Joshua 5:13-15 involving the sudden appearance of the Captain of the Host of the LORD's army are Christophanys (appearances in the Old Testament of Jesus Christ prior to His birth). Yet it was the Angel of the LORD who appeared in a dream to Joseph instructing him to take Mary and the child to Egypt in Matthew 2:13 and it was the Angel of the LORD who removed the tombstone and told the women Jesus had risen in Matthew 28:2-7. Appearing as a man among the myrtle trees in Zechariah 1:10-13ff the Angel of the LORD speaks with the LORD.

Although these translational changes of God's name explain why we do not see the name *Yehovah* or *Yahweh* or *I AM* in modern English translations of the Bible, we lose sight of the fact that God's unique name appears in the Hebrew Bible (Old Testament) over 6,000 times. Moreover, when we do not recognize God's name nor understand what the name means, we fail to see God exemplify His Name. <u>This means we tend to miss the many statements made by God about Himself and what He will do that, in essence, proclaim His Name.</u> God's nature (His inherent/permanent features), personality (the combination of characteristics and qualities that make Him distinctive) and character (His moral qualities) *are* His very name.

While the first name of God is "*I AM that I AM*," the second name of God – "*I AM*" given in Exodus 3:14 is again word #H3068 *Ehyeh* in *Strong's Concordance*. The Hebrew word *Ehyeh* is associated with the prime root word #1961 *hayah* translated in English as the irregular verb "to be." From this very commonly used verb we get the concept of "become, come to pass, exist, happen, fall out, establish, abide, continue and better for thee." There is also an aspect of the root word associated with "to breathe" which in turn is connected to life and the Spirit of God (aka Holy Spirit/Holy Ghost/the Divine Presence). The *I AM* conveys a sense of timelessness or eternal component. In fact, both names (*I AM That I AM* and *I AM*) share the same eternal quality. Phrases such as "...called on the name of the LORD, the Eternal God" (Genesis 21:33), "Him who lives forever" (Daniel 12:7), or "the first and the last" (Isaiah 46:4), all speak of the eternal constancy of God's nature and is reflected in His name.

Expanding upon the eternal component of God's name means that just as Genesis 1:1 says God was there in the beginning; this connects God as the Creator, the First Cause and the Source of all things. As the Source of Life and all living things, it is easier to recognize the connection between God's name and the meaning "to breathe" (part of the meaning of *I AM*) as in "God is the breath of Life" (Genesis 1:30, 2:7). The Eternal nature of God would naturally mean God has the ability to bring His plans to fruition and to accurately foretell events before they happen (Proverbs 19:21, Jeremiah 29:11).

Isaiah 42:5 Thus saith God the Lord, he that created the heavens, and stretched them out; he that spread forth the earth, and that which cometh out of it; he that giveth breath unto the people upon it, and spirit to them that walk therein:

God's name also conveys a connection to the life He has created in that the root word is associated with "to abide" and "to continue." When God promises to never leave us nor forsake us (Deuteronomy 31:6), this is actually who God is (the God who is connected to mankind), what God does and the meaning of His name. This aspect of God's identity directly relates to the third and fourth name/relationship God spoke of in the burning bush – where God said He is "the Lord God of your fathers and the God of Abraham, the God of Isaac and the God of Jacob. As indicated earlier the Lord God declares Him as the Eternal Creator, Master, Judge and Owner. The fourth name, "the God of Abraham, the God of Isaac, and the God of Jacob" specifically illustrates the unique individual relationship God has with each of the people He created. God's relationship with Abraham, was not the same as His relationship with Rebekah, Jacob, David, Moses, Ruth or Paul. This conveys the very real fact that each of us are unique and special to Him. Psalm 139:1-18 identifies David as always being in His presence, having been known to Him before He formed David in his mother's womb; Matthew 10:30 where God knows the number of hairs on our heads. One of the last descriptions for this word *hayah* (I AM) is "better for thee." This means that part of God's name conveys the very real reality that a relationship with God is more than good for you; it is better for you to have God in your life than not. In Genesis 2:18 this word *hayah* appears when God says it is not good that man should be (*hayah*) alone.

It is a natural conclusion that the Eternal One would have power, authority and a Mind or Intellect unlike anything we can imagine. It is mind-boggling to know that God cares so much about people that He imbues part of His power, creativity, and ability to love to millions of people who will never acknowledge His existence or will allow this part of God in them to lie dormant or underutilized. It is equally mind-boggling to think the unfathomable God can select a name for Himself that is so extraordinarily simple yet encompasses so much meaning and is so complex.

The Sacredness of God's Name

The name is not mere syllables, words, or sounds, but is God's nature, Spirit, and presence.
— *From the NIV Bible's Study notes.*

Do not profane my holy name, for I must be acknowledged as holy by the Israelites. I am the LORD, *who made you holy.*
Leviticus 22:32 NIV

God's name is sacred. The above verse says His name is holy. The God of the Bible is recognized by His name: His name identifies Him and it is part of who He is. It speaks of His character, His power and His eternal nature. When something is requested *in the name* of God, it means it is asked of God; it is done with the power and authority of God. When the name of God is blasphemed, God is blasphemed. That is what the above verse implies. When you call on the name of God, you have called on God. In II Chronicles 7:16 God said He had chosen and consecrated the temple <u>so that His name may be there forever</u>. Then He said His eyes and His heart would always be there. Where God's name is, God is. Jesus also speaks about being present when people are gathered *in His name*.

Matthew 18:20 For where two or three are gathered together in my name, there am I in the midst of them.

When we read this verse, there is a tendency to apply Jesus' statement to the present time period. However, when Jesus said it, it was not a promise of His presence after His resurrection. Rather it is a statement that declares His identity and deity: Since Jesus' name *is* the name *Yahweh* (YHVH), the eternal God, whenever any two or three people have gathered in the name of *Yahweh*, Jesus proclaimed He has been, and is there.

God is intimately related to and inseparable from His name. To use the name of God evokes a response. When young David confronted the giant, Goliath, David said he came *in the name* of the Lord so that the whole world would know there is a God (I Samuel 17:45-46 below). With the first strike, David killed the armored, professional warrior.

There is a distinct connection between God using His power and His name being proclaimed. Look at these verses that show the connection between the name of God and God Himself.

Exodus 6:3 NIV I appeared to Abraham, to Isaac and to Jacob as God Almighty, but by my name the Lord I did not make myself fully known to them. (This implies you cannot fully know God until you know the meaning of His name)

1 Samuel 17:45 and 46 NIV (when young David faced Goliath) ⁴⁵ David said to the Philistine, "You come against me with sword and spear and javelin, but I come against you in the name of the LORD Almighty, the God of the armies of Israel, whom you have defied… [that] ⁴⁶ the whole world will know that there is a God in Israel. (There is indeed power when you know the Name of God and proceed to honor God in His name.)

I Kings 9:3 NIV (and II Chronicles 7:16 NIV) The LORD said to him: "I have heard the prayer and plea you have made before me; I have consecrated this temple, which you have built, by <u>putting my Name there forever. My eyes and my heart will always be there</u>. (God is where His name is.)

I Chronicles 22:7 NIV David said to Solomon: "My son, I had it in my heart to build a house for the Name of the LORD my God.

Isaiah 12:4 NIV In that day you will say: "Give praise to the LORD, proclaim his name; make known among the nations what he has done, and proclaim that his name is exalted. (When you praise God, you will praise His name as well. <u>God's name is equal to God</u>)

Isaiah 63:14 NIV But you are our Father, though Abraham does not know us or Israel acknowledge us; <u>you, LORD, are our Father, our Redeemer from of old is your name</u>. (God's name is a part of who God is. "From of old" means from the beginning. This refers to God's eternal nature and says God's name is from the beginning just like God Himself)

Ezekiel 36:23 NIV <u>I will show the holiness of my great name</u>, which has been profaned among the nations, the name you have profaned among them. <u>Then the nations will know that I am the LORD</u>, declares the Sovereign LORD, when I am proved holy through you before their eyes. (This implies you cannot fully know God until you know/understand the meaning of His name. God's name is Holy just as God is Holy.)

There is another aspect to observing the sacredness of God's name. It is in how we treat others. We have generally not recognized that to uphold the holiness of God and His name extends to respecting and honoring all He has created. Recall from the Exodus 3:13-15 conversation with Moses God gave four names for Himself – (1) *I AM THAT I AM*, (2) the name *I AM*, (3) then the LORD God of their fathers, and (4) He identified Himself as the God of Abraham, the God of Isaac and the God of Jacob. It is in the fourth name that we discover part of God's identity is His abiding and unique individual relationship with each person who believes and follows Him.

Of the Ten Commandments that define the basic requirements of relationship between man and God, it is the fourth commandment which states do not take the name of God in vain. God goes on to say He will not leave the person unpunished who uses His name in vain (Exodus 20:7). According to *Strong's Concordance,* the term "in vain" means to make empty or worthless. This means we are not to use God's name in such a way as to make God or His name to be empty or worthless. It is not to be used in a falsehood or a joke. We are not to diminish or demean the character or power of God nor His name. Oddly enough there is an Aramaic word *-raca* – (#4469G in *Strong's Concordance*) that means empty, vain or worthless just like the Hebrew definition of "vain." Jesus gave a stern warning about the danger of speaking harshly to another. In fact, He related derogatory language toward another to murder. Jesus said this in Matthew 5:21-22 KJV and Matthew 12:35-37 NASB:

Matthew 5:21-22 KJV [21] Ye have heard that it was said of them of old time, Thou shalt not kill; and whosoever shall kill shall be in danger of the judgment: [22] But I say unto you,

That whosoever is angry with his brother without a cause shall be in danger of the judgment: and whosoever shall say to his brother, **Raca**, shall be in danger of the council: but whosoever shall say, Thou fool, shall be in danger of hell fire.

Matthew 12:35-37 NASB [35] The good man brings out of *his* good treasure what is good; and the evil man brings out of *his* evil treasure what is evil. [36] But I tell you that every careless word that people speak, they shall give an accounting for it in the day of judgment. [37] For by your words you will be justified, and by your words you will be condemned."

These two passages show not only how incredibly damaging negative names are to a person's psyche, but Jesus warned that careless and hurtful names can result in harsh consequences. Someone who is angry with a brother without cause, or says that someone has no value by calling them worthless, empty or "*raca!*" (moron, stupid, or idiot in today's language) is in danger of being judged and held accountable for their words. Someone who does not believe in God is considered godless and thereby foolish – a fool (the Hebrew definition of the word fool. See Psalm 14:1 and 53:1). Therefore, to call someone a "fool" means you have judged them, determining they will remain godless – as in having no part of God in them. This remark is insulting to God, their Creator. When we belittle, demean, harm or destroy another, we have not only sinned against the specific person, we have sinned against God, the Creator of all life. Just as an aspect of who God is His relationship with mankind, then an aspect of blasphemy is to demean or harm that which God has created.

God took offense when Cain killed his brother, Abel (Genesis 4:10 KJV "the voice of thy brother's blood crieth unto me from the ground"). Known as the worst sin of King David's life, David committed adultery with one of his soldier's wives, then after finding out she was pregnant with his child, arranged the death of that devoted soldier.

After David was confronted about his sin, in remorse and repentance David declared to God in Psalms 51:4 KJV – "against thee, thee only, have I sinned." When asked what is the greatest commandment, Jesus answered to love God with all that is within you. He said that that the second greatest commandment – to love your neighbor as yourself is like the first commandment (Matthew 22:36-40). <u>Jesus equated loving others to loving God</u>. Jesus said in Matthew 25:35-40 when we have abandoned care or provided care for others in need, we have done it unto Him! God's instructions and commands to honor, care for, respect and love others all support this premise that when we do what is right to others it is a direct reflection of our right standing with God. Likewise, when we cause harm to another (including verbally insulting, demeaning, embarrassing, bullying or harassing), our actions are subject to God's judgment. Not only do we harm others and dishonor God with the bad things we say, Jesus said the harsh and mean things we say defile us and reflect what is in our heart! Look at Matthew 15:11, 18-20:

> [11] *It is* not what enters into the mouth *that* defiles the man, but what proceeds out of the mouth, this defiles the man" … [18] But the things that proceed out of the mouth come from the heart, and those defile the man. [19] For out of the heart come evil thoughts, murders, adulteries, fornications, thefts, false witness, <u>slanders</u>. [20] These are the things which defile the man.…"

Isaiah 52:4-5 NASB makes a correlation between the mistreatment of God's people and God's name being blasphemed.

Isaiah 52:4-5 NASB [4] For thus says the Lord God, "My people went down at the first into Egypt to reside there; then the Assyrian oppressed them without cause. [5] Now therefore, what do I have here," declares the Lord, "seeing that My people have been taken away without cause?" *Again* the Lord declares, "Those who rule over them howl (the KJV says that it is the Assyrians who have made God's people howl, as in to cry out or wail), and My name is continually blasphemed all day long.

God spoke the world and all of creation into existence and it was good. Our words have power to do good but they also have far more power to do harm. (Talk to someone who has been verbally abused, they rarely remember the kind words spoken to them, but the worst statements and derogatory names are inscribed in stone in their memory.) Just as we cannot curse the name of God and not curse God, we cannot curse those He has created without disparaging God. James 3:9-10 NIV says:

> [9] With the tongue we praise our Lord and Father, and with it we curse human beings, who have been made in God's likeness. [10] Out of the same mouth come praise and cursing. My brothers and sisters, this should not be.

Respect and honor for God is not only important in how we treat people, but extends to all of God's creation – animals, those of the air and sea, the earth and the heavens. In Exodus 19:5 the LORD says, "for all the earth is mine." God cares for the fallen sparrow (Matthew 10:29), provides food for the raven when their young cry out (Job 38:41), and is concerned regarding the welfare of little children (Matthew 18:10). Genesis 6:5-6 says that God's heart is grieved by how man regards and treats others. The goal is for us, who are made in the image of God, to *become more* like God. We are to be conformed (act in accordance; comply) by what we learn of God (through His Word), enlightened (receive greater understanding and insight) by what we experience through His mercy and grace, then be transformed (to make a complete change in a good way) by what we see happen as a result of reflecting the LORD in response to situations and others. Look at these other verses regarding God's vast creation.

Deuteronomy 10:14 Behold, the heaven and the heaven of heavens is the LORD's thy God, the earth also, with all that therein is.

Isaiah 42:5 ... God the LORD, he that created the heavens, and stretched them out; he that spread forth the earth, and that which cometh out of it; he that giveth breath unto the people upon it, and spirit to them that walk therein

Psalm 148:13 Let them praise the name of the Lord: for his name alone is excellent; his glory is above the earth and heaven. (Not only is God to be praised, but this verse says His name is excellent and to be praised.)

God's Name is associated with power and glory:

Since God and His name are intimately connected and God is all powerful and thereby worthy of praise because of who He is, perhaps we can understand why the Bible says God's name is associated with God's power and glory.

Exodus 9:16 NIV But I have raised you up for this very purpose, that I might show you my power and that my name might be proclaimed in all the earth.

Psalm 106:8 NIV Yet he saved them for his name's sake, to make his mighty power known.

Jeremiah 10:6 NIV No one is like you, LORD; you are great, and your name is mighty in power.

Jeremiah 16:21 NIV "Therefore I will teach them— this time I will teach them my power and might. Then they will know that my name is the LORD. (When God has taught you about His power and might, you will know His Name)

Psalm 29:2 Give unto the Lord the glory due unto his name; worship the Lord in the beauty of holiness.

1 Chronicles 16:29 Give unto the Lord the glory due unto his name: bring an offering, and come before him: worship the Lord in the beauty of holiness.

Look at the powerful statements Jesus made regarding who He is and His power to do the work (miracles) "in my Father's name." There is no miracle in the gospels where Jesus said it was done in His Father's name. Considering Jesus' name and the Father's name are one and the same, the context of these verses has everything to do with Jesus revealing who He is and His relationship to the Name.

John 5:43 I am come[131] in my Father's name, and ye receive me not:

John 10:25 Jesus answered them, I told you, and ye believed not: the works that I do in my Father's name, they bear witness of me.

What is abundantly clear is that God's Name is not just a name as we know names to be. In fact, in Hebrew, God is often referred to as "The Name" (*HaShem*). King David wrote in Psalm 138:2 that He bowed down and gave thanks to the name of God and that God has exalted/magnified/honored (from various translations) His Name and His Word.[132] Beyond explanation, God's Name not only identifies God's eternal nature, His character and His relationship to His creation, but it also reflects who He is to such an extent that His Name is Holy, that where God is, His Name is; that even the Power of God

---

131 Note the seemingly grammatical mistake – "I am come" versus "I have come." In many English translations of the Bible, this verse is changed to "I have come." This verb tense reflects the Old English expressing an action begun in the past and is completed or continues to be completed.

132 There are several different translations on this verse.

is connected to the Name of God. The Name of God reveals God (Exodus 6:3). The Name of God reveals that He is merciful (Exodus 34:6). He loves us with an everlasting love and draws us to Him with lovingkindness (Jeremiah 31:3). He has called us to Him to be our God (Jeremiah 7:23). By His Name we become children of God (John 1:12), and because He is the Source of Eternal Life (John 10:27-28), we too will have eternal life (John 3:16). By His Name we are saved (Acts 4:12). Psalm 124:8 KJV says, "Our help is in the name of the LORD, who made heaven and earth." Therefore, when a verse uses the term, "called by" God's name (II Chronicles 7:14, Isaiah 43:7, and Jeremiah 15:16), it means that those who come to understand the character, nature and power of God (they are made aware, they believe, they have experienced the power of God), are drawn to God as one chosen, as if answering a summons, an invitation or command.

From this perspective, every time God's name is used as a punch line, a figure of speech, a slip of the tongue, an expression of surprise, pleasure or shock, or when we disparage one another, then we can understand Isaiah 52:5, which says - His Name is blasphemed all day long.

The oneness of Jesus and the LORD God

John 17:3 And this is life eternal, that they might know thee the only true God, and Jesus Christ, whom thou hast sent.

Zechariah 14:9 And the LORD shall be king over all the earth: in that day shall there be one LORD, and his name one.

Names identify. When it comes to the name of the only true God of Israel and Jesus, the Christ, the name and its meaning is essential. This book began with the question – Who is Jesus? The name of Jesus tells us He is God. Jesus' name is not the same name as the LORD God; His name *is* the LORD God with His mission to rescue, deliver and save those who are lost. It is important to God that we know Him. Several times throughout the Bible the LORD said He did certain things so that people would know that He is the LORD God (Exodus 10:2, 31:13, I King 8:43, Isaiah 37:20, John 5:39, 8:28 to name a few). From the Old Testament, God says that He is the <u>only</u> Savior; there is none other. He says, **"I am He."** From the New Testament gospels, Jesus says He and the Father are one; when you have seen Jesus, you have seen the Father. Jesus says, **"I am He."** The following verses from the Old and New Testaments speak of the LORD as the One to come, followed by statements from Jesus of His oneness with the Father.

The LORD God:

Isaiah 43:10-13 NASB "You are My witnesses," declares the LORD, "And My servant whom I have chosen,[133] So that you may know (perceive/distinguish) and believe Me (confirm) And understand (discern) that **I am He**. Before Me there was no God formed, And there will be none after Me. [11] "I, even I, am the LORD, And there is no savior besides Me. [12] "It is I who have declared and saved and proclaimed, And there was no strange *god* among you; So you are My witnesses," declares the LORD, "And I am God. [13] "Even from eternity **I am He**, And there is none who can deliver out of My hand; I act and who can reverse it?"

Isaiah 45:21 NIV Declare what is to be, present it— let them take counsel together. Who foretold this long ago, who declared it from the distant past? Was it not I, the LORD? And there is no God apart from me, a righteous God and a Savior; there is none but me.

---

[133] The LORD's Servant is the Messiah to come. See Isaiah 42:1-6, 49:6, and 53:11.

Isaiah 56:1 NASB Thus says the Lord, "Preserve justice and do righteousness, for <u>My salvation is about to come and My righteousness to be revealed</u>.

Micah 5:2 KJV But thou, Bethlehem Ephratah, though thou be little among the thousands of Judah, <u>yet out of thee shall he come forth</u> unto me that is to be ruler in Israel; <u>whose goings forth have been from of old, from everlasting</u>. (This means that out of Bethlehem will come the God who prevails, who is from eternity and who will rule, reign, and have dominion.)

The LORD God Jesus:

John 5:43 NIV "I have come in My Father's name…."

John 8:19 NIV "You do not know me or my Father," Jesus replied. "If you knew me, you would know my Father also."

John 8:23-24 NIV But he continued, "You are from below; I am from above. You are of this world; I am not of this world. ²⁴ I told you that you would die in your sins; if you do not believe **that I am he**, you will indeed die in your sins." (He is proclaiming or making judgment about the final outcome of these people; something only God can do and not be sinning.)

John 8:27-28 NIV ²⁷ They did not understand that he was telling them about his Father. ²⁸ So Jesus said, "When you have lifted up the Son of Man, then you will know **that I am he** ….

John 8:42 NIV "If God were your Father, you would love me, for I have come here from God. I have not come on my own; God sent me. ⁴³ **Why is my language not clear to you?**

John 12:45 NIV The one who looks at me is seeing the one who sent me.

John 13:19 NIV "I am telling you now before it happens, so that when it does happen you will believe that <u>I am who I am</u>. (Perhaps this is not correctly translated, but "I am who I am" is essentially God's name as given to Moses in Exodus 3:14 "I AM that/who/which/where I AM." In addition, He is claiming to be God in that He is saying He knows the future!)

John 12:28-29 NIV "Father, glorify your name!"
Then a voice came from heaven, "I have glorified it, and will glorify it again." ²⁹ The crowd that was there and heard it said it had thundered; others said an angel had spoken to him.

John 13:31-32 NIV ... Jesus said, "Now <u>the Son of Man is glorified and God is glorified in him</u>. ³² If God is glorified in him, God will glorify the Son in himself, and will glorify him at once. (Recall that Isaiah 42:8 KJV says, "I am the LORD: that is my name: and <u>my glory will I not give to another</u>, neither my praise to graven images.")

John 14:1 NIV ...You believe in God; believe also in me.

John 14:7 NIV ⁷ If you really know me, you will know my Father as well. From now on, you do know him and <u>have seen him</u>."

John 14:9 NIV ... Anyone who has seen me has seen the Father...

John 14:11 NIV Believe me when I say that I am in the Father and the Father is in me; or at least believe on the evidence of the works themselves.

John 16:15 NIV All that belongs to the Father is mine...

John 17:5 NIV ... Father, glorify me in your presence with the glory I had with you before the world began.

John 17:10 NIV All I have is yours, and all you have is mine. And glory has come to me through them.

Who is Jesus?

In Christianity people have been told it is their sins that separate them from God. They have been told in order to have Jesus become Lord of their lives, they need to acknowledge they are sinners and that Jesus died for their sins. They also need to ask Jesus into their hearts.

What if it was never our sins that separated us from God, but our unbelief, indifference and attitude that separated us and needs to be changed. What if Jesus' death was not atonement for sins but the end result of a plot by people who were afraid of what would happen if Jesus continued His teachings and healing (John 11:47-53)? What if Jesus' murder was like Joseph's enslavement to Egypt? Genesis 50:20 says what was meant for harm, God intended for good to accomplish what is now being done, the saving of many lives. What if we are separated from God because we don't know Him? What if we sin because we don't know or believe who He is, and we don't understand why we should live by His instructions on how to treat others? What if asking God into our heart is not enough if we don't know who He is, and will not follow Him, or learn what He wants of us?

When the prodigal son returned, the father did not ask what had his son done while he was away. He rejoiced that his lost son had returned to him. In the Garden of Eden, neither Eve or Adam understood the goodness of God. And when they were tempted with what they thought was a better offer, they disobeyed God's instructions. Although the Hebrew people had seen God in action exacting the plagues to obtain their freedom from Egypt, most of the Hebrew people did not know the God of their forefathers. Weeks later, they asked God not to speak to them. Soon thereafter they bowed to a golden calf statute and said this was the god that brought them out of Egypt. Later when confronted with a possible battle to enter God's Promised Land, the Hebrew people accused God of trying to get them and their children killed, and wanted to return to Egypt. The gospels indicate Jesus' friends, family and disciples were not certain about who He really was/is. Can we be certain the early fathers of the "church" have gotten it right?

God asked that His people not misuse His name, yet as God said, His name is blasphemed daily. He said His Sabbath is Holy; to observe it, to keep it. The church changed it. In Matthew 7:22-23 Jesus said of those who called Him Lord and said they did wonderful things in His name yet were immoral, perverse and committed acts of wickedness (those who work iniquity), He would say He NEVER KNEW them.

Of the poor lady who gave all she had of her meager funds, Jesus said she gave the most (Mark 12:41-44). She gave out of her trust in who God is – the God who loves, is faithful and provides. Yet the wealthy ruler who wanted to inherit eternal life and had kept the commandments from youth, did not really know God. He did not trust the God who had provided wealth was more important than any amount of money (Luke 18:18-24). In Matthew 11:28-30 Jesus said, "Come unto Me," but He also said "learn of Me." Take His "yoke"; be enjoined, connected to God. Then He will be our God, and we His people.

Jesus is the Creator of the Universe (John 1:1-3, Colossians 1:16); He is the Spirit of God (John 14:16, 14:18, 14:23). He is the One prophesied to crush the head of Satan (Genesis 3:15). He is the God of promises and the fulfillment of the promises to Abraham (Genesis 12:2-3, John 8:56-58), the Angel of the LORD, the I AM (Exodus 3), the God who provides (Genesis 22:8 and 13) and heals (Isaiah 35:5-6). He is known as the Father of Israel (Isaiah 63:16, Jeremiah 31:9), the Kinsman Redeemer, the Avenger of Death, the King of Righteousness (Genesis 49:10, Jeremiah 23:5), and the Captain of the LORD's Army (Joshua 5:14-15). He is the Redeemer (Isaiah 44:6), Savior (Isaiah 60:16), the Prince of Peace, the Everlasting Father, the Mighty God, Counselor, Wonderful (Isaiah 9:6), Immanuel (Isaiah 7:14).

The Only God (Isaiah 43:10, 44:6). Jesus is the Servant (Isaiah 42:1-6, 49:6, 53:11). He is the Good Shepherd (John 10:11, Isaiah 40:11), the true Vine and the Gardener (John 15:1), the Light of the World (John 8:12, 12:36, Isaiah 60:19-20, Revelation 21:23), the Way, the Truth, the Life (John 14:6). Jesus is the source of eternal Life and the Resurrection (John 11:25). He is the First and Last (Isaiah 44:6, 48:11-13), the Author and finisher of our faith (Hebrews 12:2). He is the One who created us for His glory, who calls us from the ends of the earth by His name (Isaiah 43:6-7). The One who will never leave (or fail) us nor forsake us (Deuteronomy 31:6, and Hebrews 13:5). The Name above all names (Philippians 2:9). Jesus is the promised Jewish Messiah (Isaiah 61:1), who has come and will return. Anointed/commissioned as King, Priest (of Israel and in Heaven), and *the* Prophet of Deuteronomy 18. Jesus is the Son of David with all rights and authority as King of Israel. He is the Son of God (II Samuel 7:12-14) whose Kingdom will never end. He is the Son of Man (Daniel 7:13), God who came to earth so that all mankind may know God is real.

In these closing scriptures, God, the LORD, the Creator of the Universe says some important things. He tells us He is with us, His seeds, His children. He has called and chosen everyone. His sons and daughters who will know Him by His Name, will come from every direction. He has formed us and made us for His glory. Those who have been physically, mentally, or spiritually blind and deaf will be healed. The LORD tells us that He is the Servant chosen to save, the Redeemer, the Deliverer, the Holy One of Israel. There is no one else.

Isaiah 43:5-14 ⁵ Fear not: for I am with thee: I will bring thy seed from the east, and gather thee from the west;

⁶ I will say to the north, Give up; and to the south, Keep not back: bring my sons from far, and my daughters from the ends of the earth;

⁷ <u>Even every one that is called by my name</u>: for I have created him for my glory, I have formed him; yea, I have made him.

⁸ Bring forth the blind people that have eyes, and the deaf that have ears.

⁹ Let all the nations be gathered together, and let the people be assembled: who among them can declare this, and shew us former things? let them bring forth their witnesses, that they may be justified: or let them hear, and say, It is truth.

¹⁰ <u>Ye are my witnesses, saith the Lord, and my servant whom I have chosen: that ye may know and believe me, and understand that I am he: before me there was no God formed, neither shall there be after me.</u>

¹¹ I, even I, am the Lord; and beside me there is no saviour.

¹² I have declared, and have saved, and I have shewed, when there was no strange god among you: therefore ye are my witnesses, saith the Lord, that I am God.

¹³ Yea, before the day was I am he; and there is none that can deliver out of my hand: I will work, and who shall let it?

¹⁴ Thus saith the Lord, your redeemer, the Holy One of Israel.

Isaiah 52:6 Therefore my people shall know my name: therefore they shall know in that day that I am he that doth speak: behold, it is I.

The End

NOTE 1

Sabbath Readings

Chapter 6 of this book entitled "Why return to Nazareth," says that the account of Jesus' return to Nazareth in Luke 4 provides enough information to determine on which Sabbath this incident occurred. This premise is based on the passage Jesus read from the scroll of Isaiah and the fact that the Jewish community[134] has had specific *Torah* (the books of Genesis through Deuteronomy) and *Haftarah*[135] readings designated for each Sabbath since the time of the scribe, Ezra nearly five hundred years before the birth of Jesus.

The Hebrew calendar in use for the Bible is based on a lunar/solar cycle that has 359 days with an extra 30-day month added to the calendar every two or three years.[136] Lunar months have either a 29 or 30-day cycle. This makes showing a definitive record of *Torah* readings difficult as certain Sabbath readings for Passover and Tabernacles change and other Sabbath readings are combined to adjust for the number of weeks in a non-leap year.

---

134 The Sephardi community dating back to around 1,000 AD have a few slightly different passages during the course of the year that usually consists of additional verses from the same book and chapter.

135 *Haftarah* (means completion) are selected passages from other books of the Hebrew Bible (Old Testament).

136 To keep the Hebrew Calendar (359 day cycle) in alignment with the Gregorian (or Western) 365 calendar, a 19 year Metonic cycle is used. In addition to the extra month added every few years, the calendar has days added or subtracted to the months Cheshvan and Kislev to adjust so that certain holy days do not occur on the regular weekly Sabbath.

Considered the start of the civil New Year, the first day of the Hebrew month *Tishrei* is Rosh HaSannah. Yet according to Exodus 12:1, the first and seventh months flopped making the new year begin in the spring month of *Nisan*, the month in which Passover occurs. **The months of the civil year are** *Tishrei, Cheshvan, Kislev, Tevet, Shevat and Adar*. In leap years, *Adar* is called *Adar I* is followed by *Adar II* or *Adar Beit*, then *Nisan, Iyar, Sivan, Tammuz, Av,* and *Elul*. Each month is said to have a theme related to the holy day that occurs during that month. For example, the month of *Nisan's* theme for Passover is redemption, *Sivan*, the month of *Shavuot* (aka Pentecost) is about the giving of the *Torah*. *Av's* theme is comfort because both temples were destroyed in that month. It is a time to reflect on the end of the exile and eventual fulfillment of God's promise to the Hebrew people. *Elul*, the month leading up to *Yom Kippur* (in the month of *Tishrei*) is about repentance.

During the year, there are 54 weekly *Torah* (Genesis through Deuteronomy) and *Haftarah* passages. There are additional readings for specific commemorative and fasting days. Although the word *Haftarah* looks like it would mean half-*Torah*, it actually means "concluding portion." The *Haftarah* passages usually complement the *Torah* portion or relate to the historical event that occurred during that time of the year. Therefore, not all the other passages that comprise the Old Testament are a part of the weekly scheduled readings.

The chart on the next page shows an approximate schedule of *Torah* and *Haftarah* readings for a year. Included are our Gregorian calendar months to give an approximate idea of when these readings take place. Passages from Isaiah occur at least sixteen times during the year including the extra reading for *Yom Kippur* that does not occur on a regular weekly Sabbath. Also note that eight of these sixteen Isaiah passages occur during an eight-week period near the end of the civil Hebrew calendar. Seven of these readings are called "*Haftarah* Consolations." They are read after the ninth day of the Hebrew month *Av* called *Tish B' Av*. *Tish B' Av* has a unique history of destruction and trouble for

Note 1 – Sabbath Readings

the Jewish people. Both temples were destroyed on *Tish B' Av*, along with the expulsion of the Jews from Spain in 1492 and the outbreak of World War I in 1914. At the time of Jesus, the people were commemorating the destruction of Jerusalem and Solomon's temple when many people died, were brutally murdered, and was followed by the 70-year exile in Babylon. The consolation passages were taken from the book of Isaiah because the book of Isaiah contained passages related to the Babylonian exile and consoled Israel with prophecies for the future return to Zion and the promise to restore the nation of Israel (Jeremiah 32:32-38).

Traditionally only priests or members of the Levi tribe read from *Torah*. Since Jesus was from the tribe of Judah, He was probably called to read a *Haftarah* portion. The passage Jesus read in Luke 4 is <u>not</u> one of the scheduled *Haftarah* readings. Therefore, it is reasonable to presume that Jesus was in the Nazareth synagogue on one of the three Sabbaths whose designated readings are within proximity of Isaiah 61:1-2 (Isaiah 57-61 and 61-65). These Sabbaths are highlighted in bold on the chart. Their close proximity would have allowed easier access to the Isaiah 61 passage without a lot of effort to adjust the scroll. As covered in Chapter 6 of this book only one of these three Isaiah Sabbath readings occurred on a holy day. That holy day is *Yom Kippur* and when *Yom Kippur* is coupled with the first day of the year of Jubilee, it is the one Sabbath when males are required to return to their hometown, family and property.

Dates by Weeks	Sabbath/ Month	*Torah* Reading	*Haftarah* Reading
Aug	3rd Sab. Av	Deuteronomy 3:23 – 7:11	Isaiah 40:1-26
Aug	4th Sab. Av	Deuteronomy 7:12 – 11:25	Isaiah 49:14 – 51:3
Aug	5th Sab. Av	Deuteronomy 11:26 – 16:17	Isaiah 54:11 – 55:5
Sept	1st Sab Elul	Deuteronomy 16:18 – 21:9	Isaiah 51:12 – 52:12
Sept	2nd Sab Elul	Deuteronomy 21:10 – 25:19	Isaiah 54:1-10
Sept	**3rd Sab Elul**	**Deuteronomy 26:1 – 29:8**	**Isaiah 60:1-22**
Sept	**4th Sab Elul**	**Deuteronomy 29:9 – 30:20**	**Isaiah 61:10 – 63:9**
Sept	5th Elul	Deuteronomy 31:1-31:30	Isaiah 55:6-56:8
Late Sept/ Early Oct	**Rosh Hashanah**	Genesis 21:1-34, Numbers 29:1-6	I Samuel 1:1 – 2:10
Oct	1st Sab. Tishrei	Deuteronomy 32:1-52	2 Samuel 22:1-51
Yom Kippur	**10 Tishrei**	**Leviticus 16:1-34 AM Leviticus 18:1-30 PM Numbers 29:7-11**	**Isaiah 57:14 – 58:14**
Oct	2nd Sab. Tishrei	Deuteronomy 33:1 – 34:12	Joshua 1:1-18
Oct	*Sukkot Holiday*	daily readings; none from Isaiah	
Oct	4th Sab. Tishrei	Genesis 1:1 – 6:8	Isaiah 42:5 – 43:11
Late Oct/ Early Nov	1st Sab Cheshvan	Genesis 6:9 – 11:32	Isaiah 54:1 – 55:5
Nov	2nd Sab. Cheshvan	Genesis 12:1 – 17:27	Isaiah 40:27 – 41:16
Nov	3rd Sab. Cheshvan	Genesis 18:1 – 22:24	2 Kings 4:1-37
Nov	4th Sab. Cheshvan	Genesis 23:1 – 25:18	1 Kings 1:1-31
Late Nov/ Early Dec	1st Sab. Kislev	Genesis 25:19 – 28:9	Malachi 1:1 – 2:7
Late Nov/ Early Dec	2nd Sab. Kislev	Genesis 28:10 – 32:3	Hosea 12:13 – 14:10

Note 1 – Sabbath Readings

Dates by Weeks	Sabbath/ Month	*Torah* Reading	*Haftarah* Reading
Dec	3rd Sab. Kislev	Genesis 32:4 – 36:43	Hosea 11:7 – 12:12
Dec	4th Sab. Kislev	Genesis 37:1 – 40:23	Amos 2:6 – 3:8
Dec	1st Sab. Tevet	Genesis 41:1 – 44:17	I Kings 3:15 – 4:1
Dec/January	2nd Sab. Tevet	Genesis 44:18 – 47:27	Ezekiel 37:15-28
Jan	3rd Sab. Tevet	Genesis 47:28 – 50:26	1 Kings 2:1-12
Jan	4th Sab. Tevet	Exodus 1:1 – 6:1	Isaiah 27:6 – 28:13, 29:22-33
Jan	1st Sab. Shevat	Exodus 6:2 – 9:35	Ezekiel 28:25 – 29:21
Jan	2nd Sab. Shevat	Exodus 10:1 – 13:16	Jeremiah 46:13-28
Late Jan/ Early Feb	3rd Sab. Shevat	Exodus 13:17 – 17:16	Judges 4:4 – 5:31
Feb	4th Sab. Shevat	Exodus 18:1 – 20:23	Isaiah 6:1 – 7:6, 9:5
Feb	1st Sab. Adar	Exodus 21:1 – 24:18	Jeremiah 34:8-22, 33:25, 26
Feb	* 2nd Sab. Adar	Exodus 25:1 – 27:19	I Kings 5:26 – 6:13
Late Feb/ Early March	3rd Sab. Adar	Exodus 27:20 – 30:10	Ezekiel 43:10-27
March	4th Sab. Adar	Exodus 30:11 – 34:35	I Kings 18:1-39
March	* 1st Sab. Adar II	Exodus 35:1 – 38:20	I Kings 7:40-50
March	2nd Sab. Adar II	Exodus 38:21 – 40:38	I Kings 7:51 – 8:21
March	3rd Sab. Adar II	Leviticus 1:1 – 5:26	Isaiah 43:21 – 44:23
Late March/ Early Apr	4th Sab. Adar II	Leviticus 6:1 – 8:36	Jeremiah 7:21 – 8:3, 9:22-23
April	1st Sab. Nisan	Leviticus 9:1 – 11:47	II Samuel 6:1 – 7:17
April	* 2nd Sab. Nisan	Leviticus 12:1 – 13:59	II Kings 4:42 – 5:19
Passover Holiday		daily readings; only one from Isaiah -- 10:32 - 12:6	
April	3rd Sab. Nisan	Leviticus 14:1 – 15:33	II Kings 7:3-20
May	* 4th Sab. Nisan	Leviticus 16:1 – 18:30	Ezekiel 22:1-19
May	1st Sab. Iyyar	Leviticus 19:1 – 20:27	Amos 9:7-15
May	2nd Sab. Iyyar	Leviticus 21:1 – 24:23	Ezekiel 44:15-31
May	* 3rd Sab. Iyyar	Leviticus 25:1 – 26:2	Jeremiah 32:6-27
May	4th Sab. Iyyar	Leviticus 26:3 – 27:34	Jeremiah 16:19 – 17:14
June	1st Sab. Sivan	Numbers 1:1 – 4:20	Hosea 2:1-22

Dates by Weeks	Sabbath/ Month	*Torah* Reading	*Haftarah* Reading
	Shavuot	Exodus 19:1 – 20:23 Numbers 28:26-31	Ezekiel 1:1-28, 3:12
	Shavuot Sab.	Deuteronomy 14:22-16:17	Habakkuk 2:20 - 3:19
June	2nd Sab. Sivan	Numbers 4:21 – 7:89	Judges 13:2-25
June	3rd Sab. Sivan	Numbers 8:1 – 12:16	Zechariah 2:14 – 4:7
June	4th Sab. Sivan	Numbers 13:1 – 15:41	Joshua 2:1-24
July	1st Sab Tammuz	Numbers 16:1 – 18:32	1 Samuel 11:14 – 12:22
July	2nd Sab Tammuz	Numbers 19:1 – 22:1	Judges 11:1-33
July	3rd Sab Tammuz	Numbers 22:2 – 25:9	Micah 5:6 – 6:8
July	4th Sab Tammuz	Numbers 25:10 – 30:1	1 Kings 18:46 – 19:21
Aug	* 1st Sab. Av	Numbers 30:2 – 32:42	Jeremiah 1:1 – 2:3
		Numbers 33:1 – 36:13	Jeremiah 2:4-28, 3:4
Aug	2nd Sab. Av	Deuteronomy 1:1 – 3:22	Isaiah 1:1-27

Glossary

Aaron, older brother to Moses and the first high priest of Israel from the tribe of Levi.

Adonai the Hebrew name meaning "lords", appears as "My Lord," "Lord," "owner" or "Master" in the English translations of the Bible. Although Adonai is plural, when the word "Adonai" is used exclusively for the God of the Bible, it is singular and is used with singular verbs or modifiers.

Adonai Elohim, the Hebrew name that appears in the English translations of the Bible as "the Lord God." Based on the definition of the individual names, Lord God conveys the meaning of the strong and powerful Creator and Judge of the Universe who is the Master and Owner.

Anoint – In Hebrew the word anoint (*mashach*) means to rub or apply a liquid for the purposes of consecration or commission for a specific task. In early Judaism priests were commissioned to serve before God in behalf of the people, kings were to lead God's people in behalf of God and prophets to deliver messages to God's people from God.

Atone, Atonement – means the covering of, or making reconciled, consistent or compatible with something else. The word can be associated with the ransom or exchange to get back as well as the cleansing, restoration or reestablishment of a damaged relationship between man and God. The Hebrew word *kaphar* is the same word translated in English as the word "reconcile."

Avenger of Blood – A kinsman whose duty is to carry out the revenge of a murder victim in behalf of the family.

Baal - The chief male god of the Phoenicians and Canaanites. The name can mean "master" or "lord." Worship of Baals extends back to the 14th century BCE among the ancient Near East cultures who were contemporary to the Semitic (Hebrew/Jewish) people.

Babylon -an ancient Akkadian/Babylonian city-state. Located in present day Iraq.

Beelzebub – literally "Lord of the flies." *Beel* is a variation of Baal.

Centurion - professional officer of the Roman army, usually in command of a few dozen soldiers.

Christ – is the English transliteration of the Greek word *christos* which means anointed. *Messiah* is the Greek transliteration of the Hebrew word *mashiyach* meaning anointed. The term came to be associated with the redeemer who would be anointed by God to bring peace and justice to the nation of Israel.

Daniel - a Jewish young man taken into captivity from Jerusalem to Babylon who became a prominent figure in the Babylonian court. Considered a major prophet, Daniel's life events are included in the Bible in the book of Daniel.

David - the second king of Israel. An ancestor of Jesus, this warrior king's story is told in the books of Samuel, I Kings, and I Chronicles. Many of the Psalms are attributed to David.

Deceiver, Devil – a evil character appearing in the Bible which says he fell from Heaven in disgrace and seduces humanity into disobedience to God. Also known as Satan and Lucifer.

Egypt – a country in Northern Africa. According to the Bible the family of Jacob went to live in Egypt in honor. Then during the next 430 years they had become slaves before God, through His prophet Moses gained the nation of Israel's freedom and release.

El Elyon – *Elyon* is an adjective that means the highest or uppermost. When speaking of God – El, God is identified as the Most High God.

El Shaddai – a Hebraic name conventionally translated as "God Almighty." The root word *Shadad* (word #H7703) conveys the ability to overpower or destroy. *Shaddai* conveys the ability to compel nature to do what is contrary to itself – suggesting absolute power to triumph over every obstacle and opposition.

Elijah – a prophet and miracle worker of the Northern Kingdom of Israel. Jewish tradition considers Elijah the forerunner of the Messiah based on Malachi 3:1 and 4:5-6.

Elisha - assistant to Elijah; a prophet and miracle worker of the Northern Kingdom of Israel.

Elohim - The Hebrew name for God, which is particularly attributed to God as the creator and judge of the Universe, implying strength, power and justice. The "El" portion of the name is considered a Semitic word meaning "god" or "deity"; the "im" suffix implies this word is plural. However, when referring to God, Elohim is singular and takes a singular verb in the Hebrew.

Epistles - documents or formal letters sent to a person or group of people. The letters written to Christians or followers of Jesus included in the New Testament are called epistles.

Exodus – the departure of a large group of people. Also the title of the second book of the Bible which tells of the exodus of the Hebrew people from Egypt.

Feast of Dedication – today known as The Festival of Lights, and *Hanukkah*. Was once also called the "Feast of the Maccabees." This is an eight-day Jewish festival that commemorates the rededication of the Jerusalem Temple after overthrowing the harsh reign of the Greek-Syrian king, Antiochus Epiphanes.

Feast of Tabernacle - instituted in Leviticus 23:22 this fall holiday is also known as the Festival of Booths, and *Sukkot*. This seven-day festival commemorates how God was with the people when they wandered in the desert for 40 years. It is one of the three biblically mandated festivals on which Hebrew people were commanded to make a pilgrimage to the Temple in Jerusalem.

Gemera – The book containing the commentaries of Rabbis from both Israel and Babylon on Mishnah, the Oral Law.

Gentile - a person of a non-Jewish culture or of non-Jewish faith

Gezerah Shavah – a Talmudic hermeneutic term which describes a theory of Biblical text interpretation. *Gezerah Shavah* refers to the verbal parallel inference of two cases of similar words or phrases where the second or subsequent appearance of similar phrases invoke the meaning or message of the first passage of scripture.

Go'el ha-dam – the Hebrew word translated to mean "blood-avenger." A kinsman whose duty is to carry out the revenge of a murder victim in behalf of the family.

Glory of God – The presence and power of God according to Deuteronomy 5:24, Exodus 16:7, 10, 24:17, 40:34, Numbers 16:19, and Ezekiel 8:4.

grace – In Hebrew #H2580 *chen* means favor, or acceptance. Greek #G5485 *charis* means goodwill, loving-kindness or favor.

Haftarah – the Hebrew word meaning parting or completion refers to selected passages from the prophets of the Old Testament that complement and follow the *Torah* portion that is read publicly each week.

Hanukkah – Means "dedication," a Jewish festival also known as the Feast of Dedication, commemorates the rededication of the Jerusalem Temple to monotheistic worship by Judah the Maccabee in 164 BCE.

HaShem – the Hebrew word many pious Jews use instead of the name of God in casual conversation. *HaShem* means "The Name."

Hebrew – refers to both a language and a member of the group of Semitic people who would later become identified as Jewish and Israeli people.

Holy Spirit – see ***Ruach Ha Kodesh***

Hypocrite - a person who pretends to have virtues, moral or religious beliefs, principles that they do not uphold.

Immanuel - the name to be given to the child of the virgin in Isaiah 7:14 and applied to Jesus in Matthew 1:23. The name means "God with us" or "God is with us."

Isaiah - a prophet of God. The Bible book of Isaiah is considered a major prophet.

Jehovah – see the entry for **Yahweh, Yehovah.**

Jairus – a synagogue leader whose young daughter Jesus restored to life.

Jesus - The Greek rendition of proper name of the Messiah and the central figure of the New Testament Bible. Also see Yahusha, Yahushua, Yehoshua or Yeshua – the Hebrew names of Jesus.

Jews – refers to a people and cultural group whose religion is Judaism. The Jews trace their origins to the ancient Hebrew people of Israel to their patriarch, Abraham.

Job – The central figure of the Bible's oldest written book with the same name.

Kabbalah, the Jewish mystical commentary of *Torah* (not to be confused with *Mishnah* or Oral *Torah*). Believed to have been written down by Rabbi Simeon during the second century, and surfaced during the 13th century in Spain. The *Kabbalah* contains mystical discussions of the nature of God, the origins of the universe, and the nature of souls among other topics.

Kinsman redeemer – A male relative who redeems that which was lost in behalf of a family member.

KJV – Abbreviation of King James Version of the Bible – first English translation of the Bible completed in 1611 commissioned by King James I.

Lazarus – The friend of Jesus and brother of Mary and Martha who was raised from the dead after four days by Jesus.

Law – the English interpretation of the Hebrew word "*Torah*." According to *Strong's Concordance Torah* in Hebrew is word #H8451 *towrah,* from the root word #H3384 *yarah*. A more accurate translation means "to instruct, to teach, to direct, to point out." In essence God's commandments, that is, His *Law* are instructions, percepts, teachings, directions for His people on how they are to live and treat others.

Glossary

Leprosy – chronic, progressive and contagious skin disease that causes skin sores, nerve damage, and muscle weakness.

Levite – a member of the priestly Hebrew tribe of Levi. The priesthood was reserved for descendants of Aaron of the tribe of Levi while other male members served in other ceremonial capacities.

LORD - the English version of the Hebrew name YHWH, also known as Yehovah, Yahweh and in modern times the J replaced the Y sound for the name Jehovah. The Hebrew name *Ehyeh* translated as (I AM) appears in most English versions of the Bible as the word "LORD" spelled with all capital letters.

lucifer - the Latin translation of the Hebrew word *heylel (Strong Concordance* word #H1966) which means light. Lucifer, referred to as the light-bearer, and the morning star is used to identify or refer to Satan.

Martha and **Mary** - two sisters of Lazarus and friends of Jesus. Their brother was raised from the dead after four days by Jesus.

Mashiyach – the Hebrew word meaning anointed, as pertaining to the Messiah.

Melchizedek – the king and priest of Salem who appeared before Abraham in Genesis 14:18. The name Melchizedek means "my king (is) righteous(ness)" or "righteous king."

mercy - in the Bible mercy means goodness, kindness or faithfulness. From the Hebrew word *checed* (word #H2617 in *Strong's Concordance*) can also mean a reproach, or shame.

Messiah – Greek transliteration of the Hebrew word *mashiyach* meaning anointed. Priests and kings of Israel were anointed with oil. The term came to be associated with the redeemer figure who would put an end of sin, make reconciliation for iniquity, bring in everlasting righteousness, and usher in the age of peace and plenty.

Mishnah –the written record of what was the Oral Law.

NASB - New American Standard Bible published first in 1995 as an updated version of the 1901 American Standard Bible.

NIV – New International Version - a completely original English translation of the Bible. The work of an international group of scholars started in 1965. The NIV is not a word for word translation but rather attempts to capture the original meaning or thought.

palsy – a medical term that describes various types of paralysis accompanied by loss of feeling, weakness or uncontrolled body movements.

Passover - The spring festival that commemorates the deliverance of the Hebrew people from slavery in Egypt as told in the book of Exodus.

Passover Lamb – In the story of the nation of Israel's Exodus from Egypt, it was the blood of the unblemished lamb over the door posts of homes that allowed "death" to *pass over* the Hebrew people.

perish is word #H6 *abad* in *Strong's Concordance*. It means destroy, vanish, to be exterminated, to blot out, to do away with. In Greek the word is #G622 *apollymi* which means to destroy, to put an end to ruin, to abolish.

Pharaoh A political and religious title for the king or ruler of ancient Egypt.

Pharisees - were at various times a political party, a social movement, and a school of thought among Jews during the Second Temple period.

Plagues of Exodus – According to the book of Exodus, there were ten plagues inflicted upon Egypt to persuade Pharaoh to release the Hebrew people from slavery. After the tenth plague – the death of the first-born males, Pharaoh said they could leave Egypt.

reconciliation – means the covering of, or making consistent or compatible with something else. The word can be associated with the cleansing, restoration or reestablishment of a damaged relationship between man and God. The Hebrew word *kaphar* is the same word translated in English as the word "atonement."

redemption – The act of redeeming or the condition of having been redeemed. Deliverance upon payment of ransom.

resurrection – the concept of a living being coming back to life after death.

righteous - word H#6662 *tsaddiyq* in *Strong's Concordance* means those who act justly, to be lawful, right and correct.

Rosh Hashanah is the autumnal festival celebrating the start of the Jewish civil New Year.

Ruach Ha Kodesh – is the Hebrew name for the Spirit of God, also referred to as the Holy Spirit, the Spirit, or Holy Ghost. *Ruach Ha Kodesh* refers to the divine aspect of prophecy and wisdom, the divine force, quality and influence of the Most High God, over the universe or over His creatures. The word is also associated with breath, to breathe and can mean either wind or some invisible moving force.

Sabbath – generally a weekly day of rest or time of worship. First mentioned in the Genesis creation narrative, where the seventh day is set aside as a day of rest and made holy by God (Genesis 2:2–3).

sacrificial death or **substitutionary atonement** The theory that atonement is attained as a result of Jesus' death as a substitute for others. This Christian concept adopted over one hundred years after the resurrection has no discernable scriptural support.

Sadducees – a sect of Jews active in Judea during the Second Temple period, starting from the second century BCE through the destruction of the Temple in 70CE. The sect was thought to be the upper social and economic echelon of Judean society who fulfilled various political, social, and religious roles, including maintaining the Temple.

salvation – As relating to Christianity, salvation is saving the soul from sin and its consequences. In the Old Testament, the word is associated with physical salvation and deliverance from those who wished to cause harm.

Samuel – The last Hebrew Judge and first major prophet. He anointed the first two kings of Israel - Saul and David. Samuel's story appears in I Samuel.

Sanhedrin - an assembly or congregation of 23 to 71 men appointed in each town to make decisions regarding political, criminal and Temple-related matters. Established after the exodus (Numbers 35:24-25), the practice of the Sanhedrin continued in Jerusalem until the destruction of the Temple in 70 CE.

Satan –an angel who fell out of favor with God. His goal is to tempt humanity into sin and unbelief. Satan is also known as Lucifer, the accuser, the deceiver, the devil and the adversary.

Savior – a person who helps people achieve salvation, or saves them from something

Glossary

Saul – (1) the first king of the united Kingdom of Israel. The main account of Saul's life and reign is found in the biblical Books of Samuel. (2) Saul, also known as Paul in the New Testament as the apostle responsible for spreading the Christian message to the Gentiles.

Scribes – a person who writes books or documents by hand as a profession and helps the city keep track of its records. In the Bible, their work involved copying sacred texts.

sheol – translated in English sometimes as "hell" means the "grave", "pit", or "abode of the dead," is the Old Testament/Hebrew Bible's the ground.

Shofar - sometimes referred to as a trumpet; a *shofar* is made from the horn of a ram.

Siddur – a Jewish prayer book, containing a set order of daily prayers. (The word *"siddur"* comes from a Hebrew root meaning "order".)

sin – is the act of violating God's will and disobedience to the commands or instructions of God. Sin is viewed as anything that violates the ideal relationship between an individual and God as in "to miss the mark." The Bible also addresses sins that cause a breach or break in a peaceful relationship. Another Hebrew word for sin is "*av, awon,* or *avon*" which indicates a perverse crookedness and/or bent and conveys the idea of blame, guilt and punishment for acts of depravity and perversion.

synoptic gospels are the first three books of the New Testament - Matthew, Mark and Luke. They are referred to as the synoptic gospels because they contain many of the same stories, often told in the same sequence. The word synoptic comes from the Greek word *synopsis* meaning "seeing all together."

Solomon – also called Jedidiah, was made king of Israel and the son of David. He was the third king of the United Monarchy, and the final king before the northern Kingdom of Israel and the southern Kingdom of Judah split. His story appears in II Samuel, the books of Kings and Chronicles.

Sukkot – the festival of Booths (Tabernacles) celebrating the forty years the Hebrew people lived in booths or tents in the desert before entering the Promised Land. It is one of the three pilgrim festivals when Jews were expected to go to Jerusalem.

Tabernacle – the portable dwelling place for the divine presence from the time of the Exodus from Egypt through the conquering of the land of Canaan. Built to specifications revealed by God to Moses at Mount Sinai, it accompanied the Israelites on their wanderings in the wilderness and their conquest of the Promised Land. The First Temple in Jerusalem replaced it as the dwelling place of God.

Tallit – a Jewish prayer shawl with twined and knotted fringes called tzitzit at its four corners.

Talmud – the book containing both the Oral Law (Mishnah) and the rabbinic commentaries (Gemara). There are two *Talmuds* – the Babylonian Talmud and the Jerusalem Talmud.

Tanakh – acronym formed from the first letters of the Hebrew Bible – *Torah* (Teaching – the first five books of the Bible), *Nevi im* (prophets and the historical books), and the *k' tuvim* (sacred writings).

Tish B' Av – Hebrew name for the 9th day of the month *Av*. It is an annual fast day regarded as the saddest day in the Jewish calendar. It commemorates among other tragedies, the destruction of both the first and second Temples in Jerusalem.

Torah "instruction," "teaching" is the central concept in the Jewish faith. It has a range of meanings: it most specifically identifies the first five books of the *Tanakh*, as well as the entire Hebrew Bible (Old Testament) or any written instructions given by God. It can also mean the rabbinic commentaries.

Tzitzit – is the name for specially knotted fringes worn by observant Jews attached to the four corners of the *tallit* (prayer shawl) fulfilling the command in Numbers 15:37-41.

unclean – Chiefly in Biblical terms means having a physical or moral blemish so as to make impure according to the instructions cited in the commandments.

Yahusha, Yahushua, Yehoshua or ***Yeshua*** –The Hebrew name for Joshua (of the Old Testament -book of Joshua and the Zechariah 3:8-9); one of which is probably the Hebrew name of Jesus. Over time the Hebrew pronunciation and spelling of this name changed slightly. The name is translated to mean "*YHVH* saves, rescues and/or delivers."

yeshu ah – salvation; part of Jesus' name in Hebrew. (Luke 2:30).

Year of Jubilee - Mentioned in the book of Leviticus (25:8-13), the Year of Jubilee occurs every fifty years. A celebratory year in which slaves and prisoners are freed, debts forgiven, property returned, and the mercies of God are manifested.

Yahweh, Yehovah - In more modern times the J replaced the Y sound for the name Jehovah. The Hebrew name representing the name of God. *Ehyeh* translated as (I AM) appears in most English versions of the Bible as the word "LORD" spelled with all capital letters.

YHWH a Tetragrammaton, meaning consisting of four letters or consonants that represent the Hebrew word for the English name of the Biblical God of Israel – *I AM*. In Hebrew the V sound is sometimes represented with the W sound.

Yom Kippur – "Day of Atonement" the annual autumn day of fasting and atonement considered the most important occasion of the Jewish religious year.

Zion – the word occurs over 150 times in the Bible. It is the name of a hill in Jerusalem on which David had built a citadel. Over time it came to identify the area where Solomon's temple was built, the city of Jerusalem, the land of Judah and the nation of Israel.

About the Authors

Anna Goodman is a wife, mother and devoted follower of the God of the Bible for over three decades. Married to Messianic Jewish archeologist, Dr. Jeffrey Goodman, Anna Goodman was exposed to the Bible from a Jewish prospective. This book originally began as a six-week summer course about Jesus for a small Bible study group and grew beyond her wildest dreams destroying many preconceptions about who Jesus is and revealing an all-powerful, loving and merciful God. Utilizing her husband's vast knowledge on anthropology, history – both general and early church history, early man traditions, and Judaic practices, this book could not have been written without his extensive assistance.

Dr. Jeffrey Goodman, an archeologist and a geologist, has devoted over thirty years to the study of the Bible. He holds a geological engineering degree from the Colorado School of Mines, a M.A. in anthropology from the University of Arizona, and a Ph.D. in anthropology from California Coast University. Dr. Goodman also earned a M.B.A. from Columbia University Graduate School of Business. He was accredited by the former Society of Professional Archeologists. Dr. Goodman is the author of four archeological titles, including *"American Genesis"* and *"The Genesis Mystery,"* which included accounts of his discovery of an early man site in the mountains outside of Flagstaff, Arizona. His last book is *"THE COMETS OF GOD-New Scientific Evidence for God: Recent archeological, geological and astronomical discoveries that shine new light on the Bible and its prophecies."* In part, *"THE COMETS OF GOD"* tells of the linguistic and scientific discoveries Goodman made within the pages of the Bible.

Goodman and his wife's research on the Bible's texts has also revealed important theological information that has largely gone unrecognized in the Bible. As the original Hebrew words of the Bible were studied and translated according to their ancient usage, and scripture was used to interpret scripture, Goodman and his wife found dramatically different interpretations of key Bible passages that provided a significantly different look at the identity of Jesus as presented in *BEHOLD! The Jesus We Never Knew.*

Additional titles from Anna A. Goodman and Dr. Jeffrey Goodman

By Anna A. Goodman
Tales of a Teller
Heart-warming and thought-provoking short stories of home life, fantasy and from working in a bank

By Dr. Jeffrey Goodman
The Comets of God – New Scientific Evidence for God: Recent archeological, geological and astronomical discoveries that shine new light on the Bible and its prophecies

The Genesis Mystery: A Startling New Theory of Outside Intervention in the Development of Modern Man

American Genesis: The American Indian and the origins of modern man

Please visit the Websites at:
www.thecometsofgod.com
www.newscientificevidenceforgod.com

www.ingramcontent.com/pod-product-compliance
Lightning Source LLC
Chambersburg PA
CBHW032057090426
42743CB00007B/155